DEMOCRACY IN LATIN AMERICA

DEMOCRACY IN LATIN AMERICA
POLITICAL CHANGE IN COMPARATIVE PERSPECTIVE

Second Edition

Peter H. Smith
University of California, San Diego

New York   Oxford
OXFORD UNIVERSITY PRESS

Oxford University Press, Inc., publishes works that further Oxford University's
objective of excellence in research, scholarship, and education.

Oxford   New York
Auckland   Cape Town   Dar es Salaam   Hong Kong   Karachi
Kuala Lumpur   Madrid   Melbourne   Mexico City   Nairobi
New Delhi   Shanghai   Taipei   Toronto

With offices in
Argentina   Austria   Brazil   Chile   Czech Republic   France   Greece
Guatemala   Hungary   Italy   Japan   Poland   Portugal   Singapore
South Korea   Switzerland   Thailand   Turkey   Ukraine   Vietnam

Published by Oxford University Press, Inc.
198 Madison Avenue, New York, New York 10016

For titles covered by Section 112 of the US Higher Education
Opportunity Act, please visit www.oup.com/us/he for the latest
information about pricing and alternate formats.

http://www.oup.com

Oxford is a registered trademark of Oxford University Press

Library of Congress Cataloging-in-Publication Data

Smith, Peter H.
   Democracy in Latin America : political change in comparative perspective /
   Peter H. Smith. — 2nd ed.
      p. cm.
Includes bibliographical references and index.
ISBN 978-0-19-538773-5
   1. Democratization—Latin America. 2. Democracy—Latin America.
3. Latin America—Politics and government—1980– I. Title.

JL966.S6 2011
320.98—dc23   2011028587

Printing number: 9 8 7 6 5 4 3 2

Printed in the United States of America
on acid-free paper

For all those ordinary citizens of Latin America
who struggled, suffered, and sacrificed
in their extraordinary quest for true democracy

BRIEF CONTENTS

CONTENTS

PART II: THE ELECTORAL ARENA

PART IV: DEMOCRACY CONSIDERED

TABLES, FIGURES, AND MAPS

FIGURES

Maps

PREFACE

This is not the book I intended to write.

My original plan was to synthesize the still-burgeoning literature on democratization in contemporary Latin America, integrate conceptual approaches, and make the results accessible to students and the general public. That seemed straightforward enough.

Once embarked on the project, however, I asked myself a near-fatal question: What is new and different about the current phase of democracy in Latin America? How does it compare with earlier episodes? Answers would require a systematic comparison of the present with the past. To my amazement, I found that existing scholarship sheds precious little light on these issues. There was only one solution: I would have to conduct original research.

This has made the whole thing harder to write and, in all probability, somewhat harder to read. The book contains an extensive amount of empirical data, which I have considered necessary in order to convey basic information and bolster my arguments. To enhance readability, I have included numerous "boxes"—which present illustrative anecdotes and personalities, explanations of methodology, and comments on conceptual approaches. Out of a sense of mercy, I have kept citations to a minimum. The result is a multifaceted volume—a contribution to scholarship, a text for college classrooms, and an analysis of current conditions in a major world region.

NEW TO THIS EDITION

This second edition contains much new substantive material and reflects careful consideration of recent trends within Latin America. The most significant additions include:

- Thorough updating of empirical information—on such present-day developments as women's representation, the empowerment of indigenous peoples, and antipoverty policies
- Interpretation of the emergence of the "new Left" as part of a recurring "dialectic" within Latin American democracy
- Evaluation of the roles of the judiciary
- Reassessment of the relative balance between "liberal" and "illiberal" democracy throughout the region
- Completely new analysis of public opinion on the basis of raw survey data

- A focus on the contemporary international environment, including attention to the rise of China

Generally speaking, the revision has been an exhaustive enterprise, and it has greatly enriched the final product. Intellectual debts have mounted over the years. Colleagues at the University of California, San Diego—Paul W. Drake, Arend Lijphart, David Mares, Michael Monteón, and Matthew Soberg Shugart—offered guidance and encouragement from the beginning. Matthew C. Kearney provided excellent research assistance for this second edition. Graduate and undergraduate students also suffered through successive renditions of the manuscript.

Academic institutions and public policy centers provided extremely useful opportunities to present ideas in the making: the Centro de Investigación y Docencia Económicas (CIDE) in Mexico City; Stanford University; the Universidad Simón Bolívar in Caracas; the University of British Columbia in Vancouver; the University of Uppsala in Sweden; the University of California, Berkeley; the University of California, Irvine; the Casa de América in Madrid; the Institute of the Americas in La Jolla, CA; the Inter-American Dialogue in Washington, DC; and the Polish Institute of International Relations in Warsaw.

For patience and support I thank my editor at Oxford University Press, Jennifer Carpenter, and her very capable assistant, Maegan Sherlock. I acknowledge contributions of reviewers, whose constructive comments have led to innumerable improvements in the final result: Jonathan A. Booth, University of North Texas; Mónica Pachón Buitrago, Universidad de los Andes; Jonathan Hartlyn, The University of North Carolina at Chapel Hill; Scott Morgenstern, University of Pittsburgh; and José M. Vadi, California State Polytechnic University, Pomona. Needless to say, any remaining errors of fact or interpretation belong to me alone.

Peter H. Smith
University of California, San Diego
phsmith@mail.ucsd.edu

DEMOCRACY IN LATIN AMERICA

INTRODUCTION

Dimensions of Democracy

Democracy is an abuse of statistics.

—JORGE LUIS BORGES

Many forms of government have been tried and will be tried in this world of sin and woe. No one pretends that democracy is perfect or all wise. Indeed, it has been said that democracy is the worst form of government, except for all the others that have been tried from time to time.

—WINSTON CHURCHILL

A TALE OF TWO PRESIDENTS

They came from everywhere. Peasants, workers, students, and families arrived by foot, bicycle, airplane, and bus. António Francisco dos Santos walked for twenty-seven days from the outskirts of São Paulo to reach his nation's capital. Francisco das Chagas Souza cycled more than 2,000 kilometers. Unable to afford hotels, entire families camped free of charge outside the city. The father of one such family fervently declared, "I wouldn't miss it for the world." What could have attracted such popular attention?

It was the inauguration of Luiz Inácio Lula da Silva as the thirty-sixth president of Brazil. His story contained elements of magic. Born into extreme poverty in the drought-stricken northeast, abandoned by his father, "Lula" and his seven siblings migrated with their mother to the industrial city of São Paulo. Rising from shoeshine boy to lathe operator to organizer for the metalworkers' union, Lula became an outspoken critic of the military regime that ruled Brazil from 1964 to 1985. A founder of the left-wing Workers' Party (known from its Portuguese initials as the PT), Lula thereafter ran unsuccessfully for president. On his fourth attempt, in 2002, he

1

January 1, 2003: Eager and optimistic, Lula strides toward the ceremonial palace for his formal inauguration as president of Brazil. (AP Photo/Eraldo Peres)

won 61 percent of the vote in a runoff election and a total of 52 million votes, a resounding triumph. As campaign posters proclaimed, "Lula's time has arrived."

This was Brazil's first transition between two democratically elected presidents in more than forty years. It was also the first time in the nation's history that a person of such humble origins had ascended to such heights. Lula was not only *for* the working class. In sharp contrast to his predecessor, the cosmopolitan intellectual Fernando Henrique Cardoso, he was *from* the working class.

Inauguration day (January 1, 2003) became a giant festival. Organizers set up huge TV screens and a stage where Brazilian pop groups started playing hours before the ceremonies. Outdoor stalls sold everything from jeans to grilled pork and beer. After a fourteen-hour bus ride from São Paulo, the pop musician João Carlos Souza stretched his legs and changed into a T-shirt reading "100 percent Lula." He had never attended any previous inaugurations, he explained, because those events "were for people in suits drinking champagne." "This time," Souza said, "it's going to be fun to participate in history."

Lula's supporters swarmed all over the city of Brasília. Under a slight drizzle, Lula and Vice President José Alencar stood in an open convertible to wave at a crowd estimated between 300,000 and 400,000. (The car was a 1952 presidential Rolls-Royce, a gift from Britain's Queen Elizabeth in 1953.) A sea of people chanted "Lula! Lula!" and raised red flags bearing the PT's colors in the air. At one point an unidentified man broke through police barriers, rushed to the car, and gave Lula a heartfelt embrace. Lula happily continued waving to the crowd. And just before the president-elect strode onto a red carpet leading into the congress building, young people jumped into an artificial lake to get closer to their hero. The vast esplanade in front of the legislative hall looked like a giant tailgate party, with tens of thousands gathering to sing, dance, eat, and drink.

Lula's acceptance speech struck a more solemn note. He wept while recalling the struggles of his childhood. He vowed to help the poor: "My life's mission will be fulfilled if, at the end of my term, every Brazilian can eat three square meals a day," he said, proclaiming that "the fight against hunger will become a great national cause." Turning to foreign policy, Lula indicated that Brazil would seek "mature relations" with the United States based on "reciprocal interest and mutual respect," while also promoting closer ties with such emerging economies as China, India, South Africa, and a resurgent Russia. Brazil would help and strengthen its neighbors: "The great foreign policy priority of my administration will be the construction of a South America that is politically stable, prosperous and united, based on democratic and social justice ideals." Above all, he would seek to serve his people. "In no way am I going to waste this unique opportunity," he said between sobs. "Voters wanted a change, and change is going to be the key word."

Despite the popular enthusiasm, Lula would encounter some difficult challenges. Brazil was a big and well-endowed country, by far the largest in South America, with a gross domestic product of well more than $500 billion. Inequality was acute, however, and nearly one quarter of the population lived in poverty. Lula's goals were to eliminate hunger, improve education, create new jobs, control inflation, reduce corruption, and boost efforts to give land to the poor. Yet he inherited rising inflation, tight public accounts, and a towering debt burden of approximately $240 billion. Meeting with his cabinet, Lula acknowledged that it might not be possible to complete his program in merely four years. "The country's situation is not good in almost any aspect," he observed, "except for the consolidation of democracy."

On hand to witness this grand celebration were hundreds of distinguished guests, among them Cuba's Fidel Castro and Venezuela's Hugo Chávez. In a calculated snub, the Bush administration had dispatched U.S. trade representative Robert Zoellick as leader of the American delegation. Only a few months before, Zoellick had quipped that Brazil would be reduced to exporting to Antarctica if it shunned U.S.-sponsored efforts to create a Free Trade Area of the Americas. Still in campaign mode, Lula had responded by sarcastically dismissing Zoellick as "the subsecretary of a subsecretary of a subsecretary." Indeed, Republicans in Washington regarded Lula with considerable unease. Representative Henry J. Hyde of Illinois had gone so far as to express public warnings that Lula was "a pro-Castro radical" who might be inclined to join with Castro and Chávez to form "an axis of evil in the Americas."

Characteristically contentious, Chávez had responded by claiming that such an alliance might create "an axis of good, good for the people, good for the future." Loudly proclaiming admiration for the new Brazilian president, Venezuela's populist leader held extensive meetings with both Lula and Fidel during the inauguration in Brasília. To all outward appearances, Chávez was self-assured and confident.

But he was in trouble back home. About a month before, the anti-Chávez opposition in Venezuela had launched a general strike that was crippling the national economy. Businesses closed, commerce declined, and oil exports plummeted, costing a total of about $50 million per day. The goal was to remove Chávez from office—he could resign, call new elections, or submit to a popular referendum on his presidency. The bottom line was clear: Chávez had to go.

His fall from grace had been spectacular. Hugo Chávez was a military officer who had led an unsuccessful coup in 1992 and as a result become a national hero. A political outsider, he denounced the country's "corrupt oligarchy" and vowed to serve the common people. Like Lula, he won the presidency with massive support, taking 56.2 percent of the vote in 1998 and 59.8 percent in 2000. Expectations were then running high. According to one opinion poll, more than three quarters of the population anticipated that personal and family life would improve within the next year and a half.

In spite (or because) of this mandate, Chávez managed to provoke the opposition. Soon after taking office he convened a special assembly dominated by his followers that rewrote the nation's constitution and greatly increased the powers of the presidency. As Venezuela's once-thriving economy sputtered, he proposed social programs that would channel resources toward the poor but reduce efficiency and competitiveness. He revamped long-standing foreign policy, extolling the virtues of Fidel Castro and other radical leaders and aligning Venezuela with Arab nations within the Organization of Petroleum Exporting Countries (OPEC). It was his confrontational attitude, perhaps, that antagonized people the most. In April 2002 a confusing welter of events led to his near-removal from power by a group of disenchanted military officers and business leaders, but mass demonstrations by his followers brought him back to power. A chastened Chávez pledged to engage in dialogue with dissidents, but he failed to keep his word on this.

Both sides resorted to incendiary rhetoric. One spokesman for the opposition, a respected sociologist, declared that Chávez's "tactics are totalitarian, similar to Stalin," alluding to the deaths of more than 10 million people in the old Soviet Union. "Hitler did the same thing in the Third Reich." A caller to a television station predicted that Chávez would do "the same thing that Hitler did to the Jews, the same thing that happened to the Americans with the Twin Towers." Carlos Ortega, a union boss and prominent opponent, dispensed with even the pretense of etiquette, regularly referring to the president as "Mr. Dictator Chávez." Pot-banging demonstrations (*cacerolazos*) against the president occurred nightly in Caracas, as opposition followers vowed to stand together to the end: *Ni un paso atrás* ("Not a step back") became the dissident slogan. For his part, Chávez responded by declaring, "What is going on in my country is not a strike. It is a coup attempt disguised as a strike," organized by "terrorists who are blocking oil and food distribution and sabotaging refineries." At every opportunity, he derided his opponents as coup-mongers, terrorists, and traitors to the fatherland. Neither side was sounding very democratic.

While attending Lula's inauguration, Chávez asked his friend for help. Lula responded with alacrity. Even before taking office, when Venezuela was obliged to import gasoline for domestic use, Lula had supported a decision to ship half a million barrels of Brazilian oil to the Chávez government. During a lengthy conversation at the inauguration, Lula encouraged Chávez to engage in more serious dialogue with his opponents. He also agreed to spearhead the formation of a group of "friends of Venezuela," an international mediation team that might ease tensions in that country. By stepping into this maelstrom, Lula was putting his newfound prestige on the line.

Thanks in part to Brazilian support, Chávez gradually regained control of power. The general strike was taking its toll on the strikers themselves, who brought it to an inconclusive end. Meanwhile the president took control of the state-run oil company by firing more than 17,000 workers and replacing the board of directors. In 2004 he survived a national referendum on his presidency. Running on a platform to establish "socialism for the twenty-first century," he triumphed again in 2006 with 63 percent of the vote. In 2008 he won approval for a proposal to lift prohibitions against reelection. Although his margins of victory might have been exaggerated by questionable practices, there was little doubt that Chávez enjoyed substantial popular support—especially from the lower classes, especially the underemployed who lived in shantytowns near major cities, and from some sectors within the middle classes. It was also true that he governed with an increasingly authoritarian style, concentrating power in the executive branch, eliminating checks and balances, purging the ranks of military officers, harassing the independent media, and intimidating the opposition.

In the international arena, Chavez staked out a strongly anti-U.S. policy. He openly accused the Bush administration of supporting the coup attempt of 2002. Expressing vigorous opposition to the U.S.-sponsored initiative for a Free Trade Area of the Americas (FTAA), he responded by proposing a "Bolivarian Alternative for the Americas" (*Alternativa Bolivariana para las Américas*). Using windfall profits from rising prices of petroleum, he showered his allies with extravagant amounts of economic assistance. Seeking support outside the Western Hemisphere, he sharply denounced U.S. policies in Iraq, Afghanistan, and the Middle East. (In a memorable speech at the United Nations in September 2006, he denounced George W. Bush as "the devil.") Thus did Hugo Chávez become a "radical" spokesperson for an anti-American, anticapitalist, proto-Marxist view of global affairs.

Lula took a different tack. While courting the private sector, he launched innovative and effective domestic programs against hunger, poverty, and inequality. Exercising tactful diplomacy, he established Brazil as a leading advocate of the economic interests of the developing world—as distinct from those of the advanced "industrialized" world. Often critical of the United States, he nonetheless hosted George Bush on official visits to Brazil and signed a bilateral pact for cooperation on the production of ethanol. Gregarious and effervescent, Lula became an extremely popular public figure. In the 2006 presidential elections he won nearly 49 percent of the vote in the first round of balloting, and 61 percent in the second round. Success continued during his second term, as Brazil discovered vast offshore deposits of petroleum and gained recognition as a rising power in the post–9/11 international order. Even as he remained on good personal terms with Chávez, Lula pursued a distinctly divergent path. Both at home and abroad, Lula was hailed as a thoughtful and constructive proponent of an independent but "moderate" approach to world affairs.

DEFINITIONS OF DEMOCRACY

This book is not about Lula and Chávez, although it will pick up their stories from time to time. It is about the quality of political democracy in Latin America. Of necessity, a focus of this kind calls for careful definition.

The term *democracy* has been widely used and frequently abused, usually for political purposes. Seeking to enhance their legitimacy, autocratic rulers have declared their regimes to be "guided" or "popular" democracies. Within the academic community, scholars have strained and stretched the concept of democracy through a plethora of adjectives, writing about such phenomena as "organic" democracy, "tutelary" democracy, "delegative" democracy, and so on. According to one recent survey, in fact, literature on this subject has spawned more than 550 adjectives used to qualify the notion of democracy.[1]

For this reason, studies of political democracy inevitably begin with a discourse on definition. What is a democracy? As used in this book, the

---

[1] David Collier and Steven Levitsky, "Democracy 'With Adjectives,'" Helen Kellogg Institute for International Studies, University of Notre Dame, Working Paper 230 (August 1996), p. 1; and "Democracy with Adjectives: Conceptual Innovation in Comparative Research," *World Politics* 49, 3 (1997): 430–451.

concept of democracy entails three principles: (1) the principle of *participation*, such that no substantial segment of the population is excluded from the effective pursuit of political power; (2) the principle of *competition*, such that there are free, fair, and regular contests for the support of the population—in other words, legitimate elections; and (3) the principle of *accountability*, such that political rulers and elected representatives serve as "agents" of their constituencies and must justify their actions and decisions to remain in office.

Principles require procedures. In other words, the application of democratic ideals depends on widely accepted agreement regarding mechanisms for their implementation. Thus, Robert Dahl has proposed what he calls a "procedural minimum" for the practical exercise of political democracy. His now-classic formulation involves eight institutional guarantees, as follows:

1. freedom to form and join organizations,
2. freedom of expression,
3. the right to vote,
4. eligibility for public office,
5. the right of political leaders to compete for support and votes,
6. alternative sources of information,
7. free and fair elections, and
8. institutions for making government policies depend on votes and other expressions of popular preference.[2]

Other scholars have extended and refined these criteria. Especially useful have been efforts to identify the limits of democratic governance, which might or might not prove to be efficient, orderly, or devoted to free-market economics.[3]

A crucial point about Dahl's procedural requisites is that, in combination, they elucidate the characteristics of a "complete" democracy. The problem is that these conditions do not always go together. (Why should we expect them to?) Countries often meet some of these criteria but not all of them. As a matter of empirical fact, variations in the combination of these features make it possible to elucidate and analyze resulting *configurations* of political democracy. This book will therefore explore the relationship between two

---

[2] Robert A. Dahl, *Polyarchy: Participation and Opposition* (New Haven: Yale University Press, 1971), 2–3; see also Dahl, *Dilemmas of Pluralist Democracy* (New Haven: Yale University Press, 1982), 11.

[3] I am especially indebted to Adam Przeworski, Michael E. Alvarez, José Antonio Cheibub, and Fernando Limongi, *Democracy and Development: Political Institutions and Well-Being in the World, 1950–1990* (Cambridge: Cambridge University Press, 2000), Ch. 1. See also Philippe C. Schmitter and Terry Lynn Karl, "What Democracy Is…And Is Not," *Journal of Democracy* 2 (1991):75–88.

Map I.1 Contemporary Latin America

key dimensions: elections and rights. According to conventional usage, elections constitute a "procedural" component of democracy; rights make up a "substantive" component.

Elections

What will here be called "electoral democracy" refers to the existence of free and fair elections—no more and no less. Most adult citizens must have the right to vote, and there must be genuine competition among rival candidates for national office.

CLASSIFYING POLITICAL REGIMES

Latin America defies traditional categories. For decades, observers struggled to find ways of summarizing (and understanding) political phenomena throughout the region. Prior to the 1980s, as will be shown in Chapter 1, only a few governments at any given time could be described as "democratic." The others were "nondemocratic" or "dictatorial"—but they were not "totalitarian," a term usually reserved for such ruthless regimes as Hitler's Germany and Stalin's Soviet Union. Nor were Latin America's autocracies necessarily moving toward imminent democracy. What were they?

In the mid-1960s Juan J. Linz, a political sociologist, resolved the difficulty by defining the concept of political *authoritarianism* as a form of rule that is conceptually and empirically distinct from democracy (characterized by free and open pluralism) and totalitarianism (characterized by "total" domination of society by the state). In contrast, Linz wrote, "Authoritarian regimes are political systems with limited, not responsible, political pluralism; without elaborate and guiding ideology (but with distinctive mentalities); without intensive nor extensive political mobilization (except at some points in their development); and in which a leader (or occasionally a small group) exercises power within formally ill-defined limits but actually quite predictable ones." Eureka!

Thus understood, authoritarianism was not just a halfway house between totalitarianism and democracy. Nor was it inherently unstable or short-lived. It was a distinctive and logical *system*, a category that could embrace a substantial variety of military governments, personalistic dictatorships, and dominant-party regimes.

Source: Juan J. Linz, "An Authoritarian Regime: Spain," in Erik Allardt and Stein Rokkan, eds., *Mass Politics: Studies in Political Sociology* (New York: Free Press, 1970), 152–183 and 374–381. The essay was first published in 1964.

The absence of elections—or the holding of patently fraudulent elections—means that a country is undemocratic. This is a distressingly common occurrence throughout the world. In Latin America, autocracy has often been the rule rather than the exception. During the twentieth century it has usually taken the form of military dictatorships that are "authoritarian" rather than "totalitarian." They concentrate power and often use it brutally, but they do not penetrate all aspects of society, as in Nazi Germany or Stalin's Soviet Union (see Box I.1).

There exist intermediate categories between electoral democracy and authoritarian dictatorship. One refers to tightly restricted elections: All candidates come from the socioeconomic elite, and suffrage extends to only a modest portion of the adult population (usually on the basis of literacy or property requirements). Such conditions describe the pattern of "competitive oligarchy" that was commonplace in late nineteenth- and early twentieth-century Latin America.

The other intermediate type consists of electoral "semidemocracy." As used in this book, the term applies to situations exhibiting one or both of two conditions: (1) elections are free but not fair—anyone is free to enter the contest, but the electoral system is rigged to favor the incumbent (or the incumbent's designated successor); or (2) elections are free and fair, but effective power does not go to the winner—instead, effective power tends to reside outside the realm of elective offices (among landowners or within the military, for instance). Under the first set of such circumstances, elected officials usually represent a dominant political party and are able to rule with considerable (sometimes excessive) authority. In the second situation, elected officeholders tend to be frustrated reformers or pliant figureheads.[4]

This focus on elections leads to an intentionally minimalist definition of democracy. Instead of assuming (or requiring) that free and fair elections are accompanied by the protection of citizens' rights—of expression, dissent, assembly, and organization—it leaves that open to question. Examination of the empirical relationship between electoral and other rights makes it possible to explore variations in the content and degree of democratic political practice.

Rights

Citizens' rights are essential to democracy. There must be constitutional protection of individual freedom and self-expression within the political arena. It is the obligation of a democratic state not only to tolerate dissent, but also to assure its unfettered expression.

According to Dahl's criteria, the notion of citizens' rights requires multiple guarantees: freedom to form and join organizations (such as labor unions and opposition parties), freedom of expression, and access to alternative sources of information (through freedom of the press). These protections enable groups and individuals not only to present their views and ideas, they also provide the basis for true competition among power contenders. Free and fair elections and citizens' rights thus seem to go hand-in-hand.

For the purposes of this analysis, governmental protection of these basic freedoms will be construed as a variable—more precisely, an ordered-nominal variable. Electoral democracies that provide "extensive" guarantees of civil liberties will be considered complete, or "liberal," democracies. Electoral democracies that provide only "partial," or "minimal," guarantees will be regarded as "illiberal" democracies. This distinction forms a central theme in this study.

---

[4] These distinctions are similar to those in Larry Diamond, *Developing Democracy: Toward Consolidation* (Baltimore: Johns Hopkins University Press, 1999), esp. 7–17.

DELEGATIVE DEMOCRACY

One of the most creative political analysts of Latin America, Guillermo O'Donnell, has coined the term *delegative democracy* to describe political practice in many new democracies around the world. Here is his depiction of this "new species":

> Delegative democracies rest on the premise that whoever wins election to the presidency is thereby entitled to govern as he or she sees fit, constrained only by the hard facts of existing power relations and by a constitutionally limited term of office. The president is taken to be the embodiment of the nation and the main custodian and definer of its interests. The policies of his government need bear no resemblance to the promises of his campaign—has not the president been authorized to govern as he (or she) thinks best? Since this paternal figure is supposed to take care of the whole nation, his political base must be a movement, the supposedly vibrant overcoming of the factionalism and conflicts associated with parties. Typically, winning presidential candidates in DDs present themselves as above both political parties and organized interests. How could it be otherwise for somebody who claims to embody the whole of the nation? In this view, other institutions—courts and legislatures, for instance—are nuisances that come attached to the domestic and international advantages of being a democratically elected president. Accountability to such institutions appears as a mere impediment to the full authority that the president has been delegated to exercise.

In other words, citizens "delegate" all effective authority and decision-making power to chief executives. Elections might be free and fair, but winning candidates govern—or at least attempt to govern—without any serious opposition and without any institutional constraints.

Source: Guillermo O'Donnell, "Delegative Democracy," *Journal of Democracy* 5, 1 (January 1994): 55–69.

The concept of "illiberal democracy" comes from the scholar, columnist, and commentator Fareed Zakaria. Scanning the world in the late 1990s, Zakaria discovered a pervasive phenomenon: "Democratically elected regimes, often ones that have been reelected or reaffirmed through referenda, are routinely ignoring constitutional limits on their power and depriving their citizens of basic rights and freedoms. From Peru to the Palestinian Authority, from Sierra Leone to Slovakia, from Pakistan to the Philippines, we see the rise of a disturbing phenomenon in international life—illiberal democracy." In almost every part of the world, he argued, elected representatives were ruling by decree, imposing restrictions on speech and assembly, and tolerating (or even inflicting) abuse on human rights. "Democracy is flourishing," in Zakaria's words; "constitutional liberalism is not."[5]

The idea of illiberal democracy bears a close resemblance to the notion of "delegative democracy," but is not quite the same. As defined by Guillermo O'Donnell, delegative democracy refers to the overweening concentration of power in the hands of chief executives, with the passive acceptance (or even active support) of national electorates (see Box I.2). This situation is likely to lead to "illiberal" policies and the denial of constitutional rights to citizens. That is a probable outcome but not a necessary one. In short, delegative democracy refers to the excessive *concentration* of power; illiberal democracy refers to the *application* of that power in restricting freedoms and rights. In either case, free and fair elections cannot (and do not) by themselves guarantee full constitutional protections and complete democracy.

OVERVIEW: FOCUS AND THEMES

This book combines historical perspective with political analysis. Part I offers an overview of political change and democratic experience in Latin America over the course of the twentieth century. Based on a new and original data set, Chapter 1 traces the rise (and fall) of electoral democracy in nineteen Latin American countries from 1900 to 2000. Chapter 2 explores variations over time—and across political regimes—in forms of transition toward political democracy. Chapter 3 examines long-term patterns of change in the political roles of Latin America's armed forces. Chapter 4 sketches ways that the international environment—and U.S. policy—encouraged or discouraged the emergence of democracy in Latin America.

Concentrating on the period from the late 1970s to the present, Part II assesses institutional attributes of Latin American democracies. Chapter 5 recounts political and constitutional debates over alternative institutional structures, with special emphasis on the relative merits of parliamentarism versus presidentialism. Chapter 6 explores varieties in contemporary political systems of Latin America, especially with regard to executive power, legislative roles, and party performance. Chapter 7 examines the conduct and consequences of elections—voter turnout, levels of competition, partisan allegiance, and implications for public policy.

Part III focuses on a broad question: Can (and do) democracies govern? Chapter 8 attempts to assess the strength of democratic states and their capacity to implement effective economic policy. Chapter 9 examines the political representation of disadvantaged groups—workers, women, and indigenous peoples. Chapter 10 explores the question of rights and, in particular, the

---

[5] Fareed Zakaria, "The Rise of Illiberal Democracy," *Foreign Affairs* 76, 6 (November/December 1997): 22–43. See also Larry Diamond, "Is the Third Wave Over?" *Journal of Democracy* 7, 3 (1996): 20–37.

prevalence of "illiberal democracy" throughout much of Latin America. Chapter 11 presents "the people's verdict," an evaluation of democratic performance as revealed by public opinion polls.

The conclusion comes in two parts. Looking back over the course of the twentieth century, Chapter 12 synthesizes principal findings and offers a qualitative interpretation of differences between the current phase of democratization and predecessor periods. An Epilogue then delves into the concept of "consolidation" and offers speculation about future prospects for improving, or "deepening," the quality of democracy in contemporary Latin America.

Interpretive Arguments

One goal of this book is to present a comprehensive picture of political democracy in contemporary Latin America. An equally important goal— indeed, the driving force behind the work—is to address a series of analytical questions: What is genuinely new and distinctive about the current pattern of democratization? Why has electoral democracy spread to so many countries? There have been earlier experiments with electoral democracy within the region, and most have not lasted very long. What makes the contemporary cycle any different from its predecessors? Is there a notable difference in quality? Will contemporary democracies prove to be more durable? Might there be a trade-off between the *depth* of democracy and *durability* of democracy?

Such queries require historical perspective. We cannot assess the "novelty" of present times without comparing them to previous eras. Conventional wisdom typically claims that democratic practices have reached "unprecedented" levels in the hemisphere. In what sense might this be true? According to what criterion? What underlying factors might account for such developments?

Focusing on these concerns, the empirical investigation reveals three distinct waves or "cycles" of democratization in Latin America: one from 1900 to approximately 1940, a second from the 1940s to the early 1970s, and a third—still continuing—from the late 1970s to the present. The first period entailed top-down experimentation with free and fair elections at the instigation of upper-class elites who were either competing with each other or seeking to co-opt rising middle-class sectors. During the 1930s many of these experiments collapsed under the weight of the Great Depression.

In the wake of World War II, the second stage reflected not only the gathering strength of middle classes but also the emergence of an urbanized working class, increasingly represented by labor unions, as well as peasant movements in the countryside. As widespread suffrage strengthened the role of competitive political parties, reformist politicians (in various guises) appealed to electoral constituencies by calling for improvements in wages and working conditions, the redistribution of agricultural land, and increased taxation (or nationalization) of foreign-owned enterprises. Public rhetoric often acquired leftist, socialist, or Marxist overtones. Within the climate of the Cold War, democracy thus came to be seen as *dangerous*—not only by the upper classes, but also by the United States. Largely as a result, democratic governments throughout the region were overthrown by military coups in the 1960s and 1970s.

Extending from the late 1970s to the present, the current phase of democratization has taken altogether different paths. Driven by what came to be known as the "Washington Consensus," economic orthodoxy has espoused free-market policies: liberalization of trade, support for the private sector, and reduction of governmental roles. The economic power of states has dissipated throughout the region, and globalization has weakened the strength of organized labor and working-class movements. Land reform disappeared as a political issue. During the 1990s, in other words, democracy was *tamed*. Given the atmosphere of the post–Cold War era, Latin American democracy no longer threatened domestic elites or international actors. On the contrary, it provided legitimacy and security for the pursuit of precisely those interests. Moreover, the imposition of "illiberal" constraints on citizen rights helped to minimize the prevalence and impact of popular protest.

It was because of these unthreatening qualities, in my view, that free and fair elections spread to so many countries and lasted for so long. Democracy became acceptable to the elites. Those who had opposed democracy during the post–World War II period came to embrace it in the post–Cold War era.

But democracy displayed flexibility as well. As the twenty-first century beckoned, mass-based movements and parties throughout Latin America sharply rejected neoliberal policies in favor of demands for social justice. They wanted not only to change the direction of policy but also to restore the historic role of the state in economic affairs. Expressing their preferences at the ballot box, popular voters threw their support to left-of-center "pink tide" presidential candidates. Thus did Chávez and Lula come to power. And thus, in years to follow, would like-minded reformers triumph in Bolivia, Ecuador, Paraguay, and elsewhere. As the record will show, significant differences arose within this overall trend, but the basic point remains: Leaders and supporters wanted to reinvigorate democracy, to amplify the range of practical policy options, and, on occasion, to challenge the interests of entrenched upper classes and international forces.

Analytical Perspectives

At the conceptual level, I attempt to draw a multifaceted picture of democracy in Latin America. Instead of relying on one or another approach, I adopt an eclectic and interdisciplinary stance.

Definitions matter. This is especially relevant to a study of *democracy*, a term that has often been carelessly used and purposely abused. In this study, the distinction between *electoral* democracy (involving free and fair elections) and *liberal* democracy (involving the protection of citizens' rights) is a central component of the overall analysis.

History matters. One of the most conspicuous weaknesses of the current literature on democratization in Latin America tends to be shortsightedness. Analyses concentrate on trends and events of the past quarter century, with only a passing nod, at most, to earlier political experience. Yet awareness of the past is vital. As the historical record indicates, democratization is by no means an inexorable process: Democracies can rise, fall, and return. History also shapes the collective imagination. In nations with long-standing and continuous democracy, such as the United States, citizens find it hard to imagine plausible alternatives. In new democracies, however, people have no reason to share this assumption: They regard democratization as an experiment, not as a culmination. Questions thus arise: How does the most recent phase of democracy fit into historical patterns? Are contemporary democracies stronger than their predecessors? Why and in what way?

Class matters. Since the end of the Cold War and the demise of the Soviet Union, the conceptual armature of Marxism has fallen out of intellectual fashion. Ideas about capitalist development, economic interests, class identity—above all, class struggle—have been relegated to the dustbin of history. This strikes me as overkill. One does not have to be a diehard Stalinist to believe that social class is a meaningful category, that class structures in Latin America (and other developing areas) influence patterns of conflict and accommodation, and that the formation (or not) of social coalitions has major implications for processes of political change. At least in Latin America, the advent of democracy does not herald the disappearance of class struggle.

Institutions matter. There is no question that recent scholarship on the "new institutionalism" has made important contributions to comprehension of the ways that electoral rules can influence voter behavior, party systems, and public policymaking. It is also true that, armed with these insights, leaders can engage in careful and deliberate modes of "political engineering." At the same time, I do not think that political institutions should be treated as a deus ex machina. They emerge from processes: Institutions are created, usually through negotiation, almost always reflecting a welter of projects and demands. Institutions are important, but so are the interests that forge them.

Performance matters. In new democracies, or in countries where democracy has failed in the past, citizens do not assume that democracy is the best (or even least bad) form of government. People want results. And if results are not forthcoming, segments of society begin exuding nostalgia for dictatorship—eras of law and order, clear-cut authority, and the no-nonsense pursuit of economic growth. Such sentiments presage real trouble.

And ideology matters. This is a controversial point. For some proponents of "rational choice," the concept of values is irrelevant: Because everyone is rational, there is no need to consider underlying beliefs and attitudes. I do not agree. To be sure, invocations of national character can be utterly meaningless, as in assertions that "Mexicans act like Mexicans because they are Mexican." On the other hand, rigorous analysis of public opinion can make essential contributions to our understanding of the depth of societal commitment to the practice of democratic politics. This is especially pertinent to the consolidation of democracy under conditions of economic and social distress.

So I here adopt a multifaceted, interdisciplinary approach. I combine political science with history, sociology, and a smattering of other fields. I blend quantitative analysis with qualitative interpretation. And instead of adopting one or another methodological posture, I seek to forge an analytical synthesis, fitting pieces together into a complex but coherent whole.

As described here, Latin America presents a variegated and multicolored political picture. That has been the case throughout its history. It will no doubt apply to the future as well.

PART I

HISTORICAL PERSPECTIVES,
1900—2000

In the strict sense of the term, a true democracy has never existed, and never will exist.

—JEAN JACQUES ROUSSEAU

It [Democracy] is a great word, whose history, I suppose, remains unwritten, because that history has yet to be enacted.

—WALT WHITMAN

Knowledge—Zzzzzp! Money—Zzzzzp!—Power! That's the cycle democracy is built on!

—TENNESSEE WILLIAMS

CHAPTER 1

CYCLES OF ELECTORAL DEMOCRACY

Democracy has faced turbulent times in Latin America. For generations the region was regarded as the province of domineering military tyrants. Civilian reformers would enter the fray, only to have their mandates interrupted by generals from the barracks. Democracy has been viewed as fragile, temporary, and superficial in content. Over the past quarter-century or so, however, democracy appears to have taken root in the region. Many observers regard this development as a sign of political maturation, the idea being that citizens of the region have (finally!) passed from adolescence to adulthood; others regard it as the inexorable and benevolent result of economic liberalization and free trade; still others credit the influence and example of the United States. The broad implication is that democracy now is vibrant, resilient, and improving with the passage of time.

Which interpretation is correct? To approach the question, this chapter explores the incidence and durability of electoral democracy in Latin America during the course of the twentieth century. The analysis traces the timing and spread of democratization, tests some key hypotheses about explanatory factors, examines the longevity of democracies within the region, and locates Latin America's patterns of political change within a broad global context. In contrast to most studies, which limit their attention to the several decades, this investigation focuses on the 100-year span from 1900 through 2000. This makes it possible to detect long-term transformations and to place recent developments within appropriate historical perspective.

Evidence clearly demonstrates that Latin America made consistent, repeated, and intensive efforts to implant electoral democracy over the course of the twentieth century. These attempts have not always succeeded: There have been coups, setbacks, failures, and mistakes. But it would be incorrect to assume that the peoples of the region are incapable of sustaining competitive politics or that democracy has come to the region only as a gift from other parts of the world. Indeed, the struggle for democracy has been one of the defining features of the region's recent history.

LEGACIES OF INDEPENDENCE

Once they achieved independence in the 1820s, the fledgling nations of Spanish America faced formidable challenges. The military campaigns left widespread destruction in their wake. Trade had come to a standstill, capital was scarce, and public debts were mounting. In many parts of the region, upper-class landowners (*creoles*, a term for Spanish descendants born in the New World) withdrew to their haciendas and concentrated on their family fortunes. Governments were run and overrun by *caudillos*, soldiers (or ex-soldiers) often with paramilitary followings who took power by force and ransacked national treasuries. Once the coffers were empty, their bands dispersed and rival caudillos took over.[1] From the 1820s until midcentury, political authority in Spanish America was weak; the state, as a central institution, did not wield much power.

This situation provoked efforts to consolidate and centralize power, usually through dictatorship. The first two decades after independence thus saw the appearance of real or would-be "strongmen," such as Diego Portales in Chile and Juan Manuel de Rosas in Argentina, who sought to impose their will on their countries and strengthen the role of the state. Struggles between provincial bosses and central authorities defined a basic theme in the political life of the new nations.[2]

The resulting confusion spawned considerable uncertainty about the most suitable forms of governance. Many leaders of the independence era, having formerly served the Spanish Crown, regarded monarchy as the most appropriate—after all, the pinnacles of civilization in Europe were ruled by royal dynasties. Others insisted that the newly independent nations should discard all traces of the old colonial regime—after all, that had been the purpose of the wars—and invest political power in the people, not the divine right of kings. Still others regarded the United States with considerable interest—and also apprehension, fearful that its democratic institutions would unleash forces of revolution and disorder in the Spanish American context. At this time, early in the nineteenth century, U.S.-style democracy was still a not-quite-tested experiment (one that would nearly collapse during a bitter civil war). There was no self-evident prescription for political success (see Box 1.1).

---

[1] See Eric R. Wolf and Edward C. Hansen, "*Caudillo* Politics: A Structural Analysis," *Comparative Studies in Society and History* 9 (1966–1967): 168–179.
[2] See Fernando López-Alves, *State Formation and Democracy in Latin America, 1810–1900* (Durham, NC: Duke University Press, 2000).

For Spanish America, the ultimate question was how to balance governmental authority with some form of representation. This led to a series of half-measures. One restricted the effective "citizenry" to the creole elite, explicitly excluding popular masses and indigenous populations. Another took the form of a punctilious insistence on constitutions and constitutionalism. At the same time, these charters gave presidents extraordinary powers to meet emergencies, assure internal security, and respond to external threats. Under what came to be known as "regimes of exception," executives and designated officials could suspend civil liberties and rights, declare states of siege, confiscate property, and establish authoritarian rule. Such provisions thus established a tradition of "constitutional dictatorship." Predictably enough, they also fostered widespread contempt for the rule of law. Constitutions were extremely fragile documents. From independence to the end of the nineteenth century, in fact, the sixteen nations of Spanish America produced 103 constitutions—for an average of more than six per country![3]

Portuguese America—that is, Brazil—traced a less tumultuous path. In 1808 the Portuguese court fled to Brazil to evade the armies of Napoleon. Years later the king resumed the throne in Portugal; his son stayed behind and in 1822 became the first emperor of an independent Brazil. Under the enlightened leadership of Pedro II, the monarchy remained intact until 1889, when it was replaced by oligarchic rule. There were struggles, to be sure, but Brazil did not face extensive economic disorder or social upheaval in the decades after independence.

As Latin America prepared to enter the twentieth century, it exhibited three distinct forms of political rule. One was *caudillismo,* the system through which military or paramilitary strongmen fought with one another to assert authority over the nation (or local region) and to enjoy the spoils of victory. These were raw struggles for power: Rules of engagement were primitive, and governments rose and fell with steady regularity. A second pattern took the form of "integrating dictatorships"—centralizing dictatorships that sought to curtail the centripetal tendencies of *caudillismo* and to establish the hegemony of the national state. Examples ranged from Portales in Chile and Rosas in Argentina to Porfirio Díaz in Mexico. Such rulers often came from the ranks of the military, and, once in power, they always relied on armed forces to uphold their rule.

The third variation, as mentioned in the introduction, might be called "competitive oligarchy" or "oligarchic republicanism." Regimes of this kind made use of regular elections for political office, and they usually complied with formal constitutional procedure. At the same time, they restricted effective competition to factions of the ruling elite. (This was accomplished through sharp restrictions on suffrage and through formidable eligibility requirements for candidates.) In effect, the system established a nonviolent means for settling disputes among contending factions of dominant elites. It was also a means of wresting power away from caudillos and military

---

[3] Brian Loveman, *The Constitution of Tyranny: Regimes of Exception in Spanish America* (Pittsburgh, PA: University of Pittsburgh Press, 1993); Paul W. Drake, *Between Tyranny and Anarchy: A History of Democracy in Latin America, 1800–2006* (Stanford, CA: Stanford University Press, 2009).

dictators. Although it boasted a democratic façade, it had little to do with rule by the people—on the contrary, it consecrated domination by the few. And in relations between elites and masses, competitive oligarchy showed precious little respect for the rule of law: In situations of class conflict, raw power prevailed.[4] This kind of regime typically flourished in societies with expansive gaps between elites and popular masses.

CYCLES AND TRENDS

What has been the incidence of electoral democracy in Latin America, and how has it changed over time? The response to these questions involves a systematic survey of nineteen countries from 1900 through 2000. As a group, these countries constitute what is commonly viewed as Latin America, stretching from the Rio Grande to the Tierra del Fuego—from Mexico to the southern tip of Argentina and Chile, including Brazil and nations of the Andes. Included are Haiti and the Dominican Republic, which occupy the island of Hispaniola. Excluded are English- and Dutch-speaking islands of the Caribbean, as well as Suriname, Guyana, French Guiana, and Belize.[5] Also omitted is Cuba, not for cultural or geographical reasons, but because it has had no meaningful experience with electoral democracy (see Box 1.2). By the year 2000, the total population of these nineteen countries was approaching 500 million.

To trace political change over time, each year for each country has been placed into one of four categories:

- "democratic," when national leaders acquired or held office as a result of free and fair elections—that is, when there was open competition for support among a substantial portion of the adult population

- "semidemocratic," under leaders who came to power through elections that were free but not fair—when only one candidate had any reasonable prospect of winning, or when elected leaders were obliged to share effective power with or cede it to nonelected groups (such as landowners or the military)

- "oligarchic," when electoral competition was essentially fair but not free—with candidates from dominant elites and suffrage restricted to a very small percentage of the adult population

- "nondemocratic," or autocratic, at all other times, or during years of military coups.

---

[4] Terminology here is not felicitous. This kind of regime could be referred to as "oligarchic constitutionalism," "oligarchic contestation," "oligarchic electoralism," or even—stretching categories—"oligarchic democracy."

[5] Additional reasons for exclusion are size, because most of these countries are very small; colonial legacy, because British and other traditions differed markedly from those of Spain and Portugal; and political experience, because many Caribbean countries acquired independence only in the 1960s and 1970s.

BOX 1.2

THE MISSING COUNTRY

Cuba is conspicuous by its absence from this book. It is, of course, a very significant country. Independent and proud, Cuba has undergone a major social revolution, endured decades of hostility from the United States, and become a complex symbol (positive and negative) in the changing world arena. Why the omission?

The answer is simple: because Cuba has virtually no democratic history. This is not to denigrate the social accomplishments of the Cuban Revolution, sometimes described as a "participatory democracy." Nor is it to say that Cuba has not given rise to eloquent appeals for democratic politics.

It is just to acknowledge the facts. Upon independence from Spain, Cuba was governed through U.S. military occupation (1898–1902). And from then until 1934 the island was an American protectorate, as the Platt Amendment to the Cuban Constitution entitled the United States to intervene in the island's domestic politics at will (it exercised this option with military expeditions in 1906–1909, 1912, and 1917–1922). Elections during this era were intermittent and could be considered "semidemocratic" at best.

Generalized protests in 1933 led to the ouster of longtime dictator Gerardo Machado and to the rise of a military sergeant named Fulgencio Batista. A relatively open election—the most nearly democratic in Cuban history—elevated an idealistic doctor-professor named Ramón Grau San Martín into the presidency. Only four months later he was ousted by Batista, who went on to dominate Cuban politics for the next quarter-century. With Cuba safely under control, U.S. president Franklin Delano Roosevelt abrogated the Platt Amendment in 1934. Batista's tyranny lasted until he finally fled the island in early 1959.

Since then the Cuban Revolution under Fidel Castro has scored some notable achievements, especially in the areas of health care, education, and race relations. It has survived countless efforts at destabilization by U.S.-sponsored operatives. Frequently, too, Castro has provided an outspoken and articulate voice for peoples of the developing world. But there have not been free and fair elections of the topmost leadership.

In practice, the nondemocratic rubric is a residual category. It could include periods of chronic instability, caudillo politics, dictatorial rule, or military occupation by a foreign power. Years of military coups are coded as nondemocratic, even if there might have been semidemocratic or democratic activity during other parts of the year. (See Appendix 1 for full explanation and details.)

Criteria for classification are relative, not absolute. They attempt to capture standards of the time. One conspicuous problem concerns disenfranchisement of women. Denial of the vote to more than half the adult population is patently undemocratic; according to fundamental principles, any regime lacking female suffrage should be classified as nondemocratic or authoritarian. Yet it is worth noting that the United States, commonly regarded as "democratic" by the 1820s, did not grant suffrage to women until 1920; within this historical context, Latin American countries with free and fair elections (and fairly broad voting rights for adult males) would be considered "democratic," too. And, in fact, Latin America gradually extended the vote to women in succeeding decades.[6]

Of necessity, application of these categories has been somewhat subjective. Chile, for example, was treated as a "competitive oligarchy" under the "parliamentary republic" that lasted from 1891 to 1923. It was classified as nondemocratic during a series of coups and dictatorial interludes that stretched from 1924 to 1932. With the onset of free and fair elections, the system became an electoral democracy from 1933 through 1972. The military coup of 1973 and ensuing dictatorship under General Augusto Pinochet placed the country under authoritarian rule through 1988. From 1989 through 2000—and well beyond, as of this writing—Chile managed to restore its democratic traditions.

The semidemocratic category is perhaps the most elusive. Argentina provides a case in point. Under the aristocratic "Generation of 1880," Argentina displayed a strong and confident system of oligarchic competition through 1915. Implementation of a major reform led to free and fair elections in 1916, marked by the victory of the opposition Radical Party and the installation of a democratic regime that was overthrown by a military coup in 1930. A dictatorial interlude then gave way to more than a decade of "patriotic fraud," under which elections were explicitly understood to be free but not fair: The official candidate was always destined to win, so the 1932 to 1942 period could be unambiguously scored as semidemocratic. After another military coup in 1943, Juan Domingo Perón triumphed in the elections of 1946. His election to a second term was tightly controlled, however, so the 1951 to 1954 phase was coded as semidemocratic. After another military intervention in 1955, elections were reinstated from 1958 through 1965, but Peronists were prohibited from either running or winning, so this period, too, was classified as semidemocratic (except for 1962, when a nondemocratic military coup prevented a Peronist victory in elections). Thereafter, Argentina endured military dictatorship from 1966 through 1972, a brief period of open democracy from 1973 through 1975, a brutally repressive military regime from 1976 through 1982, and then, from 1983 through the end of the century, an extended period of electoral democracy.

Mexico offers still another illustration. The twentieth century opened under the rule of Porfirio Díaz, an iron-fisted dictator who dominated the country's politics from 1876 until his overthrow in 1911. There followed, that

---

[6] Accordingly, the basic criterion for electoral participation was effective extension of the suffrage to at least half of the adult male citizens. In many cases this required removal of literacy requirements.

Francisco Madero of Mexico casts ballot in Latin America's first democratic election. (Editorial Trillas)

same year, relatively free elections that gave the presidency to Francisco Madero (since remembered as "the apostle of Mexican democracy").[7] Madero was ousted (and murdered) in a military coup in 1913. Years of revolutionary fighting led to alternation of military domination with a semidemocratic system that was interrupted by an assassination in 1920. In 1929, after yet another assassination, the political elite created a one-party system that lasted until the end of the century. From that point forward there were regular elections, but they were neither free nor fair. It was a foregone conclusion that the official candidate would win: In 1976, for example, the ruling party's presidential nominee ran unopposed. This situation changed when a left-wing splinter group broke off from the dominant party (the Partido Revolucionario Institucional, or PRI) and ran a strong campaign in the late 1980s—and might even have won, but was denied victory. The election of 1988 was free, in other words, but not fair. It was not until 2000 that Mexico had a genuinely free and fair presidential election, one that an opposition candidate could, and did, win.

To illustrate long-term patterns for the region as a whole, Figure 1.1 plots the incidence of democratic, semidemocratic, oligarchic, and nondemocratic regimes for Latin America from 1900 through 2000: The vertical axis

---

[7] There appears to be a widespread belief that Mexico's 1911 election was so one-sided that it could not be considered fully democratic. My authority here is John Womack, Jr., who has reported that "the Madero-Pino Suárez slate won 53 percent of the vote; four other slates shared the remainder." Womack, "The Mexican Revolution, 1910–1920," in Leslie Bethell, ed., *Mexico since Independence* (Cambridge: Cambridge University Press, 1991), 134. Essays in this volume first appeared in *The Cambridge History of Latin America.*

N Countries

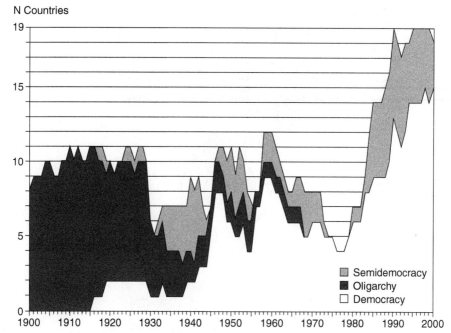

Figure 1.1 Cycles of political change in Latin America, 1900–2000

measures the number of countries with each regime type, and the horizontal axis represents year-by-year change over time.[8]

Over the span of the century, the data reveal a remarkable progression of electoral democracy in Latin America. Around 1900 there were no democracies anywhere in the region. But a process of democratization appeared early in the century, and by 2000 more than three quarters of the countries were holding free and fair elections. Democracy was on the rise. The tendency was not predetermined, inexorable, irreversible, unchangeable, or permanent. But it persisted over time, and it constitutes a fundamental fact.

Around this upward trend, the figure circumscribes three broad "cycles" of democratic change.[9] This is a crucial discovery, and it will form the basis for historical comparison throughout the remainder of this book.

The first cycle stretches from 1900 approximately through 1939, and it was dominated by oligarchic competition. At its peak, around and after 1910, intraoligarchic elections held sway in more than half the countries of Latin America—and in such influential nations as Argentina, Brazil, Chile, Colombia, and Peru. During this first cycle there were also some signs of

---

[8] The same data weighted by population size appear in Chapter 12 (see Figure 12.1). As indicated there, differences in the curve are due largely to the influence of Brazil.

[9] I use the term *cycle* in a colloquial, not a technical, sense.

Note: Argentina was democratic in 1920, semidemocratic in 1960, and democratic again by 2000; Venezuela was democratic in 1960 and semidemocratic by 2000; Ecuador was democratic in 1960 but nondemocratic in 2000.

Map 1.1 Latin America's changing political landscape: Electoral democracies in 1920, 1960, and 2000

emergent democracy—very briefly in Mexico (1911–1912) and more durably in Argentina (1916–1929) and Uruguay (1919–1933). By the early 1930s Chile also qualified as an electoral democracy. In general, however, this first phase was not a time of democratic governance; it was an era of oligarchic domination through electoral means.

Second was a cycle between 1940 and 1977 marked by the partial rise and near-complete demise of electoral democracy. To be precise, the democratic curve within this period is M-shaped. The data reveal a sharp upturn in democratic politics coinciding with end of World War II in Guatemala (1945), Peru (1945), Argentina (1946), Brazil (1946), Venezuela (1946), and Ecuador (1948) in addition to preexisting democracies in Chile, Uruguay, and Colombia (dating from 1942). There was a temporary downturn in the early 1950s, largely as a result of military coups, followed by a fairly swift recovery. By 1960, the peak year within this period, nine countries of Latin America were electoral democracies and three others were semidemocracies, bringing the total up to twelve (63 percent of countries of the region). Thereafter, the remainder of the 1960s and the early 1970s bore witness to an escalating pattern of increasingly brutal and invasive military interventions, most notably in Brazil (1964), Argentina (1966 and 1976), and Chile and Uruguay (both 1973). By the mid-1970s there were only three democracies throughout the region—in Colombia, Costa Rica, and Venezuela.

Under these unlikely circumstances a third cycle began in the late 1970s, continued through the 1980s, and crested in the late 1990s. By 1998 there were fifteen electoral democracies, four semidemocracies, and no autocratic regimes. And by 2000, nearly 90 percent of the people of Latin America were enjoying electoral democracy.

Figure 1.1 yields additional insights. One concerns the eclipse of oligarchic regimes and the rise of mass politics. As evinced by a sharp decline in the number of oligarchic arrangements around 1930, the onset of the Great Depression decimated the export–import model of economic development and led to the widespread displacement of traditional elites by military dictatorships. By the early 1950s systems of intraoligarchic competition remained only in Honduras and Panama. Throughout the rest of the region, socioeconomic development was leading to the rise of middle classes and, in larger countries, to the creation of mass-based parties and organizations, including labor unions. Such emerging sectors tended to advocate electoral reform, partly out of democratic conviction and partly because it would enhance their prospects for gaining access to power. These developments would bring permanent change to Latin America's politics. (Among other things, they would help explain the increasing reliance on semidemocratic regimes, as middle- and upper-class leaders took steps to prevent working-class movements and radical parties from triumph in the electoral process.)

A second finding relates to the predominance of nondemocratic or autocratic politics, represented by the unshaded upper portions of Figure 1.1. Of all the 1,919 country-years from 1900 through 2000, the nondemocratic

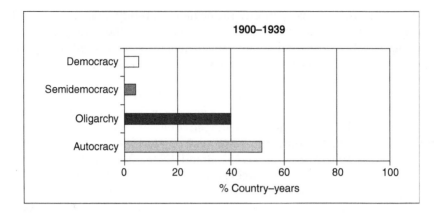

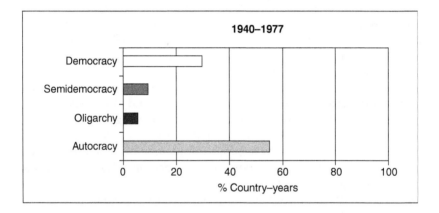

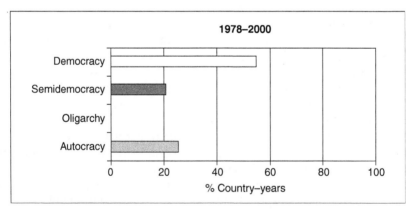

Figure 1.2   Changing incidence of political regimes, 1900–2000

category accounts for 47 percent—nearly half the total. This compares with 26 percent for electoral democracy, 10 percent for semidemocracy, and 18 percent for competitive oligarchy. This reveals another fundamental fact: By quite a wide margin, the most frequent form of political rule in twentieth-century Latin America was autocracy.

There was, of course, significant change over time. To emphasize the point, Figure 1.2 presents changing distributions of country-years in three summary periods: 1900–1939, 1940–1977, and 1978–2000. Nondemocratic rule prevailed just about half the time during the initial phase of the century (52 percent), slightly more than that during the middle period (55 percent), and then dropped to 24 percent throughout the final phase. Oligarchic regimes were widely prevalent in 1900–1939, about 40 percent of the time, and then dropped almost out of sight, falling to 6 percent in 1940–1977 and disappearing altogether by the final period. In contrast, the relative incidence of democracy climbed steadily and strongly, from 5 percent in the initial phase, to 30 percent in the second phase, to 55 percent in the third and final phase. Semidemocracy followed a similar path, but to a lesser degree, increasing from 4 percent to 9 percent to 20 percent.

Taken together, Figures 1.1 and 1.2 serve to dispel one common notion—the idea that Latin American culture is inherently undemocratic or even anti-democratic, and that peoples of the region are simply unsuited for political democracy. Undemocratic cultural traits have variously been attributed to climatic conditions (because democracy cannot flourish in the tropics), racial and ethnic legacies (especially among indigenous civilizations), the passions of Latin temperaments (which impede rational discourse), and, of course, the nefarious influence of the Roman Catholic Church (which peddles ignorance and superstition). If these pathologies were correct, there should never have been sustained experiments in political democracy anywhere in Latin America at any time. Instead, the data clearly show earnest (and temporarily successful) efforts to install democratic politics as far back as the 1910s.

Further, the data reveal that the most recent democratic wave cannot be attributed to the ending of the Cold War. The onset of current electoral democracy in Latin America began in the late 1970s and early 1980s, well before 1989 or 1990, and therefore could not have been due to the collapse of socialism or of the Berlin Wall. As shown in Chapter 4, the U.S.–Soviet rivalry exerted a powerful negative influence on prospects for democracy from the 1940s through the 1980s. The termination of the Cold War thus removed a major obstacle to democratic change but did not cause it to occur. Other factors were clearly at work.

GLOBAL AND COMPARATIVE PERSPECTIVES

Questions now arise: Was Latin America's twentieth-century political trajectory in any way unique? Was it similar to patterns in other parts of the world?

At first glance, indeed, it appears that the rhythm of political change in Latin America mirrored broad developments throughout the world. From a global perspective, Samuel P. Huntington has posited the existence of three broad "waves" of democratization:

- a "long wave" stretching from approximately 1828 to 1926, followed (and ended) by a "reverse wave" from 1922 to 1942
- a "short wave" from 1943 to 1962, with a reverse wave from 1958 to 1975
- a "third wave" from 1974 to 1990 (the time when Huntington was completing his research).

This analysis has become so widely accepted that identification of the so-called third wave has become part of the standard vocabulary of political science.[10]

Does this scheme apply to Latin America? This question merits close scrutiny. The first, long wave described by Huntington began in the United States (in 1828) and spread mostly throughout nineteenth-century Europe to Switzerland, France, and Great Britain and later Italy and Spain. Early in the twentieth century it embraced four countries of Latin America: Argentina, Chile, Colombia, and Uruguay.[11] The second wave took shape in the shadow of World War II. It began with the democratization of defeated Axis powers (Germany, Italy, Japan), gained strength through the process of decolonization (as in India), and affected Latin America with the addition of Costa Rica, Venezuela, Bolivia, Brazil, Peru, and Ecuador to democratic ranks. The third wave began with the overthrow of the Salazar dictatorship in Portugal in 1974 and moved first through southern Europe to Greece and then Spain after the death of Francisco Franco. As suggested by Figures 1.1 and 1.2 earlier, it spread to Latin America from the late 1970s through the 1990s to include Central America and parts of the Caribbean.[12] (This led Huntington to observe, with evident surprise, that the third wave was "overwhelmingly a Catholic wave.")[13] It also spread to India, the Philippines, and (once again) Korea. During the late 1980s and early 1990s the fall of communism offered subsequent opportunities for democratization to Eastern Europe, where several countries had substantial earlier experience with pluralist politics, and to portions of the former Soviet Union, where most nations had very little democratic history.

---

[10] Samuel P. Huntington, *The Third Wave: Democratization in the Late Twentieth Century* (Norman: University of Oklahoma Press, 1991), esp. Ch. 1.

[11] As shown in Appendix 1, I do not consider Colombia to be a full-fledged electoral democracy until the early 1940s.

[12] At the time that Huntington was writing, Mexico did not qualify for inclusion in the third wave.

[13] Huntington, *Third Wave*, 76.

This periodization seems appropriate for Latin America, but only with substantial caveats. One exception relates to Huntington's first phase. It would take a stretch of the imagination to interpret political change in early twentieth-century Latin America as a "wave"—more like a ripple, a cynic might say. It involved democratic experiments in only three countries. On the other hand, oligarchic republicanism was making significant advances throughout the region. To the extent that this phenomenon can be seen as protodemocratic—with free and fair elections and formalistic pronouncements of respect for constitutional procedure—it represented a qualitative shift away from caudillo politics and, to some extent, a training ground for more authentic forms of electoral democracy. In fact, Latin America's oligarchic systems bore considerable resemblance to practices in late nineteenth-century continental Europe. In this perspective—and with a considerable dose of poetic license—the 1900–1939 period might conceivably be characterized as a "wave."

Subsequent phases pose fewer complications. As mass politics came to Latin America, from the late 1930s through the 1950s, electoral democracy took root in nearly half the countries of the region. This movement was countered by two reverse waves, a brief one in the mid-1950s and a more enduring (and brutal) one in the 1960s and 1970s. The subsequent and final period, from 1978 through 2000, also reveals a clearly defined wave, one with only minor reversals, at least as of this writing.[14] Whether democracies in contemporary Latin America will become more or less permanent—and whether they will become truly "liberal" democracies instead of merely "electoral" regimes—is one of the more pressing issues of the current era.

Terminology raises difficult questions. The use of "waves" as the defining metaphor conveys the impression that the surge and decline of political democracy are natural processes: Waves mount in strength and intensity over time, they crest at their peaks, and then, under gravitational pulls, they always recede.[15] Another nettlesome problem relates to causality. Huntington's oceanographic metaphor suggests that political transitions around the world were connected to one another, or to a common cause, in some observable fashion. Thus, Latin America was simply taking part in

---

[14] See Larry Diamond, "Is the Third Wave Over?" *Journal of Democracy* 7, 3 (1996): 20–37.

[15] Paradoxically, my focus on a stable set of cases (nineteen countries) is more suitable for the detection of waves than Huntington's own approach, which uses a steadily expanding universe of cases. He thus traces variations in the absolute number of democracies, but his own data show that there was no long-term upward trend or rising pattern in the relative proportion of democracies among all states over time. See Huntington, *Third Wave*, 25–26.

global processes—later than the leading countries, and to a lesser degree—but it was nonetheless part of the overall pattern.[16]

Democratic Dominoes?

On inspection, Figure 1.1 suggests the possible existence of a regional, or "domino," effect, a process of accumulation that suggests the possible presence of common causal factors and mutual influences. Why would this be so? It would be overly mechanistic to claim that the trend is self-generating—that the incidence of democracy in any given year is a function of the incidence of democracy in the previous year. This kind of assumption does not fare well in the uncertain world of politics, nor does it spell out causal connections.

A more persuasive interpretation is that there might well have existed a process of diffusion, a demonstration effect in which the rise (or fall) of democracy in one country fostered similar outcomes in nearby or neighboring nations. This is especially plausible in societies with high levels of awareness of regional phenomena. Thus, opposition groups in Country Y could draw moral and material sustenance from the downfall of a dictatorship in Country X. It could convince them that victory is possible, inspire them to persist in their struggle, and help expand their base of support. Brazilian demands for direct elections in the latter 1980s no doubt drew inspiration from the Argentine elections of the early 1980s, for instance, and the overthrow of the Somoza regime in Nicaragua gave heart to rebels in nearby El Salvador.

Similarly, military rulers could draw lessons from developments in nearby countries. They were especially mindful of the terms under which military governments left office in other countries: If they could find ways to protect themselves and their interests once they were back in the barracks, it might be entirely acceptable to take leave of presidential palaces. As shown in Chapter 3, military leaders around the hemisphere became acutely conscious of human rights trials in Argentina in the mid-1980s. And as Paul W. Drake has observed, "the authoritarian forces learned from each toppling domino that a transition to an elected government did not necessarily usher in communism, populism, economic disaster, social chaos, the destruction of the military, or the reduction of national security. For many despots, the risks and costs of authoritarianism soon surpassed those of democratization."[17]

---

[16] This raises additional issues of cause and effect. If Latin America represented a small percentage of countries undergoing democratization, as in the first wave, then it could have been affected by developments elsewhere; but if it included most of the newcomer nations, as in the third wave, it was an internal part of the process, and cannot have been causally affected by it in the same way.

[17] Paul W. Drake, "The International Causes of Democratization, 1974–1990," in Paul W. Drake and Mathew D. McCubbins, eds., *The Origins of Liberty: Political and Economic Liberalization in the Modern World* (Princeton, NJ: Princeton University Press, 1998), 85–86.

Yet another possibility is that countries were subject to common influences and causal factors. These forces were more likely to be external than internal, in view of the broad diversity in the domestic composition of Latin American societies. They could be intellectual or ideological, including the rise (and demise) of Marxist theory and a growing conviction that electoral democracy was more promising than violent revolution. They could be economic, especially for countries so dependent on international trade and transnational capital. And they could be political, ranging from unilateral impositions by the United States to such momentous events as the conclusion of the Cold War.

Subregional Variations and the Colossus of the North

Extending the analysis, Figures 1.3 and 1.4 compare century-long patterns of change for two subregions, continental South America, on the one hand, and Mexico, Central America, and the Caribbean, on the other. As revealed by Figure 1.3, the picture for South America clearly reveals three distinct cycles: an oligarchic period (with modest but incipient democracies) from 1900 through the late 1930s, an M-shaped democratic curve from the mid-1940s through the mid-1970s, and a subsequent democratic surge from the late 1970s to (and beyond) the year 2000. Almost every country that turned toward electoral democracy in this final period had experience with a

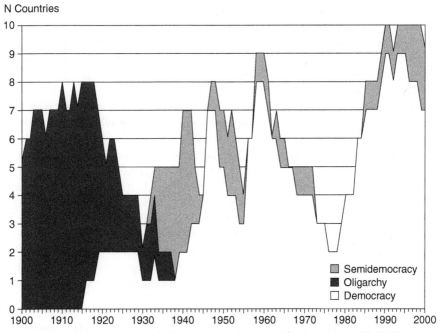

N Countries

Semidemocracy
Oligarchy
Democracy

Figure 1.3 Cycles of political change by region: South America, 1900–2000

N Countries

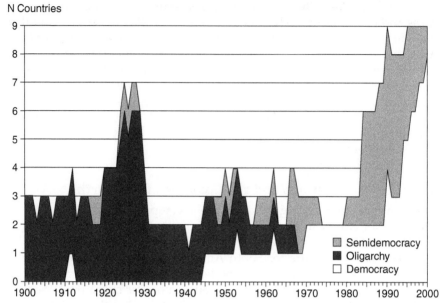

Figure 1.4 Cycles of political change by region: Mexico, Central America, and the Caribbean, 1900–2000

democratic experiment during the 1940 to 1977 period; they also had earlier experience with oligarchic competition after the turn of the century. The only newcomer to the process was Paraguay.

As shown by Figure 1.4, Mexico plus Central America and the Caribbean present a completely different picture. In this area, only one or two countries—Costa Rica and, alternatively, Guatemala and the Dominican Republic—could be described as democratic anytime between the 1940s and the 1980s. Then began a sharp rise in the incidence of democracy and semidemocracy, culminating in Mexico's free and fair election in 2000, by which time eight of the nine countries were electoral democracies.[18]

Simple inspection reveals that these two subregions might have been responding to different opportunities, pressures, and incentives. One important difference stems from alteration of the international environment. As already observed, South American nations managed to achieve democracy throughout the 1980s despite continuation of the Cold War. As argued in Chapter 4, by contrast, the ending of the Cold War helped make it possible for countries of Central America to install electoral democracies throughout the 1990s.

This analysis also yields a geopolitical observation. In the field of inter-American relations, it is axiomatic that the United States has exerted more

---

[18] Countries included in this grouping are Costa Rica, El Salvador, Guatemala, Honduras, Mexico, Nicaragua, Panama, Haiti, and the Dominican Republic.

1979: Campaign poster for Jaime Roldós of Ecuador heralds a new cycle of electoral democracy. The slogan reads: "against oppression and poverty— the force of change." (Latin America Bureau/Research and Action)

pressure, power, and influence around the Caribbean basin, including Mexico and Central America, than in South America.[19] It is plainly apparent from Figures 1.3 and 1.4 that electoral democracy started sooner and spread more widely in South America than in the Caribbean. In fact, it flourished initially in countries farthest from the United States—Argentina, Uruguay, and Chile (with the brief exception of Mexico in 1911). Although the evidence is circumstantial, it prompts speculation that U.S. influence prevented, or at least retarded, the emergence of political democracy in some countries of Latin America. Alternatively, and with more assurance, one could conclude that U.S. influence failed to guarantee the occurrence of free and fair elections. As shown in Chapter 4, such patterns thus suggest a broader point: The greater the level of U.S. involvement, the later (and

---

[19] See my *Talons of the Eagle: Latin America, the United States, and the World,* 3rd rev. ed. (New York: Oxford University Press, 2008).

probably less durable) the appearance of electoral democracy. With regard to democratization, Uncle Sam's backyard lagged far behind southern South America.

Further, Figures 1.3 and 1.4 combine to make a semantic and conceptual point: Although it is possible to speak of "redemocratization" in South America, this term cannot be applied to Mexico, Central America, or the Caribbean. To be sure, Central America had substantial experience with oligarchic republicanism early in the century, especially during the 1920s, but that was long ago, and many of those regimes gave way to military dictatorships in the early 1930s. From then until the mid-1970s, this subregion had minimal acquaintance with electoral democracy. Practically speaking, most of these citizenries were coming face-to-face with democratic practice for the first time.

Clearly, nations of South America could draw on the wellsprings of collective memory during phases of transition to democracy. This would be especially true for Argentina, Brazil, Chile, and Uruguay. Just as clearly, countries in Central America and the Caribbean could not. This difference might exert a significant impact on prospects for political consolidation.

LESSONS OVER TIME: PRIOR EXPERIENCE

An alternative approach to explaining the incidence of democracy rests on historical experience. One of the most common theorems in political science holds that countries with former democratic experience are more likely to become democratic than are countries without such experience. In contrast to the idea of regional contagion, which stresses the role of simultaneous developments in neighboring countries, this hypothesis focuses on the role of historical experience *within* individual countries.

As given, of course, the proposition begs a crucial question: How do countries initiate democracy in the first place? How do they acquire experience? Moreover, the thesis rests on a two-fold assumption: that prior democratic experience will put reinstatement of democracy at or near the top of the societal agenda, and that there will be a collective popular nostalgia for the democratic period. For this reason, though, it is of fundamental importance to consider the *qualities* of earlier democratic experiments. If the experiences were positive, it seems likely that nostalgia would exist—but what if they were negative?

In its most optimistic form, the hypothesis stipulates that countries should be able to achieve stable democracy on the basis of *one* previous democratic experience. Countries with *repeated* earlier experiences are clearly having difficulty with democracy. Countries with *no* prior experience will not have had the opportunity to absorb important lessons.

Table 1.1 attempts to test this broad idea. For nations involved in each of the three historical cycles of electoral democratization in Latin America, it summarizes information on earlier experiences—year of initiation, number

TABLE 1.1 Historical Experience with Electoral Democracy, 1900–2000

	PRIOR EXPERIENCE			CURRENT/ MOST RECENT
	Year of Initiation	N Episodes	N Years	Years[*]
Cycle I (1900–1939)				
Argentina	1916	3	22	1983–
Chile	1933	1	40	1989–
Mexico	1911	1	2	2000–
Uruguay	1919	2	49	1985–
Cycle II (1940–1977)				
Bolivia	1956	1	8	1983–
Brazil	1946	2	16	1990–
Colombia	1942	1	7	1958–
Costa Rica		_____		1953–
Dominican Republic	1962	1	1	1978–
Ecuador	1948	1	13	1979–95
Guatemala	1945	1	9	1996–
Peru	1945	3	14	1980–91
Venezuela	1945	1	3	1958–98
Cycle III (1978–2000)				
El Salvador		_____		1994
Haiti		_____		1990
Honduras		_____		1998
Nicaragua		_____		1990
Panama		_____		1994
Paraguay		_____		1993

[*]Through the year 2000.

of episodes, and total duration of episodes—together with date of initiation of the current or most recent democratic experience.

The results provide substantial confirmation of the general hypothesis. Among the thirteen countries that first became democratic during the 1900–1939 or 1940–1977 cycles, eight managed to restore democracy after just one prior episode: Bolivia, Chile, Colombia, the Dominican Republic, Ecuador, Guatemala, Mexico, and Venezuela. Among these eight, six were still democratic as of 2000 (Ecuador and Venezuela having reverted to semidemocratic status). Brazil and Uruguay regained democracy after two earlier experiences. Only Costa Rica achieved a long-lasting democracy with no prior democratic episode.

Intermediate cases are indeterminate. Argentina and Peru had numerous earlier democratic episodes and fairly extensive experience (an average of nearly twenty years each). They contradict the earlier-experience hypothesis by having multiple former episodes and suffering repeated meltdowns. Yet they were democratic by the end of the century.

A third category consists of recent cases of democratization with no prior experience. This includes virtually all countries whose initiation to democracy came during the third and final cycle of the century—Haiti, Paraguay, and four countries of Central America. But for its brief flirtation with democracy in 1911–1912, Mexico would also be in this group. At this writing it is too early to tell how durable these governments will be.

In sum, Table 1.1 provides considerable confirmation of the earlier-experience hypothesis. Yet it also reveals potential circularity within the underlying logic. Turning the thesis on its head, one might argue that countries that are especially well suited for democracy (for whatever reasons) might need only one prior episode at most: Chile, Colombia, Venezuela, Costa Rica. Countries lacking such endowments (whatever they are) would endure repeated failures: Argentina, Brazil, Peru. Other countries would not even have the opportunity until the last decade of the century: Haiti, Paraguay, Honduras. In social science argot, it is entirely possible that earlier democratic experience should be construed not as an independent variable (the cause of something else) but as a dependent variable (the result, not the cause).

Democracy and Instability

Exploration of the earlier-experience hypothesis raises questions about the notion of political stability. How long does democracy last? Have patterns of durability changed over time?

To begin the analysis, Table 1.2 presents data on the overall duration of political regimes during the course of the twentieth century, from 1900 through 2000. For each regime, the table displays the number of episodes that occurred during the course of the century, the range of duration in years, and the average (mean) duration in years.

The results are revealing. The longest-surviving type of regime was electoral democracy, with a range of 1–48 years and a mean duration of 13 years. The second-highest average belonged to nondemocratic authoritarianism, with a mean duration of 12.3 years, followed closely by competitive oligarchy, with a mean of 10.6 years. Generally speaking, the life expectancy of all three regimes was about the same, around 11 to 13 years. These time spans are very short: It must be remembered that these were changes of *regime*, not

TABLE 1.2 Duration of Electoral Regimes, 1900–2000

Regime Type	N Episodes	DURATION (YEARS)	
		Range	Average
Oligarchic	32	1–30	10.6
Democratic	38	1–48	13.0
Semidemocratic	33	1–17	5.6
Nondemocratic	73	1–90	12.3

just changes of government. And the spans are remarkably uniform: None of these regimes was inherently more durable than the others; democracy was just as vulnerable to termination as autocracy (and vice versa). As might be expected, semidemocratic regimes, with their intermediate character, had even briefer life expectancies, with an average of less than 6 years.

Survival rates for democracy underwent suggestive change. Electoral democracies that emerged during the 1900–1939 cycle lasted an average of 21 years. Democracies inaugurated during the 1940–1977 period were substantially less durable, surviving on average just 14.2 years. And although the evidence is incomplete, it appears that electoral democracies initiated in the 1978–2000 cycle are proving to be relatively stable. By 2000, democratic systems of the 1980s had already lasted an average of 14.9 years, and most of them were going fairly strong. Democracy has become increasingly durable.[20] This is a major change that sets the third cycle apart from the two earlier eras. (Yet survival was far from assured. During the 1990–2000 period alone, democratic regimes succumbed to overthrows or *auto-golpes* in Haiti, Peru, and Ecuador.)

Overall, this analysis underlines another fundamental fact: Political instability was endemic in Latin America. In fact, there were 155 regime changes over the 101-year period from 1900 through 2000—a rate of 1.53 per year. Moreover, there were no fewer than 55 *major* changes of regime—oscillations between democracy and dictatorship, with or without intermediate phases of oligarchic rule or semidemocracy—more than one every other year. These are very high rates of change. In global and comparative terms, Latin America has displayed an unusually high level of regime instability.[21]

This might seem a very bad thing. Political discourse generally attaches positive meanings to the concept of "stability" and negative associations to "instability." But stability refers only to duration in time; by itself, it does not indicate whether what lasts (or does not last) is beneficial. A brutally repressive dictatorship might well be more "stable" than an open and contentious democracy, but that does not make the world a better place; it makes it worse.

What have been the political correlates of stability and instability in Latin America? To examine this issue, Table 1.3 arrays countries of the region along two dimensions: number of regime changes (to or from democracy), as an indicator of instability, and number of years of electoral democracy, as an indicator of political experience.

---

[20] Calculation of year-to-year ratios or "probability rates" of survival for democracy makes this point another way: for both the 1900–1939 and 1940–1977 periods the probability rate was around 0.93, and for 1978–2000 it jumped to more than 0.98.

[21] For points of comparison, see Adam Przeworski, Michael E. Alvarez, José Antonio Cheibub, and Fernando Limongi, *Democracy and Development: Political Institutions and Well-Being in the World, 1950–1990* (Cambridge: Cambridge University Press, 2000), 40–49.

TABLE 1.3 Regime Stability and Electoral Democracy, 1900–2000

	N REGIME CHANGES		
Years of Democracy	1	2–3	>3
1–20	El Salvador Honduras Nicaragua Panama Paraguay	Guatemala Haiti* Mexico	
21–40		Bolivia Dominican Republic	Argentina Brazil Ecuador Peru
>40	Costa Rica	Chile Colombia Uruguay Venezuela	

*Haiti was the sole country in this category with only two major regime changes; all others had three.

Somewhat surprisingly, Table 1.3 reveals the existence of a *positive* relationship between regime instability and duration of political democracy: The higher the number of regime changes, the longer the experience with electoral democracy.[22] Or, to put it another way, there is a negative association between regime stability and levels of democracy. Five countries (El Salvador, Honduras, Nicaragua, Panama, and Paraguay) underwent only one major regime change during the twentieth century and enjoyed fewer than twenty years of democratic experience. Four countries with three regime changes (Chile, Colombia, Uruguay, and Venezuela) had more than forty years of democratic experience. All countries with more than three regime changes (Argentina, Brazil, Ecuador, and Peru) had twenty-one to forty years of democratic experience. Brazil had thirty-seven democratic years, and Argentina and Ecuador each had forty.

In sum, Table 1.3 demonstrates that instability did not promote political democracy throughout the region but did not impede it, either. After all, democratization means change, change encounters resistance, and the ensuing conflict provokes uncertainty and instability. Experiments in democracy did not always succeed, but they often yielded positive results. Only those who fought for democracy were able to reap its benefits.

---

[22] As a measure of statistical association, the gamma coefficient for this table comes out to +.425.

CHAPTER 2

TRANSITIONS AND CONTINUITIES

Transitions are complex affairs. Once a dictatorship begins to weaken, societies embark on paths of political change, with no predetermined end in sight. Authoritarian regimes can break down because of external war, economic crisis, social upheaval, or defections from the ruling coalition. Pressures can come from without, from within, or from below. Ensuing transitions can be long or short, violent or peaceful, controlled or uncontrolled. They can lead to a broad array of results, from the replacement of one tyrant by another to the installation of stable institutional democracy. To a considerable extent, outcomes depend on qualities of the transitions themselves—on surrounding circumstance, on the roles of social forces, and on decisions by key political actors. Where you go depends upon the path you take.[1]

This chapter explores modes of political transition and continuity in Latin America. It begins with a brief summation of distinctions among types of authoritarian regimes, which helps to establish starting points for paths of subsequent change. It goes on to examine conventional hypotheses about the existence of socioeconomic prerequisites for democratic change. It traces the roles of social class and organized sectors in challenging authoritarian regimes and promoting pluralistic politics. It then turns to political elites and to the bargains they might (or might not) make in the course of transitions toward democracy. A concluding section offers empirical evidence on sequential patterns of change.[2]

---

[1] See Alfred Stepan, "Paths Toward Redemocratization: Theoretical and Comparative Considerations," in Guillermo O'Donnell, Philippe Schmitter, and Laurence Whitehead, eds., *Transitions from Authoritarian Rule: Comparative Perspectives* (Baltimore: Johns Hopkins University Press, 1986), Ch. 3, 64–84.

[2] Broad comparative treatments of these issues can be found in Juan J. Linz and Alfred Stepan, eds., *Problems of Democratic Transition and Consolidation: Southern Europe, South America, and Post-Communist Europe* (Baltimore: Johns Hopkins University Press, 1996), and Geoffrey Pridham, ed., *Transitions to Democracy: Comparative Perspectives from Southern Europe, Latin America and Eastern Europe* (Aldershot, England: Dartmouth, 1995).

As its central focus, the chapter explores the roles of actors and developments within Latin America that fostered transitions toward democracy. In contrast to recent scholarship, which tends to emphasize the importance of elites, this analysis devotes a good deal of attention to conflicts and coalitions among social classes. As social structures evolved and new groups entered the political arena, demands for change emerged and provided the context for decisive action by elites. To use a theatrical metaphor, social pressures from below set the stage on which elites assumed their starring roles.

STARTING POINTS

Transitions have to start somewhere. And as a matter of definition, transitions toward democracy begin as transitions away from authoritarianism. Moreover, the authoritarian regime itself—its structure, form, and depth— can have decisive impacts on the shape and direction of the ensuing transition. To analyze these processes and their complexities, it is essential to comprehend the varieties of authoritarianism that have existed in twentieth-century Latin America.

Essentially, there have been two broad types of authoritarian rule: *personalist* and *institutional*. Each of these categories breaks down into distinctive subtypes. Figure 2.1 provides a schematic summary of the most prominent forms.

As the label indicates, personalist dictatorships are ruled by strong-willed individuals who dominate the political process. Their principal interest is power. They are tyrants. They do not subscribe to substantive ideologies and they do not have programmatic missions. They recruit collaborators, but they do not tolerate rivals or competitors. They strengthen their hold on power through combinations of fear and cooptation, liberally dispensing violence and patronage according to the situation. They possess exceptional qualities of command: intelligence, cunning, energy, strength, stamina, and, above all, ruthlessness. Often, but not always, they promote cults of

| | Power Structure | |
Leadership	Personalist	Institutionalized
Military	Traditional Caudillo or "Man on Horseback"	Collective Junta or Bureaucratic-Authoritarian Regime
Civilian	Technocratic State, Delegative Semidemocracy, or Sultanistic Despotism	One-Party State or Corporatist Regime

Figure 2.1 Types of authoritarian regime

personality, characterized by propagandistic glorification of the virtues and deeds of the ruler, and in this way they base their claims to authority on charisma.[3]

Personalist rulers often emerged from military ranks. Throughout the nineteenth and early twentieth centuries, traditional caudillos led armed bands that fought their way into power, looted the treasury, and then confronted an unending series of would-be rivals. They made generous use of patronage to purchase loyalty among their followers. Some, such as Juan Manuel de Rosas in Argentina and Porfirio Díaz in Mexico, succeeded in centralizing their rule and integrating their nation-states. Others were classic "men on horseback" who stormed into presidential palaces, imposed law and order, and, in most cases, forged close alliances with socioeconomic elites and oligarchic interests. Such figures were ubiquitous in Central America. One example among many was Maximiliano Hernández Martínez, who ruled El Salvador with conspicuous ferocity from 1931 to 1944.

Civilians could dominate personalist dictatorships. As outlined in Figure 2.1, these regimes could come in many guises. Technocratic states featured control by civilian commanders of powerful bureaucracies, such as António de Oliveira Salazar in Portugal (1932–1968). Concentrating excessive authority in chief executives, delegative semidemocracies emerged from dubious or rigged elections, as under Alberto K. Fujimori in Peru (1992–2000). Somewhat more common were satrapies, or "sultanistic" regimes, whose leaders often came from military ranks but went on to establish personalized dictatorships. A defining feature was the effort to establish the ruling family as a pseudolegitimate dynasty, so power could pass from one generation to another, usually from father to son. This had the virtue of avoiding the kind of "succession crisis" so common to caudillismo. Avarice was another signature of sultanism. Rulers would appropriate enormous shares of the national economy for themselves and family members. This enriched the dynasty and also discouraged the rise of rivals and competitors by removing the potential for any independent power base. To legitimate the dynasty, too, they cultivated myths about the virtues of the leader and the ruling family. Unlike caudillos, who tended to come and go with frequency, sultanistic rulers often prevailed for long periods.[4] Prominent examples were

---

[3] Max Weber defines charisma as "devotion to the specific and exceptional sanctity, heroism or exemplary character of an individual person, and of the normative patterns or order revealed or ordained by him." Literally, charisma means "the gift of grace." As is readily apparent, democratic politicians can possess charisma as well.

[4] Messianic movements under charismatic figureheads constituted yet another form of personalistic civilian domination, but they rarely (if ever) attained control of the state. An example might be Sendero Luminoso under the leadership of Abimael Guzmán.

the Somoza dictatorship in Nicaragua, Trujillo in the Dominican Republic, Batista in Cuba, and the Duvaliers in Haiti.[5]

Institutional authoritarian regimes were very different. Power did not belong to individuals. It belonged to committees, bureaucracies, or institutions. One example was the military junta, leaders of the armed forces who came to power through a forcible coup. Representing different branches of the military—army, navy, and air force, usually with an army general at its head—the juntas governed in the style of a committee. Decisions were collective. Traditionally, military juntas remained in power for relatively short periods. They left the civilian bureaucracy in place and did not engage in prolonged campaigns of terror or violence. Their purpose was to rectify a specific problem in the political arena and then, when their self-appointed task was finished, they would leave office peacefully. They arranged their own extrication from power, in other words, frequently setting up semidemocratic regimes for precisely this purpose. Regimes of this kind were ubiquitous from the 1930s through the 1950s, making conspicuous appearances in Argentina (1930–1932, 1943–1946, and 1955–1958) and in Brazil (1945, 1954, and 1955).

A second, more pervasive form of institutionalized authoritarianism emerged in the 1960s, what have come to be known as "bureaucratic-authoritarian" regimes. Initiated and led by the military, these regimes claimed to pursue missions of national redemption. One element in these projects was eradication of communist subversion; another was containment of the organized working class, whose irresponsibility and excess were taken to be the cause of economic stagnation. To achieve these ambitious goals, they engaged in brutal repression, waging relentless "wars against subversion" and resorting to murder, torture, and the disappearance of real and imagined dissidents. Military leaders also formed strategic alliances with economic elites—landowners and businesspeople, including foreign investors—and recruited highly educated technocrats to design and implement economic policies. It went without saying that in contrast to traditional military juntas, bureaucratic-authoritarian rulers planned to remain in power for indefinite periods of time: They were thinking in terms not of years, but of decades.[6] To the surprise of most observers, regimes of this kind emerged in the most economically developed and socially advanced parts of Latin America—Argentina, Chile, and Uruguay, the same countries that first turned toward democracy early in the century—and also Brazil.

---

[5] In addition, sultanistic leaders often consolidated power at the local level. Caciques in Mexico and *coroneis* in Brazil ruled villages and provinces as though they were personal fiefdoms. It might be noted that Stepan and Linz treat sultanism as an altogether separate category: see *Problems of Democratic Transition*, Ch. 3, "Modern Nondemocratic Regimes."

[6] See Guillermo O'Donnell, *Modernization and Bureaucratic-Authoritarianism: Studies in South American Politics* (Berkeley, CA: Institute of International Studies, 1974), and David Collier, ed., *The New Authoritarianism in Latin America* (Princeton, NJ: Princeton University Press, 1979).

Institutionalized authoritarianism under civilian leadership often consisted of one-party rule, or dominant-party rule. Power resided in the connection between state and party, which were virtually indistinguishable. There could be considerable competition and jockeying for power within the dominant party, but behind the scenes; the public stance was one of harmony and unity. Uppermost leaders were civilian politicians, who nonetheless took extravagant care to cultivate the acquiescence and good will of the armed forces. For this kind of regime, patronage was the key to survival. The classic case was Mexico from the 1930s through the 1990s. One-sided elections presented a transparent façade for authoritarian rule. The dominant party, the Partido Revolucionario Institucional (PRI), ruled in tandem with the state bureaucracy: There were no other avenues to power. Criticism was permitted but muted. Repression was used, but cooptation was favored: two carrots, even three or four, and then a stick if necessary.

Yet another version of civilian dictatorship was the "corporatist regime," a complex arrangement in which the state mobilized and regulated relations among functional pillars of society: workers, peasants, landowners, businesspeople, and so on. These functional categories derived from traditional Iberian notions of societal order. According to this view, it was the role of the state to adjudicate conflicts among competing interest groups in such a way as to achieve maximum benefits for the society a whole. The most prominent example of this genre was the Estado Novo that was imposed on Brazil by Getúlio Vargas (1937–1945). As experience elsewhere would show, corporatist schemes could also be installed by military regimes.

Such distinctions among autocratic regimes, from personalist caudillismo to institutional dominant-party systems, are purely analytical; in actual practice, most dictatorships incorporated elements of more than one type. (Mexico in the 1980s to 1990s was both a dominant-party regime and a technocratic state, almost all civilian-led autocracies relied heavily on the armed forces for support, and military governments often displayed personalist as well as institutional characteristics.) Even so, the classification demonstrates the multiplicity of starting points for alterations of political regimes. It also serves to emphasize the uncertainty of such transitions, which might or might not culminate in full democracy. They could also lead to the exchange of one kind of authoritarian regime (or ruler) for another, or to the temporary installation of democracies that might soon succumb to dictatorship. There is nothing inevitable about democracy (see Box 2.1).

ECONOMIC REQUISITES?

One of the most widely accepted—and commonly studied—propositions in contemporary social science holds that political democracy requires socioeconomic development. According to what has come to be known as modernization theory, economic progress leads to diversification of interests and diffusion of power in ways that resist monopolization by the state. Prosperity

BOX 2.1

WATCH YOUR LANGUAGE: LIBERALIZATION
OR DEMOCRATIZATION?

The variety of autocratic regimes urges caution in the use of language. It
is common to describe the breakdown of authoritarianism as a process of
"democratization." But is that necessarily correct?

The concept of "democratization" is teleological: It defines a process in
terms of its endpoint, which is presumed to be democracy. This requires more
than a little intellectual presumptuousness. How do we know where a process
will go? What did key actors think at the time?

In contrast, the notion of "liberalization" of a regime tends to focus on
movement from the starting point, rather than the arrival at an end. At the
same time, it tends to suggest that reforms have the purpose not of transform-
ing the system, but of adjusting and prolonging the regime.

There is considerable debate about the relationship between liberalization
and democratization. The question is whether liberalization can stabilize a
regime through a process of limited reform, or whether, in the long run, it
inevitably leads down a path to democratization.

Which term is most appropriate? There is no clear-cut answer to this question. The principal lesson is that it is essential to choose labels with care, rather
than adopt them uncritically.

promotes a sense of well-being that encourages people to join together in
collective pursuits, including political campaigns. Mass education enables
citizens to participate intelligently in politics, resisting demagogic appeals
and holding leaders accountable. (As Albert Einstein is reported to have said,
"An empty stomach makes a poor political advisor.") The basic idea is that
economic development leads to alterations in the social structure, which, in
turn, lay the foundations for political democracy. As Seymour Martin Lipset
once put it, "A society divided between a large impoverished mass and a
small favored elite results either in oligarchy (dictatorial rule of the small
upper stratum) or in tyranny (popular-based dictatorship)."[7]

There are, in fact, two distinct hypotheses. One asserts that socioeconomic
development is an essential precondition for the *initiation* or installation of
democracy—that is, for transitions toward democracy.[8] The other claims

---

[7] Seymour Martin Lipset, *Political Man: The Social Bases of Politics* (Garden City,
NY: Anchor Books, 1963, first published in 1960), Ch. 2, "Economic Development
and Democracy," 31.

[8] See, for example, John B. Londregran and Keith T. Poole, "Does High
Income Promote Democracy?" *World Politics* 49 (October 1996): 1–30; Samuel
P. Huntington, *The Third Wave: Democratization in the Late Twentieth Century*
(Norman: University of Oklahoma Press, 1991), 59–72; and Daron Acemoglu and
James A. Robinson, *Economic Origins of Dictatorship and Democracy* (Cambridge:
Cambridge University Press, 2006).

that development is a necessary condition for the maintenance or survival of democracy—that is, for the *consolidation* of democracy.[9] These are very different arguments, but they are often conflated or blurred.[10]

There are several ways of clearing up this confusion. Consider the following hypotheses:

H_1: Inauguration and consolidation of democracy both require the same level of socioeconomic development (it just has not been correctly determined as yet).

H_2: A lower level of development is required for inauguration, and a higher level is required for consolidation.

H_3: The relationship between democracy and development is either nonexistent or spurious, as both are consequences of another (unobserved) common factor.

There remains the possibility of reverse causation: Development does not cause democracy, it is the other way around: Democracy causes development. The empirical relationship exists. It has yet to be fully understood.

How do these arguments relate to Latin America? To approach these issues, the analysis offers a broad examination of connections between development and democracy in Latin America as they change over time. As here observed, levels of development generally precede (or are simultaneous with) movements toward democracy; development is postulated as the independent variable, and, following common convention, it is measured according to gross domestic product (GDP) per capita. As will become clear, the dependent variable is the initiation of democracy, rather than its consolidation.[11]

To begin, Table 2.1 presents data on levels of development and transitions toward democracy among thirteen countries of Latin America during the 1900 to 1939 cycle of political change. The clarity is startling. All three of the most prosperous nations of the region in this era—Argentina, Uruguay, and Chile—underwent profound and in some cases prolonged shifts toward electoral democracy (although they did not endure). No country in the lower or middle economic category made any such attempt. The proposition appears to be confirmed: The higher the level of development, the greater the prospects for transition to democracy.

---

[9] See Lipset, *Political Man*; and Mitchell A. Seligson, "Democracy in Latin America: The Current Cycle," in James M. Malloy and Mitchell A. Seligson, eds., *Authoritarians and Democrats: Regime Transition in Latin America* (Pittsburgh, PA: University of Pittsburgh Press, 1987), 6–9.

[10] As in Todd Landman, "Economic Development and Democracy: The View from Latin America," *Political Studies* 47 (1999): 607–626. For a clear distinction see Robert A. Dahl, *Polyarchy: Participation and Opposition* (New Haven, CT: Yale University Press, 1970), Ch. 5, "The Socioeconomic Order: Level of Development," 62.

[11] Transitions to semidemocracy are not included in this analysis.

TABLE 2.1 Economic Development and Democratic Change, 1900–1939

Level of Development	TRANSITION?		
	No	Yes	Total
Lower	5	0	5
Middle	5	0	5
Upper	0	3	3
Totals	**10**	**3**	**13**

Source for economic data: Figures on GDP per capita for 1913 and 1928 as reported in Victor Bulmer-Thomas, *The Economic History of Latin America since Independence* (Cambridge: Cambridge University Press, 1994), Appendix 3, 442–447; there are no data for Bolivia, the Dominican Republic, Ecuador, Haiti, Panama, or Paraguay. Cuba and Puerto Rico are not included in this analysis.

TABLE 2.2 Economic Development and Democratic Change, 1940–1977

Level of Development	Democratic as of 1940	Transition Attempted	No Democracy	Totals
Lower	0	4	4	8
Middle	1	4	3	8
Upper	1	2	0	3
Totals	**2**	**10**	**7**	**19**

Brackets are defined as follows: Lower = GDP/capita of less than $1,000 as of 1960, in constant U.S. dollars of 1995, Middle = GDP/capita of $1,000–$1,999, Upper = GDP/capita of $2,000 or more.

Source: World Bank, World Development Indicators Database, 2001.

The second broad cycle of historical change, 1940 to 1977 (see Table 2.2), reveals a somewhat similar pattern. At the outset of this period, only two countries—Chile and Uruguay, both in the upper brackets of development—were practicing democracies.[12] Among the other nations in the upper and middle categories, six would embark on transitions to democracy (Argentina, Brazil, Colombia, Costa Rica, Peru, and Venezuela), and three remained autocracies (El Salvador, Mexico, and Panama). No country in the least-developed category was democratic as of 1940. In subsequent years, four would attempt to install democracy (Bolivia, the Dominican Republic, Ecuador, and Guatemala), and four would not (Haiti, Honduras, Nicaragua, Paraguay). So there was still a positive relationship between level of development and political democracy, but it was not as strong or clear as in 1900 to 1939.[13]

---

[12] Uruguay was in the topmost bracket, with a per capita income of nearly $3,900 as of 1960 (in constant U.S. dollars of 1995); Chile just missed the $2,000 cutoff point, with a GDP per capita of $1,968.

[13] With countries classified in dichotomous fashion as "with" or "without" democratic experience during the period, gamma for 1940–1977 = +.547. The gamma coefficient for 1900–1939 was a perfect +1.000.

TABLE 2.3 Economic Development and Democratic Change, 1978–2000

Level of Development	Democratic as of 1978	Transition 1979–1989	Transition 1990–2000	Totals
Lower	0	0	3	3
Lower-middle	2	2	3	7
Upper-middle	0	2	1	3
Upper	2	2	2	6
Totals	4	6	9	19

Brackets defined as follows: Lower = GDP/capita of less than $1,000 as of 1980 in constant U.S. dollars of 1995; Lower-middle = $1,000–$1,999; Upper-middle = $2,000–$2,999; Upper = $3,000 or more.

Source: World Bank, World Development Indicators Database, 2001.

Yet most of these experiments did not survive. By 1978 there were only four democracies: Costa Rica, Colombia, Venezuela, and, by virtue of an election that same year, the Dominican Republic. Both democracies as of 1940, Chile and Uruguay, had succumbed to authoritarian regimes. Of the ten countries that attempted transitions between 1940 and 1977, five were under authoritarian rule by the end of the period.

Such findings make a crucial point: There were no economic thresholds for democratic consolidation during the 1940–1977 cycle. Countries in the lower tier, Bolivia, Ecuador, and Guatemala, managed to install electoral democracies during the 1940s and 1950s. So did nations in the middle tier, and two of them, Colombia and Costa Rica, remained democratic through the end of this era. And although every country in the upper tier had some kind of democratic experience, relatively high levels of economic development did not prevent such wealthy countries as Argentina and Uruguay from falling under military dictatorship; in the middle range, Brazil, Chile, and Peru succumbed as well. During this period, higher GDP per capita thus increased the chances that a country would attempt a democratic transition, but it did not assure survival.

During the third and most recent cycle, 1978–2000, the relationship between development and democracy weakened markedly. As revealed in Table 2.3, every country in the region, regardless of developmental level, came to enjoy a democratic experience.[14] Three electoral democracies were in place at the start of the cycle, and all of the other countries underwent some kind of transition to democracy. By the year 1999, as shown in Chapter 1, sixteen were electoral democracies, and three qualified as semidemocracies; there were no authoritarian regimes at all (with the troublesome exception of Cuba). The overall inference is clear: If countries were at different levels

---

[14] In combination, the middle brackets in Table 2.3 (lower-middle plus upper-middle) are comparable to the $1,000–$3,000 "transition zone" identified by Samuel P. Huntington in *The Third Wave: Democratization in the Late Twentieth Century* (Norman: University of Oklahoma Press, 1991), 62–64.

of economic development, which they were, and all underwent experience with democracy, which they did, then there could be no causal connection between development and the onset of democracy.

But there exists a subtle wrinkle, one that has to do with sequence, or timing, rather than the simple fact of democratic experience. Of the six countries in the uppermost economic tier, four were electoral democracies by the end of the 1980s (Colombia, Venezuela, Argentina, and Uruguay), and two more followed in the 1990s. Of three countries in the upper-middle bracket, two underwent transitions in the 1980s and one in the 1990s. In the lower-middle tier, two were democratic at the start of the period—Costa Rica and the Dominican Republic—two had early transitions, and two had late transitions. And among countries in the lowest tier, all underwent transitions in the 1990s and not the 1980s (Guatemala, Nicaragua, and Paraguay). There was a tendency, in other words, for wealthier countries to undergo transitions to democracy *before* the poorer countries.[15]

In sum, the overall relationship between development and democracy in Latin America underwent considerable change during the course of the twentieth century. In the early period, 1900–1939, the connection was powerful and clear. During the second political cycle, 1940–1977, it still existed, but to a lesser degree. And during the third and final period, 1978–2000, it vanished altogether (leaving aside the distinction between early and late democratizers in this era). Over time, the association between economic development and political democratization in Latin America lost its empirical force.[16]

Why would this be so? There could be several explanations. One is that all countries of the region had surpassed a minimal economic threshold for *transitions* to democratic politics, leaving prospects for survival or *consolidation* of democracy still much in doubt. Another is that the link between development and democracy never really existed, that the association was spurious, or that it did not reveal cause and effect. Still another possibility is that democratization in the 1980s and especially the 1990s resulted from a different set of causal factors than it did before.

SOCIAL FORCES

Political transitions result from societal demands. Regimes undergo change in response to social pressures—usually, but not always, pressures from subordinate classes or excluded sectors. On occasion, pressures from below

---

[15] By the end of 1989 there was a fairly strong relationship between development and democracy, with a gamma coefficient of +.484.

[16] Herewith a methodological caveat for analysts of this connection: Beware the time frame of the data set! At least in the Latin American context, studies covering only recent developments are likely to overlook patterns of change over time.

BOX 2.2
WHAT'S A SOCIAL CLASS?

The concept of class has a long and distinguished tradition in social science. Essentially it is an analytical construct that refers to relative position in society—the category, or "class," to which individuals or groups of people are understood to belong.

The most common criterion for defining social classes focuses on shared economic condition, although other factors, such as prestige, culture, or power, can also play determining roles. Karl Marx (1818–1883) identified divisions in society between groups bearing different relationships to the means of production (such as tools and material resources): masters and slaves, lords and serfs, and, in the capitalist era, the bourgeoisie (capitalists) and workers (the proletariat). Marx claimed, furthermore, that economic factors determined the particularities of social organization, political power, and cultural forms, and he predicted that contradictions within capitalism would lead to a "class struggle" that would eventually result in the triumph of the proletariat.

The great German sociologist Max Weber (1864–1920) challenged Marx's emphasis on the primacy of economic factors and argued for a more flexible and multifaceted interpretation of social organization. For him economic criteria remained central to the understanding of class divisions, but they were not the only ones—social status and political power were separate and relevant concerns. In this sense, class referred to a group's ability to control its "life chances" rather than just its relationship to modes of production.

Adopting a neo-Weberian approach, this book defines social class on the basis of occupational position (the primary consideration) and social status (a secondary factor). To the extent that it is independent of economic factors, prestige usually reflects social codes about cultural refinement: Teachers are modestly paid in most societies, for instance, but in some parts of the world they command widespread deference and respect.

Within Latin America, this study identifies three basic class strata: upper (wealthy industrialists, financiers, landowners), middle (white-collar employees, teachers, shopkeepers, etc.), and lower, or "popular" (workers, peasants, the unemployed, and others). For the region as a whole, the relative percentages of these strata around 2000 were approximately as follows:

	%
Upper	3–10
Middle	20–30
Lower	60–70

Latin American society is highly stratified, in other words, and what we might think of as a "middle" class actually occupies a position of relative privilege. A distinction between urban and rural components of these class strata can further enrich our understanding.

This leaves open the question of class consciousness. People might (or might not) identify themselves as members of their social class, and they might (or

> might not) feel a shared sense of collective solidarity. In the United States, class consciousness is most conspicuous by its near-complete absence. In Latin America, by contrast, it has often ignited class conflicts and struggles with enduring consequences for social and political life.

or outside can lead to overthrow of the existing regime. Alternatively, they produce fissures within the ruling elite that initiate complex patterns of political reform, modification, or transformation. Just as frequently, civic demands are met with brutal repression and perpetuation of authoritarian rule. But the bottom line is this: Democratization involves conflicts of interest, and, in most cases, this means social agitation. This is not a sufficient condition, but it is a necessary one.[17] Social groups and classes are central actors in these political dramas (see Box 2.2).

In schematic outline, successive cycles of democratization in twentieth-century Latin America reveal three broad patterns of social-class action. During the initial phase, 1900–1939, democratization was adopted by traditional elites. During the second period, 1940–1977, middle classes made effective demands for democratic change. During 1978–2000, there were several forces at work: organized labor, middle classes, and, especially in Central America, foreign powers and the international community. Negotiations between regime incumbents and opposition dissidents also played a conspicuous role in this third and final phase.

Cycle 1: 1900–1939

Traditional elites embraced political democracy not so much out of ideological conviction, although they might have claimed that was the case, but for strategic purposes. The goal was either to resolve disputes between contentious factions of the elite, to advance the interests of one elite faction against the other, or to co-opt rising middle-class groups. In actual fact, all three motivations usually came together in one combination or another.

The initial case was Argentina, which adopted the secret ballot and compulsory voting in 1912. A quintessential member of the ruling oligarchy, President Roque Sáenz Peña responded to a series of uprisings and demands from the Radical Civic Union (UCR), whose principal constituency consisted of burgeoning middle-class groups. Denouncing fraud and demanding fair elections, the UCR and its predecessors staged uprisings in 1890, 1893, and 1905 and gained support from substantial segments of society, including elements in the military. Repression of working-class movements in 1910 added to the social tension. Thinking that the UCR would not be able to win

---

[17] For a persuasive argument to this effect see Ruth Berins Collier, *Paths Toward Democracy: The Working Class and Elites in Western Europe and South America* (Cambridge: Cambridge University Press, 1999).

national elections, Sáenz Peña and his collaborators chose electoral reform as a means of co-opting the middle class, dividing the middle class from the lower class, and appeasing both groups in the process. "Whereas power had previously been parceled out to competing factions within the landed aristocracy," as one analyst has written, "it would now be shared between the aristocracy and rising middle-class groups (to the virtual exclusion of the lower classes).... There would be no class warfare: disagreements under the new system ought to be muted, controlled, undemagogic, settled gracefully by 'gentlemen'.... All the rules would stay intact." And though the Radicals promptly swept to impressive electoral victories, the reform appeared to achieve its purposes in the short run. A military coup in 1930 occurred for complex reasons, but not because middle-class rule threatened the economic interests of the aristocratic class.[18]

In contrast to Argentina, which had only one oligarchic party, Uruguay displayed two strong and competitive traditional parties, the Blancos and the Colorados. During the 1890s a faction of the Colorados wielded power through fraud; together with the Blancos, a subordinate Colorado group, based on the middle classes and headed by José Batlle y Ordóñez, began demanding electoral and political reform. Elected president in 1903, Batlle implemented key changes, including a collective executive (instead of one person) and a series of progressive social and welfare reforms that were intended to garner support from the working classes. Representing a compromise between Colorados and Blancos, a new constitution in 1918 extended the suffrage to adult males and established a quasi-parliamentary form of government. According to Ruth Berins Collier, the changes of 1918 "were brought about as a reform from above and resulted from the changing strategic calculations of Uruguay's two highly competitive, traditional political parties."[19]

Chile followed a similar pattern. Competition between upper-class factions led to numerous reforms in the late nineteenth century, but a literacy requirement placed sharp limits on effective use of voting rights. Elements of the laboring class were organized—stevedores in ports and workers in nitrate and copper mines—but they did not mount strident demands for political reform. As J. Samuel Valenzuela has explained, "Chile extended the suffrage gradually, less in response to pressures from below than as a consequence of elite strategies to maximize electoral gain."[20] As in Uruguay, traditional parliamentary parties were seeking to enhance their competitive position with one another and to increase their leverage vis-à-vis the executive power.

---

[18] Peter H. Smith, "The Breakdown of Democracy in Argentina, 1916–1930," in Juan J. Linz and Alfred Stepan, eds., *The Breakdown of Democratic Regimes: Latin America* (Baltimore: Johns Hopkins University Press, 1978), 3–27, with quote on 11–12.

[19] Berins Collier, *Paths Toward Democracy*, 73.

[20] J. Samuel Valenzuela, *Democratización via reforma: La expansión del sufragio en Chile* (Buenos Aires: IDES, 1985), 19–20.

In each of these cases, elite groups designed political reforms that granted modest shares of power to rising middle classes but not to the working classes. This strategy was made possible by specific features of their socioeconomic development. The agricultural economies of Argentina and Uruguay both focused on livestock and ranching, which did not require a large-scale rural workforce. And especially in Argentina, the overwhelming presence of foreign-born (nonvoting) laborers in the cities nullified the possibility of any significant lower-class threat to established interests. In Chile, as well, organized workers were concentrated in specific areas—ports and mining towns—so they were isolated from national politics. With the occasional use of force, elites in Argentina managed to repress or ignore the working class during this early democratic cycle. In Uruguay and Chile, elites regarded the working class as a passive social stratum available for co-optation or political exploitation by competing oligarchic elements.

In accordance with these strategies, elite-led reforms opened the way to electoral competition marked by conservatism and constraint. Elections in democratic Argentina were dominated by parties of the Center, which on average won about two thirds of the votes, and by the Right, which garnered about one sixth (64.1 percent and 14.2 percent, respectively). In Chile, electoral contests pitted a powerful Right, which averaged just over half of all votes, against a divided Left (the Left and the Center-Left each won about 20 percent of the vote). Elections in Uruguay were played out between the Center-Left and the Center-Right, with each bloc averaging nearly half the national vote. In no case did elections come close to empowering the Left.[21] These were carefully managed affairs.

Colombia straddled the first and second cycles of democratization. As in Uruguay and Chile, firmly entrenched oligarchic factions were seeking middle- and working-class support. In the 1930s the Liberal Party attempted to strengthen its position vis-à-vis Conservatives by introducing universal male suffrage and mobilizing lower classes. Apparently anticipating fraud, Conservatives elected to boycott the presidential election of 1938, which was therefore free but not fair, so it was not until 1942 that electoral democracy took hold.[22] The electoral arena witnessed restricted competition between parties of the Center (winning more than 59 percent of all votes) and the Center-Right (with about 40 percent of the vote). Yet the agricultural export sector, devoted largely to coffee, required a stable and substantial labor force, so landowners were virulently opposed to political reforms that might empower rural workers. As time went on, ruling elites failed

---

[21] Calculations based on data kindly provided by Michael Coppedge. For background see Coppedge, "A Classification of Latin American Political Parties" (Notre Dame, IN: Helen Kellogg Center for International Studies, Working Paper 244, November 1997).

[22] Frank Safford and Marco Palacios, *Colombia: Fragmented Land, Divided Society* (New York: Oxford University Press, 2002), 267.

to create mechanisms for asserting state control of burgeoning labor movements in the cities, led by communists and socialists, until a Catholic union was finally established in the mid-1940s. Class mobilization and partisan hostility culminated in the *bogotazo* of 1948, a massive riot that engulfed the capital city of Bogotá after the assassination of populist Liberal politician Jorge Gaitán. Discord within elite circles led to a political paralysis that, in turn, led to the subsequent installation of an authoritarian regime.

Cycle 2: 1940–1977

Whereas the first (and modest) democratic cycle in Latin America was initiated by upper-class elements, the second phase was instigated largely by the middle classes. From the late 1930s into the 1970s, advances in industrialization (under substantial state protection) led to the formation of entrepreneurial groups and expansion of the middle classes. Middle sector groups came to include urban professionals, public and private employees, artisans, craftsmen, and small-scale entrepreneurs, sometimes joined by small and medium farmers. Socioeconomic development resulted in mounting demands for political inclusion, especially from the business classes and the middle sectors, while also intensifying interaction between the middle classes and the working classes. Civil society thus made its entrance onto the regional scene.

At the same time, the democratic conviction of Latin America's middle classes was equivocal. Although they played a leading role in promoting transitions from authoritarianism, according to one prominent analysis, "they were frequently ambivalent concerning democracy for other subordinate classes." It was a question of tactical alliances:

> The role played by the middle classes in bringing about democracy depended upon the type of allies available. The middle classes first and foremost sought their own inclusion and formed the alliances necessary to meet this end.
>
> Where sectors of elites and/or of the military served as effective allies, the middle classes were quite content with restricted democracy. Where there was a significant working-class presence, the search for allies among the working class caused the middle classes to push for full democracy. The middle classes attempted to enlist working-class support either with appeals for electoral support for clientelistic parties or through the sponsoring of working-class organization and the formation of formal alliances with such organizations through radical mass parties. Where radical mass parties mobilized pressures for democratization, strong elite resistance resulted in preventive or reactive authoritarian regimes. Where clientelistic parties appealed for support from a sizeable working class, successful democratic openings occurred.[23]

---

[23] See Dietrich Rueschemeyer, Evelyne Huber Stephens, and John D. Stephens, *Capitalist Development and Democracy* (Chicago: University of Chicago Press, 1992), especially Chs. 5–6, with quote on 168.

In short, the middle classes in Latin America were highly opportunistic, and although the working classes were generally prodemocratic, they played a secondary role. "In a somewhat crude generalization," write Dieter Rueschemeyer and associates, "we could say that in Europe the working class in most cases needed the middle classes as allies to be successful in its push for democracy, whereas in Latin America it was the other way around."[24]

Bolstered by these social forces, democratic openings spread throughout most (but not all) of South America. Argentina, perhaps the most developed country in the region, turned toward full electoral democracy in 1946 and again in 1973. Chile and Uruguay continued to consolidate the democratic systems initiated in the 1930s. Colombia recovered from its authoritarian interlude to establish a long-lasting democratic compact in 1958. With brief interruptions in 1954 and 1955, Brazil followed democratic practice from 1946 to 1964. Exemplifying the vagaries of political instability, Peru installed democratic regimes in the 1940s, 1950s, and 1960s. Ever-surprising Ecuador, with its vigorous populist tradition, established a working democracy from 1948 to 1960. Even Bolivia, one of the poorest countries on the continent, managed to install democracy in the 1950s. Venezuela enjoyed a brief democratic experiment during the *trienio* of 1945–1948 and then, after a decade of military rule, returned to electoral democracy in 1958.

These were short-lived episodes. Latin American democracies during this period were fragile, partial, and tentative. They were interspersed with semidemocratic and nondemocratic interludes. They were consistently opposed by conservative elites, and they were tolerated, with a watchful eye, by top-ranked military officers. During times of economic downturn or paralysis, they were abandoned by the middle classes who had been their chief protagonists. Throughout South America, economic stagnation led to social tension and the emergence of class conflict: Faced with a choice, middle sectors abandoned their tactical alliance with organized labor and acquiesced in dictatorial solutions. Within such contexts, bureaucratic-authoritarian regimes seized power in Brazil (1964), Argentina (1966 and 1976), Chile and Uruguay (both 1973), and military coups toppled democratic governments in Peru (1968) and Ecuador (1972). Only Colombia and Venezuela managed to avoid this authoritarian tide.[25]

Other countries made no effort to install democracy. One category included less-developed nations still in the grip of traditional oligarchies, such as Paraguay and El Salvador, where landowning elites relied on strong alliances with the military to maintain law and order and assure a steady supply of agricultural labor. In Honduras and Nicaragua, the elites were not as domineering and the armed forces somewhat more autonomous, but they still joined together to avert the dangers of democracy. Under such conditions, ruling groups relied on either oligarchic electoralism or personalistic

---

[24] Ibid., 185.
[25] See Linz and Stepan, *Breakdown of Democracy*.

dictatorship (the Somozas in Nicaragua) to perpetuate their power. Moreover, the United States threw its support behind such regimes, with the use and threat of military force, to avoid communist takeovers or the prospect of "another Cuba" in the hemisphere.

Always the exception, Mexico retained its nondemocratic system of one-party rule. This was a large country with a growing middle class and a substantial working class. Yet the top-down organization of the PRI led to the incorporation of organized labor in the 1930s and prevented the formation of a separate working-class party (such as the Peronist movement in Argentina). As a result, Mexico managed to avoid social polarization and class conflict. Elections, often fraudulent, but elections nonetheless, provided the regime with a patina of democratic legitimacy, and repression, not extensive, but selective and effective, sharply discouraged outright opposition. In comparison with South America, indeed, Mexico from the 1940s through the 1970s looked like a paragon of political gentility: civilian leadership, no military coups, no communist threats, and, above all, institutional stability.

Cycle 3: 1978–2000

Latin America continued to achieve greater levels of socioeconomic development with the passage of time. Manufacturing increased, exports diversified, and consumer markets enlarged. As entrepreneurial sectors gained strength, traditional elites, especially landowners, declined in economic and political importance. Middle classes expanded in size, but, partly as a result, their social-class identity weakened somewhat. In a word, social forces became more diverse and diffuse: When mobilized, they often joined together under the generalized rubric of "civil society." Social groups and classes would still play a crucial role in promoting political change, but not as directly as in earlier periods.

The working class proved essential in some instances. In Peru, organized labor mounted a series of work stoppages culminating in a general strike in 1977—the largest in the country's history—that persuaded the military government to extricate itself from government by expanding suffrage and holding elections. In Argentina, where organized labor had been a major force since the 1940s, economic crisis led to growing union protests and ongoing human rights vigils that placed the military rulers under enormous pressure. The generals attempted to escape the crisis by invading the Falkland/Malvinas Islands; when that adventure ended in fiasco and humiliation, they installed a caretaker government and called elections in 1983. In both countries, as Ruth Berins Collier has written, "the labor movement mounted ongoing and escalating protest that destabilized the regime in two ways—by challenging its ability to provide a basis for social peace or order and by undermining its cohesion as it confronted this challenge."[26]

---

[26] Berins Collier, *Paths Toward Democracy*, 114.

Workers played a major role in Chile, and then—perhaps to their eventual regret—passed the baton to politicians. In the late 1970s and early 1980s it was organized labor that led opposition to the Pinochet regime and its economic and political project. Strikes and manifestations were the principal outlets for dissent. Perhaps sensing the danger, the government responded in 1983 by appointing a right-wing politician to open dialogue with traditional political parties, including Christian Democrats and Socialists but not the Communists. This multiparty alliance maintained contact with representatives of the regime and organized the "no" vote in the plebiscite of 1988 that ultimately removed Pinochet from office. Workers steadfastly opposed the military government, but the parties took over leadership of the opposition.

At the other end of the spectrum, the business sector played a major role in provoking a transition toward democracy in Brazil. Initially supportive of the bureaucratic-authoritarian regime, entrepreneurs eventually discovered that the country's military leaders were so intent on expanding the economic role of the state—and military leadership of the parastatal sector—that they were being crowded out of the national economy.[27] (Something similar happened in Chile, where business leaders were gradually excluded from economic policy formation.) In a sense, Brazilian entrepreneurs defected from the ruling coalition, and this fissure prompted incumbent leaders to embark on a gradual process of political "decompression." Within this context, labor began to mount protests of its own, staging a 41-day metalworker strike in 1980 and organizing its own political party, the Partido dos Trabalhadores (PT). Ultimately, business and labor formed parts of a broad societal front that led to the eventual removal of Brazil's military regime in 1985.

In most cases, the middle classes helped lead and strengthen these anti-authoritarian fronts. As threats of class warfare diminished and the costs of economic crisis mounted, segments of the middle classes withdrew their support for bureaucratic-authoritarian solutions. Excluded from decision-making processes, they came to realize that military leaders would not necessarily promote middle-class interests; especially in Argentina, Uruguay, and Chile, sons and daughters of the middle class—often university students—fell victim to the ravages of "dirty wars." Ultimately, the middle classes reasoned that their only hope of asserting political influence would be through elections. It would be an exaggeration to say, as does Samuel P. Huntington, that "In virtually every country the most active supporters of democratization came from the middle class."[28] But it would also be a mistake to ignore its pivotal role.

---

[27] Fernando Henrique Cardoso, "O papel dos empresariados no proceso de transiçao: O caso brasileiro," *Dados* 26 (1983): 9–27.

[28] Huntington, *Third Wave*, 67.

SLAYING GOLIATH: VICENTE FOX OF MEXICO

As both cause and effect, elections can have decisive effects on political transitions. This was nowhere more evident than in Mexico, where the ruling party, the PRI, attempted to restructure and consolidate its legitimacy through a series of electoral reforms. The original intent was to strengthen the country's long-standing authoritarian system, not overthrow it. The PRI had won every presidential election since 1929 and had every intention of staying in power. (In terms employed above, the goal was "liberalization" of the regime rather than "democratization.") Once the process of reform began, however, technical experts and opposition leaders designed electoral institutions that would lead to a free and fair presidential election in 2000.

It was in this context that Vicente Fox captured the nomination of the Partido Acción Nacional (PAN), a traditional center-right party that had opposed the PRI for more than half a century. Fox was a different breed of candidate. Tall, rugged, macho to the core, he was a private businessman and rancher. He became CEO of Coca Cola of Mexico in the late 1970s and entered politics only in 1988, when he joined the PAN and won election as a congressional representative from the small state of Guanajuato. He subsequently served as governor of Guanajuato. From that unlikely background, in his late 50s, he launched his quest for the presidency.

A charismatic campaigner, Fox pledged an honest government. He denounced the PRI as hopelessly corrupt and obsolete. Vague on specifics, Fox asserted that it was time for a change and that he would lead Mexico into a new, modern, and democratic era. In contrast the PRI nominee personified some of the party's most traditional elements, while President Ernesto Zedillo insisted that the election would have to be clean.

Fox won the presidency by a plurality, with 42.5 percent of the vote; the PRI received 38 percent. Mexico was jubilant, as though it had surprised itself. According to one observer, this was a triumph of "modern" Mexico over "traditional" Mexico, and his challenge would be to reconcile the two. Taking office in December 2000, Fox enjoyed approval ratings around 85 percent. His political honeymoon would be unusually long, but it would not last forever.

Middle-class actors expressed opposition to authoritarian rule in a variety of ways, advocating human rights, condemning corruption, forging social movements, propounding sexual equality, and demanding electoral reform. In contrast to the 1940–1977 period, when class identity was relatively firm, these prodemocratic elements did not usually represent interests of the middle class as such. Rather, they were middle-class people who took part in a broad range of dissident activities. To antiauthoritarian movements they gave voice, leadership, and political weight. Participation of middle-class elements was an essential component in the construction and emergence of civil society.

Mexico 2000: Vicente Fox flashes victory sign after his inauguration as president. (AP Photo/José Luis Magaña)

It was precisely this sort of expansive, amorphous development that helped bring electoral democracy to Mexico. By the 1990s, disappointment with the decades-long rule of the PRI reverberated throughout virtually every element of Mexican society. People were fed up with corruption, fraud, and economic crisis. Ironically, one of the groups that benefited most from PRI hegemony, the urban middle class, was a bastion of the strongest opposition. The incumbent PRI elites sought to assuage these criticisms through a series of electoral reforms—liberalizing (not democratizing) reforms, based on the assumption that the opposition could not win free and fair elections—and, as happened so often in Latin America, they were ultimately voted out of office. In a historic reversal, Vicente Fox, a former Coca-Cola executive and upstart candidate of the center-right Partido Acción Nacional, won the presidential election of 2000 (see Box 2.3).

Around the same time, the installation of electoral democracy in neighboring countries of Central America reflected, first, the emergence of a (still-modest) middle class and, second, the influence of yet another actor: the international community. One key participant was the United States, which wanted to extricate itself from its awkward immersion in the civil wars that engulfed the isthmus during the 1980s. Another was the United Nations, which agreed to perform the role of "honest broker" among contending parties. Most conspicuously in El Salvador and Guatemala, but in Honduras and Nicaragua as well, free and (more or less) fair elections gained credibility as the most viable route to peace: Ballots, not bullets, would settle political discord. Democracy came late to Central America, in fragile and partial form, but it nonetheless arrived.

END GAMES AND ELITE BARGAINS

Democratization concerns the question of *whether* an authoritarian regime comes to an end. Also important is *how* that process occurs. In this regard, there are two broad types of change: transition via *ruptura*, a complete and usually sudden and violent break with the authoritarian past, and transition via *reforma*, a process of give-and-take negotiation between incumbents and dissidents. Abrupt and comprehensive ruptures have utopian, quasi-revolutionary qualities; gradual and pragmatic changes via reform tend to be incremental, not revolutionary, and include formal or informal compacts designed to achieve political transformation with a minimum of risks.

In Latin America and elsewhere, personalistic regimes have been most susceptible to sweeping and violent overthrow. Cases in point were Batista in Cuba (ousted in 1959), Trujillo in the Dominican Republic (assassinated in 1961), Somoza in Nicaragua (ousted in 1979, assassinated in 1982), and Duvalier in Haiti (ousted in 1986). Dissidents usually believed that it was necessary to eliminate the tyrant via assassination and that with this accomplished the entire regime would crumble. There was neither room nor need for negotiations with surviving collaborators: Without the dictator, they had no remaining power base. Even so, it was not uncommon to subject them to legal proceedings or, in the case of Cuba, to extralegal peoples' courts. As a rule, sultanistic regimes rarely, if ever, gave way to transition via *reforma;* they usually fell through *ruptura*.

Other forms of autocracy had more flexible means of extrication. In dominant-party regimes, as in Mexico, members of the erstwhile ruling party could simply move into the opposition. They could take part in elections, win seats in local offices or national legislatures, claim to represent constituencies, and (depending on the circumstances) veto projects and reforms presented by newly triumphant administrations.

Military regimes also had ready exit: They could return to the barracks. In fact, many juntas from the 1930s through the 1950s announced at the outset that they would stay in office only for one or two years: Their exit strategy was thus prepared at the start. In case of more protracted interventions, military officers could always save face by declaring victory and, in the name of democracy, proclaiming a need to strengthen the vigor and vitality of the nation's patriotic armed forces. More than any other autocrats, military rulers had a place to go. This often made it easier for them to engage in negotiations with the opposition.

The Bargaining Process

Despite Latin America's reputation for tempestuous violence, the predominant form of regime change was via reform, what has come to be known as "pacted" transitions. These were agreements between consenting parties. They were complex and varied, and they frequently led to unintended as well as intended consequences.

As opposition activity begins to escalate, authoritarian rulers face two options: They can negotiate with dissidents, or they can resort to oppression. For members of the regime, the goal of negotiation is prolongation of their power in exchange for modest concessions to the opposition. The more formal the agreement, the more secure the outcome: Institutionalization is a matter of high priority. Reform is thus undertaken for the sake of continuity: *plus ça change*, as the saying goes, *plus ç'est la même chose* ("the more things change, the more they stay the same"). Despite occasional appearances to the contrary, this is not a process of democratization. It is a strategy for *liberalization* of the authoritarian regime, not its abdication.

For leaders of the opposition, by contrast, the purpose of negotiations is to achieve a change of regime—in other words, *democratization*. They can aspire to reach this goal in one of two ways: (1) by persuading the rulers that they have no other choice but to surrender their hold on power, or (2) by enticing the rulers to accept bargains that ultimately lead to subversion of the regime. An example here might be plebiscites or referenda, which the regime strategists expect to win and discover, only too late, that they have made a fatal miscalculation.

Such negotiations have been modeled as bargaining games. In one well-known version, Adam Przeworski has identified four key actors: "Hard-liners" and "Reformers" within the regime, and "Moderates" and "Radicals" in the opposition. As their labels suggest, Hard-liners want to maintain the regime without any meaningful change. Reformers are willing to accept, and might even prefer, substantial liberalization (which might strengthen their own position within the regime). Moderates are intent on democratization, even at the price of power-sharing with the military or other guarantees to the authoritarian coalition. Radicals condemn such bargains and seek unconditional democracy.

So long as the pro-regime factions and the antiregime factions stand together—Hard-liners and Moderates, Reformers and Radicals—there can be no effective bargaining. Conflict escalates, but the regime stays in place, probably with increased repression. The key to change therefore lies in an understanding between Reformers and Moderates.[29] This requires three conditions: (1) Reformers and Moderates need to assure their respective constituencies that they will have a strong presence under the new institutional arrangement; (2) Reformers have to keep the Hard-liners in line; and (3) Moderates need to keep the Radicals under control. As Przeworski has written,

> Moderate gentlemen in cravats may lead civilized negotiations in government palaces, but if streets are filled with crowds or factories are occupied by workers calling for the necks of their interlocutors,

---

[29] For practical intents and purposes, it is impossible to imagine an alliance of Hard-liners and Radicals against Moderates and Reformers.

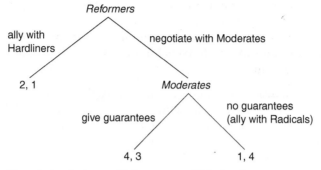

Figure 2.2 Bargaining between Reformers and Moderates

Note: The first numbers represent the value of outcomes to Reformers; the second numbers are values for Moderates (4 is better than 3, 3 is better than 2, and so on). The numbers thus establish a rank-order preference structure. Imagined outcomes are as follows: authoritarian regime survives in old form (2, 1); democracy with guarantees (4, 3); and democracy without guarantees (1, 4). Not pictured in the diagram is a fourth potential outcome—authoritarian regime holds with concessions, that is, liberalization (3, 2).

Source: Adam Przeworski, *Democracy and the Market: Political and Economic Reforms in Eastern Europe and Latin America* (New York: Cambridge University Press, 1991), 69–72.

their moderation is irrelevant. Hence, Moderates must either deliver terms tolerable to Radicals or, if they cannot obtain such terms from Reformers, they must leave enough power in the hands of the apparatus of repression to intimidate Radicals. On the one hand, Moderates need Radicals to be able to put pressure on Reformers; on the other, Moderates fear that Radicals will not consent to the deal that they work out with Reformers.[30]

For their part, Reformers require assurances that they will have a meaningful presence in any kind of democratic arrangement. Otherwise, it makes more sense for them to sustain their alliance with Hard-liners.

In a basic illustration of game theory, Figure 2.2 demonstrates the logic of this situation. Reformers have the first move and can either ally with Hard-liners, in which case the bargaining stops and the authoritarian regime survives without change; this would be the next-to-worst outcome for Reformers and the least favorite outcome for Moderates. Alternatively, Reformers can negotiate with Moderates. Initiative now passes to the Moderates. They can agree to establish a democracy with guarantees, which would give Reformers their first-place choice and Moderates their second-place preference, while risking rejection from the Radicals. Alternatively, the Moderates could align themselves with the Radicals and refuse to offer assurances. The resulting democracy without guarantees might be the first-place preference of Moderates (and Radicals) but the last-place

---

[30] Adam Przeworski, *Democracy and the Market: Political and Economic Reforms in Eastern Europe and Latin America* (Cambridge: Cambridge University Press, 1991), 69.

choice of Reformers, who could hardly be expected to accept such a result.

Guarantees are thus essential to negotiated transitions of regime. As Guillermo O'Donnell and Philippe Schmitter have observed, there are three basic types of guarantees:

> Electoral: "parties of the Right-Center and Right must be 'helped' to do well, and parties of the Left-Center and Left should not win an over-whelming majority. This often happens either 'artificially,' by rigging the rules—for example, by overrepresenting rural districts or small, periph-eral constituencies—or 'naturally,' by fragmenting the partisan choices of the Left...and consolidating those of the Center and Right.... "

> Economic: "it is forbidden to take, or even to checkmate, the king of one of the players. In other words, during the transition, the property rights of the bourgeoisie are inviolable."

> Institutional: "it is forbidden to take or even to circumscribe too closely the movements of the transitional regime's queen. In other words, to the extent that the armed forces serve as the prime protector of the rights and privi-leges covered by the first restriction, their institutional existence, assets, and hierarchy cannot be eliminated or even seriously threatened."[31]

Such assurances can result only from negotiations between Reformers and Moderates. Hard-liners (in the regime) and Radicals (in the oppo-sition) have to consent to these arrangements, and their compliance is not to be taken for granted. Both groups have the capacity to subvert compacts between Reformers and Moderates by polarizing the situa-tion. Paradoxically, Hard-liners and Radicals can tacitly join together in a game of "coup poker"—each upping the ante and daring the other to take (or precipitate) drastic action.[32] Under such conditions, the odds of miscalculation are unnervingly high.

Getting to Cases

Two conspicuous instances of "pacted" transition occurred in the late 1950s. After Marcos Pérez Jiménez was removed from power in Venezuela, his civilian opponents reached a series of agreements in 1958. One was with the then-beleaguered military: In return for a commitment to political neutrality, the armed forces would receive improvements in salaries and equipment, a pledge of amnesty, and public recognition for their patriotic services. Other agreements were binding on the victors. In the Pact of Punto Fijo, party

---

[31] Guillermo O'Donnell and Philippe C. Schmitter, *Transitions from Authoritarian Rule: Tentative Conclusions about Uncertain Democracies* (Baltimore: Johns Hopkins University Press, 1986), 62, 69.

[32] See O'Donnell and Schmitter, *Transitions*, 24–25; and Przeworski, *Democracy and the Market*, 68.

leaders agreed to respect the electoral process and, more important, to share power according to voting results. The spirit of a "prolonged political truce" would thus govern the distribution of cabinet posts, state jobs, and contracts, and the resulting spoils system would ensure the political survival of all signatories. In addition, a Minimum Program of Government obliged the parties to economic moderation: They would avoid drastic expropriations and nationalizations and support private enterprise, and the economic role of the state would expand. In effect, they exchanged the right to rule for the right to make money.[33]

Agreements in neighboring Colombia were somewhat similar. Here the leaders of two traditional parties, Liberals and Conservatives, agreed to complete parity in all branches of government for a sixteen-year period, during which time the presidency would alternate between them. As in Venezuela, the intent of this "national front" (Frente Nacional) was to fashion a political truce and bring an end to the partisan hostility—la violencia— that had ravaged the country for decades. The deal was struck in 1957 and approved in a national plebiscite by 94.8 percent of war-weary Colombian voters. In May 1958, Alberto Lleras Camargo was elected president in peaceful elections.[34]

At first glance, these compacts seem analytically distinct from the bargaining process as modeled by Przeworski and others because, with the exception of the military agreement in Venezuela, they involved civilian leaders (Moderates and Radicals) rather than direct negotiations between dissidents and authoritarians (Reformers and Hard-liners). In effect, Moderates and Radicals were committing themselves to political moderation and cooperation. In both Venezuela and Colombia, however, the armed forces were "shadow" participants in the negotiations. In both situations, civilian leaders were promising the military that they would (1) uphold law and order, (2) avoid political warfare, and (3) eschew radical programs. So long as they met these conditions, there would be no need for military intervention.

Subsequent pacts more closely followed the game-theoretic bargaining model. In Ecuador, a pro-business center-right Civic Front negotiated the extrication of a left-leaning military government in the late 1970s. In Uruguay, the Naval Club Pact of 1984 culminated ongoing discussions between the military and the opposition parties—including the Left, but excluding the communists—by establishing that (1) for army promotions, the president would choose from a list of three proposed by generals (two in the other services); (2) the National Security Council would serve as adviser to the

---

[33] Terry Lynn Karl, "Petroleum and Political Pacts: The Transition to Democracy in Venezuela," in Laurence Whitehead, Guillermo O'Donnell, and Philippe Schmitter, eds., Transitions from Authoritarian Rule: Latin America (Baltimore: Johns Hopkins University Press, 1986), Ch. 9, esp. 212–215.

[34] John D. Martz, Colombia: A Contemporary Political Survey (Chapel Hill: University of North Carolina Press, 1962), Ch. 15.

president, with a majority of government ministers; (3) parliament could vote a "state of insurrection" suspending individual guarantees; (4) a new legal mechanism, the *recurso de amparo*, would enable individuals and corporations to appeal government decisions in courts; (5) military trials would be held only for those arrested under a "state of insurrection"; (6) the National Assembly elected in November 1984 would serve as a constituent assembly; and (7) the text, if amended, would be submitted to a plebiscite in November 1985. In November 1984 the country's traditional parties, Colorados and Blancos, reasserted their preeminence in the electoral arena. All in all, the process of extrication in Uruguay was relatively smooth.[35]

Bargaining also occurred in Argentina, even though the military had engaged in horrendous dirty wars, led the economy into profound recession, and, to top it off, suffered a humiliating defeat in the Falkland/Malvinas Islands. After installing a caretaker government in June 1982, the outgoing generals carried on negotiations with leaders of the Peronist movement, long the dominant force in civilian politics, and reached an agreement that would exchange amnesty for military officers for Peronist control of labor unions. The deal came apart only because the Radicals, not the Peronists, won the elections of 1983. So the Argentine transition was (or would have been) "pacted," but the bargaining table did not offer seats to all relevant partners.

By definition, negotiations entail costs as well as benefits—and the costs to democracy have sometimes seemed exorbitant. As one analyst has observed with respect to Chile, where the military and civilians undertook negotiations in the wake of the historic plebiscite of 1988:

> Just note the price extorted by Pinochet for his consent to free elections: (1) permanent office for the current commanders in chief of the armed forces and police, (2) protection of the "prestige of members of the military and the police," (3) an "energetic struggle against terrorism," (4) respect for the opinions of a national security council to be formed of four military representatives and four civilians, (5) maintenance of the amnesty covering political crimes committed between 1973 and 1978, (6) abstention by the political authorities from intervening in the definition and application of defense policies, including not modifying the powers of military courts, the command structure, and the military budget and not interfering in the promotion of generals (normally a presidential prerogative), (7) the right to name nine members to the Senate, (8) the autonomy of the central bank, the president of which was chosen by the military, (9) acceptance of privatizations conducted during the last months of the military regime without investigation of how they were conducted, and (10) automatic allocation of 10 percent of copper revenues to the military budget.[36]

---

[35] Charles G. Gillespie, "Uruguay's Transition from Collegial Military-Technocratic Rule," in *Transitions from Authoritarian Rule: Latin America*, Ch. 8, esp. 187–192.

[36] Przeworski, *Democracy and the Market*, 78, with a correction for the percentage of copper revenues devoted to the military budget.

Compacts thus impose constraints on postauthoritarian governments. Constructed by elites, they are inherently undemocratic. This can lead to violation of the popular will. Thus conceived, democracy is born in original sin.

Although their motivation is political stability, pacted transitions tend to be unstable. Once in power, democratic forces seek to remove the guarantees granted to the authoritarians; the result is conflict and tension. And even in such cases as Colombia and Venezuela, where civilians forged consensus among themselves, agreements tend to "freeze" social and political relationships. They are meaningful only so long as the prevailing conditions and structure of power remain essentially intact—or so long as the founding generation of pact-signers remains at or near the pinnacles of power. Otherwise, the compacts become obsolete. On a positive note, revision or reversal of pacts can improve the quality of political democracy; on the negative side, the likelihood of future change can reduce the credibility of the original negotiations, thus undermining the reformers and strengthening the position of hard-line authoritarians.

PATTERNS OF CHANGE IN PERSPECTIVE

Are there clearly established pathways toward democracy? Given the regime typology set forth in Chapter 1, for instance, one could have imagined that Latin America might reveal a steady progression from authoritarianism to oligarchic democracy to semidemocracy to full electoral democracy. Would that life were so simple as that.

One might further have assumed that most regime transitions end up in democracy (or close to it). Table 2.4 sets the record straight. Over the entire course of the twentieth century, approximately one quarter of all transitions (24 percent) terminated in electoral democracy. A substantially higher proportion (39 percent) ended in autocracy. About 15 percent resulted in restoration of competitive oligarchy, and just over 20 percent led to electoral semidemocracy.

TABLE 2.4 Outcomes of Political Transitions, 1900–2000

Outcome	1900–1939 (%)	1940–1977 (%)	1978–2000 (%)	1900–2000 (%)
Autocracy	45	47	17	39
Oligarchy	36	6	—	15
Semidemocracy	11	20	40	22
Democracy	9	27	43	24
N transitions	56	64	35	155

Note: Columns may not add up to 100 because of rounding.

Source: Data in Appendix 1.

Paraguay 1989: A banner headline announces the ouster of longtime military strongman Alfredo Stroessner by another general, Andrés Rodríguez. (Universidad Católica Nuestra Señora de la Asunción)

There were revealing changes over time. The share of transitions ending in democracy climbed from 9 percent in 1900–1939 to 27 percent in 1940–1977 and 43 percent in 1978–2000, but even then, in the most "democratic" phase of Latin America's political development, less than half of all transitions culminated in electoral democracy. Correspondingly, the percentage of regime changes leading to authoritarianism dropped from 45–47 percent in 1900–1939 and 1940–1977 to merely 17 percent in 1978–2000. As oligarchic competition faded from the scene, semidemocracy emerged to take its place.

Transitions moved in every direction but one: Over the course of the entire century, democratic systems never once gave way to oligarchic regimes—not even during semidemocratic or authoritarian interludes. These were one-way affairs: Oligarchy could yield to or pave the way for democracy, but not the other way around. Once democracy took root, however temporarily, oligarchic republicanism faded out of view. It was not dictatorship that spelled the end of oligarchic dominance, it was democracy.[37]

In summary, the evidence throughout this chapter has made three emphatic points: (1) Regime transitions did not inexorably lead to

---

[37] See also Rueschemeyer et al., *Capitalist Development and Democracy*, 206–207, and Peter H. Smith and Matthew C. Kearney, "Transitions, Interrupted: Routes Toward Democracy in Latin America," *Taiwan Journal of Democracy*, 6 (July 2010): 137–163.

democracy, (2) most transitions led somewhere else, and (3) all transitions were afflicted by uncertainty. Nothing was preordained; much was the result of skill, chance, and circumstance. Yet a long-term trend persisted nonetheless. Autocracy was weakening, and electoral democracy was gaining strength.

CHAPTER 3

THE MILITARY

Heading for the Exits?

The Latin American armed forces are a source of puzzlement. Equipped to protect their countries from external threats, they have engaged in precious little major war. Charged with the defense of the nation, they have ridden roughshod over governmental authorities. Recruited from modest social sectors, they have taken the sides of privileged elites. Celebrating the nationalistic virtues of patriotic fervor, they have looked abroad for inspiration and instruction. Exalting the role of modern weaponry and military technology, they have subscribed to antiquated and anachronistic ideologies. Presenting themselves as neutral entities "above" the political fray, they dominated politics for most of the twentieth century. And then, as pressures for civilian rule intensified throughout the region, they have sheepishly retreated to their barracks. Or have they?

Such paradoxes pose numerous questions. How and why did the Latin American militaries become so involved in politics? What led to their ascendancy? How did civilian leaders of the new democracies bring the armed forces to heel? What are the resulting patterns of civil–military relations? How durable is civilian authority?

Exploration of these issues is essential not only for comprehending the changing roles of the armed forces, but also for evaluating the prospects for democratic consolidation in Latin America. Full-fledged democracy requires uncontested subordination of the military institution to elected civilian authorities. Military personnel must be subject to the rule of law. Otherwise, democracy is incomplete.

This chapter demonstrates that Latin American militaries have lowered their political profile in recent years. It also suggests that this trend is not necessarily permanent. Traditions of military power remain intact, and the armed forces enjoy considerable prestige in many countries. Rather than stepping permanently out of power, soldiers have stepped aside—for the moment. They have also discovered that they can wield substantial power without having to take over executive office.

FORGING FATHERLANDS

According to military folklore in Latin America, the armed forces are not merely part of the nation—they *created* the nation. Professional soldiers (many of whom had served under the Spanish Crown) led the forces in the wars of independence (1810–1826) that resulted in the formation of nascent states throughout Spanish America. Heroes from this glorious era dominated politics in the ensuing decades. With the exception of the church, civilian institutions were notoriously weak. Only the armed forces, despite their ragtag quality, had the capacity to impose order and stability. Insulated from civilian authority by the traditional *fuero*, stipulating the use of military courts for all disputes involving military personnel, officers saw themselves as a caste apart. In the highly stratified societies of the time, military careers also offered a unique channel for upward social mobility. The political scene subsequently gave way to violent struggles among rival caudillos, regional strongmen, not professional soldiers, who used paramilitary forces to wage campaigns and seize national governments. The nineteenth century was punctuated constantly by rebellion, conflict, and disorder.

War prevailed as well. A principal casus belli concerned the shape and form of political consolidation, particularly in Central America, the Andes, and the River Plate (where a conflict between Brazil and Argentina led to the creation of Uruguay as a buffer state). There was armed resistance to intermittent European intrusions and a major conflict between Mexico and the United States. The War of the Triple Alliance (1864–1870) pitted Paraguay against Brazil, Argentina, and Uruguay, and the War of the Pacific (1879–1884) resulted in a victory for Chile over Bolivia and Peru. Civil wars also erupted in many countries of the region.[1]

In the face of such continuing dangers, Spanish American political leaders saw an overwhelming need for strong and decisive government. Consequently, they framed constitutions that placed extraordinary powers in the hands of chief executives, even going so far as to authorize "regimes of exception." They also sought to strengthen military establishments, and for this they turned to Europe. Beginning in El Salvador in the 1860s and Guatemala in the 1870s, they contracted European officers to supervise reforms of military law and regulations, establish and staff military academies, and implement regimes for training and maneuvers. In the 1880s Chile invited an official military mission from Germany, as did Argentina in the late 1890s. Eager not to fall behind their regional rivals, Peru and Brazil soon

---

[1] See David R. Mares, *Violent Peace: Militarized Interstate Bargaining in Latin America* (New York: Columbia University Press, 2001), esp. 32–34.

invited military missions and officers from France. In all instances, the central idea was the same: to form a "professional" military, a modern fighting force capable of meeting external threats, guaranteeing national sovereignty, and upholding legal authority.

It did not work out that way. As Brian Loveman has written: "As the military institutions embarked on modernization and professionalization, they became still more politicized, more disdainful of civilian political parties and factions, more nationalistic, and more dependent on foreign doctrine, methods, and weapons."[2] Around the turn of the century, Latin American militaries came to feel ever more separate from and superior to civil society. Under the tutelage of their European mentors, they focused on the need for science, technology, and economic development; in so doing, they became increasingly conscious of defects in their own societies and of their own special talents. Service to the nation became synonymous with military tutelage of politics. In 1911 an Argentine officer went so far as to declare that "the army is the nation. It is the external armor that guarantees the cohesive operation of its parts and preserves it from shocks and falls."

All these developments combined to strengthen belief in an unwavering commitment to defense of the fatherland—*la patria*—as the grand historical mission of Latin American militaries. *La patria* became a sacred concept; it was an "entity of destiny," a transcendental basis of identity and solidarity, flexible in form but unchanging at its core. The belief possessed a quasi-religious tone, and military officers became its secular priests. According to President (General) José María Orellana of Guatemala, for instance, education in a military academy had a uniquely transformative effect—it "converts a man and transforms a citizen into a priest of a supreme cult to *la patria*, whose symbol is the flag, and whose gospel is the constitution." Professional officers were "above politics," of course, but they had an explicit political duty. (For this reason, they could not be said to "intervene" in politics, as though they were somehow external; they were part and parcel of the nation and the state.) Only the military could appropriately determine whether and when there existed a threat to the fatherland. Those who endangered *la patria* were enemies, either foreign or domestic, and they must meet with decisive retribution. Defense of the fatherland required implacable war (see Box 3.1).

As we shall see later, this brand of patriotism could lend itself to astonishing formulations, distortions, and exaggerations. It also came to focus on domestic security as well as external threats. Indeed, protection of *la patria* required vigilance against internal enemies as well as foreign powers. One might wonder whether this ideology was used merely as a convenient rationale—not a cause of action, but a justification. On the other hand, the intensity of this discourse yields the impression that at some level, many officers actually believed in it. Certainly, it became a rallying cry for institutional solidarity and a signpost of distance from (and moral superiority over) civilian society.

---

[2] Brian Loveman, *For* La Patria (Wilmington, DE: Scholarly Resources, 1999), 59.

BOX 3.1

WHAT DRIVES THE MILITARY INTO POLITICS?

There has been a great deal of scholarly debate about the causes of military intervention. A generation ago a senior historian, Lyle N. McAlister, summarized the principal arguments through an ingenious series of propositions and counterpropositions. His distillation remains relevant even today:

1. *Proposition:* As the Latin American military becomes more professional in outlook, it will by conviction and necessity eschew politics. *Counterproposition:* Historically, professionalism has been no guarantee against militarism. Samuel P. Huntington wrote of the German army, "No other officer corps achieved such high standards of professionalism, and the officer of no other major power was in the end so completely prostituted."...Recent military interventions in Peru and Argentina [both in 1962] have been by two of the most highly professionalized officer corps in Latin America.

2. *Proposition:* Latin American officers will absorb apolitical attitudes through increasing professional contacts with officers from the United States....*Counterproposition:* In the words of Senator Ernest Gruening, "Most of the Latin American military leaders will continue to react to power struggles in their own countries in accordance with their own estimates of the situation, their own ambitions, their vested privileges, and their own heritage...the military's new concept of its role has developed from circumstances within the framework of their own institutions, and not from the minute and transitory influence encountered in rubbing shoulders with U.S. military people."

3. *Proposition:* Preoccupation with and pride in public service functions will absorb the time and attention of the military. *Counterproposition:* In the long run such activities are incompatible with true professionalism and the soldier's sense of high mission. They are not "honorable" in the traditional sense, and they bring no glory.

4. *Proposition:* As enlisted men become better educated and more politically aware, their officers will not find them so easy to manipulate as in the past. *Counterpropositions:* First, they may be less easy to manipulate for reactionary ends, but easier for liberal or radical ones. Second, they may take a notion to become political groups independent of their officers.

5. *Proposition:* Recruitment of officers from middle and lower social strata will produce important changes in military values. More specifically, younger officers will tend to retain the liberal and progressive values of their families. *Counterpropositions:* Military values tend to supersede civilian ones; indeed, many young men become officers in rejection of liberal, middle-class values. In the officer's mind, the ultimate division is not between liberal and conservative but between soldier and civilian. Furthermore, although they may espouse reform, the school and laboratory officers appear just as willing as their elders to employ force to achieve their objectives.

Source: Lyle N. McAlister, "The Military," in John J. Johnson, ed., *Continuity and Change in Latin America* (Stanford, CA: Stanford University Press, 1964), 158–159.

Paradoxically, it might seem, many civilians agreed with these ideas. They viewed the armed forces as ultimate "saviors" of national honor, as bastions of dignity and discipline that could rescue society from the venality and incompetence of self-seeking politicians. In consequence, disgruntled civilians often called on the military to intervene in government and cleanse the body politic. As José Luis de Imaz once said of Argentina, reliance on the armed forces became "a tacit rule of the political game.... All will publicly deny this rule, but in private politicians cannot ignore that, at one time or another [from the 1930s to the 1960s], they have all knocked on the doors of the garrison." Recently, too, citizens have continued to express relatively high levels of confidence in the armed forces, even in countries with recent records of harsh military repression. A 2000 survey found that 38 percent of respondents in Argentina expressed "some" or "much" confidence in the military, as did 52 percent in Uruguay, 60 percent in Brazil, 61 percent in Ecuador, and 53 percent in Chile.[3] Throughout Latin America as a whole, about 40 percent of the people proclaimed confidence in the armed forces. The military has a real civilian following.

PATTERNS OF PARTICIPATION

In spite (or because) of its institutional self-image, the military has played an absolutely central role in Latin American politics. This is a massive understatement, yet the forms of participation have been complex and subject to change. Such transformations provide essential clues to its stance during the current era of democratization.

To begin the analysis, Figure 3.1 presents data on the incidence of military *golpes de estado* by decade from 1900 through 2000. By a conservative count, as indicated in Appendix 2, there were 167 successful coups—forceful overthrows of established governments—during the course of the century. That comes to an average of 1.6 per year, or 8.8 per country. Of course, the distribution was uneven: Bolivia experienced fifteen coups and Haiti fourteen, whereas Costa Rica had only two and Uruguay just one. With the exception of the 1990s, every decade in the century had nine or more coups. Military *golpes* were a fact of life.

The figure yields suggestive insights. One is decline over time, from the peak in 1910–1919 down to a low in 1990–2000. (Alternatively, the descent could be traced from the 1930s to the end of the century.) Although the reality of military coups persisted, the *incidence* of coups showed a decisive downward trend.

---

[3] According to findings in the Latinobarómetro (described in Chapter 11). Approval ratings for the military were substantially lower in Central America and Paraguay. See also Juan J. Linz and Alfred Stepan, *Problems of Democratic Transition and Consolidation: Southern Europe, South America, and Post-Communist Europe* (Baltimore: Johns Hopkins University Press, 1996), 224.

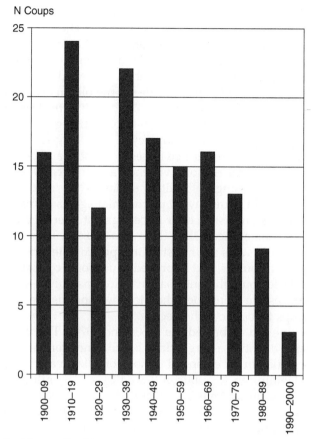

N Coups

Figure 3.1   Incidence of military coups, 1900–2000

Source: Appendix 2.

Further, Figure 3.1 reveals some key periods. One of these, the peak decade of 1910–1919, reflects what might be called a "crisis of oligarchic rule." At the beginning of the century, the region was governed mostly by competitive oligarchies, as noted in Chapter 1. These elites had promoted economic expansion on the basis of export–import development. A social consequence of this strategy was the incipient formation of a working class—miners, stevedores, and laborers in general. As the working classes expanded in size, they began to formulate demands for better wages and working conditions. Sometimes they espoused anarchist ideology; in most cases they focused on straightforward bread-and-butter issues. In country after country, proletarian agitation raised what came to be known as "the social question": What to do about these workers? With the partial exception of Argentina, which adopted an electoral reform, the oligarchic classes of Latin America were unable to come up with creative solutions to this challenge. In many instances they invited the military to take over power and impose law and order; in others, the military did not await an invitation.[4]

A second peak came in the 1930s, the era of the Great Depression. During 1930–1931 alone, *golpes* occurred in eight different countries—Argentina, Bolivia, Brazil, Chile, the Dominican Republic, Guatemala, Panama, and Peru. In a sense this represented a death rattle for the oligarchs, pushed aside in many countries for the last time. The economic crisis of the Depression called into question the viability of their export–import strategies, and widespread social suffering discredited the legitimacy of their long-standing claims on power. During this period the armed forces faced labor and peasant agitation and strikes, elections and electoral violence, and the ceaseless meddling of politicians. Whether posing as "military socialists" as in Bolivia, conservative modernizers as in Paraguay, or patrimonial agents of repression, Latin American militaries unleashed their forces against internal enemies, arresting, abusing, and sometimes killing their own citizens. They also supported public works, investments in industry and public enterprise, government control of natural resources, and improved educational opportunities. In any event, there is little doubt that international circumstances—in this case, the worldwide Depression—provided the incentive and justification for a rash of military coups throughout the decade.

A third key period embraced the 1960s and 1970s. The 1960s witnessed coups in major countries—Argentina, Brazil, and Peru—where military commanders settled in for extended periods of rule. In addition, there were coups in the Dominican Republic, followed by a U.S. military invasion in 1965; in parts of Central America, where concern about communist penetration was taking hold; and in the Andes, where military officers insisted on preventing populist politicians from taking office (especially if they had won free and fair elections). This was a period of intensifying social conflict in Latin America, and it was a time of staunch anticommunism. The success of the Cuban Revolution in 1959 had frightened and galvanized conservative sectors in Latin American society, including the armed forces. Meantime, the U.S. government, from Eisenhower to Nixon, made clear its preference for military dictatorship over weak-kneed democratic leadership. In response to these incentives, military officers performed what they saw as their duty: saving *la patria* from subversion. This pattern continued well into the 1970s, as *golpes* took place in such otherwise civilized settings as Chile and Uruguay. These were Cold War coups.

Of course, all coups were not the same. Some were low-key affairs, in which a group of officers seized power for a brief period of time to prevent an undesirable electoral outcome; these might be regarded as "veto coups."

---

[4] See Thomas E. Skidmore, "Workers and Soldiers: Urban Labor Movements and Elite Responses in Twentieth-Century Latin America," in Virginia Bernhard, ed., *Elites, Masses and Modernization in Latin America, 1850–1930* (Austin: University of Texas Press, 1979), 79–126.

Neatly capturing the ubiquity of military intervention, this 1963 cartoon shows Latin America's armed forces acting on their own—and thus overlooks the frequency of civilian collaboration. (Roy B. Justus, Minneapolis Star, 1963. Reprinted with the permission of the Minneapolis Star and Tribune Co.)

Others reflected rivalry within the armed forces, with one military faction taking steps to depose another. As time wore on, however, coups showed an increasing tendency to overthrow electoral democracies. Especially in the early years of the century, many made little use of force, but as the stakes appeared to climb, *golpes de estado* became more vicious, more encompassing, and more violent.[5] For the sheer magnitude of its brutality, the Chilean coup of 1973 stands in a category by itself.[6]

Missions and Regimes

Latin America endured well over fifty military regimes during the course of the twentieth century, and there was as much variation in patterns of

---

[5] See Martin C. Needler, "Political Development and Military Intervention in Latin America," *American Political Science Review* 40 (September 1966): 619–620.
[6] This comment refers to the coup itself, not the ensuing regime. The Argentine coup of 1976 was substantially less brutal, but (by many criteria) the subsequent regime was more repressive than the Pinochet dictatorship.

military rule as in the forms of coups. Programmatic government by a military junta is not the same as mindless tyranny by a self-indulgent dictator. Four variables are critical:

1. whether the power structure within the regime is personalistic or collegial
2. whether the military as an institution takes part in governmental decision making (for instance, holding nonmilitary cabinet posts)
3. whether the regime has a distinct ideological orientation, and, if so, what it is
4. the societal base of civilian support for military rule.

Variations along these dimensions and different combinations of variations clearly demonstrate the complexity of these phenomena.

Historically, military regimes in Latin America were highly personalistic. They were headed by a single individual—usually a general, sometimes a colonel—who issued rulings on his own authority by executive decree. These regimes relied on the armed forces for political support but did not engage the officer corps in governmental decision making. Other than invocations of *la patria* and the need for discipline, they showed little evidence of ideological commitment. Their social backing tended to come from local elites, who stood to benefit from law and order. Such were the dictatorships of Gustavo Rojas Pinilla in Colombia and Hugo Banzer in Bolivia. On occasion such regimes became so personalized that they were more "sultanistic" than military (according to terms developed in Chapter 2). Examples include Rafael Trujillo in the Dominican Republic, Anastasio Somoza in Nicaragua, and Marcos Pérez Jiménez in Venezuela. Tyrants of this sort tended to use the armed forces as patrimonial constabularies, whose main purposes were upholding domestic order and terrorizing political opponents. Precisely because of these demeaning missions, military institutions did not provide unqualified loyalty to sultanistic rulers; junior officers could often be persuaded to defect.

During the 1960s and 1970s, a new type of military regime came to the fore: institutionalized military regimes with long-term commitments to coherent ideological programs. They pledged not only to eliminate forces of subversion, real or imagined, but also to transform the economic and social structures of their nations. These were far-reaching goals.

Ideological commitments produced sharply distinctive orientations. As Karen Remmer has pointed out, *inclusionary*, or "populist," military regimes attempted "to create a popular base of support for military rule by mobilizing new sets of political actors around reformist and nationalist projects. The popular sector, which encompasses the lower middle class and lower urban and rural class, is thereby drawn actively into politics—often for the first time." As shown in Table 3.1, examples included the first Perón regime in Argentina (1946–1955),[7] the Peruvian regime under Velasco (1968–1975), Panama under Omar Torrijos (1968–1981), and the military junta in Ecuador (1972–1978). To be sure, the depth of ideological conviction among these regimes displayed substantial variation—from the concoction and occasional exploitation of a "justicialist" worldview under Perón to the avid adaptation of neo-Marxist analysis and dependency theory by the Peruvian generals.

Yet all these regimes displayed unmistakably reformist tendencies. Military rulers sought to address what they took to be the underlying causes of political unrest, particularly poverty, inequality, and economic "dependency" on foreign and transnational forces. They did not engage in large-scale campaigns of repression or wage "dirty wars" against their citizens. Instead, they mobilized lower-class groups, attempted to impose redistributionist policies, and strengthened the economic role of the state. Success was only partial. Omar Torrijos managed to negotiate an eventual U.S. turnover of the Panama Canal (effective 1999), and the Ecuadoran generals benefited from the discovery and exploitation of petroleum, but the Peruvian leaders, with perhaps the most ambitious program of all, were least able to achieve significant change.

At the opposite end of the spectrum, conservative and reactionary outlooks led to the formation of *exclusionary* regimes. In Remmer's words, "Their central thrust is demobilizational rather than mobilizational. Popular-sector groups thus become a principal source of opposition to military rule, rather than a base of support. Exclusionary authoritarianism is built instead on a foundation of middle- and upper-class support, and internationally oriented economic interests dominate the governing coalition."[8] Prime examples were the military junta in Brazil (1964–1985), the reactionary juntas in Argentina (1966–1973 and 1976–1983), and, most conspicuously, the Pinochet regime in Chile (1973–1989). In all cases the ideological commitment embraced a series of tenets—anticommunism, economic liberalism, insistence on morality, devotion to *la patria*, and belief in the inherent virtues of law and order.[9]

Although both regime types have existed, Table 3.1 makes a self-evident point: There have been many more reactionary military regimes than progressive ones. Moreover, the exclusionary regimes prevailed for extended periods in major countries such as Argentina, Brazil, and Chile. Reformist

---

[7] The Peronist regime was ambiguous in this respect: Although Perón was himself a military officer, he eventually encountered strong opposition from the armed forces and was overthrown by a military coup in 1955.

[8] Remmer, *Military Rule in Latin America* (Boulder, CO: Westview, 1991), 4–5.

[9] There is no consensus in the literature on the causal relationship between the ideology and social base of military regimes. Some writers see social base as cause and ideology as effect; others, including me, regard ideology as an independent causal factor. After all, military officers are steeped in all kinds of doctrine throughout their careers; it seems hard to imagine that they would embrace an ideological position merely as a matter of convenience.

TABLE 3.1 Prominent Military Regimes

Reformist/Inclusionary

Argentina	1946–55
Ecuador	1963–66, 1972–78
Panama	1968–81
Peru	1968–75

Reactionary/Exclusionary

Argentina	1966–73, 1976–83
Bolivia	1964–70, 1971–82
Brazil	1964–85
Chile	1973–90
El Salvador	1979–84
Guatemala	1963–85
Honduras	1972–82
Uruguay	1973–84

Source: Author's assessments and Karen Remmer, *Military Rule in Latin America* (Boulder: Westview, 1991), 4–6.

regimes were less pervasive, less effective, and less repressive. More often than not, the armed forces of Latin America have allied themselves with socioeconomic elites.

Conservative regimes showed one characteristic that progressive ones did not: recruitment of and reliance on a cadre of technocrats. Especially throughout the Southern Cone (Argentina, Chile, Uruguay), these *técnicos* assumed critical roles in the design and implementation of policy, especially economic policy. Nicknamed "the Chicago boys" because of their association with conservative economists at the University of Chicago, they provided military regimes in these countries with a civilian cast. In addition, the regimes forged close alliances with elite elements of the domestic business class. For such reasons, Guillermo O'Donnell christened these dictatorships "bureaucratic-authoritarian regimes," a label that immediately became standard usage.[10]

With regard to governance, regimes of all types have displayed personalistic as well as collegial structures of power. Within the reformist category, the Perón regime in Argentina and the Torrijos regime in Panama were highly personalistic, whereas the junta in Ecuador was essentially collegial. Within the reactionary category, the Brazilian regime was highly collegial, whereas the Pinochet regime in Chile started out as a collegial enterprise and became increasingly personalized over time. The Argentine experience

---

[10] Guillermo O'Donnell, *Modernization and Bureaucratic-Authoritarianism: Studies in South American Politics* (Berkeley: Institute of International Studies, University of California, 1973); see also David Collier, ed., *The New Authoritarianism in Latin America* (Princeton, NJ: Princeton University Press, 1979).

is illuminating here. During the 1966–1973 period, Juan Carlos Onganía was the undisputed head of government: According to one knowledgeable source, "It was made clear that the armed forces neither governed nor cogoverned. But they existed and apart from personal prestige, were his [Onganía's] only base of political support." During the 1976–1983 period, the armed forces as an institution played an active role in governance and reached decisions in a collegial manner. A careful balance was preserved among the different services, and leadership of the junta was rotated on the basis of consensus. Reflecting on the tenure of Leopoldo Galtieri, head of the junta in the early 1980s, an observer astutely noted that "Onganía was a king; Galtieri was a prime minister."

A common feature of all military regimes is their declaration that at some future point, elections will take place and democracy will take root. Indeed, they usually define their central mission as preparation of the country for democracy—"true democracy," not the incompetent pandering and self-indulgent irresponsibility that characterized earlier experiments under the fraudulent name of democracy. Military intervention could never be permanent: It was always a temporary measure, a generous response to a cry for salvation and a sacrificial gesture by members of the armed forces. Not surprisingly, military rulers reserved the right to decide whether, when, and under what conditions they should turn power over to elected civilians and go back to their barracks. As a matter of definition, however, their missions would necessarily come to an end. This gave rise to a curious paradox: the greater their success in achieving their goals, the sooner they would have to leave office.

Wars Against Subversion

As will be shown in Chapter 4, the Cold War exerted a decisive impact on hemispheric politics. Fearful of Soviet influence and inroads, the United States sought to bolster inter-American support and solidarity. The Eisenhower administration (1953–1961) masterminded the overthrow of an elected reformist government in Guatemala, launched a campaign to purge Latin American labor unions of leftist leanings, and dispatched Vice President Richard Nixon on a goodwill tour of South America in 1958. It also initiated a long-term program of cooperation with the Latin American military. As Secretary of State John Foster Dulles instructed U.S. diplomats at one point, "Do nothing to offend the dictators; they are the only people we can depend on."

The success of the Cuban Revolution in 1959 sent shock waves not only through the U.S. body politic but also through the ranks of Latin American militaries. The consummate threat to *la patria* would no longer come from an illusory Soviet invasion, but from communist ideology and its regional exponents—Fidel Castro, Che Guevara, and sympathizers everywhere. Indeed, the 1960s witnessed an explosion of more than thirty guerrilla movements throughout Latin America.[11] The Castro regime made determined efforts to destabilize the democratic government of Venezuela. Urban guerrillas staged major operations in Montevideo and other cities of South America. A revolutionary group captured and killed the U.S. ambassador to Guatemala; another kidnapped the U.S. ambassador to Brazil. In 1970 the unthinkable happened in Chile: A free and fair election resulted in the elevation of an avowed socialist to the presidency. Throughout the 1970s, guerrilla activity intensified in El Salvador, subjecting that small country to a vicious civil war, and in Nicaragua, eventually leading to the overthrow of the despised Somoza dynasty.

In response, Latin American militaries determined to repress the forces of "subversion" with all the resources at their disposal. They would closely monitor civilian governments. If existing policies seemed in any way ineffective or unsuitable, the high command would feel not only justified but *obliged* to seize power. It was their duty to *la patria*.

Embattled governments sprang into action, hoping to crush revolutionary movements and, in many cases, to forestall the likelihood of military intervention. They passed new laws augmenting the authority, jurisdiction, and internal missions of the armed forces. They increased military budgets. They expanded the size of the armed forces. In just about every conceivable way, they enlisted the military establishment in the campaign against communist ideology and guerrilla sabotage.

In the eyes of the military, the nature and magnitude of the threat called for a massive campaign. The war against subversion was not to be a temporary police action or even a surgical military operation. As Brian Loveman has explained:

> The logic and moral imperatives of war replaced those of politics, thus inevitably enhancing the role of the armed forces in policymaking and administration. Unlike law enforcement, which is focused on crimes by individual human actors, war is made on "enemies" and "targets." Sledgehammer tactics and the logic of war prevail: kill or be killed, destroy the enemy to attain victory. The logic of war replaces the niceties of civil liberties and due process. War substitutes coercion and killing for negotiation and compromise. War makes killing righteous; it is a strategic and tactical method to attain political and military objectives.[12]

Moreover, this was "total war"—war not on an open battlefield, but in the streets and schools and homes. It was a war for hearts and minds, one that would require tactics of terror, torture, and intimidation.

In effect, the antisubversive campaign amounted to the institutionalization of repression in defense of patriotism, national security—and what was

---

[11] See Timothy P. Wickham-Crowley, *Guerrillas and Revolution in Latin America: A Comparative Study of Insurgents and Regimes since 1956* (Princeton, NJ: Princeton University Press, 1992).

[12] Loveman, *For La Patria*, 184–185; see also 233–234.

repeatedly referred to as the "Western Christian way of life." Underlying this claim was an utterly bizarre interpretation of world history, one that traced the decline of Western civilization to the Reformation, the Age of Reason, the Industrial Revolution, and the rise of the bourgeoisie.[13] Modernity had bred corruption. The true age of glory was the medieval era, and the crowning achievements of nobility were the *reconquista* of Spain from the Moors and the Crusades against the infidels.

The litany stretched unbroken from Central America to the Southern Cone:

José Efraín Ríos Montt, Guatemala: "men of subversion" would "not be found murdered along the roadside; anyone who breaks the law will be shot, but not murdered."

Carlos Humberto Romero, El Salvador: all compatriots should join in "a patriotic crusade" to eradicate "dissociative, subversive, and terrorist groups."

Augusto Pinochet, Chile: "When confronted by communist penetration [that] represents the destruction of the basic moral foundations from which the Western and Christian civilizations derive...society is under the obligation of drastic self-defense."

Leopoldo Fortunato Galtieri, Argentina: "it was necessary for the Argentine Army and the other armed forces to come together to eradicate that scourge ...that jeopardized the very existence of the Fatherland....In this country there was not, and could not have been, any violations of human rights. There was a war, an absurd war, unleashed by a treacherous and criminal barbarism."

Jorge R. Videla, Argentina: "A terrorist is not just someone with a gun or a bomb, but also someone who spreads ideas that are contrary to Western and Christian civilization."

Military authorities throughout the region concurred that this would be a long-term struggle. If and when they seized power, they would establish military regimes for sufficient periods of time to cleanse society, purge politics, and initiate economic development. This would mark a major change in forms of military intervention. Instead of the "veto coups" so common in the past—short-term seizures of power intended to forestall specific outcomes, such as the election of an undesirable candidate—these *golpes* were intended to pave the way for durable military regimes. They would stay in power as long as they had to, and not one day less. Elimination of the subversive threat would be the first order of business, but by no means the only one.

Repression and reaction became the orders of the day. The trend began in Brazil, where a 1964 coup ushered in a right-wing military regime that

---

[13] See Frederick M. Nunn, "The South American Military and (Re) Democratization: Professional Thought and Self-Perception," *Journal of Interamerican Studies and World Affairs* 37, no. 2 (Summer 1995): 1–56, esp. 15.

engaged in a slow-motion campaign of repression that reached its peak between 1968 and 1972. The Brazilian officer corps subscribed broadly to a "national security doctrine" formulated by General Golbery do Couto e Silva, a notion that stressed the dangers of "indirect attack" from the Soviet Union through subversion, revolution, or both. As he argued, the concept of war was all-encompassing: "All activities are focused on one single aim: victory and only victory. No distinction is made between soldiers and civilians, men, women, and children; they face the same danger, and identical sacrifices are demanded of them. They must all abdicate the secular liberties, which had been won at such high costs, and place them in the hands of the state, the all-powerful lord of war." In this global struggle, Latin America was essential to the survival of the West, and Brazil, due to its size and the resources of the Amazon, was the most important country of Latin America. The doctrine thus appealed to traditional nationalistic ideals of *grandeza brasileira*, a predetermined destiny of greatness for Brazil.

The campaign then moved to Argentina, where the military imposed a ruthless regime in two stages: first from 1966 to 1973, then from 1976 to 1983.[14] The second phase initiated a so-called Proceso de Reorganización Nacional and sought to root out the sources of subversion with relentless efficiency. (As one of the leading generals proclaimed in 1977, "First, we'll kill all the subversives. Then we'll kill the collaborators, then the sympathizers, then the undecided. And finally, we'll kill the indifferent.") By the time they left power, Argentina's military had murdered or "disappeared" at least 9,000 citizens—and probably thousands more. It was in Argentina that the word *disappear* became an active verb, as missing compatriots were referred to as "the disappeared."

In their defense of the fatherland, Argentine leaders expressed a virulent strain of anti-Semitism as well. Attempting to identify villains, military theorists linked communist threats with alleged Jewish and Zionist conspiracies. Bigotry went hand-in-hand with repression. As illustrated in Box 3.2, it fostered absurdity.

The next front opened in Chile, where a carefully orchestrated military revolt mounted an armed attack on the presidential palace in September 1973 and imprisoned, tortured, and murdered thousands of civilian citizens. "This is not a coup d'etat," General Augusto Pinochet declared on the day of the *golpe*, "but a military movement aimed at salvaging the country." An edict promptly proclaimed that anyone displaying a "belligerent attitude" would be "executed on the spot." Soon afterward Pinochet issued another warning: "Marxist resistance is not finished. There are still extremists left. Chile continues in a state of internal war." In the name of *la patria* and civilization, the Pinochet regime would murder or disappear at least 3,000 citizens.

---

[14] This could also be considered a single military regime: 1966–1983, with a brief interlude in 1973–1976.

BOX 3.2
ANTI-SEMITIC OBSESSIONS

Jacobo Timerman was born in Ukraine and in 1928 moved with his family to Argentina, where he eventually became a prominent newspaper editor and publisher. A well-known member of the Jewish community in Buenos Aires, he was arrested without explanation by military authorities in April 1977. He later wrote an account of his detention, including a chilling summary of one of his interrogations.

"For many years," Timerman explained, "Argentine Nazi ideologues have claimed the existence of a Jewish scheme for seizing Patagonia, the southern zone of the country, and creating the Republic of Andinia. Books and pamphlets have appeared on the subject, and it's extremely difficult to convince a Nazi that the plan is, if not absurd, at least unfeasible. Naturally, my questioners wanted to know more details than were presently available to them on this matter."

QUESTION: We'd like to know some further details on the Andinia Plan. How many troops would the State of Israel be prepared to send?

ANSWER: Do you really believe in this plan, that it even exists? How can you imagine 400,000 Argentine Jews being able to seize nearly 1 million square miles in the southern part of the country? What would they do with it? . . .

QUESTION: Listen, Timerman, that's exactly what I'm asking you. Answer me this. You're a Zionist, yet you didn't go to Israel. Why?

ANSWER: Because of a long chain of circumstances, all personal and familial. . . .

QUESTION: Come on, Timerman, you're an intelligent person. Find a better answer. Let *me* give an explanation so we can get to the bottom of things. Israel has a very small territory and can't accommodate all the Jews in the world. Besides, the country is isolated in the midst of an Arab world. It needs money and support from all over the world. That's why Israel has created three power centers abroad. . . .

ANSWER: Are you going to recite the Protocols of the Elders of Zion to me?

QUESTION: Up to now, no one's proved that they're untrue. But let me go on. Israel, secure in these three centers of power, has nothing to fear. One is the United States, where Jewish power is evident. This means money and political control of capitalist countries. The second is the Kremlin, where Israel also has important influence. . . .

ANSWER: I believe the exact opposite, in fact.

QUESTION: Don't interrupt me. The opposition is totally fake. The Kremlin is still dominated by the same sectors that staged the Bolshevik Revolution, in which Jews played the principal role. This means political control of Communist countries. And the third center of power is Argentina, especially the south which, if it were well developed by Jewish immigrants from various Latin American countries, could become an economic emporium, a food and oil basket, the road to Antarctica.

Source: Jacobo Timerman, *Prisoner Without a Name, Cell Without a Number,* trans. Tony Talbot (New York: Knopf, 1981), 73–74.

Chilean soldiers on parade present a formidable image of power and determination. (AP Photo/Santiago Llanquin)

Also in 1973, the armed forces seized power in Uruguay. Here the principal threat came from urban guerrillas, especially a movement known as the Tupamaros. Like their counterparts in Argentina and Chile, the Uruguayan military imposed a reign of terror but tended to rely on torture rather than extermination. Repression was extensive but less brutal than in neighboring countries.

The struggle against subversion took other forms in other areas. Convulsed by internal discord and caught in the midst of the Cold War, Central America became the site of open warfare from the late 1970s to the mid-1990s. Unable to resist temptation, the Reagan administration intervened in this imbroglio: Washington earnestly supported *right-wing* forces attempting to overthrow a revolutionary government in Nicaragua, ardently sustained a reactionary government in El Salvador, and, somewhat casually, transformed Honduras into a military training camp. Also seized by internal strife, Guatemala endured the transformation of a civil war into a race war as the military carried out quasi-genocidal purges of indigenous communities and villages. All in all, it has been estimated that hostilities in Central America led to the deaths of at least 300,000 people and to the displacement of 2 million more (out of a regional population of less than 30 million!).

Not all this mayhem was wrought by military regimes. In the early 1980s Peru confronted a threat from Sendero Luminoso (Shining Path), a revolutionary movement originating in the Andean highlands. Sendero militants proved dedicated and effective, moving their operations from the countryside into cities and establishing strongholds in shantytowns surrounding Lima. Civilian leaders soon decided to unleash the power of the Peruvian army against Sendero rebels. As in Guatemala, the campaign acquired elements of a racist war against indigenous peoples. According to a 2003 report, the Peruvian conflict resulted in approximately 69,000 deaths.

THE DEMOCRATS' DILEMMA: TO AMNESTY OR NOT?

One of the more critical challenges for new democracies of the 1980s and 1990s was establishing authority over the military. In an ideal world, this would entail political subordination of the armed forces to the democratic regime, control over military policy by constitutionally designated civilians, and a subjection of military personnel to the rule of law. Anything less can weaken or even endanger the process of democratic consolidation.

Naturally enough, civilian authorities want to maximize their control of the armed forces. They also want to reduce the chances of another military coup. Just as naturally, military leaders want to retain as much autonomy as possible. As Alfred Stepan has argued, the resulting struggles take place along two dimensions. One concerns "contestation" over military-related policy, such as the definition of the military mission and the size of the military budget. The other dimension concerns military "prerogatives" essentially internal to the military, such as promotions, doctrines, deployments, and strategies. Bargaining between civilian and military leaders can result in significant trade-offs: Pressure on contestation might be accompanied by tolerance of prerogatives (or vice versa).[15] If the long-term goal is civilian control of the military, the near-term strategy would be acceptable accommodation and avoidance of undue antagonism.

With regard to contestation, civilian leaders achieved substantial and even remarkable success in curtailing military budgets. According to Figure 3.2, expenditures on the armed forces as a share of gross national product (GNP) began to decline in Brazil during the 1970s, when the military government was still in power. By the early 1980s, according to Stepan, Brazil had the second-lowest level of military spending among all major nations of the world.[16] Military spending would climb slightly during and after the transition to civilian democratic rule, in fact, but it would still remain at modest levels. The picture for Argentina is altogether different. Military expendi-

---

[15] Alfred Stepan, *Rethinking Military Politics: Brazil and the Southern Cone* (Princeton, NJ: Princeton University Press, 1988).
[16] Ibid., 75.

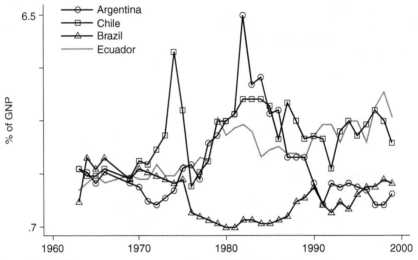

Figure 3.2 Military expenditure as share of GNP: South America

Source: United States Arms Control and Disarmament Agency, *World Military Expenditures and Arms Transfers*, various editions.

tures climbed steadily after the 1976 coup, spiked sharply in 1982, during the Falklands/Malvinas war against Great Britain, and then plummeted after the restoration of democracy. By the late 1990s, the relative size of the armed forces budget was somewhat less than in Brazil. Chile offers yet another contrast: Military spending accelerated shortly after the 1973 coup, declined briefly thereafter, then showed a steady rise throughout the 1980s, by which time the military share of GNP was several times the level in Brazil. Of the three countries in Figure 3.2, Chile had by far the largest budget throughout the 1990s—indeed, that was part of the compact that permitted the transition to democracy.

Central America reflects the traumas of war—civil war, the Cold War, and external interventions. As shown by Figure 3.3, countries of the isthmus had fairly modest military budgets during the 1960s and early 1970s, except for 1969, when Honduras and El Salvador engaged in a short but sharp conflict, the so-called soccer war. During the 1980s, however, military expenditures began a steady upward climb, reaching 6 percent of GNP in El Salvador, 4 percent in Honduras, and more than 2 percent in Guatemala. With the end of the internal wars in Nicaragua and agreements on the Esquipulas peace accords, military spending just as suddenly dropped (reflecting, in large part, reductions in U.S. military aid). Civilian leaders did not bring about these sharp reductions, but they benefited from them. By the time electoral democracy arrived, the task had already been done. By the end of the 1990s, military spending in all three countries hovered around 1 percent of GNP, much the same level as in Argentina and Brazil.

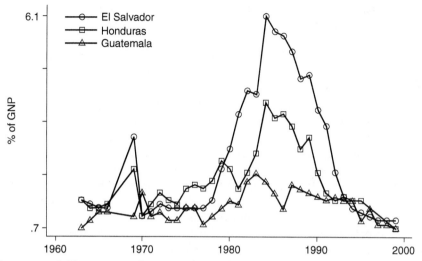

Figure 3.3 Military expenditure as share of GNP: Central America

Source: United States Arms Control and Disarmament Agency, *World Military Expenditures and Arms Transfers*, various editions.

At the same time, democratic leaders in postauthoritarian societies confronted a central dilemma: what to do about human rights abuses. In countries that suffered extensive repression, followers and support groups are likely to demand swift justice, as are friends and relatives of the dead and disappeared. For their part, military officers are bound to resist prosecution—to protect their troops as well as themselves, to uphold the honor and dignity of the military profession, and to justify the fact of military rule. This is perhaps the most critical single issue with regard to "contestation." It provokes powerful emotions, it raises fundamental questions about morality and justice, and it is the most likely to provoke military action in response.

How has this process unfolded? Argentina provides an illustrative case study. It reveals the power of the issues, the complexity of civil–military bargaining, and the uncertainty of outcome. It has also provided a template for subsequent bargains and agreements in other countries.

Precedents from Argentina

Among all nations of Latin America, Argentina appeared to have the most propitious conditions for asserting civilian control over the armed forces. By economic and social criteria, the Proceso de Reorganización Nacional had been a massive failure. Excesses of the "dirty war" had isolated the armed forces from their usual allies in civil society. Perhaps worst of all, the junta had led the country into a humiliating military defeat in the 1982 Falklands/Malvinas war against Britain. By 1983, Argentina's once-proud military was confronting a situation of unprecedented institutional and political vulnerability. Chastened officers candidly expressed chagrin. "The military [government] was a political disaster and a military disaster," said one. Concurred another: "I have witnessed every coup since the first revolt against Perón in 1951. [They] have always started with enthusiasm, with idealism, and they always ended badly."

Recognizing these realities, junta leaders took steps to protect the military during (and from) the transition to civilian rule. The armed forces issued a "Final Report on the War against Subversion and Terrorism" that offered a lengthy justification for the campaign against "terrorist aggression." Mixing self-exoneration with veiled threats, the document contended that "The actions carried out by members of the armed forces in the operations conducted in this war shall be considered acts of service; the armed forces took action and will do so again whenever it is necessary to carry out a mandate from the nation's government." An "institutional act" decreed that operations during the dirty war were undertaken under orders from the central government and that any trials for alleged human rights abuses should be conducted by military rather than civilian courts. And in September 1983, on the eve of a presidential election, the junta issued a "National Pacification Law," which provided amnesty for acts committed by all military personnel from 1973 through 1982. The idea, of course, was self-protection.

To widespread surprise, the October 1983 election was won by Raúl Alfonsín, of the Radical party, rather than by Italo Luder, of the Peronists (with whom the military had been actively negotiating behind the scenes). A champion of human rights, Alfonsín was able to take significant steps toward assertion of civilian control. He upgraded the civilian Ministry of Defense from a minor administrative office into a key instrument for military policy and planning. He replaced traditionally autonomous service commanders with chiefs of staff responsible to the president. Through a National Defense Law, he transferred primary responsibility for internal security from the armed forces to the civilian-run Ministry of the Interior. He cashiered a number of generals, including army chiefs, for making public pronouncements on what the government considered to be political questions. And as shown earlier in Figure 3.2, he halved the military budget as a share of GDP, bringing it down from nearly 4 percent to its customary pre-junta level of approximately 2 percent.

The human rights issue became convoluted and complex. Shortly after taking office, Alfonsín sent a bill to Congress that repealed the self-amnesty decreed by the military government and mandated automatic appeal of all decisions of the Supreme Military Tribunal to civilian courts. He also appointed a "truth commission," the Comisión Nacional sobre la Desaparición de Personas, under the chairmanship of the renowned writer Ernesto Sábato. The commission managed to document the existence of a clandestine military-police network of more than 300 torture and detention centers—and the disappearance of nearly 9,000 citizens. Entitled *Nunca Más*, the report was issued in July 1984. The night it was aired on TV, a bomb exploded in the broadcasting station. Several weeks later another bomb damaged the home of a commission member. Reporters who covered the story began receiving death threats.

In this highly charged atmosphere, Alfonsín chose to tread softly on the question of trials. Apparently, he wanted to focus attention on the commanders, especially the junta leaders, rather than junior officers and the rank-and-file. He was also hoping that by using its own court system, the military would manage to "cleanse itself." This was not to be. In September 1984, after the expiration of a third deadline, the Supreme Military Tribunal released a ten-page document that endorsed the dirty war and implicitly dismissed charges against the junta members.

On appeal, legal cases against the top commanders moved to the civilian courts. The ensuing series of trials—*el juicio,* as it was known—transfixed the nation for months. After dramatic hearings, the civilian courts eventually sentenced two junta members to life imprisonment, imposed varying prison terms on three others, and acquitted the rest. In a separate trial, General Ramón Camps, one of the most brutal participants in the dirty war, received a twenty-five-year prison sentence.

As the proceedings unfolded, the armed forces reacted with undisguised fury. Propaganda bombings and death threats forced the government to declare a state of siege shortly before the 1985 elections. Bitterly castigating human rights advocates in particular and civilians in general, a widely distributed flyer presented the military view:

> That we were cruel? So what! Meanwhile you have a fatherland that is not compromised for doing so. We saved it because we believed that we ought to save it. Were there other means? We did not see them, nor did we believe that with other means we would have been capable of doing what we did. Throw the blame in our face and enjoy the results. We will be the executioners, so you can be free men.[17]

It was a matter of honor and integrity. The soldiers had saved Argentina from perdition, and an ungrateful nation was making them pay for their sacrifice.

As popular pressure built up for still more trials, Alfonsín proposed to establish a date after which there could be no new charges brought against the military. Known as the Punto Final, it became law in December 1986. One of its unintended consequences, however, was to mobilize human rights groups to mount a flurry of charges before the final deadline. The issue would not go away.

A few months later, in April 1987, Major Ernesto Barreiro refused to appear in court and declared a barracks revolt. His regiment proclaimed that it would resist any effort to arrest him. Outside Buenos Aires, the Infantry School joined in the revolt; across the country, other units considered support

---

[17] Fitch, *Armed Forces and Democracy,* 138.

for the so-called Operation Dignity. Surrounded by officers in full combat gear and battle paint (which gave them the name of *carapintadas*, or "painted faces"), Lieutenant Colonel Aldo Rico called for an end to the trials, replacement of the army leadership, and a halt to government and media attacks on the military. With backing from the High Command, the president gave orders to suppress the revolt. Before a joint session of Congress and civilian leaders, Alfonsín pledged to seek a solution but not to cede to military pressure. "Here there is nothing to negotiate; Argentine democracy is not negotiable." The stalemate nonetheless continued. On Easter Sunday, Alfonsín went to a military installation where he met alone with *carapintada* leaders. To a tumultuous crowd outside the Casa Rosada, he later announced that the rebellion was over and Rico was under house arrest. "Happy Easter," he declared, "The house is in order."

Or was it? Soon after the "Easter mutiny," the army chief of staff resigned from his post. Alfonsín then sent to Congress the Law of Due Obedience, which would exonerate soldiers who were merely following orders during the course of the dirty war. In effect, it would absolve just about everyone below the rank of colonel, and it reduced the number of active proceedings from 450 to approximately 20. Congress approved the bill in June 1987. Controversy swelled and doubts arose: Had Alfonsín made a deal with Rico and the *carapintadas*?

Perhaps emboldened by this outcome, promilitary publicists continued their drumbeat of propaganda. The church was especially complicitous. The archbishop of La Plata denounced the trials as "the revenge of subversion" and came close to endorsing a military coup. A priest named Father Treviño called for "spiritual and material arms" to defend the country in clearly *golpista* language. In October 1987 Father Manuel Beltrán declared, "The military saved us from Marxism...[this antimilitary campaign] has been carried to all parts of the country...it is a well-orchestrated campaign and the instigator, basically, is Marxism and Zionist Masonry."[18]

As though on cue, *carapintada* units staged two additional revolts in 1988. These were not launched as *golpes de estado*. They were never intended to overthrow the government. Their basic goal, instead, was to reclaim the dignity, honor, and autonomy of the Argentine armed forces. In Stepan's terminology, their purpose was to enhance the influence of the military with regard to prerogatives and contestation—not to seize executive power. The rebellions seemed irrational in ways, but there was a method to their madness.

As economic chaos gripped the country in the meantime, the Alfonsín government and Radical party leadership lost credibility. The election of 1989 led to a sweeping triumph for the Peronists, whose presidential candidate, Carlos Saúl Menem, took office several months ahead of schedule.

---

[18] See J. Patrice McSherry, *Incomplete Transition: Military Power and Democracy in Argentina* (New York: St. Martin's Press, 1997), Ch. 5.

His principal concern was economic policy. Although he had himself been imprisoned by the military, Menem wanted to bring the human rights question to closure. In October 1989, shortly after his inauguration, he granted amnesty to the vast majority of officers implicated in the dirty war and in the Falklands War—and to many who took part in the uprisings under Alfonsín. In February 1990 he issued a decree reinstating a domestic security role for the military in cases of "social commotion." Seeking to assuage the military ego, he praised the armed forces at every conceivable opportunity.

Even then it was not easy. In December 1990, on the eve of a state visit by U.S. President George H. W. Bush, the *carapintadas* staged yet another revolt. Led by a fiery colonel named Mohamad Alí Seineldín, the rebels demanded not only an end to human rights proceedings but also an improvement of the status of *carapintadas* within the military and a more nationalistic stance in foreign policy. Angered by the prospect of embarrassment in front of President Bush, Menem ordered a quick end to the revolt. Loyalist troops responded vigorously. A total of sixteen rebels were killed and about fifty were wounded; Seineldín was court martialed and sentenced to life in prison. Amid the settling dust, Bush thanked Menem for Argentina's decision to send two warships to take part in the 1990 Gulf War against Iraq.

Just two weeks later, Menem issued a pardon for all convicted junta leaders of the Proceso. This move generated massive demonstrations in Buenos Aires in a so-called day of mourning and raised a storm of criticism. Menem's approval rating promptly dropped below 20 percent. In January 1991 a poll showed that 63 percent of the population thought Argentina's main problem was not economic but "moral."

Such developments had far-reaching significance. For the time being, it appeared that the most disgraced military establishment in the Americas had managed to achieve amnesty for its human rights abuses. With vivid clarity, this process revealed the complex quality of bargaining games between civilian and military authorities.[19] It showed the difficulty of imposing justice on military officers. And especially for leaders of military regimes elsewhere in Latin America, it sent a crystal-clear message: Do not submit to trials in civilian courts.

Chilean Twists

Take the case of Chile. In some ways, it was a polar opposite from Argentina. By the late 1980s, the free-market economic policies of the Pinochet regime were widely hailed for their success. Because the leftist "threat"—with a socialist president—had been relatively palpable, many sectors of civil society were willing to tolerate a dirty war. And in leaving power, the regime

---

[19] See Wendy Hunter, "Negotiating Civil-Military Relations in Post-Authoritarian Argentina and Chile," *International Studies Quarterly* 42 (1998): 295–318.

showed a touch of gentility, accepting the results of its own referendum that it was time to depart (although Pinochet himself would remain as army commander until 1998). For all these reasons, the Chilean armed forces enjoyed a much stronger bargaining position than had their Argentine counterparts.

As in Argentina, the civilian government under Patricio Aylwin (1990–1994) formed a Commission on Truth and Reconciliation (Comisión Nacional de Verdad y Reconciliación) under a jurist named Raúl Rettig. Its principal purpose was not to gather ammunition for legal proceedings against military officers; on the contrary, it was merely to document the truth and clear the air. Even then, the military government had already granted itself amnesty for abuses between 1973 and 1978, when the dirty war was at its most intense; proceedings would have to focus on actions after 1978. Unlike Alfonsín, Aylwin made no effort to repeal the self-amnesty.

After an arduous investigation, the Rettig report offered powerful testimony to the atrocities of the Pinochet regime. Released in May 1991, it documented more than 2,000 deaths at the hands of state agents. Predictably, Pinochet and his fellow commanders were apoplectic. Points 12 and 13 in the military's formal response to the commission were key:

> 12. The army and the other armed forces and police were called upon to intervene in the worst institutional crisis in this century, as the ultimate recourse against a serious threat to national sovereignty and social peace. They completed their mission, defeating the totalitarian threat; they reconstructed and modernized the economy; they restored social peace and democracy; and returned political authority to civilians in a free country....
>
> 13. The Chilean army certainly sees no reason to ask pardon from anyone for having taken part in this patriotic effort.[20]

The armed forces had entered and won a dangerous war. They had saved the country. What was there to apologize for?

Tension simmered in the years to follow. By mid-1993 there were about 800 proceedings under way against military personnel. To demonstrate their displeasure, troops marched through the streets of Santiago in the so-called *Boinazo,* a show of force named after the berets worn by the soldiers. Sensing trouble, Aylwin soon introduced a bill designed to bring a speedy conclusion to the ongoing trials and to foreclose new ones. He was learning his lessons from Alfonsín.

Two years later, in 1995, the Chilean Supreme Court upheld the lower court conviction of retired General Manuel Contreras, former chief of secret police, and second in command General Pedro Espinoza, both of whom were implicated in the 1976 assassination in Washington, DC, of Orlando Letelier, who had been Allende's foreign minister and ambassador to the United States. (Without diplomatic pressure from the United States, which

---

[20] Loveman, For La Patria, 242.

THE PINOCHET CHRONICLES

1998

March: Pinochet steps down as head of armed forces (twenty-five years after being appointed to that post by Salvador Allende), becomes senator-for-life as guaranteed to ex-presidents under 1980 constitution

September: travels to Europe on a private visit

October: undergoes back operation in a London clinic; as Pinochet awakens from surgery, agents from Scotland Yard deliver a Spanish arrest warrant; former dictator is detained in hospital room (later moves to house arrest at a country estate)

November: Spain requests extradition; Chile recalls its ambassador to Madrid

1999

March: British House of Lords denies full immunity and rules there are grounds to study extradition request

April: Britain's Home Office Secretary Jack Straw authorizes extradition proceedings

October: magistrate upholds Spain's request for extradition on charges dating from last fourteen months of military regime

2000

February: a British medical report concludes that Pinochet is suffering from a deteriorating brain condition and would be unable to understand questions at a trial

March: Straw releases Pinochet after 503 days of detention; on return to Santiago, Pinochet is welcomed by top military officials; days later, Ricardo Lagos of the Socialist Party is inaugurated as president

April: Santiago Appeals Court and Supreme Court strip Pinochet of immunity enjoyed as senator-for-life

December: Judge Juan Guzmán orders house arrest of Pinochet and charges him with masterminding the 1973 "Caravan of Death," in which seventy-five political opponents were murdered

2001

January: Chilean medical team finds Pinochet is suffering from "mild to moderate dementia" but agrees that he is fit to stand trial; Judge Guzmán interrogates Pinochet and soon afterward charges him with fifty-seven counts of murder and eighteen counts of kidnapping in connection with the Caravan of Death

March: Santiago Appeals Court rules Pinochet must stand trial to face charges related to the Caravan of Death

July: Santiago Appeals Court rules Pinochet unfit to stand trial; Sixth Tribunal suspends charges indefinitely

2002

July: by a 4-to-1 majority, Supreme Court closes case against Pinochet on charges stemming from alleged participation in the Caravan of Death.

2004

August: By a 9–8 vote, the Supreme Court rules that Pinochet should not enjoy legal immunity from charges of human rights abuses committed during Operation Condor, a shadowy alliance of right-wing South American regimes to eliminate leftists in the 1970s and 1980s

2005

Another Chilean court grants immunity to Pinochet on the basis of dementia

2006

December 10: Pinochet dies at the age of 91

---

was seeking extradition, this murder would have been covered under the 1978 amnesty.) In reply, a group of army and naval officers helped Contreras and Espinoza abscond. In fact, Contreras eluded captors for five months, during which time intensive negotiations took place. In exchange for modest concessions from military authorities, newly installed President Eduardo Frei agreed to create a special court for human rights cases.

There the matter seemed to rest. It was the international legal community that stirred up the issue again. In September 1998, as Pinochet was on a private trip to London, a Spanish magistrate named Baltazar Garzón issued a warrant for his arrest. The immediate ground was the fact that some Spanish citizens had been disappeared by the military regime; the broader ground concerned genocidal policies and "crimes against humanity." As the world watched in astonishment, agents from Scotland Yard served the papers as Pinochet was recovering in a hospital bed from back surgery.

The case became a cause célebre and dragged on for months (see Box 3.3). As a member of the European Union, Spain requested Pinochet's extradition. Eager not to upset the delicate balance that it had struck in civil–military relations, the Chilean government responded angrily, maintaining that the erstwhile dictator's legal disposition was a matter of national sovereignty. (This created the eerie spectacle of Pinochet's former opponents ardently defending him in British courts and halls of government.) As jurists decided what charges might or might not be permitted, counselors for the prosecution came up with the ingenious claim that the 1978 amnesty applied only to cases in which victims were known to be dead. As for the "disappeared," uncertainty about their fate subjected family members to cruel and continuing anguish, so these could be interpreted as ongoing transgressions (against the relatives, not the original victims), and as such they could provide a basis for legal proceedings.

In 1999 a five-person panel from the British House of Lords determined that Pinochet was not entitled to full immunity and that extradition hearings could proceed. Home Secretary Jack Straw concurred. In October a magistrate ruled that in accordance with the British statute of limitations, Pinochet could be tried only on charges dating from the last fourteen months of his regime (leaving open the question of continuing transgressions against the relatives of the disappeared). Early in 2000, however, a medical panel concluded that the octogenarian Pinochet would be unable to stand trial. At this, a visibly relieved Jack Straw released Pinochet from house arrest and authorized his return to Santiago, where he was greeted warmly by a circle of admirers.

At this point the Chilean justice system swung into action. A Santiago court and the Supreme Court stripped Pinochet of the immunity that he presumably enjoyed as senator-for-life. Magistrate Juan Guzmán placed the ex-dictator under house arrest and charged him with masterminding an infamous "Caravan of Death" in 1973. In mid-2001 the Santiago court of appeals found Pinochet unfit to stand trial, however, and the following year the Supreme Court concurred with this conclusion. Legal wrangling nonetheless continued. In August 2004, the Supreme Court voted to lift Pinochet's legal immunity (as former president) from prosecution for human rights abuses, but did not address the question of his mental capacity. Resolution finally came when the dictator died in late 2006.

The Pinochet episode had important implications. One concerned the role of international law and its challenge to the idea of state-centered sovereignty. What this meant, in effect, was that civil–military bargains, including amnesties, were subject to revision and amendment. What was determined within Chile did not necessarily hold outside Chile. Another stemmed from the changing position of Chilean courts. Initially opposed to proceedings against a former head of state, the courts adopted a major change in position and even ordered his house arrest. This revealed the increasing autonomy of the courts, which was positive for democratic development but also posed a latent threat to the compacts that had enabled the democratic transition in the first place.

There was also the question of time. Well into the twenty-first century, human rights issues were still—or again—at the center of political discourse in Argentina and Chile. The persistence of the human-rights advocates and plaintiffs in both countries was truly impressive. And at what appears to be a safe remove from military vengeance, elected civilian presidents were pressing for justice. The Argentine congress struck down both the "due obedience" and *punto final* laws and lifted a ban on extradition, leading to the detention of forty of the worst offenders from the military era. Chilean authorities were somewhat more cautious, leaving the 1978 amnesty in place but proposing legislation to oblige wrongdoers to account for their actions in courts. Clearly, the human rights issue resisted facile solution and refused to disappear.[21] The wheels of justice grind slowly, if at all, and as the adage goes, "Justice delayed is justice denied." Or is it?

MODES OF INTERACTION: THE ARMED FORCES AND DEMOCRACY

A key question for Latin America is whether the most recent cycle of democratization has assured civilian control over the armed forces. This did not occur early in the twentieth century. What about the current phase?

As suggested by the struggles over human rights, the record is ambiguous. As one analyst has said, "Military withdrawal from direct rule did not mean abject subordination to elected governments. The armed forces attempted to reassume their historical guardianship of *la patria* and made efforts to retain prerogatives assumed under military rule....To the extent that democracy means thorough control by elected civilian policymakers over military institutions and defense policy and acceptance by the armed forces of their subordination to civilian institutions such as the legislature, the courts, and the elected president, the transitions to elected government in Latin America in the 1980s did not entirely meet this criterion."[22]

Yet there were limits to military capabilities. In earlier epochs they always held one trump card: the possibility of coups. But such threats were not as credible as they had been before. The need was not as great: The Cold War was ending, the Left was weakening, and the dirty wars were done. The international context—and, in particular, the United States—would no longer be supportive. As David Pion-Berlin has succinctly stated, "the coup or no-coup question is not the defining one for this era."[23]

This does not mean that the armed forces had no influence at all. On the contrary, they continued to wield influence in a variety of ways, seeking to retain prerogatives and, on occasion, expand their policy roles through outright contestation. Variations on these themes led to a complex panorama of civil–military relations throughout the region. In the democratic climate of the 1980s and 1990s, four different patterns emerged:

Military control—political subordination of nominally civilian governments to effective military control

Military tutelage—participation of the armed forces in general policy processes and military oversight of civilian authorities

---

[21] Uruguay came to rest on this question when voters in a 1986 plebiscite decided not to repeal amnesty by a 53 to 41 percent margin. The issue has never reached central stage in Brazil, where amnesty was extended in 1979 not only to members of the armed forces but also to guerrillas—so both sides have had a stake in it.

[22] Loveman, *For La Patria*, 202, and Ch. 7.

[23] David Pion-Berlin, ed., *Civil–Military Relations in Latin America: New Analytical Perspectives* (Chapel Hill: University of North Carolina Press, 2001), 2.

TABLE 3.2 Patterns of Civil-Military Relations, 2000

Military control

None as of 2000 (with possible exception of Guatemala)

Military tutelage

Ecuador
El Salvador
Guatemala
Venezuela

Conditional military subordination

Bolivia
Brazil
Chile
Colombia
Dominican Republic
Honduras
Nicaragua
Paraguay
Peru

Civilian control

Costa Rica
Haiti
Mexico
Panama
Argentina
Uruguay

Source: Author's assessments.

Conditional military subordination—abstention by the armed forces from vert intervention in political questions, while reserving the "right" to intervene for protection of national interests and security

Civilian control—subordination of the armed forces in political and policy terms to civilian authorities, usually including a civilian minister of defense.

These are fluid categories, and distinctions between them tend to be matters of degree. Yet they provide a useful analytical scheme that underlines the complexity of civil–military relations within contexts of democratic change.[24]

---

[24] Adapted from J. Samuel Fitch, *The Armed Forces and Democracy in Latin America* (Baltimore: Johns Hopkins University Press, 1998), Chs. 2 and 5. Factors that determine the form of civil–military relations include (1) presence or absence of perceived threats to national security, (2) international geopolitical context, (3) problems of governance, and (4) degrees of unity within the armed forces.

At the risk of gross oversimplification, Table 3.2 locates nineteen Latin American countries within these classifications as of 2000. The inventory yields several significant insights. First is the virtual absence of military control. Political transformations in the 1980s and 1990s led to the removal of military regimes throughout the region, usually as a result of democratization (as in the Southern Cone), and occasionally as a result of U.S. armed intervention (as in Panama and Haiti). To be sure, it could be argued that the armed forces in Guatemala and perhaps Paraguay continued to exercise control over civilian authorities by century's end. Venezuela under Hugo Chávez also presented a complex phenomenon that has been sometimes described as an elected military regime. Yet none of these cases clearly qualifies for this category.

Even so, the possibility of military control of an elected government underlines a crucial point: You don't need to run the government to wield power. If this is so, why bother with coup plotting? On reflection, one reason for the precipitous decline in military *golpes* during the 1980s and 1990s might be that they were no longer deemed necessary. In practice, this insight goes beyond the observation that the coup–no coup question is not the defining one for the era; it might not be the right question to ask.

Military tutelage is another matter. At least four countries fell under this rubric: Guatemala and Venezuela, as mentioned earlier, and also Ecuador and El Salvador. An Ecuadoran officer spelled out the rationale: "If the armed forces are able to detect that these threats exist, one of their important roles is to make it known, to make people see, and get the necessary corrective actions taken, or avoid the problem while there is still time." In this spirit, the Ecuadoran military moved quickly to resolve institutional and constitutional crises in 2000, seizing power briefly to establish order and to oversee a presidential succession. As in Guatemala, the armed forces in El Salvador exercised continuing tutelage in the wake of a major internal war. In both countries, in fact, controlled transitions to limited democracy were part of the military's counterinsurgency strategy. As threats of conflict continued, the armed forces supervised civilian authorities and played key roles in decision making.

Armed forces exercised tutelary oversight elsewhere in Latin America, especially during transitional periods. In Peru, the outgoing military supervised the election in 1978 of a constituent assembly that worked for two years while the military retained executive power. In Brazil, the military allowed the election of a civilian to the presidency in 1985 but retained six cabinet posts for high-ranking officers. Likewise, the military continued to control its own services and national intelligence and defense systems and often took its own initiatives in social and political affairs. Under President Sarney, who treated the military "as a separate, fourth power," accountability to civilian authority was minimal. Change began only when his successor, Fernando Collor de Mello, reduced the number of military ministers, appointed a civilian to head the national intelligence service, and denounced a secret military program to build a nuclear bomb. It continued under Fernando Henrique Cardoso, who insisted that the military focus its attention on external rather than internal threats—but who also agreed to honor the 1979 amnesty law. By the late 1990s, the military still held five cabinet posts, wielded effective control over the police, and retained a significant role in domestic intelligence. As one expert observer concluded, "The 'rules of the game' for Brazilian civil–military relations remain ambiguous."[25]

The most populous category, with nine of the nineteen countries, was conditional military subordination. Here the armed forces were keeping careful watch over civilians. The policy stance was more reactive than proactive: The essential goal was to protect military prerogatives, rather than to dominate governmental initiatives. During the late 1980s, the Brazilian armed forces clearly exercised a tutelary role; by the late 1990s, their position had gravitated toward conditional subordination. Chile offered a similar picture: Pinochet and his cohorts sought a tutelary role for the armed forces after the 1989–1990 transition, but by 2000 they had to settle for conditional subordination. In these and other cases, the distinction between tutelage and conditional subordination is extremely tenuous. Armed forces in this grouping could quite easily embrace decisive tutelary roles.

The final category, civilian control, contains three pairs of countries. The first tandem includes countries that managed to curtail military influence during the course of historical crises: Mexico, where postrevolutionary disorder prevailed until the 1930s,[26] and Costa Rica, where political tumult led to the abolition of the armed forces in 1948. The second pair includes sites of U.S. military invasion: Panama, where U.S. forces ousted and captured Manuel Antonio Noriega in 1989, and Haiti, where an imminent invasion led to the resignation of General Raoul Cédras in 1994. In both cases, U.S. occupation forces dismantled existing military establishments and sought to replace them with constabularies. The third pairing consists of Argentina and Uruguay, where posttransition civilian governments managed to establish a reasonable degree of control of the armed forces. In both instances, however, the military succeeded in resisting efforts to place uniformed personnel on trial for alleged human rights abuses—through a complex pattern of bargaining and blackmail in Argentina, as described earlier, and through a more consensual process in Uruguay. Moreover, the armed forces in both countries retained substantial autonomy with regard to military organization, doctrine, and education, although they could no longer claim an independent role as "guardian" of national destiny. According to J. Samuel Fitch,

---

[25] Fitch, *Armed Forces and Democracy*, 154.
[26] See David Ronfeldt, "The Modern Mexican Military," in Abraham F. Lowenthal and J. Samuel Fitch, eds., *Armies and Politics in Latin America* (New York: Holmes and Meier, 1986), 224–261.

Argentina and Uruguay as of 2000 might best be described as instances of "partial democratic control."[27]

HAS THE MILITARY LEFT?

The history of military power in Latin America raises a fundamental question: Are the armed forces really retreating from the political arena? Are they likely to return? Why have they tolerated the rise of civilian authority?

There are several factors to consider. One is the relative absence of major threats to national security. The collapse of the Soviet Union, the implosion of world communism, and the end of the Cold War meant that there was no plausible threat of subversion. In most countries, leftist parties were weak; where they were relatively strong, they tended to espouse moderate reform rather than revolutionary transformation. *La patria* was safe. Similarly, economic elites, closely allied to armed forces in the Southern Cone, faced little immediate danger.

From the military standpoint, the armed forces have accomplished their mission. They have saved their countries. Especially in Chile and Argentina, military officers have expressed unrepentant pride in what they regard as their victory over subversive and antipatriotic enemies. Complaints from human rights groups about possible excesses only served to emphasize the difficulty of the challenge. The military had done its job and done it well. It could rest on its laurels until it was summoned again.

In this context, a return to the barracks is not a sign of defeat. On the contrary, it is the logical consequence of victory in battle. Moreover, it provides an opportunity for the military to tend to its prerogatives, enhance its sense of professional purpose, and prepare itself for challenges to come. Some officers have stressed the need for restoring discipline, dignity, and morale to their profession. Many insist that the armed forces are not in exile, limbo, retirement, or even retreat. They are honing their capabilities and enhancing their readiness.

Besides, the end of the twentieth century was not a good time for governing. In most countries there was no explicit need for military participation. And in all countries, the issues confronting civilian governments—stimulating economic growth in the context of globalization, reducing poverty and inequality, revamping the role of the state—did not lend themselves to military solutions. Better to let the businesspeople and technocrats deal with these problems and accept the blame for whatever failures might follow.

Junior officers have been especially reluctant to meddle in politics. Almost everywhere, political intervention by the military has had a distorting effect on normal promotions and advancements, as a small cadre of senior officers (and junta members) held on to top-rank positions. This reduced

---

[27] *Armed Forces and Democracy*, 41.

opportunities for junior officers, who were unable to move up their professional ladders in a timely fashion. Younger officers were often relieved to get back to the barracks, and they did not object too loudly when senior officers were retired, cashiered, or even arrested for human rights abuse; after all, it was the senior command that ordered antisubversive operations in the first place.

When all is said and done, there is no doubt about the survival of the armed forces in Latin America. They managed to escape relatively intact from human rights campaigns. They enjoyed popular support in Chile, Brazil, and some other important countries. Informally as well as formally, they were helping fight crime and strengthen public and private safety.[28]

And even in the absence of communist subversion, the armed forces were finding new missions. One was the "war against drugs." Initially, most Latin American officers were apprehensive about this idea: It was more of a police action than a military activity, it exposed soldiers to possible corruption, and, moreover, the whole problem derived from U.S. demand for illicit drugs. With strong support from Washington, Mexico has assigned approximately one fourth of its army to antidrug patrols. In Colombia and Peru, the antidrug campaigns became closely linked to antiguerrilla campaigns as, rightly or wrongly, officials decried the growing strength of narco-guerrillas. And throughout the rest of Latin America, a willingness to wage war against drugs has become a means of recuperating resources, capabilities, and new autonomy. As Argentina's defense minister declared in 1992, "If narcotraffic becomes narcoterrorism or narcosubversion [in this country], the armed forces are going to be there to smash it."

As the twentieth century drew to a close, Latin America's armed forces had not stepped entirely out of politics. They had stepped aside. In most countries they retained the option of deciding whether, when, and how to return. So long as the decision was theirs, the future remained an open question.

---

[28] Consuelo Cruz and Rut Diamint, "The New Military Autonomy in Latin America," *Journal of Democracy* (October 1998): 115–127. See also Diamint, "The Military," in Jorge I. Domínguez and Michael Shifter, eds., *Constructing Democratic Governance in Latin America*, 2nd ed. (Baltimore: Johns Hopkins University Press, 2003), 43–73.

CHAPTER 4

GLOBAL CONTEXTS, INTERNATIONAL FORCES

International factors can have serious impacts on processes and prospects for democratization. This is especially so in the case of Latin America, which is not and has never been a major global power center. Ever since independence from Spain and Portugal, the region has been subject to the designs and demands of prominent powers: first Europe, then the United States. In the global hierarchy, Latin America has occupied an essentially subordinate rank, a position that has made it conspicuously vulnerable to international pressures and trends. This situation has also affected political regimes and patterns of change. External factors have sometimes promoted processes of democratization in Latin America. And sometimes, as we shall see, they have hindered the democratic cause.

Adopting a long-range perspective, this chapter examines the impact of international factors for (or against) Latin American democracy within three broad chronological contexts: a period from the beginning of the twentieth century through the 1930s, part of what I have elsewhere called "the imperial era"; the Cold War, from the 1940s through the 1980s; and the post–Cold War decade of the 1990s. The analysis shows that international forces have mostly exerted either neutral or negative influences on processes of democratization throughout the region. Chapter 1 already expressed skepticism about the practical impact on Latin America of global "waves" of democratization during the nineteenth and twentieth centuries. And as will be shown in the conclusion to this book, the international atmosphere after the terrorist attacks of September 11, 2001, provided precious little nourishment for democracy in developing parts of the world.[1]

---

[1] Portions of this chapter have been adapted from my book *Talons of the Eagle: Latin America, the United States, and the World,* 3rd ed. (New York: Oxford University Press, 2008).

The United States has played a notably ambiguous role in this respect. As the leading power in the hemisphere, the United States has managed (or at least attempted) to exert its will on political developments throughout Latin America. At the same time, American society has long proclaimed that the nation has a moral obligation to foster democracy throughout the world; a cardinal motivation for U.S. foreign policy has therefore been the diffusion of democratic values and institutions. One question, of course, is whether U.S. policies have been effective in reaching this goal. Another is whether these noble principles actually guided U.S. actions or simply provided a convenient ideological pretext for economic, political, or other mundane purposes.

Multilateral organizations assumed key parts in this unfolding drama. Especially important were the United Nations, created at the end of World War II, and the Organization of American States, founded in 1948. Their roles have been more intermittent than continuous, but at times, especially during the 1990s, they actively promoted democratic change within the region.

Yet international interventions, even of the most benevolent kind, encountered a critical obstacle: the doctrine of national sovereignty, which has been a principal pillar of the global community. In theory, sovereignty means that nations have the right to settle internal disputes and to determine their own political order. What goes on inside a country's borders is nobody else's business; whether the government is democratic or not is a quintessentially internal matter. Any deliberate action to change a country's political regime by any external entity, such as the United Nations or the United States, therefore constitutes a breach of sovereignty. Notions of universal rights and national sovereignty thus stand in stark contradiction to one another.

IMPERIALISM AND DEMOCRACY

Imperialism entailed the policy, practice, or advocacy of the extension of control by a nation over the territory, inhabitants, and resources of areas that lay outside the nation's own boundaries. Typically, nations engaged in imperialistic behavior for two basic reasons: first, to gain access to economic benefits, such as land, labor, and minerals; and second, to increase political strength and military capability, often through the improvement of geopolitical position in relation to rival powers. Almost always, the pursuit of imperial advantage required elaborate ideological justification, ranging from the religious mission of sixteenth-century Spain, to the civilizing mission of eighteenth-century France, to the "white man's burden" that would be borne by nineteenth-century England.

As it evolved over time, imperialism fostered an informal but coherent code of international rules. Its keystone was the idea of a balance of power among the established and sovereign nation-states of Europe. Partly in reflection of this understanding, European leaders focused much of their competitive energy on imperial expansion. Preservation of a balance among metropolitan powers tended to limit the scale and scope of wars within the European theater. During the seventeenth and eighteenth centuries, battle-grounds shifted from the European continent toward the colonized areas. In effect, the extension of imperial possessions provided nations with an opportunity to enhance their power positions without having always to engage in direct hostilities with other European states. Colonial holdings became integral elements in the calculation of the power balance.

The newly independent United States eagerly joined this contest for imperial extension. Once involved, the United States adapted its policy in accordance with conditions and circumstances particular to the New World. While European powers engaged primarily in colonization of overseas pos-sessions, the United States tended to rely, first, on territorial acquisition and absorption, and, second, on the establishment and preservation of informal spheres of influence. The means thus varied, but the ends were much the same.

Circumstances were propitious in the early nineteenth century. England and France were distracted by internal strife and continental wars. Spain was in a process of precipitous decline. New nations in the hemisphere, especially in Spanish America, would be unable to offer much resistance. As Thomas Jefferson prophesied as early as the 1780s, it would eventually become possible for the United States to take over remnants of Spain's once-formidable empire "peice by peice" (sic). Under the mantle of "manifest des-tiny," a claim to heavenly benediction for westward expansion, the United States seized Texas in the 1830s and took a huge swathe of land, from New Mexico to California, from Mexico in the 1840s. There followed intermittent efforts to acquire Cuba as well, but they ultimately foundered over the issue of race: The "pearl of the Antilles" had a large population of black slaves, and American lawmakers ultimately shied away from the prospect of granting statehood and citizenship to such a society.

As the twentieth century beckoned, American strategy moved from ter-ritorial acquisition to the creation of informal spheres of influence. Between 1898 and 1934 the United States launched more than thirty military inter-ventions in Latin America. (According to one quaint but telling definition, a military intervention consists of the dispatch of armed troops from one country to another "for other than ceremonial purposes.") There were var-ied motivations for these actions. One was the protection of U.S. economic interests, especially private loans to local governments. Another was the assertion of geopolitical hegemony, assuring European powers that they need not meddle in the hemisphere. During and after World War I, pro-tection of the Panama Canal assumed special importance. In all cases, the perpetual rationalization was that the judicious application of U.S. military force would create a basis for democracy.

This component of U.S. policy focused exclusively on the greater Caribbean Basin, including Mexico and Central America. The United States launched major operations in Cuba, the Dominican Republic, Haiti, Honduras, Mexico, Nicaragua, and Panama. (There were threats of intervention on other occasions as well.) Some of these, as in Mexico, were relatively short-lived episodes. Others led to long-term military occupations. In Nicaragua, American forces occupied the country almost constantly from 1909 to 1934; in Haiti, U.S. troops lingered from 1915 to 1934; in the Dominican Republic, they established military rule from 1916 to 1924. The basic goal of U.S. policy, as commentators repeatedly said at the time, was to convert the Caribbean into an "American lake."

Washington all along insisted that it was fulfilling a high-minded political mission. The principal exponent of this view was Woodrow Wilson, who eventually defined his purpose in World War I as making the world safe for democracy. As for the hemisphere, Wilson would exclaim: "We are the friends of constitutional government in America; we are more than its friends, we are its champions." And then he sternly vowed, "I am going to teach the South American republics to elect good men!" Viewing democracy as a universal possibility, the southern-born Wilson was implicitly rejecting prejudicial theories about historical, religious, and geographical limitations on the spread of political civilization. Through instruction, example, and the judicious application of force, even Latin Americans could learn the rules of democratic conduct.

Yet even for Wilson, the conception of Latin American democracy had clear-cut limits. This was a time, it should be remembered, of substantial constraints on American democracy: Women acquired the right to vote only in 1920, organized labor was struggling to assert itself, and racial segregation meant the virtual exclusion of blacks from political life. And in view of popular skepticism about the political capability of Latin American peoples, the United States had precious little interest in promoting highly participative politics throughout the region. Instead, the preference was for an "aristocratic republic" under the aegis of an upper-class elite—a "competitive oligarchy," as defined elsewhere in this book. The priority was not on the democratic interplay of social interests; it was on the maintenance of law and order under presumably enlightened leadership.

Most U.S. interventions followed a consistent pattern. Military forces would arrive amid considerable fanfare; depose rulers, often with minimal force; install a hand-picked provisional government; supervise national elections; and then depart, mission accomplished. The political key to these operations was the holding of elections, which, as tangible signs of democracy at work, justified both the fact of intervention and the decision to lift the occupation. U.S. supervision of these contests was often overbearing, sometimes to the point of preselection of the winner, but the holding of elections was an essential step in the process. As one U.S. ambassador explained to his bewildered British counterparts, the United States would intervene as necessary in Latin America to "Make 'em vote and live by their decisions." If rebellions follow, "We'll go in and make 'em vote again."

American efforts to promote democracy underwent a sharp reversal after the 1932 election of Franklin Delano Roosevelt, who promptly declared the adoption of a "Good Neighbor" policy toward nations of the hemisphere. In spirit, this outlook indicated a diplomatic priority on relations with Latin America and a generally benevolent stance toward governments and peoples in the region. In substance, it entailed strict respect for national sovereignty and, more important, a policy of nonintervention. The type of political regime no longer mattered; the concern was on the friendliness of the relationship. (To be fair, U.S. policymakers might have figured they had little choice; by the mid-1930s, there were only two or three electoral democracies in the entire region.) This point received stunning emphasis in 1940, when FDR welcomed the ruthless tyrant of Nicaragua, Anastasio Somoza, on a state visit to Washington. "He's a son of a bitch," the U.S. president is said to have remarked, "but at least he's our son of a bitch."

THE ANTICOMMUNIST CRUSADES

World War II led to realignment of the global arena. After the defeat of Nazi Germany and imperialist Japan, the victorious Allies split into hostile camps. On one side were the United States and Western Europe, capitalist societies with democratic governments; on the other were the Soviet Union, its Eastern European satellites, and (eventually) the People's Republic of China, communist societies with totalitarian regimes. In March 1946 Winston Churchill denounced the lowering of an "iron curtain" in the midst of continental Europe and called for liberation from communist rule. In 1948 there came a Soviet-sponsored coup in Czechoslovakia; later in the year Josef Stalin sought to cordon off the occupied city of Berlin, which required a months-long airlift of food and supplies by the Allies. In 1949 the USSR announced successful detonation of its own atomic bomb, thus shattering America's postwar monopoly. That same year, communist insurgents under Mao Zedong surged to victory in China.

What would Washington do? The answer came in 1947, when Harry S. Truman decided to support the government of Greece in its struggle with a leftist insurgency. In a momentous address to Congress, the president declared that "it must be the policy of the United States to support free peoples who are resisting attempted subjugation by armed minorities or by outside pressures." This phrasing implied a remarkably capacious mandate. It committed the United States to assist "free peoples" (however defined) in struggles against external or internal foes. This called for both defense against outside threats and intervention against domestic challenges. In effect, the Truman Doctrine proclaimed that the United States would assume the role of global policeman. For the next forty years, Washington's principal goal would be to halt the spread of communism. The policy came to be known as one of "containment."

In paradoxical ways, the waging of the Cold War led to a series of tacit understandings, or rules of the game. First, each side strove mightily to establish military superiority over the other; in view of the potential for nuclear retaliation, however, neither side could take the risk of attacking the other. The United States and the USSR thus found themselves locked in a stand-off, accumulating arsenals they could never use. Second, each side defined its purpose in the name of high and principled causes. The Soviet Union sought to extend communist influence in support of social solidarity and economic justice. The United States positioned itself as leader of the "free" and democratic world. Third, there could be constant conflict, but always on the periphery. The principal contenders never fought among themselves; they assigned that task to clients and surrogates in what came to be known as the "third world." Such struggles were assumed to represent a "zero-sum" game, in which one side's gain would be another's loss. This prompted U.S. formulation of a "domino" theory, in which the loss of one country would immediately and automatically endanger its neighbors. Conflicts within or among small countries were therefore resistant to negotiation; because they entailed symbolic contests between the superpowers, neither side had much interest in accommodation.

In time the Cold War came to the Americas, and the United States braced itself to contend with communist threats. In May 1950 President Truman approved a National Security Council memorandum on "Inter-American Military Collaboration," which insisted that "the cold war is in fact a real war in which the survival of the free world is at stake." Later in the year, an official statement declared that "U.S. security is the objective of our world-wide foreign policy today," and "U.S. security is synonymous with hemisphere security."

Around this same time George Kennan, chief architect of the containment policy, offered his conception of the goals of U.S. policy in Latin America:

1. the protection of our [sic!] raw materials
2. the prevention of military exploitation of Latin America by the enemy
3. the prevention of the psychological mobilization of Latin America against us.

Communists "represent our most serious problem in the area," Kennan insisted, and they "have progressed to the point where they must be regarded as an urgent, major problem." Under no circumstances could they be allowed to take power. "The final answer might be an unpleasant one," Kennan conceded, "but...we should not hesitate before police repression by the local government. This is not shameful since the Communists are essentially traitors....It is better to have a strong regime in power than a liberal one if it is indulgent and relaxed and penetrated by Communists." Democracy was less important than security.

As Cold War perceptions hardened in Washington, the United States strengthened its ties with Latin American military establishments. As President Eisenhower argued, apparently with reference to a potential conventional war (rather than a nuclear exchange), it was important to bolster armed forces throughout the region because "we can't defend South America if this Communist war starts." By mid-1954 Congress approved $105 million in military aid for Latin America. In fact, the strategic benefits were slight, notwithstanding Eisenhower's military judgment, but the anticipated political benefits were substantial. As U.S. Army Chief of Staff J. Lawton Collins explained, "the Latin American officers who work with us and some of whom come to this country and see what we have and what we can do are frequently our most useful friends in those countries."

The U.S. embrace of dictatorship did not reflect a value judgment in favor of authoritarianism over democracy. It represented, instead, a cold-blooded calculation: that authoritarian regimes would be more predictably and efficiently anticommunist than other types of governance, including democratic systems. As the Cold War unfolded, the United States and military rulers in Latin America joined together in a three-part crusade to staunch the influence of communists through (1) virtual elimination of Latin American communist parties, (2) assertion (or reassertion) of state control over labor movements, and (3) diplomatic exclusion of the Soviet Union from the Western Hemisphere.

The 1959 triumph of the Cuban Revolution created a new sense of urgency. From the outset, long before Fidel Castro declared himself to be a Marxist-Leninist, the United States regarded his regime with apprehension and disdain. Castro's nationalist rhetoric, his confiscation of U.S.-held companies, and his program for land reform all provoked a predictably negative response in U.S. policy circles. To Washington, his movement was both an insult and a challenge.

In 1961 the newly elected president, John F. Kennedy, responded by launching the Alliance for Progress, a ten-year effort designed to stimulate economic growth, social development, and political democracy throughout Latin America. "We propose to complete the revolution of the Americas," the president proclaimed, "to build a hemisphere where all men can hope for a suitable standard of living, and all can live out their lives in freedom and dignity.... Let us once again awaken our American revolution until it guides the struggle of people everywhere—not with an imperialism of force or fear, but the rule of courage and freedom and hope for the future of man." As the rhetoric made clear, the Alliance for Progress, not the Fidelista movement, held out the true promise of "revolutionary" change. Achievement of these goals would require Latin American governments to design national development plans and undertake redistributive reform, including agrarian reform; for its part, the United States would channel $20 billion in foreign assistance to Latin America, "with priority to the less developed countries."

From Washington's point of view, the ultimate purpose of the Alliance for Progress was explicitly political. According to official documents, a principal goal was "to improve and strengthen democratic institutions through application of the principle of self-determination by the people." It was furthermore a "basic principle" that "free men working through the institutions of representative democracy can best satisfy man's aspirations." As was so often the case, President Kennedy offered the most lucid explanation of U.S. motivations. "Latin America is seething with discontent and unrest," he observed. "We must act to relieve large-scale distress immediately if free institutions are to be given a chance to work out long-term solutions." The point, in other words, was to bolster reformist democratic regimes and to forestall revolutionary threats. Such centrist parties as Acción Democrática in Venezuela and Christian Democracy in Chile offered desirable models for political reform and leadership. Support for the Center would prevent the rise of the Left.

Partly as a result of the alliance, the 1960s witnessed a marked acceleration in economic growth. The record on social reform was mixed; agrarian reform was especially intractable. But the most striking failure occurred in the political realm. Instead of promoting and consolidating reformist civilian rule, the 1960s witnessed a rash of military coups (see Figure 3.1 on page 77). By the end of the decade dictators were holding sway in Argentina, Brazil, Peru, Paraguay, and most of Central America; Bolivia and Ecuador were controlled by the military; and Mexico remained under the rule of its unique, dominant-party, civilian-led, but unmistakably authoritarian regime.

The Alliance for Progress and other programs were intended to prevent the rise of communist, socialist, and left-wing states in the Americas. On occasion, however, Washington found itself face to face with what it regarded as an unacceptably "leftist" regime within the hemisphere. In such cases, U.S. policymakers felt obliged to take action, which meant overthrowing the government in question. Exigencies of the Cold War thus led the United States to adopt a tacit but consistent policy of political intervention in Latin America as well as other third world areas, among them Vietnam.

Stemming the Tides of Revolution

The most conspicuous targets of American wrath were revolutionary governments. Leftist or socialist regimes presented the United States with political and ideological challenges, and in view of their links to the USSR, real or imagined, they were believed to endanger U.S. security as well. The only solution was to forestall or overthrow them.

In April 1961, shortly after the unveiling of the Alliance for Progress, Kennedy authorized a paramilitary invasion of Cuba at the Bay of Pigs. The assault force consisted of nearly 1,300 anti-Castro dissidents who had been recruited, trained, and supported by the U.S. government. Planners blithely assumed that news of a rebel landing would spark sympathetic uprisings among the Cuban people. Instead, Fidelista forces captured almost all the attackers and held them as prisoners for more than a year and a half. Contrary to its intention, the Bay of Pigs assault only strengthened Castro's hold on political power in Cuba and bolstered his stature throughout the third world.

In 1983, the Ronald Reagan administration launched an attack on the tiny Caribbean nation of Grenada, where a once-moderate reformist government under the New Jewel Movement was taking a radical turn. Official Washington declared that this otherwise lovely and inconsequential island was becoming "a Soviet-Cuban colony being readied as a major military bastion to export terror and undermine democracy." In one of the most bizarre episodes of the Cold War, nearly 2,000 U.S. Marines and airborne forces stormed and occupied the island. Order was restored and a new government installed.

Also in the 1980s, the United States became deeply involved in Central America. In El Salvador, a revolutionary movement called the Farabundo Martí Liberation Front (FMLN), named for the leader of a popular uprising in 1932, challenged the country's right-wing regime. The Reagan White House saw the conflict as a sign of alien communist agitation and devoted unequivocal support to the government, including large amounts of military aid. In February 1981, the State Department released a report purporting to offer "definitive evidence of the clandestine military support given by the Soviet Union, Cuba, and their Communist allies to Marxist-Leninist guerillas now fighting to overthrow the established government of El Salvador." According to this analysis, the Salvadoran insurgency represented a "textbook case" of communist interference within the hemisphere. With considerable bravado, Secretary of State Alexander Haig declared that the United States would have to go to "the source" of the trouble—by which he meant Cuba.

Washington also regarded Nicaragua as a source of danger. After years of fighting, the reactionary regime of Anastasio Somoza suddenly collapsed in 1979, just as Batista had given way in Cuba two decades before. Once in power, the youthful leaders of the victorious Sandinista movement proclaimed two broad policy goals: creation of a "mixed economy" as a foundation for social justice, and an "independent and nonaligned" foreign policy. The 1980 Republican Party platform openly denounced "the Marxist Sandinista takeover of Nicaragua," and the Reagan administration came to view the Sandinista government with fervent hostility. As the Central Intelligence Agency (CIA) mounted clandestine operations to destabilize the Nicaraguan government, the Reagan administration openly supported anti-Sandinista paramilitary rebels known as "Contras" (from the term *counter* revolutionaries). In one covert operation, officials on the National Security Council, including Lt. Col. Oliver North, assisted the Contras with funds diverted from the (equally covert) sale of arms to allegedly moderate groups in fundamentalist Iran. The Sandinistas managed to resist these onslaughts, despite extensive human suffering and economic dislocation, and peace eventually came to Nicaragua as a result of painstaking negotiations mediated by President Oscar Arias of Costa Rica. Ironically, an opposition movement led by Violeta Barrios de Chamorro triumphed in the elections of 1990. President Reagan's Contra wars thus achieved their principal goal, more by gradual attrition than by military conquest: ouster of the Sandinistas.

Displacing Inconvenient Democracies

In the grip of Cold War ideology, the United States also intervened against democratic governments—in cases, to quote George Kennan again, where a "liberal" administration showed signs of being "indulgent and relaxed and penetrated by Communists." The pattern began in 1954 in Guatemala, where a moderate government under elected president Jacobo Arbenz was attempting to implement agrarian reform, a program that provoked the ire of the United Fruit Company, an American firm that held enormous tracts of land throughout the country. Analysts responded with alarm: "The battle of the Western Hemisphere has begun," wrote journalist Daniel James. "We face, for the first time, the prospect of continuous struggle against Communism on a hemispheric scale." The CIA organized an exile force that seized the capital city, toppled Arbenz, and eventually installed a military regime. Partly as a result of U.S. action, Guatemala fell into a decades-long civil war that was characterized by brutal authoritarian repression.

Another democratic movement came under U.S. assault in 1965 in the Dominican Republic, where a group of "constitutionalists" were challenging right-wing "loyalists" in an effort to restore the freely elected Juan Bosch to the presidency. (Bosch had been ousted in late 1963.) Washington decided to side with the loyalists. As disorder mounted, the Lyndon Johnson administration took military action against "a Moscow-financed, Havana-directed plot to take over the Dominican Republic." Within days there were nearly 23,000 American troops on Dominican soil, with thousands more on alert. A military occupation then led to installation of a puppet president who was soon followed by Joaquín Balaguer, a longtime collaborator of the Trujillo dictatorship. Ever the politician, Johnson obtained diplomatic support from the Organization of American States (OAS), which obligingly confirmed claims of communist activity in the Dominican Republic and legitimized the U.S. operation. Not surprisingly, the OAS would suffer a major loss in credibility.

The most brazen U.S. attack on democracy took place in Chile in 1973. The presidential election of 1970 resulted in the victory of Salvador Allende, leader of the Unidad Popular (UP) movement with backing from both socialists and communists. Even more clearly than with Bosch in the Dominican Republic, the prospect of an Allende presidency presented Washington with its worst-case scenario—a free and fair election that gave power to the Left. Cold War ideology construed this as a logical impossibility: Communists could come to power only through conquest or subversion; by definition, free-thinking citizens would *always* cast their ballots against left-wing radicals. This would be the beginning of the end. As Henry Kissinger darkly predicted, there would never again be any free and fair elections in Chile.

The United States sprang into action. Once Allende took office, the Nixon administration developed a multifaceted campaign to destabilize the government of Chile. One component was an "invisible" economic and financial blockade, what Nixon described as an effort "to make the economy scream" and provoke a military coup. A second element entailed covert support for electoral opposition to the UP government. Third, explicit support and encouragement were provided for a military coup, which finally occurred on September 11, 1973. Brutal crackdowns followed. At least 3,000 Chileans were killed or disappeared in the aftermath of the *golpe*. Soldiers ransacked the headquarters of communist and socialist parties, imposed a strict curfew, dissolved labor unions, and took over once-proud universities. Under the leadership of General Augusto Pinochet, the military would dominate the country for years to come. Washington could barely contain its glee.

The United States appeared to shift course in the late 1970s, when President Jimmy Carter proclaimed that U.S. policy would henceforth work for the defense of human rights on a global level. The promotion of democratic values would take priority over the containment of godless communism. In this spirit, Carter called on the State Department to produce annual (and rigorous) reports on human rights conditions around the world. Within the hemisphere, the president and his youthful collaborators denounced right-wing brutality in Guatemala, Argentina, Uruguay, and Chile and lent passive encouragement to leftist revolutionaries who toppled the Somoza dynasty in Nicaragua in 1979.[2]

One of the Carter administration's most effective pro-democracy stands involved the Dominican Republic, where the United States led international condemnation of military attempts to subvert the 1978 election on behalf of strongman Joaquín Balaguer. Most decisive was Carter's direct presidential threat to reduce U.S. military and economic support. Balaguer eventually relented and his opponent took office, although not without significant concessions and constraints.[3]

In retrospect, however, it must be said that even Jimmy Carter was willing to overlook human rights violations in countries outside the hemisphere that were viewed as crucial to U.S. security, most notably Iran under the Shah and

[2] For a thoughtful assessment of the Carter policy see Kathryn Sikkink, *Mixed Signals: U.S. Human Rights Policy and Latin America* (Ithaca, NY: Cornell University Press, 2004), Ch. 6.

[3] Michael J. Kryzanek, "The 1978 Election in the Dominican Republic: Opposition Politics, Intervention and the Carter Administration," *Caribbean Studies* 19, nos. 1–2 (April–July 1979): 51–73.

BOX 4.1

THE COLD WAR AND U.S. PROMOTION OF DEMOCRACY

Throughout the Cold War the United States consistently maintained that it was promoting and defending democracy from threats of communist subversion. The historical record does not quite confirm this claim. A distinguished expert on inter-American affairs, Abraham F. Lowenthal, has codified as follows the conditions under which Washington would foster democratic change in the region.

> The United States has been more likely to push actively for democratic opening in a Latin American nation when:
>
> a. An incumbent authoritarian regime is pursuing specific policies perceived by U.S. officials as anti-American; or
> b. An incumbent authoritarian regime is pursuing specific policies perceived by Washington officials as contrary to U.S. interests; or
> c. A high priority effort to dislodge or pressure one regime qualifying under condition *a* or *b* requires consistent attempts to promote democratic opening in other nations that can easily be portrayed as comparable; or
> d. Democratic opening, or at least a "democratic election," is needed as a means of legitimizing a significant diminution of the U.S presence in and influence upon a country where Washington has heretofore been deeply engaged; or
> e. Local democratic forces by themselves are so close to obtaining power that a timely identification of U.S. policies with their fortunes is opportune; or
> f. Local political forces are particularly adept at mobilizing groups within the United States to pressure for the alignment of U.S. policies with their movement; or
> g. No important U.S. economic or security interests are engaged in a particular country, and the underlying U.S. cultural and ideological preference for democratic politics has recently been strongly reinforced in the minds of policy makers in a broader international context; *and,*
> h. The left in the specific country is either thought to be insignificant or else understood to be committed to democratic and nonviolent forms of political competition.

Source: Abraham F. Lowenthal, ed., Exporting Democracy: The United States and Latin America, Themes and Issues (Baltimore: Johns Hopkins University Press, 1991), 259–260.

the Philippines under the Marcos family. To this degree, the Carter policy ratified long-standing principles: to oppose dictators in Latin America only if they (1) became a serious embarrassment to Washington, (2) ran a risk of being overthrown by radical movements, or (3) both (see Box 4.1).

In pursuit of this same logic, the United States eventually elected to abandon Pinochet, as it had abandoned other dictators in times past. The central reason for this switch was fear of "another Nicaragua," a concern that polarization in Chile would lead to instability and pave the way for a leftist takeover. As the archconservative analyst Mark Falcoff asserted in congressional testimony, "If the way to democracy is closed and the democratic forces destroyed, there is no doubt that before the end of this century, Chile will be a Marxist-Leninist state, allied to the Soviet Union." And while Washington sought to take credit for "the new wave of democracy" sweeping Latin America, as President Reagan claimed in 1984, the retrograde Pinochet regime became something of an embarrassment. In 1988 the U.S.-funded National Endowment for Democracy openly threw its support to the "no" vote on continuation of Pinochet's rule. The opposition triumphed, the old man stepped aside, and Washington escaped from its entanglement.[4]

As a global factor initially external to the region, the Cold War had a decisively negative impact on prospects for democracy in Latin America. As the U.S.–Soviet conflict reached into the hemisphere, it tended to polarize political forces, galvanizing the revolutionary Left, strengthening the reactionary Right, and weakening the moderate Center. Among these currents, it was the Center that had the greatest incentive to foster and sustain electoral democracy. And if Fidel Castro's Cuba sometimes supported revolutionary movements, the United States frequently resorted to intervention—covertly or openly, either through the CIA or the armed forces. Few if any of these American intrusions were undertaken for the purpose of installing or protecting political democracy. This was not a positive development.

ECONOMIC ISSUES: DEBT AND STRUCTURAL REFORM

In addition to being treated as a geopolitical pawn in the Cold War, Latin America endured major economic setbacks. What came to be known as the "debt crisis" of the 1980s had its origins in the 1970s. Seeking to increase their profits and exert their political power, members of the Organization of Petroleum Exporting Countries (OPEC) halted production in 1973–1974 and again in 1979–1981. The result on both occasions was a shortage of petroleum throughout the West, long waiting lines at gas stations in Europe and the United States, sharp increases in prices, and windfall profits for oil-producing countries. Unable to absorb all these funds, OPEC governments deposited massive amounts of dollars into U.S. and European banks. Obliged to pay interest on these deposits, the banks then had to lend these sums out to borrowers who would pay profitable rates of interest.

---

[4] See Paul E. Sigmund, *The United States and Democracy in Chile* (Baltimore: Johns Hopkins University Press, 1993).

The moneylenders turned to Latin America. Because advanced industrial countries were facing recession, the most logical targets for lending were relatively unsophisticated borrowers who could be tempted by temporarily low interest rates. This meant especially the so-called upper tier of third world countries—nations such as Argentina, Brazil, Venezuela, and Mexico. Under these circumstances, Latin America's total foreign debt swelled from around $30 billion in 1970 to more than $240 billion in 1980.

Conditions soon took a turn for the worse. First, economic stagnation in the industrialized world reduced demand for imports of raw materials; for Latin American countries, this led to a substantial decline in export earnings, which were required to service their loans. Second, rising interest rates led to sharp increases in the cost of debt service: Actual interest rates paid by Latin America climbed from 10 percent in 1978 to 15 percent in 1980 and 18 percent in 1981. Third, the value as well as the volume of traditional exports, from coffee to nonferrous metals to petroleum, was plummeting. As the cost of debt service was rising, in other words, Latin America's capacity to pay was declining. By the early 1980s, lenders and borrowers both were overextended.

In August 1982, one of the prime borrowers, Mexico, announced that it could no longer meet obligations on its foreign debt. Frantic negotiations with U.S. authorities and the International Monetary Fund (IMF) led to a short-term rescue package and, later, a longer-term restructuring of Mexico's debt. As other countries announced their inability to meet debt obligations, the international community sought to fashion a workable response. During the early 1980s, they attempted to "muddle through" what they regarded as problems of "liquidity" (a cash squeeze, rather than a basic inability to pay). To implement this strategy, the IMF served as catalyst and monitor. Once a country proclaimed inability to pay, the IMF would negotiate an austerity package designed to reduce inflation and public sector deficits. Approval of an IMF package would then persuade otherwise reluctant creditor banks to provide fresh loans, which enabled debtor countries to keep up their payments. These tactics assured successful rescue of the banks. As the international economist Pedro-Pablo Kuczynski observed, no major bank failed because of its Latin American loans.[5]

Yet for Latin America, the 1980s were an unmitigated nightmare and would come to be remembered as the "lost decade." Economic and social progress was negligible at best, and negative at worst. Renegotiations and restructurings led to reliance on continuous lending (and borrowing), which forced the region's external debt up from $242 billion in 1980 to $431 billion by 1990. To meet contractual obligations, Latin American nations transferred a net amount of more than $200 billion to advanced industrial countries. Economic growth came to a virtual halt. For the decade as a

---

[5] Pedro-Pablo Kuczynski, *Latin American Debt* (Baltimore: Johns Hopkins University Press/Twentieth Century Fund, 1988), 86.

whole, per capita output declined by 8.3 percent, and for individual countries the performance was much worse: –23.5 percent for Argentina, –24.9
percent for Venezuela, and, largely because of the Contra war, –33.1 percent
for Nicaragua. Unemployment swelled and wages plummeted. In Mexico,
whose conduct set a model of good behavior for other debtor countries, real
wages declined by nearly 50 percent. Poverty spread, especially in cities, as
did inequality.

The economic devastation had political impacts as well. Throughout
Latin America, the debt crisis undermined the legitimacy and efficacy of
established governments, which tended to be authoritarian regimes. Partly
as a result of economic pressure, military dictatorships gave way to civilian
governments in Argentina (1983), Brazil (1985), Chile (1989), and elsewhere.
This is not to say that the economic crisis promoted democratization; on
the contrary, it posed a threat to whatever regime happened to be in place
at the time the crisis struck. Indeed, the economic problems inherited by
democratic leaders posed significant challenges to their own survival, as
shown by Raúl Alfonsín's early departure from the presidency of Argentina
in 1989.

By the late 1980s, the international financial community determined that
Latin America suffered not only from liquidity problems but from structural
deficiencies. To address these problems, analysts and policymakers forged
what came to be known as the Washington Consensus on economic policy.
The package entailed three sets of prescriptions for developing areas and, in
particular, for Latin America. First, it called for reduction and revision in the
economic role of the state. Governments should exercise fiscal discipline, as
commonly preached but rarely practiced by Washington itself. Second, the
consensus advocated active support for the private sector. Latin American
governments should sell off state-owned enterprises, remove restrictions
on foreign capital, and encourage economic competition in the marketplace.
Third, Latin American governments should drastically revise policies on
trade. They should look outward, not inward, for markets. Excessive protection of domestic industry created costly distortions that penalized exports,
punished domestic consumers, and encouraged inefficiencies. Trade policy and the encouragement of private investment went hand in hand: Both
would stimulate competition, efficiency, and active participation in the international economy.

Faced with international pressures and the threat of marginalization,
Latin America's leaders hastened to impose reformist policies. Out of necessity or choice, they lowered tariff and nontariff barriers to trade, opened
doors to foreign investment, and sold off public enterprises. This had yet
another political consequence: reduction in the power and role of the state.
As a result, Latin American policymakers would have fewer resources at
their disposal for addressing economic and social problems. In other words,
the democratic states of the 1990s would be weaker than were the authoritarian states of the 1970s and 1980s.

The Political Economy of Globalization

The end of the Cold War ushered in a period of optimism—and uncertainty. The fall of the Berlin Wall, the reunification of Germany, the liberation of Eastern Europe, and the eventual implosion of the Soviet Union transformed the international arena and established the United States as the sole remaining superpower. Many regarded these developments as a final triumph of capitalism over communism, of democracy over autocracy. Francis Fukuyama gave highbrow formulation to this impulse in his celebrated 1989 essay "The End of History," which claimed that the world was bearing witness "not to an 'end of ideology' or a convergence between capitalism and communism, but to an unabashed victory of economic and political liberalism."

Economic matters moved to the forefront of the inter-American agenda, and officials throughout the hemisphere came to agree that the Cold War had distorted U.S.–Latin American relations by introducing an ideological factor that was extraneous, superficial, and deleterious. Moreover, they concurred, the economic interests of Latin America and the United States were converging with one another. Steadfast pursuit of economic goals would lead to a happy and harmonious relationship.

The watchword of the 1990s was "globalization," a catchphrase used to describe the rapidly accelerating flow of goods, capital, information, and people around the world. The process was heralded as the defining characteristic of a totally new era, one that promised to bring prosperity and freedom to all peoples of the world. All good things would go together. As a market-driven phenomenon, globalization would have extensive ramifications in social and political arenas.

A primary claim was that economic globalization would foster political democracy. The liberalization of markets would lead to the liberalization of politics: The dismantling of state monopolies would break up old ruling cliques, the deregulation of business would encourage entrepreneurship, and economic competition would foster political competition. Moreover, broader access to information, enabled by the spread of information technologies, would bypass governmental controls and empower dissident groups and citizens. Such developments would establish foundations for democracy. In the form of a hypothesis, the proposition would be this: the greater the impact of globalization on any given society, the greater the degree (or probability) of democratization.

DRUGS, DICTATORS, AND U.S. POLICY

Despite its position of world primacy, the United States played a relatively modest—and intermittent—role in promoting Latin American democracy throughout the 1990s. There were several reasons for this reticence. One was the legacy of the Cold War: America's military interventions and diplomatic high-handedness had created much resentment throughout the region, so the United States was lacking credibility. Another was the fact that Latin American societies were promoting processes of democratic transition and consolidation for their own domestic reasons. Third was the fact that, as we shall later see, international organizations were willing and able to pick up the slack.

As the Cold War was coming to its end, the United States launched two more military interventions. The first occurred in Panama in 1989. A quasi-colony of the United States, this tiny country had been under the sway of authoritarian rule for nearly twenty years. Moreover, the then-current strongman, Manuel Noriega, had close links with Washington, allowing the Reagan administration to use Panama as a staging area for military operations in Nicaragua and assisting the CIA in efforts to destabilize the Sandinista regime. Ever the opportunist, Noriega opened Panama to money laundering for profits from illicit drug trafficking and established working relations with cocaine cartels in Colombia. He also made the mistake of rigging presidential elections and unleashing thuggish "Dignity Battalions" that administered a public bloody beating to an opposition candidate.

It was the drugs that caused the trouble. By this time the United States had been engaged in a decade-long "war on drugs" with precious little to show for its efforts. In September 1989 President George H. W. Bush denounced illegal drugs as the country's "gravest threat." In mid-December Panama's pro-Noriega government proclaimed that a "state of war" existed with the United States and installed the military leader for the first time as chief of state. The next day members of the Panama Defense Force opened fire on a group of U.S. military officers. Professing "enormous outrage," Bush authorized a military strike. Employing overwhelming firepower, U.S. forces secured control of the country within five days (see Box 4.2). Noriega surrendered shortly after that. Intoned Republican Senate leader Bob Dole: "Noriega's bad news is good news for our war on drugs. It proves America won't cave in to anyone, no matter how powerful or corrupt."

The second episode took place in Haiti, the poorest country in the hemisphere. After the fall of the murderous Duvalier dynasty in 1986, Haiti finally held a free and fair election in 1990. The undisputed winner was Jean-Bertrand Aristide, a thirty-seven-year-old Catholic priest and devotee of liberation theology. Inaugurated in February 1991, Aristide proceeded to antagonize opponents without consolidating power. Less than nine months into his term, he was forced into exile by a military coup. Haiti once again fell under the heel of the armed forces, now led by General Raoul Cédras.

As repression mounted, thousands of Haitians set out for the United States on homemade rafts. Efforts to find a diplomatic solution to the brewing crisis stretched over months and years. In September 1994 a frustrated President Bill Clinton denounced the Cédras government as "the most

BOX 4.2

OVERWHELMING FORCE—WAS IT REALLY NECESSARY?

Shortly after midnight on December 20, 1989, U.S. armed forces launched Operation Just Cause against the tiny republic of Panama. Its central goal was to capture General Manuel Antonio Noriega and remove him from power. Instead of using a SWAT team or a squad of commandos, the Bush administration chose to apply the doctrine of "overwhelming force," which in this case included thousands of troops, scores of jet planes, teams of Navy SEALs, and two Stealth fighter-bombers, each armed with a 2,000-pound bomb. The assault on Noriega's headquarters (the Comandancia) inflicted widespread devastation on the nearby El Chorrillo section of Panama City, as described in this report:

> Exploding shells and tracer bullets set fires that were clearly visible from the other side of the city within just a few minutes. U.S. loudspeakers told residents to stay in their houses, but U.S. gunships fired directly into one building after another as crews tried to kill the snipers scattered throughout the neighborhood. Wooden structures blazed and collapsed, and when people ran into the streets many fell under the torrent of firepower from the sky. The assault continued until approximately 6:00 a.m., when U.S. troops moved up to the pockmarked, scorched, but still standing Comandancia. It was 10:00 a.m. before they entered the structure and counted the bodies, many of which were clad only in underwear.
>
> In densely packed El Chorrillo, fires razed nearly 2,000 dwellings, making some 15,000 residents homeless. Many of them crowded into an open field in front of Balboa High School. Hospitals, such as Santo Tomás, filled up. The counting of the civilian dead began, and it continued for a long time.

Source: *Kevin Buckley, Panama: The Whole Story* (New York: Simon & Schuster, 1991), 240.

---

violent regime in our hemisphere" and cited several reasons for concern: "to stop the brutal atrocities that threaten tens of thousands of Haitians, to secure our borders, to preserve stability and promote democracy in our hemisphere, and to uphold the reliability of the commitments we make and the commitments others make to us." He went on to define the imminent threat: "As long as Cédras rules, Haitians will continue to seek sanctuary in our nation....Three hundred thousand more Haitians, 5 percent of their entire population, are in hiding in their own country. If we don't act, they could be the next wave of refugees at our door. We will continue to face the threat of a mass exodus of refugees and its constant threat to stability in our region and control of our borders."

Cédras countered Clinton's warning with defiance, and Clinton prepared a military strike. At the very last minute Cédras and his associates accepted a deal exchanging their own amnesty for Aristide's return to power. American troops still arrived, but as a peacekeeping force rather than as an invasion. In less than a week there were more than 15,000 American troops on the ground, and there would eventually be more than 20,000 in place. What began as a limited military occupation eventually developed into a temporary takeover of the governmental apparatus. In early 1995, a relieved President Clinton celebrated the replacement of U.S. troops by a UN peacekeeping force of 6,000 troops, with 2,400 American soldiers and a U.S. commander in charge. Elections followed in orderly fashion. Aristide resisted the temptation to succeed himself, and René Preval, one of his former associates and ex-prime minister, took office in February 1996.

The American operations in Panama and Haiti cast much light on the dynamics of the post–Cold War era. They were both undertaken in the name of democratic restoration, which imbued them with an aura of Wilsonian high-mindedness. Yet the restitution of democracy itself was insufficient cause for military action; were that the case, American troops would have been scattered all over the globe. In each of these two cases, there were pressing political considerations: the need for visible progress in the drug wars and the clamor for an end to illegal immigration. Democracy alone was not enough; democracy plus a domestic political problem could provide a recipe for intervention.

These efforts to impose democracy were modestly successful. The nature and extent of democratic practice would be restricted, but it was nonetheless true that elections resulted in peaceful transfers of power (in the short run for Haiti, in the long run for Panama). One reason for this happy outcome was that Panama and Haiti were small countries with small military services that could not begin to thwart the power of the United States. A second reason was that the United States retained a strong political and institutional presence in both instances, with military units overseeing the Panama Canal for the following decade and with U.S. troops spearheading multinational and subsequent UN operations in Haiti. Yet these same factors revealed the uniqueness of these cases. The installations of democracy in Panama and Haiti were not suitable precedents for U.S. action elsewhere.

For the remainder of the 1990s, the United States was content to rely on the claim that economic liberalization would foster political liberalization. Accepting a principal tenet of proglobalization ideology, the Clinton administration promoted free trade with Latin America in the name of democratization. In 1993 the Democratic president achieved congressional ratification for the North American Free Trade Agreement (NAFTA), an economic compact binding the United States with Canada and Mexico in part on the ground that it would help achieve political change in Mexico. A year later, at the first Summit of the Americas, Clinton and other hemispheric heads of state agreed to begin work on the creation of a Free Trade Area of the Americas (FTAA) by 2005. Confidently predicting that the FTAA would stretch "from Alaska to Argentina," Clinton boasted that the accord marked "a watershed in the history of the hemisphere." With the glaring exception of Cuba, he exulted, Latin America had "freed itself from dictatorship and debt, and embraced democracy and development." Negotiations over FTAA subsequently encountered major delays, and the whole project engendered major controversy in Latin America: Would it be a good thing or not?

By the end of the century, Clinton's optimism seemed overstated. Mexico finally held a free and fair presidential election in 2000—but in response to domestic developments, not as a consequence of NAFTA. And despite its pursuit of neoliberal economic reform, South America would plunge into troubled waters. Peru spent most of the 1990s under the iron grip of Alberto Fujimori. Venezuela succumbed to the blandishments of the semiauthoritarian Hugo Chávez. Ecuador endured a military coup. Argentina's economic and political system utterly collapsed in 2001–2002. Only Chile and Brazil seemed to weather the storms. Free markets were not living up to their political expectations.

INTERNATIONAL ORGANIZATIONS

Beyond unilateral actions by the United States and other significant powers, international organizations have also affected processes of democratization in Latin America. By representing the collective will of the international community, multilateral institutions possess exceptional moral and political authority. They can claim to be fair and impartial, yet they confront an unavoidable dilemma: the contradiction between democracy promotion and national sovereignty. Because their memberships consist of nation-states large and small, multilateral institutions must tread this line with caution.

This dilemma consistently plagued the OAS, an assembly of hemispheric countries founded in 1948. The OAS charter solemnly declared that "representative democracy is an indispensable condition for the stability, peace and development of the region" and proclaimed the intention "to promote and consolidate representative democracy, *with due respect to the principle of non-intervention*" (italics added). With equal solemnity, other chapters enshrined the principle of national sovereignty: according to Article 18, for instance, "No State or group of States has the right to intervene, directly or indirectly, for any reason whatever, in the internal affairs of any other State." In short, the OAS came down on both sides of the issue. This is not uncommon in the diplomatic world.[6]

From the beginning, many Latin Americans suspected that the OAS would be controlled by the United States. Their fears were ultimately justi-

---

[6] See Domingo E. Acevedo and Claudio Grossman, "The Organization of American States and the Protection of Democracy," in Tom Farer, ed., *Beyond Sovereignty: Collectively Defending Democracy in the Americas* (Baltimore: Johns Hopkins University Press, 1996), 132–149.

fied by the organization's one-sided endorsement of the U.S. invasion of the Dominican Republic in 1965. As a result, the organization became quiescent throughout the remainder of the Cold War. It took few decisions, offended hardly anyone, and exerted only modest efforts. It lost its institutional legitimacy. Largely for this reason, nations of Central America—under the leadership of President Oscar Arias of Costa Rica—turned years later to the United Nations, not the OAS, for assistance in monitoring peace agreements in that troubled region. The other main reason was that members of the European Community, notably Spain, had become deeply involved in diplomatic efforts to end the conflicts that were ravaging the isthmus, and European states would have been excluded by the OAS.[7]

In 1989 Arias and his colleagues asked the UN to verify the electoral process in Nicaragua and the prohibition on cross-border support for irregular or dissident movements. (This second provision was aimed directly at Nicaragua, accused of aiding guerrilla groups in El Salvador, and at the United States, which was backing counterrevolutionary movements attempting to depose the Sandinistas.) The UN secretary general, Javier Pérez de Cuéllar of Peru, boldly accepted these roles. The diplomatic field ahead was literally full of land mines.[8]

Oversight of the Nicaraguan elections turned out to be the easy part. To the surprise of most observers (and pollsters), a conservative opposition candidate defeated the Sandinista leader, Daniel Ortega, who gracefully accepted the loss after late-night urging from former U.S. president Jimmy Carter. The UN then helped promote a process of national reconciliation. El Salvador proved to be another matter. By the early 1990s, the internationalized civil war in that country had claimed 75,000 lives. The opposing sides—revolutionary guerrillas versus a reactionary military—had fought to a standstill. In July 1990, the UN mediator persuaded both parties to sign a human rights accord, which provided the justification for dispatching international observers throughout the country. With the Cold War winding down, both Washington and Moscow signaled their readiness to accept a full-blown peace accord. This was finally accomplished in late 1991–early 1992.[9]

The UN's involvement in Central America extended to Guatemala, where a civil war had persisted since the 1960s. As in El Salvador, the military conflict had ground to a stalemate, which prompted both the government and the guerrillas to engage in negotiations. The two sides invited the UN

---

[7] See Robin Rosenberg, *Spain and Central America: Democracy and Foreign Policy* (New York: Greenwood Press, 1992).
[8] See David P. Forsythe, "The United Nations, Democracy, and the Americas," in Tom Farer, ed., *Beyond Sovereignty: Collectively Defending Democracy in the Americas* (Baltimore: Johns Hopkins University Press, 1996), 107–131.
[9] See Terry Lynn Karl, "El Salvador's Negotiated Solution," *Foreign Affairs* 71 (1992): 147–164.

to moderate in late 1993. Negotiations stretched out for years, and peace accords were finally signed in December 1996.[10]

The OAS then made a comeback. Two factors helped rescue the OAS from oblivion. One was the ending of the Cold War. The other was the installation of electoral democracy throughout the region, especially in major countries—Argentina, Brazil, and Chile. Democratic leaders in Latin America suddenly regarded the OAS as an institution with significant potential, one that might help *defend* established democracy, if not actually promote the process of democratization.

As a result, the OAS in 1990 created the Unit for the Promotion of Democracy, whose principal task was monitoring elections. In 1991 the OAS adopted Resolution 1080, which was designed to bring states back onto the path of constitutional democracy "in the event of any occurrences giving rise to the sudden or irregular interruption of the domestic, political institutional process or the legitimate exercise of power by the democratically elected government in any of the Organization's member states." A parallel document, the Santiago Commitment to Democracy and the Renewal of the Inter-American System, declared "its uncompromising commitment to the defense and promotion of representative democracy and of human rights in the region"—and then added, almost as an afterthought, "within the parameters of respect for the principles of self-determination and non-intervention." A year later the substance of Resolution 1080 was inserted into the constitution of the OAS, which now threatened that any member country "whose democratically constituted government has been overthrown by force" could be suspended from the organization. And one year after that, the OAS Declaration of Managua went one step further by emphasizing the need not only to restore legitimate democracies but also "to prevent and anticipate the very causes of the problems that work against democratic rule."

These high-minded declarations at first found only timid application. The OAS responded to the Haitian crisis by enacting Resolution 1080 and helping to negotiate Aristide's return to power in 1994, although that was accomplished mainly by the use of U.S. military force. After Alberto Fujimori's 1992 *autogolpe* in Peru, the OAS voiced its disapproval, enacted Resolution 1080 again, urged the immediate restoration of democratic institutions, and dispatched high-level missions, to little apparent effect. And in 1993, the OAS condemned another "self-coup," this time in Guatemala, and made a modest contribution to the maintenance of fragile democracy in that long-beleaguered country.

Under a new and dynamic leader, former president César Gaviria of Colombia, the OAS began gaining credibility and strength. In 1996 the

---

[10] Susanne Jonas, "Between Two Worlds: The United Nations in Guatemala," in Tommie Sue Montgomery, ed., *Peacekeeping and Democratization in the Western Hemisphere* (Miami, FL: North-South Center Press, 2000), 91–106.

democratically elected president of Paraguay, Juan Carlos Wasmosy, requested the resignation of General Lino César Oviedo from the post of army commander; Oviedo's refusal precipitated a constitutional crisis. Ambassadors from the United States, Brazil, and Argentina quickly condemned the challenge to democratic authority. Oviedo was contacted by foreign colleagues, including his counterpart in Brazil, who urged him to desist; Wasmosy received supportive calls from neighboring countries, Europe, and U.S. president Bill Clinton; Gaviria also hurried to the scene. An emergency meeting of the OAS proclaimed "full and resolute" support for Wasmosy and condemned "the threat to constitutional order posed by the army's commander." During the course of subsequent negotiations, Oviedo resigned as commander in erroneous anticipation of another high-level appointment. Wasmosy quickly accepted the resignation, a disgruntled Oviedo went into retirement, and the democratic order was restored. According to the U.S. scholar-diplomat Arturo Valenzuela, the outcome was "a triumph for the international community."[11]

It was also an achievement for MERCOSUR, the four-country compact for regional economic integration embracing Argentina, Brazil, Paraguay, and Uruguay. Established as the "Common Market of the South," MERCOSUR had from its inception a political agenda: the preservation of peace and the consolidation of democracy among its members. Swift action by MERCOSUR partners, especially Argentina and Brazil, helped defuse the crisis in Paraguay. In recognition of this fact and in anticipation of the possibility of future needs, MERCOSUR adopted a full-blown "democracy clause" within months of the Paraguayan affair, proclaiming that "any alteration of the democratic order" would present an "insuperable obstacle" to participation in the integration process—in other words, military coups would bring suspension or expulsion from the group. The agreement also called for consultation in the case of any "threat" to continuation of the democratic order in any member country.

In 2000 the OAS took even more decisive action in a complex situation in Peru. Ever since his successful "self-coup" in the early 1990s, Alberto Fujimori had been assiduously manipulating the political system to assume a third presidential term. Elections took place in April and May 2000, and, according to an OAS observation team, they reeked of intimidation and fraud. (Things were so bad that the opposition challenger, Alejandro Toledo, decided to boycott the runoff round.) Shortly thereafter delegates to an OAS meeting in Canada refrained from invoking Resolution 1080 but, as a compromise, agreed to dispatch a high-level mission to Lima for the euphemistically defined purpose of "exploring, with the Government of Peru and other sectors of the political community, options and recommendations aimed at further strengthening democracy in that country." Within weeks the OAS

---

[11] Arturo Valenzuela, "Paraguay: The Coup That Didn't Happen," *Journal of Democracy* 8, no. 1 (1997): 43–55.

mission presented the Fujimori government with broad recommendations for political reform and, more important, announced the creation of *mesas de diálogo*—forums for "dialogue" among key political actors, including dissidents and representatives of civil society as well as government officials. (The *mesas* would continue from August 2000 through January 2001.) Despite OAS disapproval, Fujimori was inaugurated in late July. At this point he seemed to have weathered the storm.

Then a bombshell struck: In mid-September 2000 a tape was released to the public showing Vladimiro Montesinos, Fujimori's top adviser and intelligence official, bribing an opposition congressman to support the president's reelection. The public outcry was deafening. Montesinos and Fujimori were hopelessly exposed. Late in November, while on a visit to East Asia, Fujimori suddenly resigned from the presidency and sought asylum in Japan. No longer did the OAS have to confront a recalcitrant executive. Instead, it could assist the successor government with the tasks of consolidating authority and holding new elections, eventually won by Toledo. Clearly, the restoration of democracy in Peru was a cardinal achievement for the OAS.[12]

Yet the Peruvian affair also underlined the limitations of the OAS. On reflection, it appears that the OAS could have effectively defended democracy under only two specific conditions. One held that the president of the country in question must not be resistant to the OAS. Plainly, Paraguay's Wasmosy was in need of help; that was not the case for Fujimori, who could probably have outlasted pressure from the OAS without the revelation of the Montesinos tapes. The second condition was that the United States must not be a party to the conflict. Washington hardly knew or cared about Paraguay and managed to steer clear of much involvement in Peru; indeed, Canada played a much more active role in resolving the Fujimori furor than did the United States. For the OAS to perform decisive roles, *both* conditions had to be present.

Even so, the Peruvian episode led to subsequent developments. In December 2000 the country's new foreign minister, Javier Pérez de Cuéllar, suggested the adoption by nations of the hemisphere of an "inter-American democracy charter." Soon thereafter the idea was officially presented to the OAS. In April 2001 it gained additional momentum at a Summit of the Americas meeting in Quebec City, Canada, which declared that any "interruption of the democratic order" could lead to exclusion from "the Summit of the Americas process"—meaning, specifically, exclusion from the FTAA. OAS task forces then developed drafts for a charter, stipulating that member states would risk banishment from the OAS in the event of "an unconstitutional interruption of the democratic order or an unconstitutional alteration of the constitutional regime that seriously impairs the democratic order in a member state."

---

[12] Andrew F. Cooper and Thomas Legler, "The OAS in Peru: A Model for the Future?" *Journal of Democracy* 12, no. 4 (October 2001): 123–136.

BOX 4.3

POSTSCRIPT: U.S. SUPPORT FOR A COUP?

Venezuela's President Hugo Chávez was ousted by a coup in April 2002—and restored to office within forty-eight hours. It has ever since been rumored that the U.S. government under George W. Bush aided, abetted, and encouraged the illegal overthrow of a democratically elected president.

The crisis culminated more than a week of protests and violence within Venezuela. Opposition leaders demanded Chávez's resignation. On April 11 the president responded by shutting down five private television stations, denouncing demonstrators as "subversives" and "traitors," and declaring that he had no intention of dealing with them. As he spoke, violence escalated outside the presidential palace. Gunmen opened fire on the crowds, killing at least fourteen people. The next day, April 12, military leaders arrested Chávez and took him into captivity, accusing him of ordering thugs to open fire on unarmed demonstrators.

A prominent businessman, Pedro Carmona Estanga, became interim president and moved at once to undo Chávez's policies. He abrogated the 1999 constitution, dissolved the legislature and supreme court, repealed key economic laws, announced a probe into Chávez's role in the April 11 killings, and announced that it would be nearly a year before new presidential elections. Such sweeping decrees immediately splintered the coalition that had supported the coup in the first place. By this time it was reported that Chávez had not resigned from office, as originally claimed. Buoyed by the news, *chavista* leaders mobilized hundreds of thousands of loyalists, who swarmed to the presidential palace to demand his return.

On the day of the coup, leaders of the nineteen-nation Rio Group of Latin American countries issued a statement strongly condemning "the interruption of constitutional order" in Venezuela. Argentina and Paraguay called the Carmona government illegitimate. Vicente Fox of Mexico said his administration would not recognize the new government unless elections were held.

U.S. officials, however, did not condemn the coup. Instead they suggested that Chávez had brought the developments upon himself. "We know the action encouraged by the Chávez government provoked this crisis," said presidential spokesman Ari Fleischer on April 12. Further, Fleisher refused to label the ouster a coup, saying that the Chavez administration had "suppressed what was a peaceful demonstration of the people," which led to "a combustible situation in which Chávez resigned." "What happened in Venezuela was a change in government," Fleisher affirmed. The Bush administration immediately embraced the Carmona regime.

On April 13 the OAS invoked its own "democratic charter" to endorse a resolution rebuking "the alteration of the constitutional order" in Venezuela. The United States voted for the resolution only after lobbying behind the scenes for a milder statement.

A few days later, U.S. officials acknowledged contact with anti-Chávez opposition leaders, but insisted that they had not supported the coup. They further admitted that officials from the White House and the Departments of Defense and State had hosted a range of Venezuelan opposition figures during the months that led up to the overthrow. It later emerged that the National Endowment for Democracy, a nonprofit organization supported by the U.S. government, had funneled some $877,000 to anti-Chávez groups.

Given the Bush administration's disdain for Chávez and his policies, many observers concluded that Washington had tacitly supported the coup. Editorialized the *Los Angeles Times*: "The Bush administration insisted that it did not give a green light to the attempted ouster. If so, the signals from Washington do not seem to have been treated seriously. Whatever its intentions, the White House failed to stay on the side of democracy." Added Mara Liasson on Fox News: "Either we stand for democratically elected governments or we don't. What happens the next time the military overthrows someone in Latin America? We have less credibility." Wrote Tim Wiener of the *New York Times*: "When is a coup not a coup? When the United States says so, it seems—especially if the fallen leader is no friend to American interests."

Months later the text was submitted to a special assembly of the OAS in Lima, Peru. After receiving word of a catastrophe in his home country, U.S. Secretary of State Colin Powell eloquently urged approval of the document and then hurried back to Washington. The date was September 11, 2001.

In retrospect, the post–Cold War context consisted of two phases. Extending from 1990–1991 to 2001, the first period was generally supportive of democracy. Centrist moderates reclaimed control of national agendas. The United States spoke earnestly about the importance of democracy; if its actions were not as instrumental as spokespersons claimed, at least they did not inhibit or impede democratic transitions. Such organizations as the UN and the OAS managed to make constructive contributions to democratic development. The second phase started on September 11, 2001 and has lasted to the present. As shown in the conclusion to this book, it has been much less supportive of democracy and more tolerant of autocracy. Security has become more important than rights, and alignment with (or against) the United States more significant than the practice of democracy (see Box 4.3). One of the central questions of the twenty-first century was whether and when that might change.

PART II

THE ELECTORAL ARENA

The people made the Constitution, and the people can unmake it. It is the creature of their own will, and lives only by their will.
—JOHN MARSHALL, CHIEF JUSTICE OF THE U.S. SUPREME COURT

Democracy is the recurrent suspicion that more than half of the people are right more than half the time.
—ELWYN BROOKS WHITE

A man that'd expect to thrain lobsters to fly in a year is called a loonytic; but a man that thinks men can be tu-rrned into angels be an iliction is called a rayformer an' remains at large.
—FINLEY PETER DONNE [MR. DOOLEY]

CHAPTER 5

PRESIDENTS OR PARLIAMENTS?

Democratization posed a stark challenge for late twentieth-century Latin America: How to assure the survival of democracy? How to reduce the likelihood of institutional collapse and military intervention? Such issues were all the more salient in the wake of bureaucratic-authoritarian regimes in South America, where "dirty wars" against imagined subversion led to the death or disappearance of tens of thousands of citizens, and in the aftermath of vicious civil wars in Central America, which claimed approximately 300,000 lives. These brutal experiences seared the conscience of political society and provoked extended bouts of vigorous denial and anguished soul searching. Citizens, leaders, and activists loftily vowed that such cycles of murder had come to an end, but the specter of retrogression nonetheless loomed large. How to prevent a reversal?

This question prompted an intense round of intellectual and political debates in Latin America. This chapter explores these discussions, particularly as they focused on the relative merits of presidentialist and parliamentary forms of government, and examines real-world efforts to achieve systemic reform in three major nations: Brazil, Argentina, and Chile. In the end, none of these countries—or any other in Latin America—replaced presidential democracy with a parliamentary system. The arguments nonetheless reveal extremely high levels of discussion, meaningful attention to the practical significance of academic analysis, and serious concern about the role of political institutions. Throughout Latin America, leaders and thinkers were seeking ways to assure the survival of still-fragile democracies.

THE TERMS OF DEBATE

The process of introspection first focused on the past, especially on the democratic breakdowns of the 1960s and 1970s. What had gone so very wrong? What lessons could be extracted from reexamination of this era? Predictably, and not without reason, there were denunciations of Latin America's armed forces and their indiscriminate use of violence in the name of bizarre and extremist ideologies. Military institutions had become increasingly distanced from mainstream society and intolerant of disputation. Politically insulated and intellectually isolated, they came to see their nations as key battlefronts in global struggles between virtue and vice, discipline and sin, and capitalism and communism. Doctrines of "national security" informed the conviction that principal threats came from internal "subversion" rather than external assault. Often intensified by racist or anti-Semitic sentiments, these worldviews served as both motive and pretext for waging open warfare against domestic civilian populations. Somehow, the new democracies would have to find ways to bring the armed forces under control.

Just as predictably, and also with reason, there were condemnations of the United States. Time and again, Washington had chosen to abandon democratic leadership in support of hard-line anticommunist dictatorships. Examples were manifold: Guatemala (1954), Brazil (1964), the Dominican Republic (1965), Chile (1973). In this interpretation, Latin American democracies succumbed to unyielding pressure from the "Colossus of the North," whose obsessive crusade against communism had come to dominate and distort the inter-American agenda.

More dispassionate analyses concentrated on internal social conflicts, especially the intensification of class conflicts. Socioeconomic processes—industrialization, urbanization, education, and communications—had led to the expansion and organization of working classes in the cities and, in many cases, to the mobilization of peasant groups in the countryside. These developments brought new and escalating demands on the political system: recognition of labor rights, promulgation of agrarian reform, and a host of measures to improve the conditions of the poor (often at the expense of the rich). Economic growth made it (more or less) possible to accommodate such demands, even if with only token responses; economic stagnation exacerbated tensions. Politics degenerated into a zero-sum game, and there followed the inevitable antidemocratic reaction of privileged elites against the institutions that permitted mass challenges to the existing socioeconomic order. Often at the behest of upper classes, the military intervened to restore the status quo ante. Democracy became a victim of class struggle.

But the most compelling arguments dealt not with exogenous factors—the military, the United States, and societal conflict—but with endogenous political factors. Was there something wrong with Latin American democracy itself? Democracies in other parts of the world had succeeded in taming powerful militaries, coexisting with dominant powers, and surviving economic crises and long-term depressions. Did the problem lie within?

One concern focused on failures of democratic leadership and, in particular, on the self-destructive choices that often transformed crises of *governments* into crises of *regimes*. As Juan J. Linz contended, political actors "have certain choices that can increase or decrease the probability of the persistence and stability of the regime." In point of fact, democratic leaders often manufacture conditions of crisis because they "are likely to be tempted to place all unsolved problems of the society on their agenda simultaneously, presumably to maximize support, without realizing that in doing so they also maximize the number of persons likely to be affected negatively by their reforms." This tendency was due partly to hubris and ambition and partly to a misplaced conviction that all existing problems resulted from neglect by the previous regime rather than from the intractability of social reality. Democratic rulers thus became confronted with "unsolvable problems" just as their popular support diminished—and as aggrieved social sectors moved into the ranks of a "disloyal opposition." In many instances, it was the action or inaction of democratic leaders that led to institutional breakdown and ultimately to overthrow.[1]

It was not long, however, before attention turned from leadership to systems—in particular, to the "presidentialist" form that was characteristic of Latin American democracies. Perhaps the problem lay not in specific policy choices but in the broad institutional features of the regime. Instead of dissecting political behavior per se, the idea would be to analyze the institutional incentives that encouraged such behavior. Change the incentives, the argument went, and you could change the behavior. Analysts and politicians alike thus focused on matters of what has come to be known as "institutional design" (see Box 5.1). Within this context, there emerged a sweeping proposal for Latin America: replace the presidential system with a European-style parliamentary regime. This prompted an arduous, intense, and still-continuing debate in academic and political circles.

ENVISIONING ALTERNATIVES

What was the fuss all about?

It was about the relative merits of two distinct forms of political democracy. As its label suggests, a presidential regime invests independent authority in a chief executive, or head of state. A defining feature is that the head of government, usually called a president, is popularly elected directly by the citizens. Moreover, the president has a fixed, constitutionally prescribed term in office and in normal circumstances cannot be forced to resign by the legislature (except through impeachment). Presidents wield executive power alone. They have complete authority to select and dismiss cabinet members, who serve them as advisers and subordinates, not as equals.

In parliamentary governments, by contrast, ultimate authority resides in the legislature. Voters elect members of the parliament (MPs), and the MPs select a head of government, usually known as prime minister, premier, or chancellor, from within their own ranks. There is no popular vote for the

---

[1] Linz, "Crisis, Breakdown, and Reequilibration," in Juan J. Linz and Alfred Stepan, eds., *The Breakdown of Democratic Regimes* (Baltimore: Johns Hopkins University Press, 1978), 3–124, with quotes on 4 and 41.

BOX 5.1

THE NEW INSTITUTIONALISM

The emergence of the "new institutionalism" in the 1980s showed that modes of analysis in political science had come full circle—almost.

Early in the twentieth century American political science focused heavily on formal institutions, especially on constitutions, together with the history of political thought. In response the midcentury witnessed a "behavioral revolution," a trend that sought to examine what political actors actually did (rather than what they said or were supposed to do). Behavioralism also promoted the use of quantitative methods and rigorous testing of hypotheses.

Yet another movement took place in the 1960s and 1970s (and continues today)—the rational choice revolution. As summarized by Kenneth Shepsle, "The behavioral revolution in political science was a triumph of sociology and psychology. The rational choice revolution...is a triumph of economics." (And as another scholar once quipped, "Economics is all about how people make choices; sociology is all about how they don't have any choices to make.") As its name suggests, rational choice analyzes the choices made by political actors and tends to assume that such actors take rational actions to maximize the probabilities of reelection, career advancement, or some other positive benefit. Again according to Shepsle, "A rational agent is one who comes to a social situation with preferences over possible social states, beliefs about the world around him, and a capability to employ these data intelligently....But rational man [or woman]...is an atom unconnected to the social structure in which he or she is embedded."

The new institutionalism arose in reaction to both the behavioral and rational choice paradigms. Its central idea was to bring the study of institutions back into mainstream political science and to invest it with new theoretical rigor. This approach flourished in studies of the U.S. Congress, where it became self-evident that rules, procedures, and institutional arrangements were important determinants of collective decision making. In established democracies, the new institutionalism helped explain the outcomes of different electoral rules. And as democratization took place through the 1980s and 1990s, it provided the intellectual foundation for practical debates over the relative merits of presidentialism and parliamentarism (and smaller scale issues as well).

The new institutionalism incorporates rather than rejects rational choice. It posits that political actors make (rational) choices within the context of institutional inducements and constraints. In other words, institutions present actors with sets of incentives; actors make rational choices in response to those incentives.

Clearly, the new institutionalism has yielded important intellectual advances, but it has not yet solved a central puzzle: Where do institutions come from? In addition, some skeptics note that institutions—or institutional reforms—can have unpredictable (or at least unpredicted) consequences in new democracies. Other critics maintain that the paradigm's practitioners sometimes pay insufficient attention to informal institutions, and that advocates simply claim too much for the approach. As illustrated by Chapters 5 to 7 of this book, however, the "new institutionalism" has made significant (and growing) inroads into the study of Latin American politics.

Key sources: James G. March and Johan P. Olsen, "The New Institutionalism: Organizational Factors in Political Life," *American Political Science Review* 78, no. 3 (September 1984): 734–749; Kenneth A. Shepsle, "Studying Institutions: Some Lessons from the Rational Choice Approach," *Journal of Theoretical Politics* 1, no. 2 (1989): 131–417; and Douglass C. North, *Institutions, Institutional Change and Economic Performance* (Cambridge: Cambridge University Press, 1990).

head of state. Cabinet members are also selected with the approval of the legislature, so parliamentary systems tend to have collective, or collegial, executives; a strong prime minister can be first among equals, but there is usually a high degree of collegiality in decision making. The tenure of the prime minister and the cabinet are dependent on the continuing confidence of the parliament; they can be removed from office by a legislative vote of no confidence or censure.

Chief executives in presidential systems have dual functions: they are heads of government *and* they are heads of state. Prime ministers are merely heads of government. In some parliamentary systems, such as in England and Spain, the head of state remains a monarch; in others, as in Germany, the head of state is determined by popular election. In either case, the head of state does not determine national policy but instead provides a basis and symbol for continuity. If and when a parliamentary government falls, the state remains intact.

In theory, presidential regimes entail a *separation* of powers between the legislative and executive branches, which are both determined by popular election. Again in contrast, parliamentary regimes represent a *fusion* of powers, as the executive branch emerges from and is determined by the legislature. (In all democracies, presidential and parliamentary alike, the judicial branch is substantially independent.)

There are paradoxes here. In principle, the separation of powers is designed to impose limitations on presidential power. At the same time, the concentration of authority in a one-person executive would appear to strengthen presidential power. And although the fusion of powers in parliamentary systems is designed to assure dependence of the executive on the legislature, it turns out that parliamentary majorities usually go to great lengths to support their cabinet ministers. (The nineteenth-century British writer Walter Bagehot termed this the "efficient secret.")

As Latin America turned from authoritarianism toward democracy, especially throughout the 1980s, this question then arose: Was presidentialism responsible for the historic problems of governance and democratic stability throughout the region? With only two significant exceptions—Brazil, which retained a monarchy through most of the nineteenth century, and Uruguay, which experimented with a "collegial executive" in more recent times—most countries of Latin America had had presidential systems ever since the acquisition of national independence. Could this have been the source of the problem?

Proparliamentary Arguments

A distinguished cadre of analysts, among them Juan Linz, mounted a penetrating critique of presidentialism in practice.[2] One concern focused on the problem of "temporal rigidity." As Linz wrote in a seminal essay, the fixed length of the presidential term "breaks the political process into discontinuous, rigidly demarcated periods, leaving no room for the continuous adjustment that events may demand." Under presidential systems, there was no regular constitutional means of removing chief executives who had lost their bases of popular support, not even in moments of crisis. Parliamentarism could meet such problems through its more fluid mechanisms for replacing governments, especially through votes of no confidence.

A second claim was that presidentialism led to "winner-take-all" politics. Only one candidate can win the presidency; everyone else loses. Further, the concentration of power in the presidential executive creates little incentive for the formation of coalition cabinets or other power-sharing arrangements that are common in parliamentary regimes. As a result, presidentialist politics tends to become a zero-sum game. This leads to fragmentation and polarization. In time, it can encourage perpetual losers—"outs" who might have formed the core of a loyal opposition—to doubt the legitimacy and fairness of the democratic system. Once this happens, they are likely to move into the ranks of a "disloyal opposition." This is a source of great danger.

A third issue concerned the prevalence of executive-legislative deadlock, the inevitable result of the coexistence of independent organs that might be in disagreement. It stems from what has been termed the "dual democratic legitimacy" of the presidency and the legislature: Both can claim to represent the will of the people, and there is no legal prescription for resolving stalemates. (Parliamentary systems can meet these problems through votes of no confidence.) Political scientist Scott Mainwaring has described the problem of deadlock, or "immobilism," as the most serious challenge for Latin American countries that are unambiguously democratic:

> Effective executive power is almost indispensable if democracy is to thrive, yet the history of presidential democracies in Latin America has often

---

[2] See especially Juan J. Linz, "Presidential or Parliamentary Democracy: Does It Make a Difference?" in Linz and Arturo Valenzuela, eds., *The Failure of Presidential Democracy* (Baltimore: Johns Hopkins University Press, 1994), 3–87. As a piece of intellectual history, it is interesting to note that this whole issue received only a four-page "excursus" in Linz's 1978 essay on "Crisis, Breakdown, and Reequilibration," 71–74.

A spate of books and reports by prominent authors expressed strong support for adoption of a parliamentary form of government.

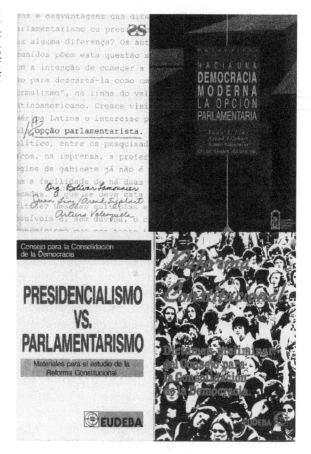

been one of immobilized executives. Immobilism in turn has often contributed to democratic breakdown. Many scholars have insisted on the importance of strengthening congresses in order to bolster democracy in Latin America, but it may be even more important to create effective executives—a point that has received little attention. Unfortunately, in presidential systems, especially those with fragmented party systems, strengthening congress can exacerbate executive immobilism.[3]

Ironically, countries usually adopt (or sustain) presidentialist systems in hopes of having strong governments, but executive–legislative gridlock actually tends to make them weak.

In response to such impasses, democratic presidents resort to a variety of tactics. They buy the support of opposition parties with pork-barrel handouts

---

[3] Scott Mainwaring, "Presidentialism in Latin America," in Arend Lijphart, ed., *Parliamentary versus Presidential Government* (Oxford: Oxford University Press, 1992), 113.

or outright corruption. They skirt legislatures and issue executive decrees. They present direct, often emotional appeals to the public, seeking a mantle of "plebiscitarian legitimacy" that would justify additional (often extralegal) assertions of presidential authority. Typically such measures increase the likelihood of military intervention. As employed by Hugo Chávez in Venezuela, they led to the replacement of electoral democracy by a semidemocratic regime.

Advocates of parliamentarist reform offered extensive evidence in support of their position. They noted that more states had parliamentary governments instead of presidential systems and implied that there must be solid reasons for such preferences (see Box 5.2). And they observed that outside the United States, very few presidential democracies had ever endured for more than twenty-five years: Chile, Colombia, Costa Rica, Uruguay, and Venezuela. (In Chile and Uruguay, presidentialism gave way to military dictatorships during the 1970s; in Venezuela, it succumbed to semidemocratic rule in the late 1990s.) In contrast, parliamentary systems displayed far superior records of survival. Among fifty-three developing countries with at least one year of democracy between 1973 and 1989, for instance, only 20 percent of the presidential democracies lasted for ten consecutive years, compared with 61 percent of parliamentary regimes.[4]

Counterarguments

It took time for a propresidentialist position to emerge.[5] One central argument focused on the virtues of executive stability. In contrast to the continual uncertainty inherent in parliamentary regimes, the constitutional stipulation of a fixed presidential term would strengthen executive accountability, encourage long-term policymaking, and discourage partisan maneuvering. Political horizons would be clear. Unhappy voters could always await the next election. In some cases it might be desirable to reduce the length of presidential terms, say, from six years to four, but that was insufficient reason to discard the system altogether.

A second counterargument asserted that the separation of executive and legislative powers under presidentialism would "promote more limited government, institutionalize checks and balances, and thus protect individual liberties against the ever-present possibility of governmental domination and abuse." By contrast, the fusion of powers under parliamentarism posed a serious threat of a "tyranny of the majority." Even with its imperfections, the separation of powers would help guarantee citizens' rights.

---

[4] Alfred Stepan and Cindy Skach, "Constitutional Frameworks and Democratic Consolidation," *World Politics* 46, no. 1 (October 1993): 1–22.

[5] Within academic circles this position first appeared in Matthew Soberg Shugart and John M. Carey, *Presidents and Assemblies: Constitutional Design and Electoral Dynamics* (Cambridge: Cambridge University Press, 1992).

A third and especially persuasive point maintained that popular election of the chief executive was inherently more democratic than indirect selection through a parliament. Direct election allowed the people themselves to choose their head of government, rather than delegating that role to a gaggle of MPs. Besides, a divided government, in which the president's party lacks a legislative majority, was not inherently bad. People might want it that way, because it would provide another means of curtailing the potential for abuse of governmental power.

Moreover, the problems associated with presidentialism were not the result of presidentialism itself. They stemmed from other factors. Take the issue of legislative–executive stalemate, or "immobilism." This came not from presidentialism per se, according to this line of argument, but from the *combination* of presidential government with a multiparty system. Presidential systems functioned rather well with strong two-party systems; immobilism was more likely to result from multiparty systems, especially when legislative seats were awarded on the basis of proportional representation (see explanation in Chapter 6). In demonstration of this point, Chile was the exception that proved the rule: It was "the only case in the world of a multi-party presidential democracy that endured for twenty-five years or more"—and we all know how that story came to an end![6]

---

[6] Mainwaring, "Presidentialism," 114.

Weak and fragmented parties would only exacerbate this problem. As one commentator hypothesized:

> Where parties are weak, it is not obvious that institutional reform can single-handedly prevent democratic breakdown *and* enhance governability, as its proponents purport [with reference to such countries as Brazil and Peru]....But their failure to consider the alternative—that had Brazil and Peru had parliamentary government, the result might have been a *succession* of weak governments headed by prime ministers no more capable of marshaling support for austere economic policies than a president—diminishes not only the attractiveness of the proposed reform but also its credibility as a possible explanation for incomplete democratic consolidation.
>
> ...If the scramble for state jobs and resources that accompanies the frequent formation of cabinets is instructive, negotiation among parties to form parliamentary majorities would only intensify the rampant state clientelism that has destroyed the nation's fiscal health. Proposing electoral reforms could similarly produce ambiguous effects. Adopting a closed-list system of proportional representation may indeed be desirable from the point of view of strengthening party discipline, but it is not at all clear that such reform in Brazil would attenuate intraparty competition and clientelism. Intraparty competition is sometimes strident not only because candidates for deputy base their electoral appeals on their ability to deliver state patronage to their constituents, rather than on their party platform.[7]

Echoed a subsequent analysis: "We are less than sanguine about the effects of shifting to parliamentary government in countries with undisciplined parties. Undisciplined parties create problems in presidential democracies, but they create even more daunting problems in parliamentary systems."[8] In general, it was claimed, the prevailing party systems in Latin America were inimical to parliamentary governance.

Finally, the empirical claims of the proparliamentarist side were held to result from systematic "selection bias." As one prominent essay asserted, "Presidentialism is more likely to be adopted in Latin America and Africa than in other parts of the world, and these parts of the world may have more formidable obstacles to democracy regardless of the form of government. On the other hand, parliamentarism has been the regime form of choice in most of Europe and in former British colonies (a large percentage of which are microstates), where conditions for democracy may generally be more favorable."[9] So misfortunes stemmed not so much from presidentialism per

---

[7] Frances Hagopian, "After Regime Change: Authoritarian Legacies, Political Representation, and the Democratic Future of South America," *World Politics* 45, no. 3 (April 1993): 464–600, with quote on 481.

[8] Scott Mainwaring and Matthew Soberg Shugart, eds., *Presidentialism and Democracy in Latin America* (Cambridge: Cambridge University Press, 1997), 53.

[9] Ibid., 29.

se but from societal conditions in the areas of its adoption. Thus challenging the proparliamentary position, this argument represented a tacit but major concession to the socioeconomic interpretation of democratic breakdowns.

Semipresidentialism/Semiparliamentarism?

Amid the swirl of these arguments, there emerged considerable support for a synthesis, usually known as "semipresidentialism," also referred to as "semiparliamentarism" and "premier-presidentialism." The general formula called for two elements: a president elected by direct vote of the citizenry, and a prime minister (and cabinet) selected by and beholden to the legislature. In principle, this would combine the advantages of direct democratic election and stable tenure (for the president) with the flexibility of a parliamentary cabinet and prime minister.

The question, of course, was who would really govern—the president or the prime minister? As Arend Lijphart has pointed out, semipresidentialism might not represent a real "synthesis" but an alternation of presidential and parliamentary phases. If the president's party held a majority in the legislature, decision making would be largely presidential; if not, decision making would be mostly parliamentary.

This idea appeared to capture the best of both worlds and attracted considerable support in much of Latin America. It became the basis, in fact, for significant reform proposals in key countries of the region.

ATTEMPTS AT REFORM

The debates on institutional alternatives led to intense speculation throughout Latin America. Much of the discussion was purely hypothetical. For all its European influence, in fact, Latin America had rarely—or never—experienced "pure" parliamentarism. Within traditional oligarchic settings, it was the nominal form of government under the monarchy in nineteenth-century Brazil and, with modifications, a de facto form of government in Chile from 1891 to 1925. Under highly contested circumstances, it was briefly attempted (and promptly discarded) in Brazil, again, in 1961–1962. Peru installed a semipresidential system in 1962, with a prime minister responsible to the legislature, but the power of the presidency and the weakness of the congress made this an ineffectual experiment.[10]

The debates of the 1980s flourished especially in South America, where democratic transitions took place in the wake of long-term military regimes. Discussions led to serious and plausible proposals.

---

[10] See Julio Cotler, "A Historical-Structural Approach to the Breakdown of Democratic Institutions: Peru," in Linz and Stepan, eds., *Breakdown of Democratic Regimes.*

Brazil: Voice of the Voters

One was in Brazil, where a Constitutional Congress of 1987–1988 gave careful consideration to the installation of a semipresidential system, under which a president elected by the people and a prime minister elected by the legislature would share executive power. The president would function as head of state and enjoy formal prerogatives as, for instance, commander of the armed forces; the prime minister would serve as head of government and manage day-to-day policy issues. Only the legislature, not the president, could decide to dismiss the prime minister. The proposal came to a vote in March 1988 and was defeated 344 to 212, a margin of roughly 60 to 40 percent. At the same time, it was stipulated that there should be a popular referendum on the entire issue five years later.

The plebiscite was scheduled for April 1993. Opinion polls showed considerable support for the parliamentary alternative, and at times it looked as if it would pass—almost anything would have seemed an improvement over the prevailing situation! For example, Robert de Souza, a well-known social activist, declared his opposition to pure presidentialism because "that would represent more of the same. Parliamentarism is at least a chance for change." (Yet he also predicted that Brazilians would vote to retain the presidency because of the country's culture of "salvationism—delegating citizenship to a savior," much along the lines of what has come to be known as "delegative democracy.")[11] "Brazilians have the idea," de Souza continued, "that the president is a substitute for God," and they tend to leave everything for the president to solve.

As the campaign mounted, propresidential forces insistently argued that a parliamentary system would deprive Brazilian voters of their time-honored (and recently reachieved) right to choose the chief executive through direct elections. Perhaps in response, surveys began to reveal a consistent 60 to 40 percent split in favor of presidentialism.

The referendum itself had two parts. The first asked whether voters wanted Brazil to have a republican or monarchical form of government (see Box 5.3). More than two thirds (69 percent) supported a republican form of government, 10 percent voted for a monarchy, and 20 percent cast blank or null votes. The second offered a choice between presidentialism and pure parliamentarism: 59 percent voted for presidentialism, 24 percent for parliamentarism, and 16 percent voted for neither (however that might be interpreted). Although the results seemed decisive, polls revealed that nearly two thirds of the voters did not fully understand the difference between parliamentarism and presidentialism—not to mention semipresidentialism!

According to Bolivar Lamounier, participants in the referendum succumbed to three arguments. One was that a fixed term would lead to stability and programmatic unity (this was especially effective in the wake of

---

[11] See Box I.2 in the introduction to this book.

BOX 5.3

A PLETHORA OF PRINCES IN BRAZIL

The inclusion of monarchy as a choice in Brazil's 1993 referendum on institutional regime offered a nostalgic reminder of the nineteenth-century empire under Dom Pedro II, fondly remembered in many quarters as an enlightened and benevolent ruler. It also raised questions about who might qualify as a legitimate heir to the throne. Many observers believed that a courtly octogenarian named Pedro de Alcantara de Orleans e Bragança would be the most acceptable choice. But as a journalist wryly noted, there was "no shortage of pretenders to this phantom throne."

Pedro II's descendants were the Orleans e Bragança family, who over time split into two rival clans: the Vassouras and the Petropolis, who took their respective names from the cities where they established themselves. Rivalries between these two aristocratic families who aspire to the Brazilian crown are further complicated by the fact that the founder of the Petropolis branch renounced his claim to the throne. However, his descendants do not accept his renunciation, which forms the very basis of the claim made by their cousins, the Vassouras.

The eldest son of the Vassouras branch, Prince Luis of Orleans e Bragança, is known as "Luis the chaste" because he took a vow of celibacy when he joined the ultra-conservative Catholic group "Tradition, Family, and Property." But "Luis the chaste" is unlikely to win support for his bid. Apart from his unappealing political views, the 50 year-old prince was born in France, has no heirs, and speaks Portuguese with a heavy French accent—like the rest of his family.

By contrast, his cousins from Petropolis present a young, modern image. The best known family member, João de Orleans e Bragança—nicknamed "Johnny the surfer" after his favorite sport—is now in the hotel business and is a keen environmental photographer. João is one of the few members of the royal dynasty who was born and bred in Brazil, speaks Portuguese like a native, and is married with two children.

Matters have been further complicated by the recent appearance of another claimant, this time an Austrian with a thick Germanic accent named Saxen-Coburg. As a descendant of Pedro II's daughter, he is also staking his claim to the throne.

The dispute has also been enlivened by the arrival on the scene of a black "ogan" (priest) Neninho de Obaluaye, president of São Paulo's Center for Black Resistance. Obaluaye insists that the kingdom built upon the sweat and blood of African slaves during the colonial era should be handed over to their descendants. He argues that blacks have a greater claim to the throne than Pedro II's family because their forefathers arrived first....

Alcides da Silva Souza, the grandson of Fulnio Indians, does not want to hear talk about European or African families or even kings: he wants to see an indigenous "cacique" (chief) ruling Brazil. "The imperial crown represents a band of assassins and thieves who killed our forefathers and stole our gold," declares Alcides, who intends to ask the Supreme Electoral Tribunal to include the option of a "cacique" on the ballot papers. "I'm practically alone in this struggle, but I will not back down. Our system is the indigenous system: justice must be just, cleanliness must be clean and purity, pure. And if the cacique does not respond to the people's expectations, he should go," declared Alcides.

Source: Ricardo de Bittencourt, "Brazil: Princes, Blacks and Indians Lay Claim to Phantom Throne," InterPress Third World News Agency (April 1993).

the recent impeachment of a sitting president). Second was the assertion that Brazil had an identifiable presidentialist "tradition" and, more important, that this tradition was "congruent with the style of authority embedded in the country's political culture...." Third, and perhaps most persuasive, was the idea that "resistance to military rule was closely linked to the idea of direct presidential elections; the huge mobilization of 1984, called *diretas-já* or 'direct elections now,' was the symbolic climax. Redemocratization became virtually synonymous with the voters' right to choose a president with full powers, and hence a shift to parliamentary government would be regarded as a fraud with immense risks for the very legitimacy of democratic government."[12]

The Brazilian result conveyed a powerful moral: Where people had once enjoyed the right to vote directly for the president, it would be politically impossible to install a pure parliamentary regime. The only plausible alternative would be some form of semipresidentialism, as in France or Germany.

Argentina: Calculating Political Odds

Apparently heeding this lesson, reformers in Argentina adopted a more cautious path. Seeking ways to secure the survival of civilian politics, democratic president Raúl Alfonsín established a Council for the Consolidation of Democracy in the mid-1980s. Under the able and indefatigable leadership of Carlos Santiago Nino, the council issued two book-length reports detailing the problems of presidentialism. One issue was the "inability to channel political tensions" properly, which led disaffected sectors to seek solutions outside the system. Another was the concentration of power in the chief executive, which made the president the central figure in times of crisis—and his or her removal from office thus became a tempting solution. Yet another problem was the intractability of executive relations with the

---

[12] Bolivar Lamounier, "Presidentialism and Parliamentarism in Brazil," in Lijphart, ed., *Parliamentary versus Presidential Government*, 134. See also Bolívar Lamounier, ed., *A opçao parlamentarista* (São Paulo: IDESP, 1991).

legislature, where party discipline (known as "verticality" among the die-hard Peronists) often led to immobilism and zero-sum politics.

To meet these difficulties, the council proposed a "mixed" system in which a directly elected president would select a prime minister from the majority party (or dominant coalition) in the House of Representatives. (Note how this differed from the Brazilian proposal, in which the legislature would choose the prime minister.) The prime minister would have responsibility for national policy. The president would appoint and remove the prime minister; on the recommendation of the prime minister, the president would also appoint and remove cabinet ministers. Standing above the political fray, the president would possess all those powers "relating to the maintenance of institutions and the continuity of the nation," including the nomination of judges, ambassadors, and the highest military officers. Exerting a moderating influence, the president could even dissolve the House of Representatives and call for new elections in moments of crisis.

As Nino and his colleagues maintained, this kind of semipresidential system would provide crucial elements of flexibility. Under such an arrangement, "the prime minister and the government serve as 'circuit-breakers' that 'break' in cases of tension." That is, the prime minister and cabinet would have to leave office if they lost the confidence of the president or the legislature. Individual governments might fall, but the democratic system would endure.[13]

Carefully argued and handsomely packaged, the council's proposals appeared to have a strong chance of adoption. It was assumed, at the time, that the still-popular Alfonsín could win election to the newly defined presidency. The question was whether Alfonsín's Radical Party or the dissident Peronists would dominate the House of Representatives and thus claim the prime ministership.

According to reliable reports, the Peronists were on the brink of accepting the council's plan on the ground that a potential share of executive power would be far better than none. But then the party leadership commissioned a series of public opinion polls that showed that, contrary to original expectations, the Peronists had a very good chance of winning the old-fashioned presidency for themselves. In a straightforward political calculation, of course, this would be vastly preferable to a mere prime ministership.

So in the end, the Peronists scuttled the council's plan. As Alfonsín's presidency later crumbled under the weight of economic crisis, Carlos Saúl Menem of the Peronist party went on to win the presidency by a landslide vote in 1989. Semipresidentialism was no longer a consideration. Within a short time, as we shall see in Chapter 6, Menem set about plans to prolong his stay in office.

---

[13] See also *Reforma constitucional: Dictamen preliminar del Consejo para la Consolidación de la Democracia* (Buenos Aires: Eudeba, 1986), and *Reforma constitucional: Segundo dictamen del Consejo para la Consolidación de la Democracia* (Buenos Aires: Eudeba, 1987).

Chile: A Pact for Presidentialism

In addition to Brazil and Argentina, there was extensive discussion about the desirability of bringing parliamentary democracy to Chile. It seemed to be a promising context. After all, Chile had a strong and stable party system organized around three ideological poles—Left, Center, and Right. It had a history of legislative competence and prestige. It drew cultural inspiration from both the United Kingdom and continental Europe. It served witness to an underlying paradox, the inverse correlation between the power of the presidency and the success of presidential government: "The stronger the president, the weaker the presidential system." And it had suffered the brutal consequences of presidentialist rigidities in 1973: "Had Chile been governed by a parliamentary regime," Arturo Valenzuela has written, "Allende's government might have fallen, but democracy would have survived" (see Box 5.4).

In theory, it was argued, a parliamentary system could bring numerous benefits to Chile. It would eliminate the need to construct "high-stakes coalitions around a winner-take-all presidential option." It would ameliorate the tensions and hostilities characteristic of executive–legislative relations in twentieth-century Chile. And as a result, it would contribute to the further moderation of Chilean politics.[14]

Yet it was not to be. The explanation is straightforward. Part of the price of Chile's democratic transition in 1988–1989 was acceptance of the 1980 constitution laid down by the military government. This was a highly presidentialist charter—"hyperpresidentialist," many critics have said—drafted on the assumption that General Pinochet would one day win election as the country's chief executive. In the wake of the shocking defeat in the plebiscite of 1988, military architects made some crucial alterations in the constitution, but they insisted on keeping control of the process. They were hardly about to turn the whole enterprise over to an as-yet-unknown constitutional committee or convention. Ultimately, broad considerations of institutional design were sacrificed to the expediencies of regime transition.

In practical terms, political outcomes in the ABC countries (Argentina, Brazil, and Chile) brought the parliamentary–presidentialist debate to an end. These nations offered the most propitious sites for adoption of the parliamentary model. They all had fairly strong congressional traditions, Argentina and especially Chile had institutionalized party systems, and they all had reason to seek major reforms in the institutional arrangements

---

[14] Arturo Valenzuela, "Party Politics and the Crisis of Presidentialism in Chile: A Proposal for a Parliamentary Form of Government," Ch. 6 in *Failure of Presidential Democracy*, 91–150. See also Oscar Godoy Arcara, ed., *Hacia una democracia moderna: La opción parlamentaria* (Santiago: Ediciones Universidad Católica de Chile, 1990).

BOX 5.4

WHAT IF? THE CASE OF CHILE

One of the key elements in institutional debates has involved "counterfactual" speculation—in other words, guesstimating what would have happened if Latin American country X had had a parliamentary rather than presidential-ist framework. Would things have worked out differently? One of the most explicit examples concerns the breakdown of democracy in Chile in the early 1970s. As analyzed by Arturo Valenzuela:

> In Chile, there was an inverse correlation between the power of the presidency and the success of presidential government. The stronger the president, the weaker the presidential system—a perverse logic that came to a head in the Allende years. A parliamentary system of govern-ment would have defused the enormous pressures for structuring high-stakes coalitions around a winner-take-all presidential option, which only reinforced political polarization. At the same time, it would have eliminated the stalemate and confrontation in executive-legislative rela-tions. Had Chile had a parliamentary regime in the early 1970s, Allende's government might have fallen, but democracy would have survived. The working majority in Congress that elected Allende to the presidential post would have had to continue for him to retain his position. This was not out of the question....Had the coalition collapsed, it is quite likely that a Christian Democrat, or perhaps a member of the small left-ist Radical Party, would have formed a new government with support from elements on the right.
>
> It is important to stress that parliamentary politics...would have contributed to moderating Chilean politics by reinforcing the time-honored traditions of compromise honed by generations of politicians. Moderate leaders on both sides of the congressional aisle would have gained strength, encouraging centripetal drives toward coalition and compromise, rather than being outclassed by maximalist leaders who thrived in the public arenas of high-stakes electoral battles. Moreover, leaders of all parties would have thought twice about abandoning hard-fought coalition arrangements if they had faced the prospect of imme-diate reelection, and the greater accountability of having been part of an agreement to structure executive authority.

Source: Arturo Valenzuela, "Chile: Origins and Consolidation of a Latin American Democracy," in Larry Diamond, Jonathan Hartlyn, Juan J. Linz, and Seymour Martin Lipset, eds., *Democracy in Developing Countries: Latin America*, 2nd ed. (Boulder, CO: Lynne Rienner, 1999), 221–222.

that had led to such catastrophic breakdowns in the 1960s and 1970s. Such deliberations seemed somehow irrelevant in Central America, where the question was not what kind of democracy ought to prevail, but whether there would be any democracy at all.

WHY NOT?

The 1980s and early 1990s were heady times for Latin America, especially South America. The removal of hard-line dictatorships created a vivid sense of empowerment and possibility. Bitter experiences with military brutality in Argentina, Brazil, Chile, and Uruguay led to widespread belief in the norms and virtues of political democracy. Examples of heroic resistance also conveyed a sense of obligation, a determination among survivors that the courageous sacrifices of noble citizens should not have been in vain. These and other sentiments gave exalted meaning and moral significance to the quest for democratic consolidation.

They also led to an intensive search for institutional formulas that might promote this goal. And this, in turn, led to a remarkable blending of academic research with public policy. Building on accumulated findings in the field of comparative politics, analysts and activists in Latin America devoted serious attention to the possibility and desirability of replacing presidentialist systems with parliamentary democracies. They served on commissions, drafted proposals, sat in constitutional conventions, and argued their case with elegance. Why did they not succeed?

There were several reasons. One was the near-impossibility of discarding direct presidential elections where they had existed before. This was explicitly apparent in the case of Brazil and implicitly relevant everywhere else. Such a move would seem patently "antidemocratic" and threatened to undermine the legitimacy of still-fragile democratic transitions. It was simply unthinkable.

This limited the range of options to semipresidential government. But even here, as demonstrated in the case of Argentina, barriers proved to be formidable.

One problem accompanied the advent of public opinion polling, which exploded throughout Latin America during the course of democratic transitions in the 1980s. In analytical terms, the rise and widespread use of polling led to a reduction of uncertainty in the minds of political actors. And uncertainty is an essential prerequisite for power sharing; or, to put it more precisely, power sharing seems desirable only to those who face the likelihood of losing a winner-take-all competition. Polling permitted political strategists to make their calculations with more confidence—or at least with the appearance of more confidence. If any party (or coalition) has a reasonable prospect of winning a presidency outright, as the Peronists discovered, it will staunchly oppose a semipresidentialist reform.

Another factor was low popular esteem for congress. Legislatures and legislators had not distinguished themselves over the course of previous decades. For the most part, they were either subservient to presidential will or unreasonably resistant to presidential persuasion. They appeared to place party above nation, loyalty above rationality, and short-term personal gain above long-term national interest. They often seemed venal, sycophantic, and corrupt. In no case had legislatures acted decisively and constructively to assure the survival of second-cycle democracies in the 1960s and 1970s. Parliamentarism, even in semipresidentialist form, meant expanding the authority and role of the legislative branch. On the basis of past experience, who would want to do that?

The same held true for political parties. As many analysts insisted, a parliamentary formula could succeed only through the performance of strong and disciplined parties. The only country that could boast such parties was Chile. Elsewhere, they were too aloof and centralized, as in Venezuela, or too fragmented and disorganized, as in Ecuador and Brazil. And as surveys repeatedly showed, they did not enjoy the confidence of citizens.

A final consideration, more cultural than practical, stemmed from the politics of nostalgia. While under military rule, it was natural and common for citizens to romanticize preexisting eras of democratic government. Things in the past might not have been perfect, the feeling went, but they were a far sight better than they are now. Leaders of those bygone democracies assumed heroic proportions, and, even more commonly, democratic constitutions became sacred documents, durable testaments to the nation's will and capacity for civilized self-government.

In this way, earlier institutional arrangements became key elements in the ethos of regime transitions, one of the "necessary myths" in support of the idea that democracy could come to a deserving populace. Reinstatement of those institutions thus became a moral obligation. Departure from these traditions would be a form of blasphemy. Political transitions are moments of uplift and inventiveness, but at the same time—and ironically so—they can also be profoundly conservative.

CHAPTER 6

INSTITUTIONAL VARIATIONS

By no means did the retention of presidentialism terminate efforts at institutional reform in Latin America. On the contrary, democratic transitions prompted an extensive series of inquiries, adjustments, and modifications. During the 1990s, seven countries adopted completely new constitutions; others used amendments as means of reform.[1] In most cases, the intent was to understand the workings of the system, identify its strengths and weaknesses, and make adjustments that would improve the quality of political democracy and help assure its survival. As a system, presidentialism turned out to be a capacious concept; it could have a broad range of subtypes and varieties. The question for Latin America was not *whether* presidentialism—it was *what kind*.

This chapter examines key institutional features of presidentialist systems in Latin America, including commonalities and differences, and the scope of recent reforms. It focuses on three major electoral institutions: the presidency, the legislature, and political parties. (The judicial branch is analyzed in Chapter 10.) For the most part, the institutional reforms of the 1990s have led to expected results, but also to some unanticipated consequences. And while they have altered the rules of political contestation, they have not changed the overall balance of power or means of representation. The presidency continues to be the most effective locus of power; legislatures have made significant strides but are not well equipped to initiate major legislation; as vehicles for popular representation, political parties leave much to be desired in most instances. Checks and balances do not function efficiently in most countries of the region.

---

[1] See Matthew Soberg Shugart, "Towards a Representation Revolution: Constitutional Reform, Electoral Systems, and the Challenges of Democracy in Latin America" (The Carter Center, Atlanta, GA, October 2000).

EXECUTIVE POWER

The presidency has always been the epicenter of Latin American politics. Exercising authority both de jure and de facto, presidents have defined national priorities, framed policy alternatives, and implemented strategies. Power has emanated from both the trappings of the office and from the strength of personality. Commonly possessed of unusual energy, intelligence, and social skills, sometimes magnetic or mysterious, and almost always men, presidents have been dominant players in the political arena. Governing administrations and historical eras have come to be closely identified with presidential personas.

This came about for several reasons. One was the relative absence of alternative power centers. During the nineteenth century and well into the twentieth century in many countries, the only coherent institutions in Latin America were the Roman Catholic Church and the military, which was purportedly under the control of the president. Legislative and judiciary authorities were weak and notoriously subject to persuasion or corruption. Coups were frequent, and violence was an integral part of political life. Chronic regime instability meant that political commitments tended to focus on individual personalities and face-to-face relationships rather than on ideological missions or policy programs. Cultural emphasis on loyalty and trust enhanced the myth of *personalismo*, the celebration of a person rather than a cause.

There were presidents, of course, and then there were *presidents*. As shown in Chapter 1, some ruled over democratic polities, mainly in the Southern Cone during the first cycle of democratization (1900–1939) and in South America during the second cycle (1940–1977). Elsewhere and at other times, however, rulers known as "presidents" tended to govern through systems that were autocratic, oligarchic, or semidemocratic. *El señor presidente* was an awesome figure, ruthless and effective, feared, respected, and sometimes despised by his obedient subjects. It is because of these circumstances that Latin American presidents have been indiscriminately regarded as omnipotent, intolerant, and authoritarian.

There were two basic means of assuring rotation of chief executives. One was through *golpes de estado*, the use or threat of force, often by dissident leaders or factions of the military. The other was through a constitutional prohibition on presidential reelection, a provision dating from the early years of Spanish American independence. The basic idea was to prevent long-term monopolies of power (*continuismo*). By assuring ambitious rivals that their chances would come within a foreseeable future, it tended to discourage rebellions and coups. Some presidents respected this rule, but others did not: Porfirio Díaz of Mexico was notorious for constitutional tinkering that enabled him to stay in office for decades (see Box 6.1).

BOX 6.1

USES (AND ABUSES) OF CONSTITUTIONS IN LATIN AMERICA

Constitutions are widely viewed as sacred documents. They spell out procedures, specify rules, allocate powers, and, in modern democracies, define the rights of citizens. They are subject to interpretation and reinterpretation but are nonetheless revered as timeless charters. What about constitutions in developing societies undergoing rapid change? Here is one picture of Latin America:

> Quite clearly, many constitutional provisions are honored only in the breach; and yet great stress is placed upon constitutional forms and procedures, even where these mask political realities quite discordant with their intent. National constitutions are heavily eulogized in popular oratory, and key provisions are well known and frequently cited; yet existing constitutions are frequently discarded and replaced—in fact the average life span of Latin American constitutions has been slightly less than 20 years....
>
> The clauses that organize the public powers, prescribing the mechanisms of constitutional succession and establishing the organs of government, on the other hand, are literally followed in practice. It may well be that the constitutional forms do not correspond to political realities; the legislature is supposed to act independently of the President, although everyone knows that it has no will of its own; the judiciary is supposed to be nonpolitical, although everyone understands that its decisions are guided by political savoir-faire rather than principles of jurisprudence. Nevertheless, the forms are observed, even where they seem to the onlooker merely ceremonial: the President proposes legislation, which the parliament goes through the motions of debating; the court hears evidence and hands down a learned decision that coincidentally favors the position of the President.
>
> Often the divergence between constitutional form and political reality is so great, however, that what occurs politically can simply not be contained within the terms of the fundamental law. When this happens, one does not simply violate the constitution; he rewrites it, to extend the dignity of constitutionality to the new situation. Normally, the dictator who wants to have a second term as President, when the constitution limits him to one, calls a constitutional convention to produce a new document; a successful revolution justifies itself retroactively by writing itself a new constitution; and so on....

Source: Martin C. Needler, *Latin American Politics in Perspective* (New York: Van Nostrand, 1967), 124–125.

Since the late 1970s, it has become the norm for Latin American presidents to govern through electoral democracies. They have, for the most part, respected the letter, if not always the spirit, of institutional constraints on their authority. What are the bases of presidential power in modern-day democracy throughout the region?

Means of Election

The most basic question deals with popular mandate. Having rejected parliamentary alternatives, countries of the region select their chief executives through direct election. This is a cardinal tenet of Latin American democracy.

There are variations on this theme. A "plurality" system stipulates that the candidate with the largest number of votes shall be declared the winner, with or without an absolute majority of 50 percent or more. This seems straightforward enough (especially in two-party democracies such as the United States). A problem arises when there are more than two serious candidates, because the winning plurality might be rather modest—and the president's mandate correspondingly weakened. In the 1970 elections in Chile, for instance, Salvador Allende triumphed with only 36.5 percent of the vote.[2] His administration thus started out with a serious birth defect and would later collapse in disaster.

Second is a majority runoff (MRO) system, which calls for a second-round runoff if no one wins a majority in the first round. Usually the top two candidates compete in the second round. A principal goal is to make sure that the eventual winner obtains a majority of voter support and thus secures a strong mandate to govern. For this reason, it has gained popularity in recent years. By 2010, as shown in Table 6.1, all but five countries had adopted some form of runoff requirement. MRO thus became a basic norm throughout the region.

MRO has other effects. One is to encourage small and marginal parties to enter candidates in the first round; they have nothing to lose, and a respectable finish might enable them to strike advantageous deals with finalists in the second round. A related consequence is to promote all manner of bargaining between the first and second round, as finalists seek to forge winning coalitions. As a result, it is entirely possible that the top vote-getter in the first round, the one with a plurality but not a majority, will be defeated in the second round. A third effect is to encourage centrist politics. Deal making tends to dilute programmatic purity, and the logic of a two-way race means that the finalists are likely to compete for voters at the center of the political spectrum.

MRO has thus become a force for moderation. This is a defining feature. One motive for its widespread adoption has been to reduce the likelihood that "extremist" candidates—of Left or Right, but especially the Left—can win presidential elections. The specter of Salvador Allende loomed large over Latin America's restored democracies; under an MRO system, he would

---

[2] Under the Chilean constitution then in force, a joint session of the national congress was to name a winner from the top two candidates; in keeping with tradition, the legislators agreed to respect Allende's plurality. Until recently Bolivia had a similar provision, allowing the congress to choose among the top three finishers.

TABLE 6.1 Systems for Presidential Elections, 2010

Simple Plurality	Runoff for ≤50%	Runoff for ≤40%
Honduras	Argentina*	Costa Rica
Mexico	Bolivia*	Nicaragua**
Panama	Brazil	
Paraguay	Chile	
Venezuela	Colombia	
	Dominican Republic	
	Ecuador*	
	El Salvador	
	Guatemala	
	Haiti	
	Peru	
	Uruguay	

*Winner needs only 45 percent of vote in Argentina; in Argentina, Bolivia, and Ecuador, no runoff if leading candidate gets over 40 percent of total vote and at least 10 percent more than runner-up.
**No runoff if leading candidate gets 35 percent of total vote and at least 5 percent more than runner-up.

probably never have become the president of Chile (assuming that parties of the Center and the Right would have restored their historic alliance for the runoff election itself). And even if leftist candidates succeeded under MRO, they would have to moderate their platforms and policies to win the second round. Here Lula of Brazil might be a case in point. MRO favors the center of the ideological spectrum. Not surprisingly, it has been adopted in countries with recent histories of political polarization or military rule: Argentina, Brazil, Chile, and Nicaragua.

There are permutations of the MRO formula. One asserts that the leading candidate in first-round elections could be declared a winner by achieving a specified portion of votes: In Argentina the minimum threshold is 48 percent and in Costa Rica and Nicaragua it is 40 percent. Another is the "double complement" rule, adopted in several countries, according to which the leading candidate could become a winner if the distance between his or her vote and a majority is less than half the distance by which the second-place candidate falls short.[3] Under this system, a plurality candidate could win only if his or her vote were significantly stronger than the vote share for the leading competitor. Otherwise, a second-round runoff would then take place.

Whatever the precise formulation, MRO has gained widespread support. To a substantial degree it has eclipsed the 1980s and 1990s debate over system reform, as it appears to provide many of the benefits associated with parliamentarism without exacting any (or all) of the costs. It has thus enabled querulous leaders to avoid excruciating struggles over fundamental insti-

---

[3] Where v_1 is the vote share for the first-place candidate and v_2 is the vote share for the second-place candidate, a winner would be declared if $(50 - v_2) > 2 (50 - v_1)$.

tutional change. Indeed, MRO has become something of a silver bullet for Latin American politics.

To Reelect or Not?

The question of presidential reelection has attracted a great deal of attention. Throughout Latin American history, as mentioned earlier, the principal means of restraining executive power was through a constitutional ban on reelection. As a compromise, some charters stipulated that presidents would have to wait out one or two "interim terms" before seeking reelection. Only a few countries in the region, mostly during autocratic eras, have permitted unlimited reelection. Presidential terms have varied in length between four and six years—the longer the term, as a rule, the less likely the provision for consecutive reelection.

In the democratic context of the 1990s, however, the no-reelection rule seemed more impediment than safeguard. It prevented citizens from retaining competent executives in office, it restricted accountability, and it made all elected presidents into lame ducks, which gave them little reason to attend to citizens' preferences. Out of such considerations, and as the result of elite bargaining, prohibitions on immediate reelection were overturned in Argentina (1994) and Brazil (1996). These modifications enabled Carlos Saúl Menem to win reelection in 1996 and Fernando Henrique Cardoso to follow suit in 1998. Also in 1998 a new constitution for Ecuador allowed for presidential reelection after one interim term; in 2008 yet another constitution permitted immediate reelection to a second term.

Other changes resulted more from imposition than transaction. After engineering an infamous *autogolpe* in Peru, Alberto Fujimori put through a law enabling reelection in 1993; with the collusion of a subservient court, he would interpret the statute in such a way as to allow his own reelection in 1995 and again in 2000. Similarly, Hugo Chávez of Venezuela convened a constitutional convention (of questionable legality) that lifted the ban on presidential reelection in 1999. He would, of course, become the first chief executive to benefit from this decision.[4] In both instances, the electoral system became "semidemocratic": In essence, subsequent elections would be free but not fair.

Yet these modifications did not herald a region-wide rush to reinstate *continuismo*. In 1991 Colombia imposed a lifetime one-term limit without reelection. Similarly, the Dominican Republic, Nicaragua, and Paraguay, countries with painful histories of prolonged dictatorship, adopted total bans on reelection. Other countries made smaller adjustments: Colombia (1991) disallowed reelection after an intervening term out of office, which

---

[4] See John M. Carey, "The Reelection Debate in Latin America," *Latin American Politics and Society* 45, no. 1 (April 2003): 119–133.

TABLE 6.2 Rules on Presidential Reelection, 2010

No Reelection	After One Interim Term	After Two Interim Term	Two Consecutive Terms, Then No Reelection	Two Consecutive Terms, Then One Interim Term	No Limits
Costa Rica	Chile	Panama	Bolivia	Argentina	Venezuela
Guatemala	Dominican Republic		Brazil		
Honduras	El Salvador		Colombia		
Mexico	Haiti*		Ecuador		
Paraguay	Nicaragua*				
	Peru				
	Uruguay				

*Maximum of two total terms. Legal status of term limits currently under dispute in Nicaragua.

Source: John M. Carey, "Presidentialism and Representative Institutions," in Jorge I. Domínguez and Michael Shifter, eds., *Constructing Democratic Governance in Latin America*, 2d ed. (Baltimore: Johns Hopkins University Press, 2003), 19, with updates by author.

had previously been permitted. Panama (1994) increased the sitting-out interim period from one to two terms.

By 2010, as shown in Table 6.2, Latin America presented a broad array of rules regarding presidential reelection. Five countries, most conspicuously Mexico, retained total bans on reelection. Seven, including Chile, insisted on one interim term; Panama stipulated two. Bolivia, Brazil, Colombia, and Ecuador would allow two consecutive terms, but no reelection thereafter. Argentina had perhaps the most arcane provision: A president could serve for two consecutive terms but would then have to wait out one interim term before running again. In testimony to Hugo Chavez's demagogic appeals, Venezuela—alone by itself—imposed no term limits at all.

Although it might seem a reasonable compromise, the provision for interim terms—or "punctuated reelection"—could have complex implications. One potential consequence is the possibility that an incumbent president might attempt to undermine his own party's immediate electoral success. If another politician from the president's party wins, then the outgoing president would almost certainly fade into retirement, but if the party loses, the outgoing executive might retain authority as the leader of the opposition and run for reelection in a subsequent campaign. Sitting-out requirements thus pose "moral hazard" problems for ambitious politicians and their parties. Examples of this situation include Venezuela before 1999, where presidents and co-Acción Democrática party members Jaime Lusinchi and Carlos Andrés Pérez competed vigorously with each other, and Argentina, where Carlos Saúl Menem failed to support Eduardo Duhalde in 1999 because of his own desire to regain the presidency in 2003.

Sources of Power

Once in office, democratic presidents in contemporary Latin America wield two forms of power, *constitutional* and *partisan*. The first comes from the designation of roles, authority, and responsibilities according to the national constitution (and, less formally, from tacit rules of the game as understood by political actors). With regard to legislation, presidents can be either "proactive," submitting bills and dispatching executive decrees, or "reactive," using vetoes and other instruments to block congressional initiatives. Extremely powerful executives can become dominant in legislative matters, whereas weak ones might end up as marginal.

As the label implies, partisan powers derive from parties and party systems. More specifically, they reflect the extent to which the president's party dominates the legislature, the extent of party discipline, and the extent of presidential influence over his or her own party. The ultimate question, of course, is whether the president can use these powers to get whatever is wanted from congress.[5]

There are other arenas in which Latin American presidents can exert enormous authority. One is the bureaucracy, through which executives enjoy wide discretion in powers of appointment. Another is the judiciary, which has tended to be responsive to presidential preferences. Yet another, in some countries, is local and regional government, especially if presidents are able to influence nomination procedures within their political parties. And finally, presidents are commanders-in-chief of the armed forces. In a region where the military has long been a major political force, as shown in Chapter 3, this can be a significant source of executive strength. This was especially relevant because of the frequency of states of siege (or "regimes of exception"), which entailed the suspension of constitutional guarantees. During the decade of the 1950s, for instance, there were more than 100 declarations or extensions of states of siege in Latin America—all prior to the Cuban Revolution! Colombia was in a state of siege for about three quarters of the time between 1958 and 1974, as well as most of the 1990s.

An especially explicit form of proactive power is presidential authority to issue decrees. By this means, presidents are able to establish laws at their own discretion (technically, in lieu of congressional action). In most countries, executive decrees enter into immediate and permanent effect without any legislative action or ratification. Thus, the Colombian president has the authority to declare a state of economic emergency and issue decrees to restore "economic order" (Art. 215); the Peruvian president can exercise decree authority "on economic and financial matters, when so required by the national interest" (Art. 118); and the Chilean president can decree budgetary expenditures of up to 1 percent of total appropriations (Art. 32:22).

---

[5] Scott Mainwaring and Matthew Soberg Shugart, eds., *Presidentialism and Democracy in Latin America* (Cambridge: Cambridge University Press, 1997).

In Argentina, Brazil, and Colombia, presidents have the ability to issue laws by decree in almost any policy area.[6]

Chief executives have employed decree authority to proclaim drastic and far-reaching economic reforms such as Alfonsín's Plan Austral, Sarney's Plano Cruzado, and Collor's Plano Brasil Novo. They did so to skirt legislative resistance and, more specifically, to avoid modifications that could undermine the package as a whole. Leaving aside the fact that these programs proved to be ineffective, government by decree has unsettling implications. As Adam Przeworski has noted,

> Democracy is thus weakened. The political process is reduced to elections, executive decrees, and sporadic outbursts of protest. The government rules by decree, in an authoritarian fashion but often without much repression. All the power in the state is concentrated in the executive, which is nevertheless ineffectual in managing the economy. People get a regular chance to vote, but not to choose.[7]

On many occasions presidents could unilaterally declare states of siege, especially if the legislature was not in session. Taken to an extreme, decree authority becomes a key element in "delegative democracy" as defined by Guillermo O'Donnell (see Box I.2 in the Introduction to this book).

Consider the case of Carlos Saúl Menem, who tended to govern Argentina through so-called *decretazo* during his first term. Taking advantage of a constitutional provision that authorized the president to emit decrees in cases of "urgency and necessity" (*decretos de urgencia y necesidad*, or NUDs in an English-language acronym), Menem managed to impose neoliberal economic reforms without engaging congress. A cooperative legislature then permitted him to pack the Supreme Court, which promptly approved his use of decrees. Thus emboldened, Menem went on to make unprecedented use of this authority. (Earlier governments had shown substantial restraint. From 1853 to 1983, constitutional governments in Argentina issued about twenty NUDs in total; during his six years in office, Alfonsín issued ten; between July 1989 and August 1994, Menem issued no fewer than 336 NUDs.) In 1993 his economics minister, Domingo Cavallo, acknowledged that the government would have achieved only 20 percent of its economic program without the use of decrees.

Abuse of constitutional authority would take its toll on Argentine democracy. According to one thoughtful analysis:

> Emergency government in Argentina has given birth to a new institutional balance of power. The presidency has accumulated authorities that previously had been distributed among the other branches. Moreover, Menem

---

[6] See John M. Carey and Matthew Soberg Shugart, eds., *Executive Decree Authority* (Cambridge: Cambridge University Press, 1998).

[7] *Democracy and the Market: Political and Economic Reforms in Eastern Europe and Latin America* (Cambridge: Cambridge University Press, 1991), 186–187.

has exhibited a new style of decision making—discretionary, informal, sometimes arbitrary, and with a low commitment to the sanctity of formal political institutions—one resembling the style of old local leaders, or *caudillos*. Concurrently, Congress has lost legitimacy and political capacity, reducing its ability to act in reaction to presidential initiatives. All these developments were responses to public opinion and public demands for quick and effective policy making. The presidency was better prepared, both structurally and in terms of leadership capacity, to satisfy those demands than Congress, which faces formidable collective action problems. As a consequence, reactions against presidential decree authority have been isolated and uncoordinated—they have primarily been responses to presidential measures that directly hurt specific political and economic interests.[8]

The constitutional reform of 1994 established limits on the use and scope of NUDs. As part of the bargain, however, the reform also permitted presidential reelection for a second term. This was Menem's cherished prize.

Menem was not alone. Even Fernando Henrique Cardoso, a more capable leader and a much more committed democrat, made extensive use of decrees in Brazil. Article 62 of the 1988 constitution allowed the president to decree "provisional measures with the force of law." In years to follow, presidents issued between six and nineteen decrees per month—until Cardoso, who proclaimed an average of thirty-six per month. Then there is the case of Peru, described with passion (and hyperbole) by Hernando de Soto and Deborah Orsini: "The only element of democracy in Peru today is the electoral process, which gives Peruvians the privilege of choosing a dictator every five years. Rule making is subsequently carried out in a vacuum, with the executive branch enacting new rules and regulations at a clip of 134,000 every five years (an average of 106 each working day) without any feedback from the population." Despite the overstatement, they seemed to have a point.[9]

THE LEGISLATIVE BRANCH

As presidents dominated Latin America's political scene, legislatures historically did very little lawmaking. Duly enshrined in constitutions, they extended an aura of legitimation for whatever government might be in power. They were outlets for extensive oratory and occasional debate. They served as training grounds for aspiring politicians and as arenas for personal networking. On occasion they exercised oversight over the executive power,

---

[8] Delia Ferreira Rubio and Matteo Goretti, "When the President Governs Alone: The *Decretazo* in Argentina, 1989–93," in Carey and Shugart, *Executive Decree Authority*, 58.

[9] The simple number of decrees can be a misleading indicator, as some are procedural and mundane, and on occasion legislatures delegate decree authority to presidents.

criticizing cabinet ministers more sharply and frequently than presidents, usually within well-defined limits of decorum. But they did not make many laws.

As a result, analysts routinely dismissed the congressional branch, especially during the second cycle of democratization (1940–1977). In the late 1950s, one prominent scholar declared that "in most countries congress does not participate in determining national policy in the independent manner and to the extent usually deemed necessary to the successful operation of democratic and responsible government." A decade later, another writer proclaimed that in most nations "the legislatures are merely rubber stamps.... The legislatures ordinarily kowtow to the president, cater to his slightest whims, and enjoy no more independence or popular respect than political sycophants could expect to." And in the 1970s, legislatures were again dismissed as "marginal" and as "rubber-stamp legitimizers."

Such one-sided portraits reflected a kind of optical illusion. It is entirely true that authoritarian regimes established and maintained legislative branches to claim a mantle of democratic legitimacy. The most durable example was Mexico, where a pliant congress routinely approved executive bills by unanimous vote from the 1930s through the 1970s; even as late as the 1980s, presidential proposals received nearly 100 percent approval. The military regime in Brazil also installed a national congress. Such legislatures served as handmaidens to undemocratic regimes. Understandably, they acquired little respect or prestige.

By contrast, others played significant roles in democratic systems. Typical examples during the 1940–1977 period were Chile, up to the coup of 1973; Brazil during most of the period from 1946 to 1964; Costa Rica and Venezuela after the installation of democracy in the 1950s; and the venerable instance of Uruguay.[10] Argentina was a complex case, with intermittent democratic experience in the postwar era, although its national congress had a rich and complex history that stretched back to the early twentieth century.[11]

For many years, in other words, the perception of Latin American legislatures as irrelevant and ineffectual reflected the extent of electoral democracy. The relationship is clear: The weaker the democracy, the more likely that legislatures would be coopted (or closed) by authoritarian rulers; the stronger the democracy, the more respectable and meaningful the roles of congress.

It has been during only the third and most recent cycle of political change, starting in the late 1970s, that electoral democracy has become widespread throughout the region. As a result of this fact, plus the growing fascination

---

[10] See Weston H. Agor, ed., *Latin American Legislatures: Their Role and Influence* (New York: Praeger, 1971).

[11] Peter H. Smith, *The Failure of Democracy in Argentina: Conflict among Political Elites, 1904–1955* (Madison: University of Wisconsin Press, 1974), esp. 16–22.

with institutional engineering, congressional politics has begun to receive serious attention from analysts, activists, and politicians.

Electoral Systems and Rules of Representation

A good deal of recent scholarship has focused on means of electing congressional members. Proponents of institutional analysis argue that electoral arrangements shape the incentives for legislative behavior, including preferences for policy and party alignments.

The U.S. House of Representatives and the British Parliament have what are known as single-member districts (SMDs), with one legislative seat for each voting district. According to Duverger's Law, this arrangement encourages the formation of two-party systems, as small parties have no chance of winning the only available seat. It also leads to moderate politics, as the two main parties compete for votes at the center of the political spectrum.[12]

Along with most of continental Europe, Latin American countries have opted instead for proportional representation (PR). Under this formula, parties receive legislative seats according to their share of the total popular vote. In theory, therefore, 15 percent of the vote leads to 15 percent of the seats, whereas it would yield no seats at all in an SMD system. (There are different ways of calculating proportionality, but the principle remains the same.)[13] In practice, PR thus tends to encourage small parties, as they can aspire to obtain at least a modest share of power. This is the basis of Duverger's Hypothesis, which holds that PR is likely to result in multiparty politics.

An important factor in determining the actual distribution of legislative seats is the number of legislative seats allocated to a given district, what political scientists have labeled as district magnitude (M). The lower the ratio of seats to votes, the greater the potential for disproportionality. There exists a continuum, of course, from $M = 1$ (that is, SMD) to $M = S$ (where S is the total number of seats in the legislature, as is the case in Israel). A pattern thus emerges: The higher the M, the greater the number of parties winning seats and the more precise the proportionality of the resulting representation.[14]

Seeking the best of both worlds, some countries have forged "mixed" systems that combine SMD elections for most seats in the legislature with a highly proportional electoral formula for the remaining slots. This was adopted in authoritarian Mexico, of all places, at a time when the dominant regime was intent on coopting small but vocal opposition parties. It was also

---

[12] Maurice Duverger (1917–) is a French political scientist who published classic works on political parties in the 1950s.

[13] See Gary W. Cox, *Making Votes Count: Strategic Coordination in the World's Electoral Systems* (Cambridge: Cambridge University Press, 1997), 56–58.

[14] John M. Carey, "Institutional Design and Party Systems," in *Consolidating Third World Democracies*, eds. Larry Diamond, Marc F. Plattner, Yun-han Chu, and Hung-mao Tien (Baltimore: Johns Hopkins University Press, 1997), 67–92.

embraced in Venezuela as of 1993, when it was hoped that the SMD formula would diminish the power of the party bosses (the *partidocracia*, or "partyocracy"), who had long controlled nomination procedures. As explained by one advocate, "Elected representatives ought to act in the interests of those who elected them, ought to attend to their complaints and demands, ought to respond to their correspondence.... The SMD does not guarantee the proportional representation of parties, but in exchange it is the best at allowing the representation of the interests that really stir society."

Postauthoritarian Chile displays a transparent manipulation of district magnitude. There are two legislative seats per district (in other words, $M = 2$). The first seat goes to the party with the highest number of votes—a plurality. To win the second seat, however, the first-place party has to win at least twice the vote of the second-place party. Hence, the system favors the second-largest vote getter. This was not a mistake; it was an integral part of the country's "pacted" transition toward democracy. According to one prominent analyst, "The system was designed so that parties of the Right, with only one-third of the vote, could aspire to gaining half of the seats."[15] In the 1990 congressional elections, for instance, parties of the Center received forty-three seats, the Left got twenty-nine, and the Right emerged with thirty-eight seats. (Recall Schmitter and O'Donnell's observation in Chapter 2 that posttransition regimes might need to "cheat" to favor the Right.)

An additional question concerns the structure of the ballot, which in turn reflects the level of party control over nomination procedures. One common form is a "closed list," prevalent in Western Europe, under which voters cast ballots not for individual candidates but for political parties. Seats then go to individuals in the order in which their names appear on internal party lists. (In a case in which $M = 3$, for instance, the number one candidate from Party X has a much better chance of winning a seat than the number three candidate.) The closed-list system is used in Argentina, Central America, and Peru and was a bastion of power for party bosses in Venezuela up until the reform of 1993.

An alternative is the "open list," which allows voters to cast their ballots for individual candidates from competing parties. This gives voters greater choice, and it weakens the strength of party bosses. In Colombia, for instance, individuals can now use a party label to run for office merely by compiling signatures and paying a registration fee, without any input from the party hierarchy. And in Brazil, it is understood that incumbents have a guaranteed "right" to run for reelection, whether party leaders want them to do so or not.

What difference does it make? The argument is that even at this level of detail, institutional design has a significant impact on the quality of political

---

[15] Arturo Valenzuela, "Party Politics and the Crisis of Presidentialism in Chile," in Juan J. Linz and Arturo Valenzuela, eds., *The Failure of Presidential Democracy: The Case of Latin America* (Baltimore: Johns Hopkins University Press, 1994), 114.

This closed-list ballot from Venezuela in the 1990s presented voters with each party's name, logo, and presidential candidate. The larger ballot was for the presidential election; the smaller one served for both houses of the legislature. Congressional votes were cast for parties, not individuals—and there were over thirty parties in this race!

representation. At question is whether the ultimate interests of legislators concern (1) policy issues, (2) clientelistic relations with voters, or (3) promotion of their parties. On the one hand, exclusive promotion of personal followings leads legislators to concentrate on particularistic goods and services—"pork," such as public works—that tend to be costly and inefficient. On the other hand, slavish devotion to party machineries increases the distance between legislators and the districts they represent. Both of these extremes distract attention from broad questions of national policy.

One broad-based study has concluded that given widespread use of closed-list ballots, Latin American electoral systems offer little incentive for legislators to serve constituents—less than in Asia, Africa, and Eastern Europe. "The evidence suggests that politicians in Latin America have more incentives to be on good terms with party leaders than do politicians anywhere else in the world. So Latin American parties are strong in this particular sense—they hold the keys to political power."[16] The implication, however, is that they use this power to maintain their positions of strength

---

[16] Inter-American Development Bank, *Development Beyond Economics: Economic and Social Progress in Latin America* (Washington, DC: Johns Hopkins University Press for the Inter-American Development Bank, 2000), 175.

An open-list ballot for a senate election in Colombia offers a dizzying array of individual candidates—with multiple candidates from the same parties. Voters could cast their ballots for only one candidate. Confusing!

rather than to serve constituents or to formulate serious positions on issues of national import.

Still another significant factor is the degree of malapportionment—in other words, the extent to which voters are over- or underrepresented in the overall distribution of legislative seats. This is a common problem in contemporary democracies. In the United States, for instance, it is widely thought (and confirmed by demographic studies) that inner cities do not have as much representation in legislative bodies as they rightfully should. And if it is severe, malapportionment can have serious impacts on policy and politics. It tends to promote a distinctive rural and conservative bias, it can lead to estrangement between executive and legislative branches, it can enable local bosses to hold national governments hostage on important policy issues, and, by rewarding districts with minimal competition, it can preserve and protect authoritarian enclaves at local and regional levels.

A recent study reveals that malapportionment is rampant in Latin America and much higher than in other parts of the world. Argentina's senate is the most malapportioned legislative chamber in the world; Ecuador's lower chamber is the third-most malapportioned lower chamber in the world. High levels of malapportionment also exist in Bolivia, Brazil, Chile, and Colombia. One effect has been ideological imbalance. In the 1998 congressional elections in Brazil, for instance, leftist parties captured 26 percent of all votes but earned only 22 percent of the seats. In Argentina, the persistent overrepresentation of rural districts in the lower chamber has protected the Peronist party and its conservative allies.[17] At least in Latin America, malapportionment favors the forces of reaction. In some cases, this situation might result from patterns of demographic concentration or dispersion; in others, it might constitute implicit elements of transitional pacts.

In addition, electoral cycles can have important consequences for legislative–executive relations. When elections are concurrent—that is, when voters cast ballots for president and representatives at the same time—the results tend to strengthen the president's support in the congress. When they are asynchronous—as with midterm elections in the United States— outcomes tend to weaken the executive's hand. And the greater the distance in time from the beginning of a presidential term, the less the support for the president.[18]

This brings back the question of MRO formulas for presidential election. As a matter of tradition, legislative elections are usually concurrent with the *first round* of the presidential election. This tends to attract small parties, as indicated earlier, especially because they might be able to win some seats under proportional representation. But as John M. Carey has pointed out, this provision can also lead to gridlock and immobilism: "To the extent that MRO contributes to fragmentation of the legislative party system...it makes legislative coalition building more difficult and thus undermines the ability of its presidents to act."[19]

Reelection and Term Limits

Legislators react, in part, to prospects for reelection. It is widely believed that reelection makes it possible for legislators to develop expertise, build relationships among themselves, concentrate on long-term issues, and, perhaps most important, achieve autonomy from party leaders and chief executives. Low reelection rates tend to impede the professionalization of legislatures. In most Latin American countries, reelection is legal but relatively rare, ranging from 59 percent in Chile, to 43 percent in Brazil, to 17 percent in Argentina, compared with 83 percent in the United States. This situation reveals a vicious circle: if legislatures are weak, members will be inclined to move on to more important positions instead of seeking reelection; if reelection rates are very low, legislatures will remain weak.

---

[17] Richard Snyder and David Samuels, "Devaluing the Vote in Latin America," *Journal of Democracy* 12, no. 1 (January 2001): 146–159; see also David Samuels and Richard Snyder, "The Value of a Vote: Malapportionment in Comparative Perspective," *British Journal of Political Science*, 31, no. 4 (October 2001): 651–667.

[18] See Matthew S. Shugart, "The Electoral Cycle and Institutional Sources of Divided Government," *American Political Science Review*, 89, no. 2 (June 1995): 327–343.

[19] Carey, "Institutional Design and Party Systems," 72–73.

Strict term limits can have especially deleterious effects. The most conspicuous case is Mexico, where members of the lower house serve three-year terms without the possibility of consecutive election. As a result, deputies tend to focus their energies not on policy issues but on searches for their next positions. Under the traditional system, this meant that they were utterly beholden to the president and to the PRI; term limits strengthened the control of central party leaders over rank-and-file legislators. Under democratic governments since the year 2000, it has led to populist grandstanding and resolute obstructionism. The only other case is Costa Rica, where a ban on legislative reelection was adopted by a post–civil war constituent assembly in the 1940s. Costa Rica resembles Mexico in the sense that ambitious deputies seek postlegislative political career opportunities through executive branch appointments, so they are dependent on presidential patronage. It differs from Mexico, however, because incumbent presidents do not control appointments, and, in view of intense electoral competition, it is never clear who the next president will be. In consequence, legislators look out for themselves, and party discipline is weak. As the leader of one party lamented, "Because of term limits...I have no stick to beat anyone with."

Faced with such incentives, up-and-coming legislators do not always want to make their voting records public. To the extent that they depend on presidential largesse for future career enhancement, they are reluctant to take sides on controversial measures—and then be held accountable.

As a result, roll-call voting, with formal tallies of individual yeas and nays, is uncommon. The traditional means of expressing the will of the chamber, still widely used in Latin America, is "signal voting"—raising hands, standing up to be counted, or pounding on desks (loudest noise wins). Such procedures allow legislators to preserve anonymity and avoid responsibility. In "public voting," by contrast, the roll is called and each position recorded. Depending on the country, name-by-name votes (*votaciones nominales*) can be requested by either a handful of legislators or a majority of those present. In view of the logistics, manual tallies have turned out to be cumbersome, time-consuming, and inconvenient.

Then came electronic voting machines, first installed in Costa Rica in the mid-1970s. Electronic systems were thereafter adopted with the restoration of democracy in Argentina, Brazil, and Chile. Colombia, Mexico, Panama, and Peru soon followed suit. Yet the machinery has been unevenly employed. Colombia, Costa Rica, and Venezuela have never put their equipment to use. In Peru the issue came to a head in 1998, when an exasperated opposition delegate demanded utilization ("It's an instrument of democracy and transparency....It has to be used, sir"). And with or without electronic machines, voting records are not always made public. Argentina and Nicaragua bury results in congressional archives. The Mexican Senate posts votes on the Internet but only overnight. "In Latin America," as John Carey has observed, "recorded voting is negligible in the absence of electronic voting. It is increasingly common—but not a given—where electronic systems reduce procedural costs."[20] Clientelistic norms and arcane rules conspire to impede public scrutiny.

The rhetorical rationale for secrecy is that it helps insulate legislators from outside pressures, either from the people or the president, and permits them to reach decisions on the basis of personal commitment and mutual enlightenment. In other words, it protects legislative autonomy. The underlying reason, of course, is protection of the legislators. It eliminates accountability, promotes duplicity, and fosters opportunism.

Institutional Performance

What do legislatures do? Have they become more effective? Has the current (post-1978) cycle of democratization in Latin America brought about significant changes in the roles and functions of legislative bodies?

Recent research has begun to explore the workings of Latin American legislatures with rigor and detail. It shows that congressional bodies have played positive roles in dealing with tax reform (Mexico and Argentina), promoting economic reform (Brazil), and uncovering corruption (Brazil, again). The general view, however, is that Latin American legislatures still tend to be "reactive" rather than "proactive."[21]

In the case of Argentina, Ana María Mustapic has argued that congress has the ability to amend, delay, or veto executive proposals. Both Raúl Alfonsín and Carlos Saúl Menem faced congressional opposition during at least part of their presidential terms. Alfonsín won approval for 69 percent of the bills he presented to congress, and Menem managed to pass 60 percent of his proposals. These are high rates of executive success. Yet they also mean that 30 to 40 percent of presidential initiatives were not approved, indicating a substantial degree of legislative autonomy from the executive branch. To some extent, this was overridden by Menem's extensive use of *decretos de urgencia y necesidad*, as described earlier, but it nonetheless shows that Argentina's legislature had a will of its own.

Up to the mid-1990s, the same could not be said of the Mexican congress. Although the legislature has considerable law-making and law-checking authority, according to the constitution, representatives did not exercise their power during the reign of the PRI. And the PRI, it should be remembered, was a highly disciplined party with centralized control over nominations; the president of the nation functioned as president of the party, which gave him a nearly infinite reserve of partisan powers; and the prohibition on reelection made it impossible for deputies to carve out legislative careers.

---

[20] John M. Carey, *Legislative Voting and Accountability* (New York: Cambridge University Press, 2009), Ch. 3, with quote on 65.

[21] See Scott Morgenstern and Benito Nacif, eds., *Legislative Politics in Latin America* (Cambridge: Cambridge University Press, 2002).

The increasing presence of opposition parties in the late 1990s led to greater congressional activism. Passage of bills proposed by legislators, rather than by the executive, jumped from 7 percent in 1982–1985 to 20 percent in 1997–2000. President Ernesto Zedillo thus found himself obliged to negotiate with, instead of ignore, the opposition. As María Amparo Casar reports, "These developments showed that Congress—especially the Chamber of Deputies—was beginning to acquire an importance that would not have been dreamt of just a few years earlier."[22]

With its legacy of multiparty politics, Chile presents yet another scenario. During the 1990s, presidents worked hard (and made concessions) to maintain the ruling coalition of the *Concertación*. They respected the role of the oppositionist Right, and they were mindful of the need to uphold a delicate balance in executive–legislative relations. They did not abuse decree authority.

Even so, the Chilean congress has displayed only modest initiative. During the presidency of Patricio Aylwin (1990–1994), the executive branch submitted 637 bills, while legislators presented only 529. Out of more than 400 bills that were passed into law, more than 90 percent originated in the executive branch. Especially telling is the subject matter of the thirty-three bills submitted by legislators that gained final approval. They dealt with the establishment of monuments to political and literary figures and the designation of holidays (to be sure, these could be significant gestures of national reconciliation). They established criteria for local scholarships. They delegated power or authority to the president or cabinet ministers in specific areas. "The rest of the laws dealt with issues of national scope," according to Peter Siavelis, "although not necessarily with issues of the same magnitude that characterized executive initiatives.... The only real significant legislation proposed by members of Congress was that of raising the legal age of adulthood, and some substantial changes to the penal code."[23] This is pretty trivial stuff.

On balance, Latin American legislatures thus tend to be reactive. With the exception of pre-1997 Mexico, however, they are not subservient—they are mostly "workable," to borrow a phrase from Scott Morgenstern and Gary Cox, and sometimes "recalcitrant." Most countries of the region would probably fit somewhere within these categories at different points in time. Venezuela under Chávez would qualify as being subservient, as might some of the Central American cases; Ecuador and Peru have been recalcitrant at times; and, despite its state of continuing crisis, Colombia has been mostly workable.

---

[22] Ma. Amparo Casar, "Executive-Legislative Relations: The Case of Mexico (1946–1997)," in Morgenstern and Nacif, *Legislative Politics*, 130.

[23] Peter M. Siavelis, "Exaggerated Presidentialism and Moderate Presidents: Executive-Legislative Relations in Chile," in Morgenstern and Nacif, *Legislative Politics*, 88–89.

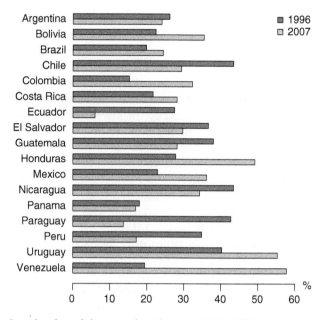

Figure 6.1 Levels of confidence in legislatures, 1996–2007

Note: Scales depict percentages expressing "some" or "a lot" of confidence in national legislatures.

Source: Latinobarómetro.

According to public opinion surveys, the people of Latin America regard their national legislatures with only modest esteem. Figure 6.1 presents data on the proportions of respondents expressing "some" or "a lot" of confidence in congressional institutions through surveys in 1996 and 2007. In 1996 the highest score went to Nicaragua, with 43 percent approval, and the lowest was in Panama, with only 18 percent. Among major countries, Brazil, Colombia, and Venezuela had less than 20 percent, Argentina and Mexico had less than 30 percent, and Peru had less than 40 percent. The average score was 29 percent.

Although scores shifted for individual countries over the subsequent decade—increasing in eight countries, declining in nine—the overall pattern was almost unchanged. After a full decade of democratic politics, the average approval score as of 2007 came to merely 30 percent. Scores had declined in Peru, Chile, and Argentina, while climbing upward in Brazil, Mexico, and Venezuela. Generally speaking, legislatures throughout the region had not gained great prestige.

Toppling Presidents?

Such findings might appear to contradict one of the most visible trends of the 1990s, the removal of elected presidents from constitutional office by extraordinary legislative action—impeachment or "quasi-impeachment." As Carey has noted, "one could argue that the assertion of legislative authority over the executive marks a regional resurgence of checks and balances over *presidencialismo*."[24]

Legislatures succeeded in removing three incumbent executives. One instance occurred in Brazil in 1992, when President Fernando Collor de Mello chose to resign after being impeached by the lower house for corruption and while facing certain conviction in the Senate. In Venezuela the following year, the congress removed Carlos Andrés Pérez from office on charges of misappropriation and embezzlement. And in Ecuador, the legislature in 1997 voted to remove Abdalá Bucaram from the presidency for "mental incompetence" and installed congressional president Fabio Alarcón as chief executive. In all three cases, it should be noted, there was widespread opposition to presidential efforts to impose neoliberal economic austerity programs.

On other occasions, presidents either prevailed or survived. In Peru and Venezuela, Alberto Fujimori (in 1992) and Hugo Chávez (in 1999) succeeded in disbanding the incumbent legislatures; through such actions, both leaders went on to impose "semidemocratic" political systems. In Colombia, the lower house voted in 1996 not to pursue the well-founded allegation that President Ernesto Samper had accepted drug trafficking money for use in his election campaign. In Nicaragua, assembly opponents charged President Arnoldo Alemán with corruption and illegal enrichment but failed to muster sufficient votes.

What accounts for this phenomenon? First, efforts to remove chief executives emerged within divided governments, in which presidents could not command congressional majorities. Divided government was a necessary but not sufficient condition for effective impeachment or quasi-impeachment proceedings. Second, accusations of corruption were common but failed to gain the ouster of two of the most conspicuous offenders, Samper and Alemán. (And even in Brazil, Collor was later acquitted by the Supreme Court because the overwhelming evidence against him was acquired illegally.) Third, as already mentioned, disagreements over economic policy played fundamental parts in the removals of Collor, Pérez, and Bucaram.

These episodes convey ambiguous messages about expansion of congressional authority.[25] They demonstrate that under certain circumstances, legislatures possess the capacity to remove unpopular executives, but they cannot

---

[24] John M. Carey, "Presidentialism and Representative Institutions," in Jorge I. Domínguez and Michael Shifter, eds., *Constructing Democratic Governance in Latin America*, 2d ed. (Baltimore: Johns Hopkins University Press, 2003), 12.

[25] Here I focus only on instances where legislatures played primary roles; in some cases the congress merely confirmed or acquiesced in decisions. For a full inventory see Carey, "Presidentialism," 23–24.

always do so, even when charges against the presidents appear compelling at face value. Whether they ought to be in the business of removing chief executives is another question. On the contrary, it could be argued that democratic presidents should have the opportunity to govern if their elections were free and fair.

In retrospect, Latin America's legislatures have made substantial advances over earlier eras, but perhaps not as many as one might expect. Those legislatures that functioned under electoral democracy in the years between 1940 and 1977—in Brazil, Chile, Costa Rica, Colombia, and Venezuela—were also "reactive" in many respects. They made few laws, but they provided a public forum for debate, discussion, and criticism. In Brazil and especially Chile, too, they were capable of paralyzing the executive and (unintentionally) contributing to democratic breakdown.

PARTIES AND PARTY SYSTEMS

Like legislatures, political parties of Latin America have only recently become the object of sustained scholarly analysis. Parties acquired new relevance (and opportunities) with the post-1978 expansion of electoral democracy. Popular disenchantment with economic conditions encouraged the formation of dissident opposition parties, while traditional machines, most conspicuously in Mexico and Venezuela, suffered from vociferous splinter movements.

Taking the Measure of Parties

One of the most striking features of party systems in Latin America is their diversity and breadth. From the 1950s through the 1990s Mexico displayed a dominant-party system, Chile and Brazil had extensive multiparty systems, and the continuing democracies—Colombia, Costa Rica, and Venezuela—came close to having two-party systems. As the twentieth century drew to a close, the number of "effective" parties ranged from 2.0 in Chile to more than 7.1 in Brazil. According to Table 6.3, nine countries had two or three effective parties; five countries had between three and five; and four countries, including Brazil, displayed more than five. (See Box 6.2 for a technical definition of effective political parties.)

As important as it is, the measurable expanse of a party system—that is, the effective number of parties—constitutes only one element. Equally significant is its quality, what Scott Mainwaring and Timothy Scully have defined as the level of "institutionalization." As they argue,

> Whether or not an institutionalized party system exists makes a big difference in the functioning of democratic politics. It is difficult to sustain modern mass democracy without an institutionalized party system. The nature of parties and party systems shapes the prospects that stable democracy

TABLE 6.3 Effective Numbers of Political Parties, 1996–2000

Effective Number of Parties	
< 3.0	
Chile	2.01*
Honduras	2.18
Paraguay	2.27
Dominican Republic	2.32
Guatemala	2.35
Mexico	2.55
Argentina	2.56
Costa Rica	2.56
Nicaragua	2.79
3.0–5.0	
Uruguay	3.07
Colombia	3.17
Panama	3.26
Venezuela	3.44
El Salvador	3.47
Peru	3.97
> 5.0	
Bolivia	5.36
Ecuador	5.73
Brazil	7.13
Average	3.34

Note: Calculations based on distribution of seats in the lower chamber.

*The *Concertación* coalition is here treated as a single party; with member parties counted as separate entities, the figure for Chile rises to 5.08.

Source: "Party Systems and Democratic Governability," in J. Mark Payne et al., *Democracies in Development: Politics and Reform in Latin America* (Inter-American Development Bank: Washington, DC, 2002), 145; see also Scott Mortgenstern and Javier Vázquez-D'Elía, "Electoral Laws, Parties, and Party Systems in Latin America," *Annual Review of Political Science*, 10 (2007): 143–168.

will emerge, whether it will be accorded legitimacy, and whether effective policy-making will result.[26]

After all, democratic governments are elected through parties. Through the use of labels and platforms, parties help citizens make their choices in the polling booths (in technical terms, they "reduce information costs" for voters). Parties offer vehicles for expressing, channeling, and aggregating interests of citizens and groups. And they often serve as training grounds for future leaders.

To achieve high levels of institutionalization, parties should exhibit (1) a relatively stable base of electoral support over time, (2) relatively strong and deep roots in society, and (3) a popular perception that they are central

---

[26] Scott Mainwaring and Timothy R. Scully, eds., *Building Democratic Institutions: Party Systems in Latin America* (Stanford, CA: Stanford University Press, 1995), 1–2.

BOX 6.2

COUNTING POLITICAL PARTIES

This ought to be a simple matter: Find a list of registered parties and count them up. But what if one party wins all the time? Is a party that wins 3 to 5 percent of the votes the same as a party that wins 45 to 50 percent? To deal with such questions Markku Laakso and Rein Taagepera developed an index to measure the "effective" number of political parties, N. Its formula is:

$$N = 1/\Sigma p_i^2$$

where p_i is the proportion of votes earned by the i-th party. (Alternatively, it can stand for the proportion of seats earned in the legislature.)

So if two parties each win 50 percent of the vote, the index comes out to

$$N = 1/(.25 + .25) = 2$$

meaning that two parties are equally "effective" at winning votes.

But if one party wins 80 percent of the vote and the other gets 20 percent, the index comes out to

$$N = 1/(.64 + .04) = 1.47$$

showing that one party is very effective, and the other one is not.

In all cases in which the parties are exactly equal, the effective number will be the same as the raw numerical count. When the parties are not equal in strength, the effective number will be lower than the raw number.

and positive elements in the political process. On the basis of such criteria, Mainwaring and Scully determined that there were relatively "high" levels of party institutionalization by the early 1990s in five countries: Costa Rica, Chile, Uruguay, Venezuela, and Colombia. They found "intermediate" levels for party systems in three countries: Argentina, Mexico, and Paraguay. And they detected "low" levels of institutionalization in four countries: Bolivia, Ecuador, Brazil, and Peru, which could be described as having "inchoate" party systems.[27] These are meaningful differences:

> Where the party system is more institutionalized, parties are key actors that structure the political process; where it is less institutionalized, parties are not so dominant, they do not structure the political process as much, and politics tend to be less institutionalized and therefore more unpredictable. Democratic politics is more erratic, establishing legitimacy is more difficult, and governing is more complicated. Powerful economic elites tend to have privileged access to policy makers. In the absence of well-developed institutional checks and balances, patrimonial practices often prevail, and legislatures tend to be weakly developed.[28]

---

[27] They include strength of party organization as a fourth criterion; it is operationalized in an impressionistic manner.
[28] Mainwaring and Scully, *Building Democratic Institutions*, 22.

TABLE 6.4 Structures of Party Systems, Mid-1990s

Level of Institutionalization	N Parties[a]		
	< 3.0	3.0–5.0	> 5.0
Low		Bolivia	Peru Ecuador Brazil
Medium	Argentina Mexico Paraguay		
High	Costa Rica Colombia	Uruguay Venezuela	Chile

[a]Number of parties based on Laakso-Taagepera index, calculated according to shares of seats in lower chamber of legislature. Participants in the Chilean *Concertación* are here treated as separate parties.

Source: Adapted from Scott Mainwaring and Timothy R. Scully, eds., *Building Democratic Institutions: Party Systems in Latin America* (Stanford, CA: Stanford University Press, 1995), 17, 30.

Moreover, inchoate party systems frequently make room for demagogic personalism and antisystem populism. They impede accountability and encourage corruption.

Table 6.4 presents summary data on levels of institutionalization and effective numbers of political parties in key countries of Latin America by the mid-1990s. It reveals a clear and negative association: The higher the number of parties, the lower the level of institutionalization. Of the four countries with five or more effective parties, three showed the lowest level of institutionalization; among the five countries with fewer than three parties, none displayed low levels of institutionalization, three had medium levels, and two had high levels. Yet it also shows that high levels of institutionalization can coexist with a fairly high number of parties, Chile being the clearest example.[29] To put it another way, the sheer number of parties does not completely determine the level of institutionalization.[30]

Gauging Public Distrust

As for legislatures, public opinion surveys offer direct means of assessing voter attachment to parties. Figure 6.2 displays the proportion of Latin American citizens expressing "some" or "a lot of" confidence in political parties in 1996 and 2007. The results are startling. In both years, the

---

[29] Member parties in the then-ruling coalition are here counted as separate parties; if the *Concertación* is treated as a single entity, the number of effective parties for Chile approximates 2.0 (see Table 6.3).

[30] There is considerable uncertainty over the "optimal" number of political parties in presidential regimes. Some analysts favor two-party systems; others think that multiparty systems (with, say, three to five parties) would accommodate more interests and promote stability.

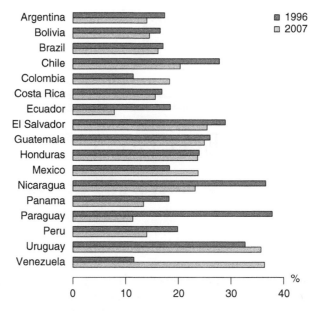

Figure 6.2 Levels of confidence in political parties, 1996–2007

Note: Scales depict percentages expressing "some" or "a lot" of confidence in political parties.

Source: Latinobarómetro.

average score hovered around 20 percent. Confidence was greatest—and most enduring—in Uruguay. It increased strongly in Venezuela, where Hugo Chávez had undertaken to dismantle the traditional party system and create an entirely new scheme, and in Mexico, which became a democracy during the interim period. Everywhere else, citizen confidence plummeted, from a temporary high of more than 35 percent in Paraguay to just over 10 percent, from nearly 20 percent in Peru to less than 15 percent, from 18 percent in Ecuador to less a dismal 8 percent, from 28 percent in Chile to 20 percent, and from 17 percent in Argentina to 13 percent. Brazil held even around 16 to 17 percent.

To conclude, these findings paint a discouraging picture of political parties in Latin America. Most showed low levels of institutionalization. And of the four "highly" institutionalized party systems in the mid-1990s, two would suffer serious setbacks. Frontally challenged by Hugo Chávez, traditional parties would collapse almost completely in Venezuela; undermined by changes in electoral rules, traditional parties would decline in salience and authority in Colombia. Outside of Chile, Costa Rica, and Uruguay, political parties were not providing effective channels of popular representation. This condition could severely compromise the quality of democracy throughout the region.

CHAPTER 7

ELECTIONS

Voters, Winners, and Losers

Elections are the hallmark of democracy. They provide regular opportunities for people to choose their political leaders. Elections thus enshrine the basic tenets of democracy: the principle of competition, as candidates strive to win office and authority; the principle of participation, as citizens join together in the selection of leaders and programs; and the principle of accountability, as voters cast judgment on the performance of rulers and their parties.[1] There can be elections without democracy, as in the case of fraudulent or rubber-stamp ratification of authoritarian regimes, but there cannot be democracy without free and fair elections. As one authority has written, "There is a widespread consensus that the presence of competitive elections, more than any other feature, identifies a contemporary nation-state as a democratic political system."[2]

This chapter examines elections in contemporary Latin America. One set of questions concerns the quality of the process. How democratic are these elections in practice? The analysis explores three general issues—voter turnout, levels of competition, and ideological breadth. Do people take advantage of the opportunity to vote? How contested are elections? What is the range of platforms and ideas? A second set of questions relates to governance. Here the analysis focuses on three additional themes—governmental turnover, divided government, and political gridlock. Once election returns are in hand, what are the prospects for governance?

The analysis traces electoral patterns in Latin America from the 1940s to the present. It was in the era around World War II that suffrage became

---

[1] Accountability is only partially observed through elections; it is most explicit in cases of reelection (or recall, as in Venezuela and the U.S. state of California).
[2] G. Bingham Powell, Jr., *Elections as Instruments of Democracy: Majoritarian and Proportional Visions* (New Haven, CT: Yale University Press, 2000), 4.

available to most adults—at least, most adult males—in a significant number of countries. This provides the basis for the comparison of voting trends and behavior in popular electoral democracies.

This exploration reveals paradoxical results. Although there are significant restrictions in practice, the right to vote is in principle extensive throughout Latin America. Among eligible voters, turnout tends to be strong. In casting their votes, Latin American citizens thus enforce the legitimacy of the democratic system, but they often use their ballots to express disapproval of ruling presidents, parties, and elites. Voting has thus become an institutionalized channel for the expression of popular discontent.

EXPANDING THE ELECTORATE

The right to vote is a keystone of democracy, and it is not to be taken for granted. In Latin America, as in the United States and elsewhere, the extension of suffrage has been a sharply contested political issue. And as might be expected, it has followed distinct rhythms in countries of the region.

During periods of oligarchic competition in the late nineteenth and early twentieth centuries, elections were tightly restricted. For the most part, only members of the propertied elite—landowners in the countryside and professionals in cities, lawyers and merchants among them—possessed the right to vote. On average, just over 2 percent of the population took part in national elections.[3] These were carefully managed affairs.

Signs of change appeared after the turn of the century, but only in a few countries. The earliest and most far-reaching reform occurred in Argentina, where President Roque Sáenz Peña won approval in 1912 for a proposal to extend suffrage to all male adult citizens (at a time when most working-class men were foreign nationals), establish secret balloting, and make voting compulsory. As shown in Figure 7.1, this reform expanded the Argentine electorate to approximately 15 percent of the total population. Other countries lagged substantially behind, including Peru and Chile, also depicted in Figure 7.1. For Latin America as a whole, voters constituted about 5 to 6 percent of the total population during the period 1900–1930.

Expansion followed from the 1940s through the 1960s. Urbanization, industrialization, and a host of associated social transformations led to the emergence of "mass politics" in much of Latin America. Often seeking tactical

---

[3] See Enrique C. Ochoa, "The Rapid Expansion of Voter Participation in Latin America: Presidential Elections, 1845–1986," *Statistical Abstract of Latin America* 25, ed. James W. Wilkie and David Lorey (Los Angeles: UCLA Latin American Center Publications, 1987), 862–910. Calculations are based on entire populations, rather than adult populations, as reliable age breakdowns were not available in most censuses of the time.

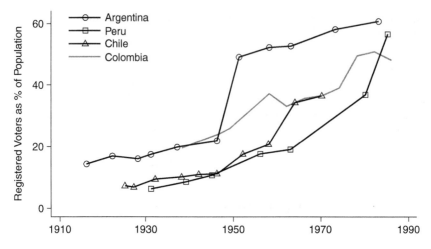

Figure 7.1 Expansion of the electorate: Selected countries

Source: International IDEA Voter Turnout Website.

advantage, rival politicians extended suffrage to burgeoning middle- and lower-class sectors. Such was the case of Colombia, where Liberal politicians abolished literacy requirements in the mid-1930s and introduced universal male suffrage (according to Figure 7.1, nearly 20 percent of the nation's population became eligible to vote). Even where electoral competition was restrained by fraud or otherwise subject to manipulation, as in Mexico and Brazil, populist leaders granted rights to vote in order to consolidate the social foundations of their regimes. In addition, the second cycle of democratization led to intensive electoral competition in Costa Rica, Venezuela, Brazil, and other countries of the region.

As elementary arithmetic would suggest, extension of the vote to women virtually doubled the size of the electorate. Ecuador took this step as early as 1929. Four other countries, including Brazil and Cuba, followed suit during the 1930s. Seven countries, including Chile, Venezuela, and Argentina, did so in the 1940s, as did seven more, including Mexico, in the 1950s. Paraguay was the last to comply in 1961.

As revealed in Table 7.1, a comparison of voter participation before and after the reform shows that women's suffrage had an enormous impact on voter turnout. On average, according to one set of calculations, women's suffrage increased the effective number of voters by nearly 140 percent! This could have been due to several factors: in demographic terms, women tend to outnumber men; in political terms, they might have voted at higher rates than men, especially in their first opportunity to exercise the suffrage; and campaign issues might have galvanized electorates in general. It is also conceivable that willful women persuaded, cajoled, challenged, or otherwise convinced more men to take part as well.

TABLE 7.1 Impact of Women's Suffrage on Voter Participation

Country	Year of Women's Suffrage	% Change in Voter Participation
Argentina	1947	+146.0
Bolivia	1952	+705.0
Brazil	1932	+509.0
Chile	1949	+77.6
Colombia	1957	+108.7
Costa Rica	1949	+63.1
Dominican Republic	1942	+63.1
Ecuador	1929	−50.0
El Salvador	1939	+258.0
Guatemala	1945	+31.1
Haiti	1950	+443.5
Honduras	1955	+46.1
Mexico	1953	+69.5
Nicaragua	1955	+61.8
Panama	1945	+29.5
Paraguay	1961	−9.3
Peru	1955	+113.0
Uruguay	1932	−73.9
Venezuela	1947	+53.8

Source: Enrique C. Ochoa, "The Rapid Expansion of Voter Participation in Latin America: Presidential Elections, 1845–1986," *Statistical Abstract of Latin America* 25, ed. James W. Wilkie and David Lorey (Los Angeles: UCLA Latin American Center Publications, 1987), 904.

Although women's electoral participation would mark a crucial step on the path toward democracy, it was often the autocrats, not democrats, who initially opted for women's suffrage. They were seeking to mobilize and organize new bases of political support. Such was the case in Argentina under Perón, the Dominican Republic under Trujillo, El Salvador under Hernández Martinez, Mexico under the PRI, Nicaragua under Somoza, and Paraguay under Stroessner. Wives of the autocrats suddenly became "first ladies" with symbolic and sometimes extensive roles in the creation of women's organizations. Eva Duarte de Perón in Argentina was perhaps the most glamorous such figure, but she was by no means the only one. In more recent times, Lucía Hiriart Rodríguez de Pinochet in Chile played an important role in mobilizing support groups for the dictatorship among upper- and middle-class women.

Mandatory voting proved to be another double-edged sword. In principle, it upheld the idea that citizens have a responsibility to engage in democratic processes. Such was the spirit behind compulsory voting rules that have been in place in Argentina since 1912, Chile since 1958, and Peru since 1963. In practice, though, mandatory voting often became a pretext for legitimation of undemocratic or fraudulent elections. In the absence of meaningful competition, it permitted autocrats to claim that their elections (or reelections) were based on extensive participation of the populace, thus fulfilling at least part of the basic criteria for political democracy. Revealingly enough, voting was mandatory under patently nondemocratic regimes in Mexico, Paraguay, and much of Central America.[4]

By the 1980s, as the third and current cycle of democratization was getting under way, eligibility requirements for voting were relatively uniform throughout Latin America. Suffrage was generally available to all adult citizens, female and male. The minimum age tended to vary between eighteen and twenty-one. There were no property requirements and, in most nations, no literacy requirements (in Brazil, illiterates had the right to vote, but they were not obliged to exercise that right). Active-duty members of the military and the police were not allowed to vote in many countries. Voting was mandatory in most countries but abstention was rarely subject to punishment. In theory, national electorates were thus open and expansive.

Yet there were significant restrictions in practice. Almost everywhere, citizens could vote only if they were formally registered. The process of voter registration could be cumbersome, slow, bureaucratic, and socially biased. In Chile before 1962, potential voters could register only during a two-hour period on eight prescribed days each month. Here is a description of Colombia:

> Months before the election prospective voters must assure that their national identification cards are in order. If they wish to vote anywhere other than the place where the card was issued they must go through a separate procedure. On election day all roads are closed, so that persons who need to vote in their hometowns must take three days off in order to vote. Furthermore, the actual casting of the vote is an elaborate procedure.[5]

Despite such obstacles, more than 60 percent of Argentina's population possessed the right to vote by the early 1980s, according to Figure 7.1, as did more than 50 percent of the population in Brazil, Costa Rica, Chile, and elsewhere. In some countries, however, the registration rate was extremely low: less than 30 percent in Bolivia and less than 40 percent in El Salvador and Guatemala. Not surprisingly, perhaps, indigenous populations were sharply underrepresented on the electoral rolls.

PARTICIPATION

Turnout is a major issue. When citizens vote, they exercise the right to select political leaders, and, in so doing, they confer legitimacy on the electoral

---

[4] Countries with compulsory voting now include Argentina, Brazil, Chile, Costa Rica, the Dominican Republic, Ecuador, El Salvador, Guatemala, Honduras, Mexico, Paraguay, Peru, Uruguay, and Venezuela. Panama, Colombia, and Bolivia do not have such provisions.

[5] John A. Peeler, *Latin American Democracies* (Chapel Hill: University of North Carolina Press, 1985), 97–98.

process itself. When they abstain, either because of disinterest or disenchantment, they dilute the competitive process and undermine the legitimacy of the outcome. The greater the turnout, ceteris paribus, the stronger the democracy.

As in other parts of the world, voter participation varies with type of election. As "presidential" regimes, countries of Latin America hold elections for chief executives who serve fixed terms in office. Most nations also have bicameral legislatures, with a directly elected upper chamber (usually called a senate) that is endowed with constitutional authority comparable to that of the lower chamber (usually called a chamber of deputies or representatives). And throughout the region, the composition of the legislature—especially the lower house—is based on some form of proportional representation (PR).

Among registered voters, participation has been strong in much of Latin America. In many countries of the region, turnout in presidential elections (as a share of registered voters) has customarily exceeded 70 or even 80 percent. This stands in sharp contrast to the United States, where turnout has generally hovered around 55 percent.

Table 7.2 presents data on registration and turnout in presidential elections for eighteen countries of Latin America in 1988–1990.[6] Five nations—Argentina, Brazil, Costa Rica, Chile, and Uruguay—displayed "high" levels of voter registration (more than half the total population) and "high" levels of turnout (more than three quarters of registered voters). At the other extreme, six countries, including Colombia and Mexico, showed low rates of registration and participation: Only one fifth to one quarter of the population was taking part in national elections.[7] Even where turnout was high, as in Bolivia, modest rates of registration led to effective restrictions on suffrage.

Historical perspective sheds further light on this phenomenon. One of the most striking findings is that, as a share of registered voters, average levels of turnout in democratic (and semidemocratic) elections were generally as high during the 1940–1977 cycle as in the 1978–2000 phase, and sometimes perceptibly higher. Average turnout in Argentina was 86 percent during 1940–1977 and 82 percent in 1978–2000; in Brazil, turnout was 77 percent during 1940–1977 and 84 percent during 1978–2000; in Chile, the respective figures were 84 percent and 92 percent. In Venezuela, by contrast, average turnout was 95 percent during the 1940–1977 cycle and only 74 percent in 1978–2000; and in Guatemala, where restrictions on voting had long been acute, average participation was 61 percent among registered voters in the first period and 45 percent in the second. It is to be noted, as well, that several countries of the region, Mexico and Nicaragua among them, did not hold democratic or even semidemocratic elections anytime before 1977, so there can be no comparisons over time.

---

[6] Reliable data on Haiti are not available.

[7] These results might be affected by variations in age structure, as countries with high population growth would have large youth cohorts not yet eligible to vote.

TABLE 7.2 Voter Eligibility and Turnout, 1988–1990

	REGISTERED	VOTERS	
	% Population	*% Registered*	*% Population*
Category I: High registration, high turnout			
Argentina	62.7	85.0	53.3
Brazil	55.6	85.6	47.6
Costa Rica	57.9	81.8	47.4
Chile	58.3	94.7	55.2
Uruguay	78.7	88.7	69.8
Category II: High registration, low turnout			
Panama*	51.0	64.0	32.7
Paraguay*	53.5	52.0	27.9
Category III: Low registration, high turnout			
Ecuador	45.4	78.1	35.5
Honduras*	49.3	76.0	37.5
Nicaragua	46.1	86.3	39.8
Peru	45.0	78.3	35.2
Venezuela	49.0	81.9	40.1
Category IV: Low registration, low turnout			
Bolivia	29.8	73.7	21.9
Colombia	46.2	43.5	20.1
Dominican Republic	45.6	59.4	26.9
El Salvador*	35.2	54.7	19.3
Guatemala*	34.4	56.4	19.4
Mexico*	46.0	50.1	23.1

Note: Threshold for registration was 50 percent; for voters, 75 percent (of registered voters). All results refer to presidential (or general) elections.

*Semidemocratic elections.

Source: Dieter Nohlen, ed., *Enciclopedia electoral latinoamericana y del caribe* (San José, Costa Rica: Instituto Interamericano de Derechos Humanos, 1993).

Extending beyond the turn of the century, Figure 7.2 displays data on turnout (as share of the voting-age population) in selected countries over the past decade or so. Uruguay achieved absolutely remarkable levels of more than 90 percent in 1999 and 2004; participation exceeded 80 percent in Brazil in 1998 to 2006, and in both Ecuador and Peru in 2006. Argentina stood well above 70 percent in 1999 and 2007, as did Venezuela in 2006. Bolivia, Chile, and Mexico fell in the 60 to 70 percent range. Among the nations in the table, only Colombia fell below 50 percent (as did Guatemala). In comparison with other regions of the world, including the United States, voter participation in Latin America has been very strong.

What accounts for such high levels of turnout? Part of the explanation lies in provisions for mandatory voting. According to one broad-gauged study, compulsory voting laws increase turnout by about 10 percentage

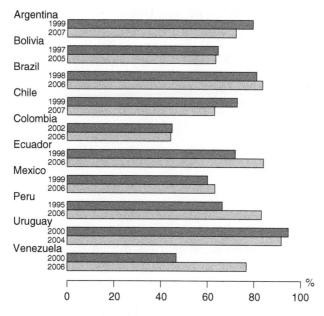

Figure 7.2 Voter turnout in presidential elections, 1997–2007

Source: International IDEA Voter Turnout Website.

points over the average, but because these laws are variably and incompletely enforced, their actual effect is difficult to discern.[8] In addition, elections in Latin America usually take place on Sundays rather than during the week, thus making it easier for working people to vote.

Another factor is societal: The more developed the society, the greater the level of voter participation. Table 7.3 displays correlation coefficients for zero-order relationships between voter turnout (per voting age population) and indicators of socioeconomic development (GNP per capita, percent of school-age children in secondary school, and level of urbanization). The associations are uniformly positive and relatively strong, ranging from +.354 to +.507.[9] It thus appears that there has been a clear "development effect" at work on voter turnout. This connection presumably works in two ways: First, socioeconomic development generates demands for meaningful political participation; second, members of the middle class, fairly prosperous and often well educated, might be more likely to take advantage of the opportunity to vote than less-privileged compatriots.

---

[8] Inter-American Development Bank, *Development Beyond Economics: Economic and Social Progress in Latin America* (Washington, DC: Johns Hopkins Press for the Inter-American Development Bank, 2000), 177.

[9] It was not possible to construct a multiple regression model because of multicollinearity among the social development indicators.

TABLE 7.3 Turnout and Development, 1940–2000

Variable	Time Period	Correlation Coefficient	N Observations
GDP per capita	1940–1977	+.382	50
	1978–2000	+.507	87
	1940–2000	+.475	137
Urban population (%)	1940–2000	+.380	29
	1978–2000	+.383	25
Secondary school enrollment (%)	1940–2000	+.390	29
	1978–2000	+.354	25

Note: Turnout is calculated as (N voters/Voting Age Population) in presidential elections only.

Source: Author's calculations.

These linear relationships apply only to Latin America. According to one study, the worldwide pattern appears to be curvilinear: Voter participation is low in underdeveloped societies, rises during the process of development, and then declines in advanced industrial societies.[10] As a region, Latin America encompasses nations that are either poor or in the process of development. It is entirely conceivable that if and as countries become more advanced and prosperous, levels of voter turnout will decline as a result.

But in the meantime, what accounts for fluctuations over time within individual countries? Some obvious factors are circumstantial or transitory: the intensity of campaigns, the content of platforms, the personalities of candidates, and so on. Among structural determinants, one of the most revealing explanations concerns the novelty of political democracy. In elections that mark the restoration (or initiation) of democracy—so-called "founding elections"—voter turnout tends to be very high. After years of repression, citizens are enthused, eager to express themselves, and anxious to cast their ballots. And major issues often are at stake: the nature of the constitution, the form of civil–military relations, the acceptability of "pacts" reached in the course of transition, and the partisan balance of electoral strength. These are moments of real and imagined "people power." As reality sinks in and issues become more mundane, however, enthusiasm fades, and so does voter turnout.

This pattern is clearly apparent in Table 7.4, which shows trends in voting during founding elections and in subsequent years (and in comparison to voter turnout in the last election prior to the authoritarian interlude). A general pattern emerges: Turnout in founding elections rises to new heights, higher than in the last previous election, and then enters a process of steady decline. Prototypical cases are Chile, where nearly 95 percent of the registered population cast ballots in the founding election of 1989, and Venezuela, where 93 percent of voters took part in the founding election of 1958. But in both countries, turnout then dropped off—drastically in Venezuela, where

---

[10] Inter-American Development Bank, *Development Beyond Economics*, 177.

TABLE 7.4 Founding Elections and Voter Turnout

Country*	Vote as % of Registered Voters in Presidential Elections									
	−1	0	+1	+2	+3	+4	+5	+6	+7	+8
South America										
Argentina (1983)	83.2	83.3	85.0	81.0	78.6					
Brazil (1989)	81.0 (82.3)**	88.1	84.9	78.5						
Chile (1989)	83.5	94.7	90.5	90.6						
Venezuela (1958)	na	93.4	92.3	96.7	96.5	87.5	87.3	81.9	58.3	56.5
Central America										
Costa Rica (1953)	60.0	67.2	64.7	80.9	81.4	83.3	79.9	81.3	78.6	84.9
El Salvador (1989)	72.0	54.7	46.2	38.6						
Guatemala (1990)	60.2	56.4	45.3	36.9	40.4					
Honduras (1981)	67.5	78.0	84.0	76.0	65.0	72.1				
Nicaragua (1984)	69.4	75.4	86.2	76.4						

*Parentheses indicate year of founding election.
**Figures in parentheses refer to turnout in elections of 1982, which determined membership in the electoral college—which decided on the presidency in 1985.
Key: 0 = founding election for democratic regime.
    −1 = last election prior to authoritarian regime.
    +1…+8 = elections subsequent to founding election.

it plummeted to U.S.-style levels in the 1990s. A similar pattern obtained in Brazil. Argentina sustained its high level of voter turnout during the first election subsequent to the founding election, and then began slipping to less than 80 percent.

In other words, voters grow weary of political contests, and, in many cases, disillusionment sets in. As it becomes clear that democratic institutions and even democratic leaders cannot solve long-term problems of economic growth, equity, and development, voters appear to conclude that voting is not worth the trouble. Slick partisan campaigns and get-out-the-vote efforts generally bring only modest improvements in turnout (see Box 7.1). Rising levels of abstention remain a troublesome indicator for contemporary democracy in Latin America.

COMPETITIVENESS

Like participation, competition is a central attribute of authentic democracies. During the course of elections, voters should have meaningful opportunities to select their political leaders. In practice as well as in theory, rival candidates must have plausible chances to prevail. If the conclusion is foregone—if there can be only one winner—the significance of any election is seriously compromised. To be truly democratic, in other words, elections must be truly competitive.

"AMERICANIZING" POLITICAL CAMPAIGNS—UP TO A POINT

During the 1990s many observers reached the conclusion that political campaigns in Latin America were becoming "Americanized"—replete with consultants, pollsters, and spinmeisters, often imported from abroad. Campaigns would emphasize personalities rather than platforms. Media influence would take priority over contacts with voters. Citizenship would become a form of spectatorship. Money, not competence, would become the key to victory.

The 1999–2000 presidential contest in Chile looked like a case in point. With Ricardo Lagos as candidate, the Center-Left *Concertación* recruited consultants from Germany and France; the opposition Center-Right, with Joaquín Lavín as candidate, sought advice from Puerto Rico–based Bruno Haring. Moreover, the conservative Lavín was supported by both main newspaper groups and was able to lavish hospitality on TV journalists and camera crews. The total cost of his campaign was said to be approximately U.S. $120 million, compared with only $40 million for the Lagos team.

On these grounds alone, one might have anticipated a Lavín victory. But as Roberto Espíndola has pointed out, modern and "American" campaign techniques were less decisive than were time-tested tactics:

> Both coalitions fought hard for the traditional ground by which campaigning success has been measured in that country since the 1950s: the streets. All the techniques that characterize professionalized campaigning in the US and Western Europe were there (even the consultants were the same), but the main asset remained the ability to field party activists or "volunteers," to hold mass rallies and to cover every wall, lamp, and any bit of public space with posters or just plain paintings of the candidates names. "Grassroots gladiators"...remain central to campaigns in the Southern Cone.
>
> Candidates may engage in media-staged debates, but nothing has replaced the attraction of the mass rally or the razzmatazz of the candidates' visits to villages or to populous neighborhoods. The campaign becomes the only game in town in a very literal sense, with all forms of commercial marketing adopting electoral themes, showing their centrality to social life. This is particularly the case in Chile, the only Latin American country without a Carnival, where campaign activities are the closest thing to a street party most people experience.

The well-heeled Lavín campaign made intensive use of media and marketing techniques. "On the other hand, the center-left *Concertación*'s campaign style stressed door-to-door canvassing, motorcades, and neighborhood meetings that combined carnival style bands, performances by local artistes, games for children, chess competitions, and free services provided by *Concertación* supporters, from legal, medical and social work advice, to hairdressing and fortune-telling. In other words, the *Concertación* unleashed its infantry." And it won—but by the razor-thin margin of 51.3 percent to 48.7 percent.

Source: Roberto Espíndola, "Electoral Campaigning and the Consolidation of Democracy in Latin America: The Southern Cone" (March 2002).

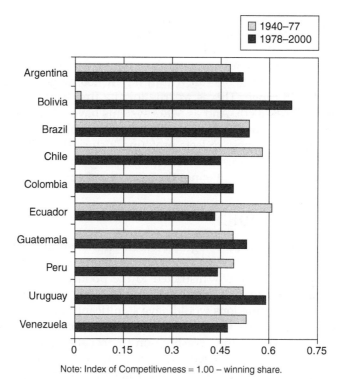

Figure 7.3 Competitiveness in presidential elections, 1940–1977 and 1978–2000

Source: Author's calculations based on data in International IDEA Voter Turnout Website.

What is the record in Latin America? Does the opposition really have a chance to win? These questions will be explored through a simple index: the proportion of the vote for all losing candidates in presidential elections (or, in operational terms, 1.0 minus the winner's share of the vote). Calculated thus, a score of .50 means that the losers received the same total share of the vote as did the winner. A score exceeding .50 means that the winner won only by plurality, not by majority. Any score of more than .40 suggests that the election was reasonably competitive; a score of less than .40 means that the election was lopsided; a score of less than .30 reveals a runaway election that was essentially uncompetitive.

Figure 7.3 presents average competition scores in presidential elections for ten Latin American countries by electoral cycle. In the case of Argentina, for instance, the index rose slightly from .48 in 1940–1977 to .52 in 1978–2000. In Brazil it stayed level, at .54 in both periods; it declined somewhat in Chile, from .58 to .45, as the post-Pinochet *Concertación* came to dominate national elections; and in Venezuela it dropped from .53 to .47 but stayed within a highly competitive range. As a multiparty semidemocracy, Mexico obtained a score of .50.[11] Nicaragua received a modest score of .39, as anti-Sandinista coalitions dominated presidential elections in the 1990s by convincing margins.

The figures suggest that Latin American elections have been quite competitive. Almost all indicators fall within the .40–.60 range, and many fall within the .45–.55 range. This is as true for the first wave (1940–1977) as for the second (1978–2000). And as MRO systems have taken root in recent years, second-round runoff elections have become ubiquitous throughout the region. Competitiveness reflects profound historical traditions in Latin American electoral practices. If there is something new about the current stage of democratic politics, it is not the intensity of competition.

THE RANGE OF CHOICE

Still another issue concerns ideological breadth. How open and inclusive were the contests among political ideas? Were all viewpoints represented? Or were ideological positions narrowly restricted to the political center? What was the ideological spectrum, in other words, and how did it change over time?

Contextual transformations would have significant impacts on the range and content of choices for voters in Latin America. For instance, economic pressures and the rise of the "Washington Consensus" privileged private enterprise and thus strengthened the social base of conservative parties. Around the same time, the end of the Cold War discredited Marxist ideology and, at least in the short run, weakened parties of the political Left.

Statistical analysis (not presented here) has traced average votes for major ideological blocs according to a conventional Left–Right dimension—Left, Center-Left, Center, Center-Right, and Right.[12] The findings contain a rich array of insights. One simply relates to the observable span of ideas within the political arena. It extends all the way from the Left to the Right, from doctrinaire socialism to reactionary conservatism. Ideological contestation in Latin America has been remarkably broad—much broader than in the United States, for example, where Republicans and Democrats cluster around the political center. At least in part, this stems from institutional differences: It is a well-known adage of political science that single-member districts tend to produce two-party systems with centrist tendencies, whereas proportional representation, as in Latin America, encourages the formation of multiparty systems with substantial ideological diversity. The pattern also

---

[11] Calculations do not include the Mexican election of 2000, which Vicente Fox won with a plurality.

[12] Religiously based "Christian" movements (e.g., Christian Democratic parties) are joined together with secular blocs within this Left–Right spectrum. On criteria and methods for the categories see Michael Coppedge, "A Classification of Latin American Political Parties," (Notre Dame, IN: Helen Kellogg Institute for International Studies, Working Paper 244, November 1997).

reflects societal norms: For voters in Latin America, ideas matter as much as interests.

Moreover, the scope of ideology related to the severity of the authoritarian experience and compacts (if any) reached during the course of the transition. There were two rules at work.

Rule 1: The more brutal the prior military regime, the greater the premium on ideological moderation.

Rule 2: The greater the risk of renewed military intervention, the greater the premium on political moderation.

As a result, parties of the Left were likely to soften their discourse, abandon extremist positions, and, in effect, adopt more moderate platforms. And without extremist challenges from the Left, parties of the Right could conduct themselves in more moderate fashion as well. The legacy of dictatorship was a tendency toward ideological centrism.

Impacts of Bureaucratic-Authoritarianism

Bureaucratic-authoritarian (BA) regimes had complex effects. As an initial hypothesis, one might have expected BA interludes to weaken the Left and strengthen the Right. The Left would lose electoral strength as a result of imprisonment or assassination of its leaders and unceasing intimidation of its followers; consistently negative publicity might also diminish its appeal. On the other hand, the Right might be emboldened by the programs and tactics of the military dictatorship, especially if they met with some degree of success. Bureaucratic-authoritarianism would thus lead to electoral realignment.

This was most emphatically the case in Chile. In a country where a socialist candidate had actually won the presidency in 1970, the far-Left bloc dropped from 26.7 percent during the 1940s–1970s cycle to merely 7.0 percent after the reinstitution of democracy, a decline of 19.7 points. In the meantime, parties of the Right increased their average electoral share from 29.4 percent to 35 percent, a gain of more than 5 points. Parties of the Center and Center-Left scored even greater advances, increasing their respective shares by 10 percent and 13 percent. Overall, the electoral pendulum made a decisive swing from the Left toward the Center and the Right.[13] Chilean elections became a good deal more conservative than they were before.

---

[13] This finding contrasts with orthodox interpretations of Chile, which tend to stress the continuity of party voting strength. See Arturo Valenzuela, "Chile: Origins and Consolidation of a Latin American Democracy," in Larry Diamond, Jonathan Hartlyn, Juan J. Linz, and Seymour Martin Lipset, eds., *Democracy in Developing Countries: Latin America*, 2d ed. (Boulder, CO: Lynne Rienner, 1999), 202; and Peter M. Siavelis, "Executive-Legislative Relations in Post-Pinochet Chile: A Preliminary Assessment," in Mainwaring and Shugart, *Presidentialism and Democracy*, 346. The principal difference stems from my use of a five-point Left–Right scale, whereas other authors rely on a conventional three-point scale.

Parties of the Left also lost ground in Argentina, where they were never of major importance, and parties of the Right and Center-Right, also of minor importance, underwent some modest shifts. Spectacular advances were made by Peronist parties, labor-based movements with paradoxically conservative ideologies, which nearly doubled their average vote share (from 25 percent to almost 48 percent). Although Argentina's realignment defies categorization on a simple Left–Right spectrum, it clearly does not confirm hypothetical expectations.

Brazil and Uruguay add further complications. In Brazil three blocs gained electoral ground: the Left (+7 points), the Center (+20 points), and the Right (+9 points). In Uruguay, too, the Left made remarkable gains, increasing its average electoral share from 7.3 percent to 24.4 percent, largely at the expense of the Center-Left, which suffered a catastrophic drop of nearly 40 points. Meanwhile, the Center gained nearly 30 points, and the Center-Right slipped 6.6 points but remained a major electoral force.

Such variation in the durability of the political Left under BA regimes appears to reflect the importance of three factors. One was the extent of repression during the "dirty wars" that erupted in all of these countries; second was the role of organized labor in resisting military rule and guiding the transition toward democracy; and third was the extrication of the authoritarian regime and the perception of success or failure.

In Chile the repression was extensive, and labor unions were displaced by political parties as leaders of the opposition; both factors tended to weaken the far Left, and the relative "success" of Pinochet's economic policies and the orderliness of the transition prevented a backlash against the regime. In Brazil and Uruguay, where transitions were carefully negotiated, repression was less severe, and labor retained a major role. Under Lula's leadership, organized labor created what would become the most institutionalized party in Brazil, the Partido dos Trabalhadores (PT), and in Uruguay it became the critical base for preexisting socialist parties. As a result, the Left gained ground in both of these nations.

As always, Argentina defies simple classification. There was extensive repression, but organized labor remained a significant force—and the generals left office in near-total disarray, especially after the humiliating military defeat at the hands of Great Britain in the ill-starred conflict over the Malvinas/Falklands Islands. The backlash effect was severe: Improvement in the electoral fortunes of the Peronist party reflected the continuing power of organized labor, the progressive decay of traditional parties, and popular displeasure over the performance of the military regime.

Legacies of Military Populism

In contrast to right-wing BA regimes, populist military regimes in the Andes might have been expected to strengthen the political Left. Such governments claimed to represent downtrodden masses and exuded radical-sounding appeals on their behalf. One of their defining features was the effort to mobilize and organize popular groups and worker organizations (sometimes in opposition to preexisting labor unions). A common result was polarization. It could thus be anticipated that such regimes would invigorate the Left, weaken the Center, and, by antithesis, provoke the political Right.

As voting patterns show, the secular Left gained strength in each and every case—by more than 8 points in Ecuador and more than 13 in Peru. (The Left also gained more than 7 electoral points in Bolivia, which did not have a reformist military experience, but where organized labor was strong and where ideological legacies of the 1952 revolution might have opened political space at the radical end of the spectrum.) As expected, the Center remained a negligible factor in all three countries. The Center-Left was also demolished in Bolivia and Peru, with shares dropping from around 70 percent in both cases to the mid-20-percent range, whereas it became a substantial force in Ecuador. The far Right fared very poorly in Ecuador and Peru, losing 17 to 18 points in each case, although it made modest gains in Bolivia. In contrast, the Center-Right made impressive gains in Bolivia (more than 31 points) and Peru (more than 17 points) but not so much in Ecuador (only 2 points).

On balance, expectations were mostly confirmed. Populist-military regimes bequeathed societies with electoral alignments that exhibited (1) strengthened left-wing movements, (2) combined Left and Center-Left blocs that accounted for 30 to 40 percent of average vote shares, (3) virtually nonexistent political centers, and (4) right-wing blocs that were moderate in ideology (as shown by Center-Right gains) and in overall strength. As a result, postpopulist politics was more competitive than before: The once-dominant Center-Left Movimiento Nacionalista Revolucionario (MNR) in Bolivia gave way to a loose Right plus Center-Right coalition, and Ecuador and Peru would have more or less evenly matched leftist-versus-rightist coalitions (along with substantial personalist followings in both instances).

In contrast to countries undergoing military rule, democracies that survived the 1960s and 1970s (Colombia, Costa Rica, and Venezuela) showed a clear-cut tendency toward continuity in partisan alignments. Most ideological blocs showed remarkably little change in average vote shares between the two periods. Venezuela witnessed a substantial drop in the electoral power of the Center-Left, the once-hegemonic Acción Democrática, and a corresponding shift toward the Center-Right, the Christian Democratic COPEI (Comité de Organización Política Electoral Independiente), but this largely reflected the power-sharing arrangements adopted by those two parties. Overall, the prevailing theme was continuity: survival of the democratic systems and perpetuation of electoral blocs.

In retrospect, the political Left remained rather modest across Latin America as a whole. Despite the region's reputation for radical extremism, parties of the far Left accounted for less than 10 percent of the average vote in most countries. Only in Chile and in Uruguay (after 1978) did the Left obtain more than 20 percent of the average vote. In Ecuador the leftist bloc expanded from only 5 percent to 13.4 percent, and in Peru it grew from 1.2 percent to 14.6 percent. And these Andean countries continued to be plagued by widespread poverty, increasing inequality, and weak systems of governance—conditions that might well have encouraged the appeal of leftist ideologies.[14] With a few conspicuous exceptions, however, the political Left was not faring well in Latin American polling booths.

Moreover, the combined strength of the Left plus the Center-Left, what might be thought of as "progressive" political movements, revealed a conspicuous downward tendency. Among ten countries of the region, seven show a decline in combined electoral shares of the Left and Center-Left (Argentina,[15] Bolivia, Chile, Costa Rica, Peru, Uruguay, and Venezuela), and only three register gains (Brazil, Colombia, and Ecuador). And even here, the Left plus Center-Left became a prominent force only in Ecuador, rising from an average vote of 5.1 percent to 38.0 percent.

In addition, as Scott Mainwaring and Timothy Scully have argued, the "renovation" of the Left—meaning its ideological moderation and its rejection of violence—would have complex implications for party politics in Latin America:

> On the one hand, the stakes of party competition have been reduced. Politics is no longer conceived of as a war in which radically opposed sides try to vanquish each other. This salutary transformation favored the compromise and moderation that are necessary ingredients in democratic politics. Conservative parties and groups are generally less fearful that electoral defeat will lead to radical social, economic, and political change at their expense. On the other hand, the moderation of the Left resulted in quieting the voices that spoke for wider political participation and greater social equity in a region marked by egregious inequalities. Poverty and inequality in most countries remain more pressing issues than ever before, but they are less effectively voiced now.[16]

Who would represent the poor?

In sum, Latin American elections accommodated a broad spectrum of ideological tendencies, but the spectrum shifted over the years. Forces of the Left (i.e., Left plus Center-Left) declined in overall strength. So did personalist movements. Forces of the Center and the Right gained in strength. Over time, Latin American voters became increasingly cautious and conservative. By the decade of the 1990s, Latin American democracy had become docile, timid, and tame.

---

[14] Communist parties were outlawed in many countries during the post–World War II cycle, so one might have anticipated that legalization would lead to an increase in vote shares for the Left.

[15] Peronists are not here considered part of the Left. On this, see Coppedge, "Classification."

[16] Scott Mainwaring and Timothy R. Scully, *Building Democratic Institutions: Party Systems in Latin America* (Stanford, CA: Stanford University Press, 1995), 466.

A RESURGENCE OF THE LEFT

Conditions were changing as the twenty-first century beckoned. Conventional wisdom stoutly maintained that the demise of the Soviet Union would discredit Marxist ideology and weaken the political Left—socialist as well as communist—around the world. But as Jorge Castañeda has astutely argued, there could also be "a silver lining...in the vanishing socialist cloud." Progressive leftist movements would no longer feel obliged to align themselves with Soviet (and/or Cuban) foreign policy, to adopt rigid anti-American stances on international and geopolitical issues, and, perhaps most important, to reject democratic politics for the sake of violent revolution. And in spite (or because) of the imposition of neoliberal policies, grievous economic and social injustices continued to persist throughout the region. Ironically, Castañeda surmised, the ending of the Cold War "could thus achieve what nothing and no one else has: the 'Latin Americanization' of the Left and its definitive rooting in the hemisphere's still barren native land."[17]

And in time, a political Left—a so-called "new Left"—made a dramatic appearance on the electoral stage. In country after country, it managed to defeat the Center and the Right in free and fair elections. Left-of-center candidates succeeded in overcoming the resistance of entrenched elites, opposition from the United States, and, especially, institutional impediments designed to prevent just such a dénouement (as explained in Chapter 6). As a result, one of the most striking developments of the time was the emergence of what came to be known as Latin America's "pink tide."

Starting with Venezuela in 1998, the region witnessed a surge of leftist electoral triumphs—in Brazil, Argentina, Bolivia, Ecuador, Nicaragua, and Uruguay. Some observers believed (and many hoped) that the tide crested in 2006, with narrow losses for populist candidates in Peru and Mexico. But in 2008 voters in Paraguay threw their support to Fernando Lugo, a former Catholic bishop and advocate of "liberation theology" whose victory ended the sixty-two-year reign of the Colorado Party, his country's equivalent of the Mexican PRI. And as shown in Table 7.5, citizens of El Salvador in 2009 elected Mauricio Funes, a candidate of the once-revolutionary FMLN, while Uruguayans opted for José Mujica, a former member of their country's Tupamaro guerrilla movement. In 2010 Brazilians cast decisive votes in favor of the PT's Dilma Rousseff and in 2011 Peruvians gave their backing to Ollanta Humala (whom they had rejected in 2006). Despite occasional setbacks, the "new Left" persevered.

What was this trend, and what did it mean? First and foremost, the pink tide was a protest movement. It was a protest against conditions of poverty, inequality, and corruption. It was a protest against the inability (or

---

[17] Jorge G. Castañeda, *Utopia Unarmed: The Latin American Left After the Cold War* (New York: Alfred A. Knopf, 1993), 252–253, 266.

TABLE 7.5 The Rise of the New Left

Country	President	Election Years
Venezuela	Hugo Chávez	1998, 2004, 2006
Brazil	Luis Inácio Lula da Silva	2002, 2006
	Dilma Rousseff	2010
Argentina	Néstor Kirchner	2003
	Cristina Fernández de Kirchner	2007
Bolivia	Evo Morales	2005, 2009
Ecuador	Rafael Correa	2006, 2009
Nicaragua	Daniel Ortega	2006, 2011
Paraguay	Fernando Lugo	2008
Peru	Ollanta Humala	2011
El Salvador	Mauricio Funes	2009
Uruguay	Tabaré Vázquez	2004
	José Mujica	2009
Near-Misses		
Peru	Ollanta Humala	2006
Mexico	Andrés Manuel López Obrador	2006

unwillingness) of governments to promote effective social justice. It was a protest of citizens against impersonal economic forces and uncaring political leaders. It was neither organized nor orchestrated. It was an outpouring of popular will.

In ideological terms, the pink tide represented a cluster of values rather than a clear-cut formulation. It was far from doctrinaire—inspiration came from such diverse sources as nationalism, populism, indigenous tradition, Catholicism, and, not surprisingly, diluted forms of Marxism. In contrast to the "radical" movements of the 1960s and 1970s, it did not seek "revolutionary" change.[18] Instead it expressed a general commitment to social justice, support for the poor, and a compassionate world system. In contrast to the modern-day Right, with its emphasis on individual rights and free-market competition, the new Left stressed the importance of communal well-being, social solidarity, and state responsibility.[19]

More specifically, the movement amounted to a rejection of the neoliberal policies propounded by the Washington Consensus—pro-market policies designed to promote free trade, foreign investment, and the reduction of state power. Poor people had come to believe that the Consensus favored privileged elites at the expense of suffering masses. They were demanding more active protection and promotion of their interests from the state.

---

[18] For this reason Kurt Weyland refers to the new Left as "contestatory" rather than "radical." Kurt Weyland, Raúl L. Madrid, and Wendy Hunter, eds., *Leftist Governments in Latin America: Successes and Shortcomings* (New York: Cambridge University Press, 2010), Ch. 1.

[19] Peter H. Smith, "Perspectivas de la izquierda política latinoamericana," in Pedro Pérez Herrero, ed., *La "izquierda" en América Latina* (Madrid: Editorial Pablo Iglesias, 2006), 291–305.

As candidate, Hugo Chávez of Venezuela was greeted by adoring crowds throughout his campaigns for the presidency; as president, he encountered determined opposition. (AP Photo/ Ricardo Mazalan)

Critiques of the Washington Consensus helped give the movement an anti-American flavor, augmented by deep-seated resentment of the George W. Bush administration's unilateral style and, more particularly, from opposition to the U.S.-led war in Iraq. Citizens of Latin America were judging U.S. policies around the world, not only in the Western Hemisphere, and many were losing their respect for American society. This sentiment softened greatly after the 2008 election of Barack Obama, despite subsequent disappointment over his apparent lack of interest in the region.

Fundamentally, the pink tide was a democratic trend. Its leaders came to power through free and fair elections. They represented citizens. To be sure, Hugo Chávez of Venezuela would move in authoritarian directions—but others did not. And they were by no means all *chavistas*—they might admire his ability to yank George Bush's chains and envy his petrodollar windfalls, but they sought to emulate neither his pronouncements nor his policies. Over time, Lula of Brazil steadily distanced himself from Chávez and became his principal rival for the leadership of South America.

Generally speaking, Latin America's pink tide meant that angry and disenchanted masses were expressing their discontent at the ballot box. They were not taking up arms, going to the hills, planting bombs, or engaging in terrorist conspiracies. They were voting. They were not rejecting democratic politics. On the contrary, they were using the most basic instruments of democracy to express their demands and seek far-reaching reform. In this sense they posed a crucial question: whether electoral democracy in the developing world would be capable of promoting true social justice.

Ultimately, the leftist trend represented a protest against timid democracy throughout the region. The relentless accumulation of popular grievances and the progressive decay of traditional institutions created demands and opportunities for a new style of political movements. The people wanted stronger and bolder agendas, leaders who would be willing and able to challenge established elites, conventional wisdoms, and free-market nostrums. In a dialectical sense, it was the docility of Latin American democracy in the 1990s that paved the way for the audacity of the Left in the 2000s.

How to assess the strength of the pink tide? The orthodox approach has been to count the number of left-of-center chief executives, but this criterion ignores pink-tide candidates who fell just short of electoral victory. More important, this short-sighted view overlooks the breadth and depth of popular demands for structural change. Wherever there was social injustice, there was support for the new Left. As a rough estimate, it has been surmised that 30 to 40 percent of all Latin American citizens supported the values of the "new Left" around the year 2005. Whatever the precise figure, the methodological point stresses the need to focus on the overall social base, not merely on electoral outcomes.

Digression: Schisms on the Left

A broad commitment to left-of-center worldviews did not inspire unity among all pink-tide regimes. Ideological breadth provided ample room for disagreements over tactics and strategy. Traditional geopolitical interests provoked underlying tensions, and personality differences could lead to policy differences. As a result, the emergence of "new Left" proved to be a changeable development, a phenomenon marked by opportunistic allegiances, divided loyalties, and broken campaign promises.

In time the movement produced two basic camps: a "moderate" trend, led by Lula of Brazil, and a "radical" (or "contestatory") contingent, led by Hugo Chávez of Venezuela. Although the two leaders remained on good personal terms, they pursued diverging paths in politics and economics.

Blending realism with pragmatism, the moderate approach was committed to work within existing democratic institutions, to make incremental progress toward socioeconomic goals, and to acknowledge constraints imposed by the forces of globalization. The basic idea was to impose a "human" face on market-oriented economics, laying viable foundations for long-term development and constructing effective safety nets for marginal sectors and the poor. This strategy usually entailed coalition-building, tolerance of political opposition, legislative maneuvering, positive relations with the private sector (domestic and international), and prudence in foreign policy.

In sharp contrast, the radical approach was bold, impatient, and argumentative. Rather than work within existing institutions, or even reform them, radicals sought to replace them. Expressing deep distrust of the market, they wanted to expand the economic roles of the state. They sought to redistribute income and wealth, usually through generous forms of governmental subsidies. They were distrustful of the opposition. Rather than build foundations for an equitable future, they wanted to initiate change right away.

These differences showed up in visible ways. As a moderate, Lula decided to give maximum priority to macroeconomic stability soon after taking office. He courted the private sector, cut political deals (often behind closed doors), and displayed a willingness to compromise. Within the international arena he defended the economic interests of developing countries, forged alliances with emerging giants like China and India, and hosted visits to Brazil by George W. Bush.

Chávez adopted a contrasting style. Proclaiming his intention to forge "socialism for the twenty-first century," he discarded traditional restraints and institutions. He denounced Venezuela's long-standing elite as a "rancid oligarchy." In the name of "participatory democracy," he promoted constitutional amendments that removed prohibitions on his own reelection. He harassed the media and intimidated the opposition. He seized control of the state-owned petroleum company and later went on to confiscate private properties and firms (sometimes to punish political opponents). He used international forums to ridicule George W. Bush, referring to him as "the devil" in a memorable UN speech, and constantly denounced the imperialist intentions of the Colossus of the North.

Beyond these political differences, Lula and Chávez harbored competing geopolitical aspirations. Both wanted recognition as the undisputed political leader of Latin America, especially of the regional Left. Toward this end, Chávez joined together with Fidel Castro in 2004 to launch a so-called Bolivarian Alternative for the Americas (Alternativa Bolivariana para las Américas, or ALBA)—a project offering an "alternative" to the U.S.-sponsored proposal for a Free Trade Area of the Americas (FTAA). ALBA thus proposed to counter both the Washington Consensus and U.S. hegemony.

With tacit Brazilian support, Chávez led the successful charge against FTAA in 2005. As petroleum prices climbed, he expended state revenues on economic assistance programs designed to expand ALBA's membership. Bolivia joined in 2006, as did Nicaragua in 2007 and Ecuador in 2009. (Honduras was a short-lived member from 2008 to 2010, at which point the country withdrew.) Small island states in the Caribbean also joined the group, and several other nations—Haiti, Grenada, Paraguay, Uruguay, and Syria (!)—held "observer" status. In addition ALBA received expressions of moral support from other leaders, most prominently the Kirchner couple in Argentina. In June 2009, with FTAA long out of the way, the movement's name was changed from "alternative" to "alliance" (formally speaking, the Alianza Bolivariana para los Pueblos de Nuestra América). By 2010 the total membership embraced about 70 million people, but ALBA appeared to have reached its plateau.

In the meantime, Lula's star was on the rise. Under his leadership, Brazil came to be hailed as an emerging world power. The nation's long-standing demand for a permanent seat on the UN Security Council received widespread statements of support. At the regional level, Brazil spearheaded the formation in 2008 of a "Union of South American Nations" (*Unión de Naciones Suramericanas*, or UNASUR). This organization began as an intergovernmental union of two existing customs unions, MERCOSUR and the Andean Community. It included virtually all of continental South America (with the exception of French Guiana, an overseas department of France), with a total population exceeding 385 million.[20] UNASUR was explicitly modeled after the European Union, with the ultimate goals of forging a single economic market with a common currency, a parliament, and a continental passport.

Possessing roughly half the Union's total population, Brazil became the unquestioned leader of the group. Because of its power and scope, UNASUR eclipsed ALBA (as a member of both, Venezuela thus found itself in a corner). In effect, UNASUR established an institutional vehicle for one of Brazil's traditional foreign policy aims: hegemony in South America. Competition lingered in the background of the handshakes and the photo ops. As of late 2010, Brazil and the "moderate" trend of the Left were in the ascendancy, while Chávez and the "radical" side were in retreat.

DILEMMAS OF DEMOCRACY: REPRESENTATION VS. GOVERNANCE

How have Latin America's elections affected governance? Have they strengthened or diminished prospects for effective public policy? Have they provided officeholders with clear mandates for change?

As a general rule, Latin American citizens have placed significant constraints on chief executives. For one thing, they have not endowed their presidents with working majorities in congress. This was not a meaningful issue from 1940 through 1977, when most Latin American legislatures were weak and insignificant. But from the 1980s onward, as shown in Chapter 6, national legislatures have made substantial gains in authority and effectiveness. And if presidents are unable to forge working majorities, they are unable to implement decisive public policy.

---

[20] Although claimed by Argentina, the Falkland Islands are an overseas possession of the United Kingdom. Mexico and Panama have observer status in UNASUR.

TABLE 7.6 Average Share of Congressional Seats of Party of the President (in percent)

Country	Period	N Elections	PRESIDENT'S PARTY Lower Chamber	PRESIDENT'S PARTY Upper Chamber
Argentina	1983–1997	8	48.5	52.9
Bolivia	1980–1997	5	31.6	47.4
Brazil	1985–1998	6	23.2	23.2
Chile	1989–1997	3	28.8	28.6
Colombia	1945–1949, 1974–1998	12	53.5	54.5
Costa Rica	1953–1998	12	48.9	—
Ecuador	1978–1998	8	22.9	—
Peru	1980–1995	4	48.9	41.1
Uruguay	1984–1994	3	37.7	—
Venezuela	1958–1998	8	39.2	44.5

Source: Inter-American Development Bank, *Development Beyond Economics*, 185.

Table 7.6 illustrates the situation. In only a handful of countries—Colombia, Honduras, Nicaragua, and Paraguay—did the presidents enjoy a majority in lower houses of the congress. And in major countries—Brazil and Venezuela among them—the president's party controlled less than 30 percent of seats in the legislature. (Although this was technically true of Chile, the governing coalition, the *Concertación,* enjoyed comfortable majorities in congress.) In many instances, divided government became the norm.

Figure 7.4 shows that the degree of gridlock varied widely among the Latin American countries.[21] Ecuador, Chile, and Bolivia had the worst tendency for gridlock. Costa Rica and Paraguay had the least, with the remaining countries tightly packed in the center. Notwithstanding this variation, Latin America as a whole displayed a higher level of political gridlock than any other developing region in the world. Some of this might have been due to interparty competition rather than a propensity toward gridlock per

---

[21] Degrees of political gridlock are measured as "the probability that disagreements between the executive and the legislature will preclude changes in the status quo." If the president's party controls two thirds or more of the congress, it is assumed that there can be complete agreement between the executive and legislature; if the opposition controls two thirds or more of the seats, it is assumed that the two branches will hardly ever agree. Points in between are gauged by the distribution of seats between the president's party and the opposition. The higher the index, the greater the likelihood of disagreement between the executive and the legislature. An index at or near zero suggests that there are few if any constraints on the executive's policy initiatives. An index of 0.20 means that, on average, 20 percent of all policies are off limits; an index of 0.40 means that 40 percent of all policies are out of bounds; and so on, up to 1.0.

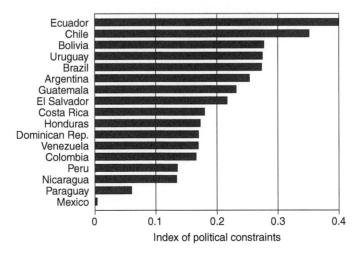

Figure 7.4   Degrees of political gridlock, 1985–1994

Source: Inter-American Development Bank, *Development Beyond Economics*, 184.

se, but the basic point is clear: Elections in Latin America often resulted in paralysis on policy. This was a serious problem.

This propensity toward executive–legislative gridlock, or "immobilism," had institutional roots. As revealed in Chapter 6, the use of proportional representation (PR) tends to encourage multiparty politics, especially if district magnitudes are large, and a proliferation of political parties makes it difficult for presidents to muster working majorities in congress. In short, the legislative strength of opposition parties not only reflected potential discontent with presidential leadership, it also revealed the mechanics of the electoral system itself. Working in combination, these two factors can lead to harsh results (see Box 7.2).

Adding insult to injury, Latin American voters have not only tied the hands of chief executives. Perhaps in response to the policy gridlock, they consistently turned presidents (or their parties) out of power. A study of thirty-four democracies around the world has found governmental turnover—that is, replacement of chief executives—in 68.4 percent of Latin America's elections, compared with just 30.3 percent of elections in advanced industrial societies. When incumbents are barred from reelection (as in Mexico, for instance), party turnover in Latin America climbed to 77.8 percent of cases, whereas it declined to 25 percent in industrialized countries.[22] When incumbents were running for reelection, turnover occurred in 52.4 percent of Latin American elections and 31.9 percent of elections in advanced

---

[22] Apparently, this means that in industrialized countries, citizens were more likely to vote for the incumbent's political party with executives themselves barred from reelection.

BOX 7.2

STANDOFF IN MEXICO

The 2003 congressional elections in Mexico were a disaster for President Vicente Fox, whose policy initiatives had been crippled throughout the first half of his term by recalcitrant opposition from the PRI. It was essential for Fox's party, the Partido Acción Nacional (PAN), to strengthen its position in the Chamber of Deputies, where it held only 202 out of 500 seats. The PRI held 207 seats, and the left-wing Partido de la Revolución Democrática (PRD) had 56.

No such luck. Across the country, the PAN garnered only 30.6 percent of the total vote, and its congressional delegation declined by more than 50 seats. The PRI picked up 17 additional seats, and the PRD—the big winner—stood to gain 43 seats. As determined by the Federal Electoral Institute, the final results were as follows:

- The PRI went up from 207 to 224
- The PAN went down from 202 to 151
- The PRD went up from 56 to 97.

(Other small parties shared a total of 28 seats.) This was a classic recipe for gridlock.

Commentators agreed that this was a devastating outcome for the charismatic and still-popular Fox. "The congressional races were very much a resounding slap in the face to Fox," said George Grayson of the College of William and Mary. "They told him: 'You promised change, and you didn't deliver.'"

"Fox is very well liked by voters, who seem fond of him for having ushered in political change," said a respected pollster in Mexico City. "But that doesn't necessarily mean that they see him as an effective leader. He's like a great friend, but a not-so-great president."

"The presidency of Vicente Fox is over," wrote political analyst Denise Dresser in the newspaper *Reforma*. "The president will continue to live in Los Pinos [the presidential residence], but he won't be orchestrating any changes from there. He'll leave his office like every other day, but he'll be a political corpse."

---

democracies. The conclusion is inescapable: "Turnover is more frequent in non-industrialized countries than in industrialized ones, whether there is reelection or not."[23]

This pattern also affected parties in power. On average, the incumbent party lost nearly 10 percentage points (-9.3) from one election to the next

---

[23] José Molina, "The Electoral Effect of Underdevelopment: Government Turnover and Its Causes in Latin-American, Caribbean, and Industrialized Countries," *Electoral Studies* 20 (2001): 427–446, esp. 436–437. See also Aníbal Pérez-Liñán, *Presidential Impeachment and the New Political Instability in Latin America* (New York: Cambridge University Press, 2007).

in Latin America, compared with less than 2 percent (-1.7) in advanced industrial societies. Reelection mitigated these results to some extent; when reelection was prohibited, incumbent parties lost nearly 12 points in Latin America (-11.7) and more than 3 points (-3.2) in advanced democracies. Not only the chief executive was being punished at the polls, so were incumbent presidential parties. In legislative as well as presidential elections, citizens were voting all the rascals out.

It is not entirely clear why this should have been the case. Because of its pervasiveness throughout Latin America, the principle of no-reelection surely accounts for part of this phenomenon. As Robert H. Dix noted some time ago,

> a presidential coalition is more readily held together by an incumbent who has personal control over the budget and the administrative machinery of government and who can take immediate action on behalf of supporters, as opposed to a nonincumbent candidate of the same party who can merely promise such action. Concomitantly, the machinery of the governing party may be less surely under the control of a nonincumbent candidate, and a chain of personal and partisan loyalties less certainly or less broadly established, especially if the candidate of the incumbent party should be a factional rival of the president's. In fact, a principal reason for constitutional strictures against reelection is undoubtedly the recognition that, given such presidential potential for manipulation as well as influence, electoral turnover might be unlikely to occur at all in their absence.[24]

Desertion and betrayal become commonplace, as erstwhile supporters seek out new candidates who will be able to wield political power and dispense governmental favors in the future. One-time loyalists might even join the opposition. With the approaching end of presidential terms, the power of incumbent executives steadily evaporates. As shown in Chapter 6, this was one of the reasons why a number of Latin American countries removed prohibitions on presidential reelection.

A second explanation focuses on accelerating social change, especially increases in literacy and urbanization, and the relationship between demands and resources. As Dix observed, heightened demands complicate the tasks of governing: "Indeed, it may be that any government in a country where increasing demand outruns available resources would be likely to have difficulty holding onto its popular support. Therefore, it may be that incumbent turnover and diminished pluralities reflect the markedly more difficult job of governing or of holding together governing coalitions in countries like those of Latin America."[25] Building on this general point, Venezuelan political scientist José Molina has described much of Latin America as exhibiting

---

[24] Robert H. Dix, "Incumbency and Electoral Turnover in Latin America," *Journal of Interamerican Studies and World Affairs* 26, no. 4 (November 1984): 435–448, with quote on 440.
[25] Ibid., 441–442.

"endemic discontent." In his words, "a population plagued with high levels of poverty, deficient public services, and with its basic necessities unsatisfied…lives in a state of 'endemic discontent.' Because of this, it becomes difficult for a government to satisfy the majority of voters, or even those who supported the party during the election. As a consequence, it is quite normal to expect that the party in power will lose the next election and suffer a decrease in its share of the vote (electoral attrition). The exception would be that it win or better its share of the vote."[26]

Whatever the cause of this phenomenon, one of its effects is plain: It obstructs the policymaking process. As Molina again points out, high rates of turnover tend to shorten the horizon for planning and policymaking.

> While in industrialized countries a political project tends to have various periods in which to be developed, in nonindustrialized countries, most probably it will be discarded after four or five years, except in those cases where there is consensus among the major parties. It may be true that political continuity is not necessarily an advantage, but the fact that the political environment may be an obstacle to the execution of government programs, whether good or bad, cannot be considered as positive….In non-industrialized countries, political continuity is excessively difficult. These difficulties are a barrier to the development of even the most positive and plausible projects. And this in turn implies that, except in cases of complete consensus, even the continuity of programs which lead to higher levels of well-being for the population are more difficult to maintain in the societies which would benefit most from them. In this sense, the lack of continuity which is derived from frequent turnover seems to be a factor which contributes to widening the gap of well-being between rich and poor countries.[27]

In this way, political factors could hamper the process of economic development.

There is, of course, a positive side to this coin. Displacement of incumbents and constraints on ruling parties suggest that Latin American voters were making critical judgments about governmental effectiveness: They were holding leaders accountable. Further, these outcomes demonstrate that electoral processes were sufficiently free and fair to empower dissident voices (or, at the very least, they show that *oficialista* efforts at intimidation and fraud did not have much effect). Oppositions managed to carry the day. To this extent, democracy in Latin America was working rather well.

All in all, this outcome illustrates one of the fundamental dilemmas of contemporary democracy, not only in Latin America but everywhere around the world: the choice between efficiency and representation. For the sake of efficient policymaking, democracies need to provide leaders with mandates and the resources to fulfill them; in practical terms, this means working

---

[26] Molina, "Electoral Effect," 428.
[27] Ibid., 444.

majorities in congress. But for the sake of representation, democracies need to provide citizens with the opportunity to express their grievances and hold leaders to account; in practical terms, this means tying their hands or voting them out of office. Democracy must offer outlets for disenchantment. As Latin America moved through its third cycle of political democracy, the choice between efficiency and representation presented the region with a deep and enduring dilemma.

PART III

QUALITIES OF DEMOCRACY

Democracy, which is a charming form of government, full of variety and disorder, and dispensing a sort of equality to equals and unequals alike.

—PLATO

Law is order, and good law is good order.

—ARISTOTLE

The death of democracy is not likely to be an assassination from ambush. It will be a slow extinction from apathy, indifference, and undernourishment.

—ROBERT MAYNARD HUTCHINS

CHAPTER 8

STATE CAPACITY AND POLICY PERFORMANCE

Citizens savor well-being. They seek regular employment, a decent wage, prospects for advancement—in short, a dignified standard of living. They want governments to promote economic growth, create effective institutions, and furnish protection in times of downturn or crisis. They want adequate health care for families and educational opportunities for children. Yet states find it hard to meet all these demands. Such tasks require substantial resources, usually obtained through taxation, which citizens are often reluctant to provide. But if people do not see results—if they regard governments as ineffective, incompetent, or parasitical—they are likely to withdraw support from public authorities and, in time, from the incumbent political regime.

These concerns are especially pressing for modern-day democracies in Latin America. Governments need to prove themselves. Questions thus arise: Are democracies throughout the region producing tangible benefits? And are they more (or less) effective than nondemocracies? Especially where democratic experiments are new, partial, and incomplete, governmental performance provides a litmus test for viability.

This chapter begins with an overview of changing roles and capacities of the state in Latin America. It then examines hypotheses about the economic merits of dictatorship and democracy, and proceeds to analyze policy performance in key areas: economic growth, health care and education, poverty alleviation, and income distribution. With regard to economics, the analysis shows that democracies have been faring just as well (or just as badly) as nondemocracies. With regard to health care and education, however, democracies have outperformed autocracies. Whether this outcome will sustain popular support for democratic rule is a wholly different question. For many people in the region, authoritarian rule might remain a tempting alternative.

THE LATIN AMERICAN STATE: ROLES AND CAPACITIES

The worldwide Great Depression of the 1930s exerted a devastating impact on Latin American countries that relied on the export of raw materials to foreign markets in Europe and the United States. In response to this calamity, states throughout the region adopted an activist stance in economic affairs. Essentially, they sought to protect their economies from the vagaries of the international market by nurturing and protecting national industries. This broad policy of "import-substitution industrialization" (ISI) had three basic goals: to assert economic independence, to create jobs for a burgeoning work force, and to promote economic growth. From the 1940s to the mid-1970s the strategy met with considerable success, as growth rates hovered in the 5 to 6 percent range for much of the period (the annual average was 5.1 percent in the 1950s, 5.4 percent in the 1960s, and 6.7 percent in the early 1970s). The international community responded with praise for economic "miracles" in Mexico, Brazil, and elsewhere. ISI was working, and interventionist states were leading the way.

Success, ironically, sowed the seeds of subsequent failure. Because state-directed ISI promoted spurts of growth, governments continued to expand their economic roles (if a little bit of state intervention was a good thing, more could only be better). Overprotected and inefficient industries passed inflated production costs on to captive consumer markets, which eventually became saturated. Populist leaders sought to sustain business-plus-worker coalitions by creating or acquiring enterprises in a rapidly expanding "para-statal" sector and by becoming employers of last resort. Patronage bloated government payrolls and weakened policymaking capacity.[1] As Javier Corrales has argued, the steady rise of "statism" eventually led to a decline in "stateness" (see Box 8.1).

The debt crisis of the 1980s brought a final reckoning. Tempted by modest interest rates during the 1970s, countries of Latin America—both their private and public sectors—borrowed massive amounts of money. Mexico suddenly announced that it would not be able to service its loans in 1982, sending shock waves through the international financial community. As shown in Chapter 4, ripple effects from the debt crisis had devastating impacts on Latin American economies. The 1980s became a "lost decade" for the entire region.

As the crisis deepened, a bevy of international economists concluded that the long-term cure for Latin America's ills lay in a package of policies that came to be known as the "Washington Consensus." Their prescription contained three basic elements: Latin American governments should support

---

[1] Peter H. Smith, "The Rise and Fall of the Developmental State in Latin America," in Menno Vellinga, ed., *The Changing Role of the State in Latin America* (Boulder, CO: Westview Press, 1998), 51–73.

ON STATES, STATISM, AND STATENESS

One of the most trenchant analyses of the economic roles of Latin American states has come from Javier Corrales, a political scientist who offers a distinction between "statism" and "stateness." Ultimately, he writes, excessive economic intervention by governments (statism) led to a reduction in the capacity to govern (stateness). In his words:

> Latin America prior to the 1990s was an example of increasing statism accompanied, paradoxically, by declining stateness. *Statism* refers to the tendency of states to intervene in the economy.... *Stateness* refers to the capacity of states to assert themselves over the national territory. Stateness is a measure of the extent to which states can design policies and elicit the necessary consensus—at home and abroad—to ensure implementation....
>
> [During the 1980s] state and societal actors were in the business of muddling through the crisis by trying to outsmart or cheat each other, which in the end ate away public assets. Indexes of political and civil liberties were thriving in many countries, but indexes of public mindedness were collapsing. Latin America was suffering the consequences of a deficit of stateness. Crucial standards of stateness—bureaucratic competence, extractive capacity, international backing, and control over economic affairs—were wiped out, paradoxically, by excessive statism. State presence in the economy was pervasive, but ineffective and perverse. Rather than promote savings, investment, and economic well-being, states became creators of distortions, disavings, and special privileges. Rather than inspire faith, they destroyed credibility. Citizens turned into pirates of public assets, and states, into agents of disinformation. Latin America in the late 1980s faced an urgent need to restore stateness.

Source: Javier Corrales, "Market Reforms," in Jorge I. Domínguez and Michael Shifter, eds., *Constructing Democratic Governance in Latin America*, 2d ed. (Baltimore: Johns Hopkins University Press, 2003), 75–76, 80.

the private sector (foreign as well as domestic), they should liberalize policies on trade, and, perhaps most important, they should reduce the economic role of the state. ISI must give way to neoliberalism. Often pressured by international lending agencies, particularly the International Monetary Fund, Latin American leaders duly adopted these market reforms.[2]

A core element in the Washington Consensus called for reductions in government expenditures. To illustrate such trends, Figure 8.1 presents data on public spending as a share of gross domestic product (GDP) in four major

---

2 See Susan Stokes, *Mandates and Democracy: Neoliberalism by Surprise in Latin America* (Cambridge: Cambridge University Press, 2001).

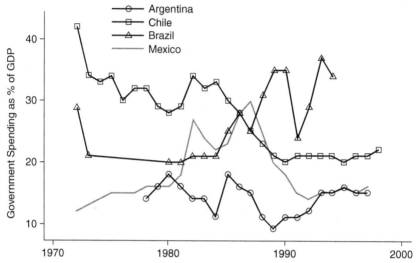

Figure 8.1 Public spending as share of GDP: ABC countries and Mexico, 1970–2000

Source: International Monetary Fund, Government Finance Statistics 2001.

countries: Argentina, Brazil, Chile, and Mexico. The data reveal substantial declines in Chile (from a high of more than 40 percent in the early 1970s) and Mexico (from a high around 30 percent in the mid-1980s), both ending up in the 15 to 20 percent range. Starting at a much more modest level, government expenditures in Argentina dropped sharply from 1980 to 1984, recovered temporarily, and declined again through the remainder of the decade. Brazil dropped from 30 percent to 20 percent in the 1970s and then returned to the 30-plus percent range in the late 1980s. This increase reflected mounting payments for debt service and earmarked expenditures (including transfers to local governments) and did little to enhance the discretionary power of the state. As the exception, Brazil thus proves the rule.

Reductions in public expenditures reflected two dynamics. One was the need to eliminate excessive statism and, in so doing, establish a foundation for effective governance. Yet the reductions were often undertaken too rapidly and mindlessly. Social programs suffered. Human capital was wasted. Privatization of state-owned industries often spawned corruption and, in many instances, led to the replacement of state monopolies with private monopolies.

Results turned out to be uneven. As Menno Vellinga has observed, application of the Washington Consensus

> often had drastic consequences. "Reform" amounted, in practice, to a demolition of institutions involving massive dismissals of personnel, resulting in a debilitating influence on state policymaking regarding "core obligations" that will not easily be taken care of by other institutions. The

technical capacity and expertise that could have been mobilized to help define policies and systems in these core areas were lost, thus hindering the search for an efficient way to alleviate *the* basic problem of Latin American society: the structural inequalities imbedded in the organization of economy and society and the social, economic, and political exclusion of the poor.[3]

Moreover, it became clear that the successful implementation of neoliberal market reforms, or any other coherent economic policy, would require an efficient and capable state. Analysts at the World Bank were especially quick to recognize the import of these lessons.[4]

The building (or rebuilding) of effective states would require resources. Strong economies are able to produce strong states; weak economies cannot. Table 8.1 presents information on population size and per capita income for nations of Latin America and three indisputably wealthy countries (Canada, Japan, and the United States) as of 2005. The data reveal great diversity in Latin America, with countries ranging in population size from 186 million inhabitants (Brazil) to less than 4 million (Panama and Uruguay). Table 8.1 also shows that some nations were a good deal more prosperous (or poorer) than others, with per capita annual incomes ranging from $8,000 in Mexico to $900 in Nicaragua. The average for the region as a whole was around $3,500.[5]

Latin America is not a wealthy area; far from it. The average per capita income was about one tenth that of Canada and Japan and around one twelfth that of the United States (adjustments for "purchasing power parity" (PPP) do not alter these results in any meaningful way). Per capita incomes in the uppermost tier—in Argentina, Brazil, Chile, Mexico, Uruguay, and Venezuela—averaged around $5,200. More than half the countries of the region had per capita incomes of less than $3,000, and four—Bolivia, Haiti, Honduras, and Nicaragua—had per capita incomes of less than $1,500.[6]

How much "stateness" could emerge in such societies? How would democratic governments fare under these circumstances? Would they do better or worse than autocratic regimes?

---

[3] Introduction to Vellinga, ed., *Changing Role*, 2.

[4] World Bank, *World Development Report 1997: The State in a Changing World* (New York: Oxford University Press, 1997); and Shahid Javed Burki and Guillermo E. Perry, *Beyond the Washington Consensus: Institutions Matter* (Washington, DC: The World Bank, 1998).

[5] Estimates of per capita incomes in U.S. dollars tend to be unstable, as they fluctuate with prevailing exchange rates. This point also applies to the calculations of "purchasing power parity" (PPP), which adjust raw dollar figures in terms of relative purchasing power.

[6] This source presented no data on Haiti, but its per capita income was thought to be around $500.

TABLE 8.1 Population and Per Capita Income: Latin America and Selected Countries, 2005

	POPULATION (Millions)	PER CAPITA INCOME	
		U.S. Dollars	PPP Adjusted
Upper tier			
Argentina	38.7	4,460	10,430
Brazil	186.4	4,020	8,380
Chile	16.3	5,920	11,090
Costa Rica	4.3	4,660	8,650
Mexico	107.0	8,090	12,380
Panama	3.2	4,650	8,520
Uruguay	3.5	4,820	9,400
Venezuela	26.7	4,950	9,770
Middle tier			
Colombia	45.6	2,870	6,930
Dominican Republic	8.9	2,810	5,850
Ecuador	13.2	2,700	6,380
El Salvador	6.9	2,890	5,690
Guatemala	12.6	2,080	4,010
Peru	28.0	2,650	5,910
Lower tier			
Bolivia	9.2	1,260	4,320
Haiti	8.5	—	—
Honduras	7.2	1,400	3,120
Nicaragua	5.5	890	2,250
Paraguay	6.2	1,230	3,900
Comparison cases			
Canada	32.3	33,430	34,450
Japan	128.1	38,910	31,000
United States	298.2	44,030	42,780

Note: Upper tier = raw per capita incomes of $4,000 or more; middle tier = per capita incomes between $2,000 and $4,000; lower tier = per capita incomes below $2,000.

Source: World Bank, World Development Indicators, 2005.

DEMOCRACY VS. DICTATORSHIP: GENERAL HYPOTHESES

What are the political determinants of economic development? Posed in this fashion, the question presumes that political regime—democratic, authoritarian, or otherwise—could exert a causal effect on patterns of economic change. It goes without saying that economic development results from a complex variety of structural and situational factors, including the domestic level of education, alterations in consumer preferences (at home and abroad), and, more generally, the state of the global economy. So this interrogation actually has two facets: first, ascertaining *whether* a political regime actually has an independent impact on patterns of development, and second, determining *the form and strength* of that relationship.

One school of thought argues that authoritarian regimes are more effective at economic management than are democracies. Because autocratic leaders do not have to worry about prospects for reelection, they can make difficult decisions. They enjoy considerable degrees of autonomy from social pressures, including lobbyists and interest groups as well as the popular masses. They can design and implement policies for the sake of long-term benefits rather than short-term gratification. They can engage in coherent planning, they can impose (and collect) taxes as needed, and they can shift emphasis or course as changing conditions might require. In particular, they can stimulate investment, whereas democratic politicians tend to favor consumption. Success stories of this genre include the "developmental states" of East Asia—Taiwan and South Korea prior to their recent democratic transitions, the city-state of Singapore, and the People's Republic of China in its current mode.[7]

Autocrats turn such arguments to their own advantage. In times of crisis, they claim, nations require firm and decisive leadership. Countries need leaders who can stand above the partisan fray, who can define and pursue broad national interests, and who can provide essential benefits for society at large. According to this view, military officers are especially well equipped to rescue economic policy from the contradictions of populism, restore investor confidence, and return the country to a path of self-sustaining growth. (It is also claimed that armed forces personnel do not succumb to the temptations of corruption, an assertion that does not stand up to close inspection.) The bottom line is this: Authoritarian governments can and will be more effective. Within Latin America, this interpretation gained support from Mexico's "stabilizing development" in the 1960s, the rapid expansion of the Brazilian economy in the early 1970s, and from Chile's remarkable turnaround under General Pinochet in the 1980s.

As electoral democracy spread throughout the region, advocates of pluralistic politics developed a series of counterarguments. They assert that democracies are better able to tailor policies to citizens' wants and needs. Moreover, they say, democratic policymaking is a transparent process: People can see how decisions are made, and they therefore know what to expect. And once decisions are made, they are likely to remain in place—at the very least, they are not subject to the whims and caprices of a junta or a dictator. By representing the popular will, democratic governments can thus provide investors, workers, and consumers with assurances into the future.

---

[7] See Chalmers Johnson, "Political Institutions and Economic Performance: The Government-Business Relationship in Japan, South Korea, and Taiwan," in Frederic C. Deyo, ed., *The Political Economy of the New Asian Industrialism* (Ithaca, NY: Cornell University Press, 1987), 136–164.

As a result, these proponents insist, democracies are more effective at promoting growth because of "allocative efficiency"—that is, democracies can better allocate available resources to productive uses. By protecting property rights, democracies encourage investment. And according to some, the free flow of information improves the quality of economic decisions. In support of this claim, analysts are fond of observing that no democracy has ever experienced a famine, presumably because of the likelihood of protests from the media and the opposition, which would make the political costs for those in power absolutely unbearable.

As Adam Przeworski and his associates have pointed out, some of these propositions are not necessarily incompatible:

> The arguments against democracy claim that it hinders growth by reducing investment; the arguments in its favor maintain that it fosters growth by promoting allocative efficiency. Both may be true: The rate at which productive factors grow may be higher under dictatorship, but the use of resources may be more efficient under democracy. And because these mechanisms work in opposite directions, the net effect may be that there is no difference between the two regimes in the average rates of growth they generate. The patterns of growth may differ, but the average rates of growth may still be the same.[8]

This insight raises yet another possibility: There might be no observable difference in growth rates between dictatorship and democracy.

As it has taken shape in recent years, the prodemocracy argument has often assumed, or asserted, that democratic regimes support neoliberal economic policies as a matter of definition. The idea seems to be that freedom in the political arena will naturally lead to freedom in the economic arena— that democratic governments will leave economic matters to the interplay of market forces. (Officials enamored of this view thus tend to speak of "market democracies.") There is, however, no inherent reason why this should be so. Democratic leaders might liberalize economic policy not because they want to, but because they have no practical choice. At the same time, politicians might win elections because they promise to use the power of the state to contravene the capitalist marketplace and provide social justice for the disadvantaged. At any rate, this is an empirical question, not something to be resolved by definitional fiat.

THE POLITICS OF ECONOMIC GROWTH

Economic growth in Latin America has been highly uneven. Figure 8.2 displays annual rates of GDP growth from 1980 to 2010 for the region as a whole

---

[8] Adam Przeworski, Michael E. Alvarez, José Antonio Cheibub, and Fernando Limongi, *Democracy and Development: Political Institutions and Well-Being in the World, 1950–1990* (Cambridge: Cambridge University Press, 2000), 144–145.

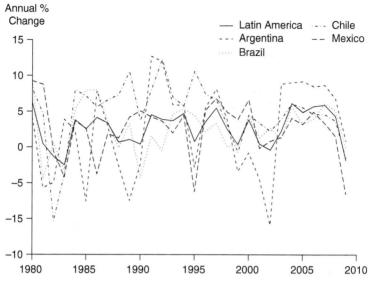

Figure 8.2 Patterns of GDP growth: ABC countries and Mexico, 1980–2010

Source: Economic Commission for Latin America and the Caribbean (ECLAC).

plus four individual countries: Argentina, Brazil, Chile, and Mexico. As the data show, Latin America suffered a sharp decline with the onset of the debt crisis in the early 1980s: Growth rates became negative (as economists are wont to say, meaning that output actually shrank), as employment, wages, and per capita incomes plummeted. A partial recovery in the late 1980s and early 1990s achieved growth rates of 1 to 4 percent, levels that were significantly lower than those of the 1960s. During the 1990s, the era of the Washington Consensus, the region's record was uneven: Most years hovered around 3 to 4 percent, but there was a sharp drop from 5 percent in 1998 to just over 1 percent in 2000. Upward trends resumed around 2003, as a result of increasing demand (especially from China) for Latin American exports, such as minerals and soybeans and other agricultural products. For the next several years, growth rates climbed to 5 to 6 percent. The global financial crisis of 2008–2009 brought this halcyon phase to an abrupt end, however, and regional output fell once again below zero in 2009.

While these general patterns applied to all countries, some experienced more drastic fluctuations than others. Mexico proved to be especially prone to economic crisis, suffering from sharp contractions in the early 1980s (the debt crisis), the mid-1990s (the peso crisis), and 2009 (the global crisis plus spiraling drug-related violence). Likewise, Argentina endured a sharp drop in the late 1980s, positive growth throughout the 1990s, a massive contraction (to –11 percent) in 2002, then a surge of growth in following years. Chile and Brazil experienced less volatility. After an excruciating contraction in

TABLE 8.2 Electoral Regimes and GDP Growth, 1960s–2000s

	ELECTORAL REGIME		
GDP Growth	Autocracy (%)	Semidemocracy (%)	Democracy (%)
Low	27	26	24
Medium-low	20	31	29
Medium-high	24	26	26
High	30	18	22
Total %	101	101	101
N	306	109	319

Note: Columns do not add up to 100 because of rounding.

Source of economic data: World Bank, World Development Indicators 2001.

the early 1980s, Chile achieved strong and generally consistent growth from 1990 to 2008 (thus becoming the "poster child" for neoliberal reform). After ups and downs throughout the 1990s, Brazil also attained fairly stable patterns of expansion and development.

Such fluctuations pose a key question: Are variations in growth associated with variations in political regime? As explained earlier, one line of argument holds that authoritarian regimes can promote growth more effectively than can democracies. Another maintains that democracies are more effective than are dictatorships. Which position is correct?

One way to test these hypotheses is by comparing average rates of annual GDP growth for different types of political regime. From the early 1960s through 2000, a period of nearly forty years, the average rate of growth for electoral democracies and autocratic regimes was identical, both rounding off at 3.7 percent. Over this entire stretch of time, the economic performance of dictatorships and democracies was virtually indistinguishable. Neither was more effective than the other.[9]

In further illustration of this point, Table 8.2 presents data on the relationship between electoral regime (autocracy, semidemocracy, and democracy) and annual rates of growth, now grouped into quartiles as low, medium-low, medium-high, and high.[10] This makes it possible to examine the dispersion, or "spread," of values as well as the central tendencies (as reflected in the averages). Entries are computed as column percentages.

---

[9] This finding is consistent with other prominent studies. See Przeworski et al., *Democracy and Development,* 158 and passim; and Karen L. Remmer, "Democracy and Economic Crisis: The Latin American Experience," *World Politics* 42, 3 (April 1990): 315–335.

[10] The data are grouped into quartiles. For the 1940–1977 period, low rates are 1.45 or lower (including negative rates); medium-low are between 1.5 and 4.15; medium-high are between 4.16 and 6.39; and high growth is 6.40 or above (with a maximum value of 13.46).

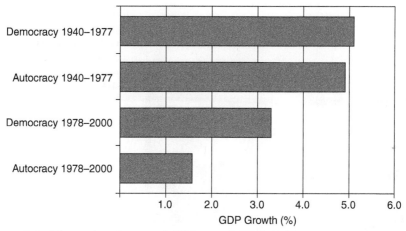

Figure 8.3 Electoral regimes and GDP growth, 1940–2000

There was no strong relationship. Dictatorships were more erratic than democracies, producing more low-growth years (27 percent vs. 24 percent) and also more high-growth years (30 percent vs. 22 percent). Autocracies showed 47 percent of low or medium-low rates of growth and 54 percent of medium-high or high rates of growth. Democracies performed slightly less well in this respect, with 53 percent of country-years at low or medium-low rates of growth and 48 percent with medium-high or high rates of growth. These findings come out in favor of dictatorship, but only by a modest margin. The overall conclusion is inescapable: Democracies were not performing better than dictatorships, but not worse, either.

A chronological breakdown according to political cycles sheds additional light on this question. As revealed in Figure 8.3, the average annual rate of GDP growth for electoral democracies during the 1940–1977 era came to 5.1 percent. For autocratic regimes, the corresponding figure was 4.9 percent, just about the same. Surprisingly, though, a significant gap in performance emerged during the subsequent cycle of democratization (1978–2000), when the average rate of growth for democracies was 3.3 percent, compared with only 1.6 percent for dictatorships. According to this criterion, democracies were doing twice as well as dictatorships![11]

Figure 8.3 yields other interpretations as well. One might explain the dismal performance of autocratic regimes during the post-1978 period as a result of the debt crisis, which struck the region when dictatorships happened to be in power (e.g., in Argentina, Brazil, Chile, and Mexico). It could be said, in fact, that the 1980s debt crisis played a major role in undermining authoritarian claims to legitimacy. Such an argument reverses the line of causality:

---

[11] A word of caution: For the 1978–2000 period, type of electoral regime explained less than 2 percent of the total variance in GDP growth.

Buenos Aires 2001: Economic crisis and a freeze on bank accounts provoked massive demonstrations of popular outrage. (AP Photo/Walter Astrada)

Instead of viewing GDP growth as a result of political regime, it considers change in political regime as a result of (declines in) GDP growth.

Still another view would focus not so much on the differences between political regimes as on the differences between chronological periods. The average rate of growth during the 1940–1977 cycle was more than 5 percent. For the 1978–2000 period, the average rate of growth was only 2.6 percent, about half the prior level. By this standard, post-1978 democracies were performing significantly less well than pre-1978 democracies *and dictatorships*. This would prompt nostalgia for the "developmental decades" of the past.

Nor did transitions toward democracy provide protection from economic crisis. Democratic Argentina suffered devastating downturns in 1988–1989 and again in 2001–2002. Even under the enlightened leadership of Fernando Henrique Cardoso, Brazil endured a crisis in 1998–1999. Partly as a consequence, post-Pinochet Chile underwent a short-lived recession in 1999. And Mexico, under semidemocracy, suffered a massive currency crisis in 1995 and, under democracy, faced an equally severe downturn in 2009. All these episodes led to sharp drops in economic output, employment, and wages. So if the debt crisis of the early 1980s exerted its impact on authoritarian regimes, subsequent crises posed sharp challenges to the credibility and capability of democratic governments. As the twentieth century came to a close, neither kind of regime could boast a stellar record of strong and sustained growth.

SOCIAL IMPACTS: HEALTH AND EDUCATION

Democracy promotes societal well-being, or so it is often assumed. Officials face incentives to improve the living condition of their constituents, thus earning public gratitude and enhancing prospects for reelection. They therefore advocate such programs as education and public health. Dictatorships and dictators are not dependent on voter approval and therefore have little reason to invest in social welfare.

Does this proposition withstand empirical analysis? To address this question, the inquiry turns to an assessment of democratic and autocratic performance in two key issue areas: health and education.

The analysis begins with policy. Persuasive bodies of evidence suggest that democratic regimes devote more resources to social programs (health, education, and welfare) than do dictatorships. A path-breaking exploration of Latin America from 1945 to 1980 has shown that heightened electoral competition in democratic contexts tended to increase social expenditures.[12] More recently, a rigorous follow-up study of data from 1980 to 1992 reveals that democratic regimes allocated more resources to social programs than did nondemocracies, especially at lower levels of development. In general, the authors conclude, "authoritarian governments place greater weight on addressing the exigencies of the market, whereas democratic governments respond more to political pressures." It is less a matter of virtue, they continue, than a question of practical interest:

> Politicians who deliver social benefits to their constituents hope to garner votes and ensure political survival. Providing a collective good by resolving the debt problems or establishing macroeconomic stability is not likely to have that effect.... Also, even if a given politician does not continue in office, political cronies and party allies can often benefit electorally from the patronage and programs s/he delivered while in power. At the same time, no individual politician—except for possibly a president, whom the citizenry holds responsible for the welfare of the country as a whole—has an incentive to cut back on social spending and forgo building clienteles in order to contribute to the broader cause of financial solvency.[13]

---

[12] Barry Ames, *Political Survival: Politicians and Public Policy in Latin America* (Berkeley: University of California Press, 1987).

[13] David S. Brown and Wendy Hunter, "Democracy and Social Spending in Latin America, 1980–92," *American Political Science Review* 93, 4 (December 1999): 779–790.

TABLE 8.3 Electoral Regimes and Infant Mortality, 1960s–1990s

Infant Mortality	ELECTORAL REGIME		
	Autocracy (%)	Semidemocracy (%)	Democracy (%)
High	48	17	12
Medium-high	22	32	24
Medium-low	22	32	25
Low	8	19	39
Total %	**100**	**102**	**100**
N	128	53	186

Note: Columns may not add up to 100 because of rounding.

Source of data on infant mortality: World Bank, World development indicators Database, 2001.

In contrast, dictators need not be concerned with popularity or prospects for reelection, so they can cut back on social programs in response to debt burdens or other economic pressures.

Were these expenditures effective? Apparently so. One of the most poignant indicators of social deprivation is infant mortality (measured here as deaths within the first year per 1,000 live births). From years with available data from the 1960s through the 1990s, the average rate for authoritarian regimes was 83.9, compared with 46.8 for democratic country-years. Infant mortality was nearly twice as high under dictatorship as under electoral democracy. This is a substantial margin.[14]

In pursuit of this point, Table 8.3 displays the relationship between regime type and levels of infant mortality (here divided into quartiles). Under authoritarian regimes, infant mortality rates reached high levels nearly half the time (48 percent), compared with only 12 percent of the time under democracies. Conversely, mortality rates were low under dictatorships less than 10 percent of the time, compared with nearly 40 percent under democracies. This is a strong and significant relationship.[15]

A related issue concerns education. For individuals, schooling is an essential platform for upward mobility; for societies, schooling is the most basic means of forming social capital. Within democracies, politicians confront the same kind of incentives as with regard to public health: Citizens want their children to have educational opportunities, and they are likely to reward leaders who provide this public good with votes and other forms of support. Again, dictators have no need for electoral payoffs. This does not mean that they are oblivious to the question of public support—quite the contrary—but they do not seek it in the same way and to the same extent as do the democrats.

---

[14] Analysis of variance shows that regime type explains more than 20 percent of the variance in infant mortality.

[15] A similar relationship emerges from an analysis of regime type and child mortality defined as deaths per 1,000 children under the age of five.

TABLE 8.4 Electoral Regimes and Primary School Enrollment, 1980s–1990s

Primary School Enrollment	ELECTORAL REGIME		
	Autocracy (%)	Semidemocracy (%)	Democracy (%)
Low	40	27	14
Medium-low	15	14	38
Medium-high	31	14	27
High	13	45	22
Total %	**99**	**100**	**101**
N	67	44	101

Source of data on school enrollment: World Bank, World Development Indicators Database, 2001.

One key indicator of governmental performance is attendance at primary school (measured by the percentage of age-eligible children enrolled in school). Attendance in primary school is responsive to public policy, whereas secondary and higher education attendance levels take years to affect, and it represents a clear-cut social benefit.

According to this criterion, democracies outperform dictatorships. Average primary school attendance under electoral democracy was 85 percent, compared with 75 percent under authoritarian regimes. And as shown by Table 8.4, school enrollment appeared in the top category more than 20 percent of the time under democracies, compared with 13 percent of the time under autocracies. At the other end of the spectrum, the lowest level of enrollment occurred just 14 percent of the time under democracies, compared with 40 percent under dictatorships. Interestingly, semidemocracies showed a sharply bipolar distribution, with most values in the upper- and lower-end categories, rather than the middle.

Overall, the broad implication seems clear: Democracies do better than dictatorships with regard to primary education. (They also do better with regard to secondary education, but by a smaller margin, probably because it takes longer to achieve results in this area.) And in general, democracies outperform dictatorships with regard to social policy. They are healthier places to live and more congenial places to learn. They nurture their children and send them to school. They might not be much more prosperous, at least in the immediate term, but they are kinder and gentler to their citizens.[16]

---

[16] Peter H. Smith and Melissa R. Ziegler, "Governmental Performance and Political Regimes: Latin America in Comparative Perspective, 1990–2004," *Taiwan Journal of Democracy* 3, 2 (December 2007): 101–118. See also John Sloan and Kent L. Tedin, "The Consequences of Regime Type for Public Policy Outputs," *Comparative Political Studies* 20 (April 1987): 98–124; and Matthew A. Baum and David A. Lake, "The Political Economy of Growth: Democracy and Human Capital," *American Journal of Political Science* 47, 2 (April 2003): 333–347.

THE PROBLEM OF POVERTY

One of the most pervasive challenges for Latin American governments has been the persistence of poverty. As a human condition it is degrading, dehumanizing, and demoralizing, especially when passed from one generation to another—from anguished parents to suffering children. As an economic factor, it represents a massive underutilization of resources and poses a substantial drag on growth and development. As a political consideration, it has (rightly or wrongly) been seen as a source of instability or even revolution, a "powderkeg" that could ignite without warning, a societal danger that cries out for preventive action.

For all these reasons, political leaders proclaim that poverty reduction is a major policy goal. It has been a recurring theme in electoral democracies. For parties of the Left and Center-Left, from socialists to Christian Democrats, it has been an article of political faith. From Salvador Allende in Chile to Lula in Brazil, poverty alleviation has been a central mission. Nowadays, conservative candidates also bemoan the persistence of poverty and proclaim their intent to attack it.

This unanimity stems from two major factors. One is a political calculation. For the most part, poor people do not vote—not very often, anyway. They thus represent a "reserve electorate," a potential source of political strength that would be likely to support whoever is able to improve their condition. From this standpoint, rival parties seek to mobilize poor voters on their own behalf or, if that proves impossible, to prevent competitors from establishing a partisan monopoly among the voting poor.

The other factor is moral. There is no choice but to oppose poverty. The electoral marketplace no longer tolerates traditional claims that people are poor because of their human failings—that they are lazy, indulgent, and undeserving. Instead, poverty has come to be seen as a source of collective shame and as a blight on the entire society. The need to reduce poverty is a recurrent theme in modern political discourse. Questions therefore arise: Have democracies made much headway in eradicating poverty? Have they been more effective than dictatorships?[17]

Figures 8.4 and 8.5 present summary data on overall levels of poverty for Latin America from 1980 to 2010. By all accounts, this was the most democratic phase in the region's history. And in light of incentives confronting

---

[17] The Washington Consensus did not offer explicit policy prescriptions for reducing poverty, apparently on the assumption that growth and efficiency would lead to long-term improvements in this area. As the synthesizer of the consensus later acknowledged, "I deliberately excluded from the list anything that was primarily redistributive...because I felt the Washington of the 1980s to be a city that was essentially contemptuous of equity concerns." Quoted in Terry Lynn Karl, "The Vicious Cycle of Inequality," in Susan Eva Eckstein and Timothy P. Wickham-Crowley, eds., *What Justice? Whose Justice? Fighting for Fairness in Latin America* (Berkeley and Los Angeles: University of California Press, 2003), 134.

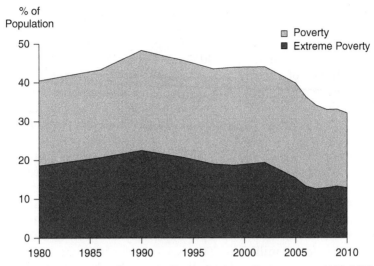

Figure 8.4 Poverty and indigence in Latin America: Percentages, 1980–2010

Source: Economic Commission for Latin America and the Caribbean (ECLAC), and *Social Panorama of Latin America, 2010.*

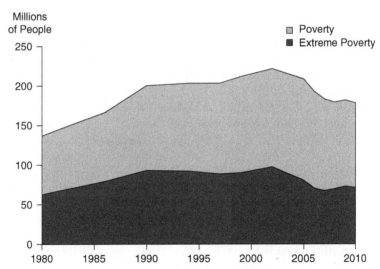

Figure 8.5 Poverty and indigence in Latin America: Absolute numbers, 1980–2010

Source: Economic Commission for Latin America and the Caribbean (ECLAC), and *Social Panorama of Latin America, 2010.*

elected leaders, one might reach a hypothetical expectation: As the incidence of electoral democracy increases, the level of poverty ought to decline.

So it did—to an extent. Overall levels of poverty have remained at staggering levels. As of 1980 more than 40 percent of the region's population lived under conditions of poverty. As a result of the debt crisis, this proportion rose to 48 percent (with more than 20 percent enduring from "extreme poverty" or indigence). By 2002, the poor and indigent population had declined to 44 percent of the overall population, with the indigent share declining to roughly 18 percent. As economic growth thereafter resumed, the total share of poor dropped to 34 percent by 2007 and to 32 percent in 2010.

As a result of population growth, meanwhile, the *absolute number* of people living in poverty was still very high. Despite fluctuations in percentages, the size of the poverty-stricken population swelled from 136 million in 1980 to 221 million in 2002, including 95 million indigents. Conditions thereafter improved and the number of people in poverty dropped to 180 million in 2008, climbing to 183 million in 2009—as a result of the international financial crisis—and returning to 180 million as of 2010. This figure was a good deal lower than in 2002, but substantially higher than it was in 1980.

Despite such caveats, the relative decline in poverty—from one half the region's population to one third—could only be seen as a welcome development. It appeared to stem from two causes. One was the post-2002 global increase in prices of commodities, due in large part to rising demand from China, as growth rates climbed into the 5 to 6 percent range. And if it is true that rising tides lift all boats, as the adage goes, poverty declined as a result. This brings us back to the relationship between democratization and economic growth. As shown at the outset of this chapter, democracies have been only marginally, if at all, more successful than dictatorships at stimulating economic growth.

Social policy also played a crucial role. One of the most remarkable innovations in recent years has been the adoption of "conditional cash transfer" programs, known as CCTs. Essentially these involve modest cash payments to poor families, usually the mothers, who agree to meet specified conditions—such as sending their children to school, providing nutritional meals, and getting proper medical attention. The goals are to reduce levels of poverty in the short run, to break cycles of intergenerational poverty, and to increase human capital in the long run. In effect, CCTs amount to "social contracts" between the states and needy citizens. As such, they confront governments with substantial logistical challenges—determining eligibility, overseeing compliance, and tracking practical outcomes. Even so they have proven to be cost-effective, with budgetary outlays well under 1 percent of GDP in virtually all cases.

One landmark program was launched in 1997 in Mexico under the name of Progresa. Renamed "Oportunidades" in 2001, the strategy has emphasized health, nutrition, and education, especially for children. As of 2009 the Oportunidades program was covering about one fifth of household expenses for more than 5 million poverty-stricken families, or about 25 million people. This was a major endeavor.

A similar effort emerged in Brazil. Initially launched under Fernando Henrique Cardoso, the program was greatly expanded under Lula and came to be known as Bolsa Família. With expenditures amounting to 0.5 percent of GDP, it offers monthly payments of about U.S. $12 per child in school up to a maximum of three children, plus an additional flat sum to indigent families. Now the largest CCT in the world, Bolsa Família covers about 12 million families, more than 45 million people.

Evidence suggests that CCTs have led to substantial reductions in poverty. "I think these programs are as close as you can come to a magic bullet in development," says Nancy Birdsall, a well-known economist. "They're creating an incentive for families to invest in their own children's futures. Every decade or so, we see something that can really make a difference, and this is one of those things." Given the apparent effectiveness of CCTs, spin-off programs have emerged in such varied locations as Nicaragua, Honduras, Jamaica, Chile, Malawi, Nigeria, Zambia—and New York City.

Of course the CCTs have provided political benefits as well. Most analysts believe that the high-profile success of Bolsa Família provided a substantial boost to Lula's reelection campaign in 2006. After purchasing flip-flop sandals for her previously barefoot children, one grateful recipient stated the matter bluntly. "First, I thank God," said the mother. "Second, I thank President Lula."

Traditional social assistance programs have also flourished under more left-of-center regimes. In particular, the Chávez government in Venezuela launched a series of "missions to save the people" in 2003, initially focusing on health care in shantytowns around the cities (Misión Barrio Adentro). Subsequent "missions" have promoted literacy (Misión Robinson) and educational opportunity (Misión Ribas). Others have constructed discount grocery stores throughout the country (Misión Mercal) and fostered job creation through local cooperatives (Misión Vuelvan Caras). All these programs have been financed by the allocation of oil revenues to a special fund managed directly by the presidency, possibly as much as 2.5 percent of GDP. This has provided Chávez with enormous amounts of discretionary power. In contrast to the CCTs, especially in Mexico, decision making for the "missions" has proven to be arbitrary and accountability has been opaque. There is little doubt that Chávez has used the programs to build popular support and bolster his political fortunes.

Even so, the missions have improved the lives of Venezuela's poor. Between 1998 and 2009, according to official statistics, the nation's poverty rate declined from 49 percent to 26 percent, and unemployment fell from 15 percent to 7 percent. Extreme poverty and overall inequality declined as well. Such trends have sparked debate about patterns of cause-and-effect (and the reliability of governmental data), but it is widely recognized that the "missions" have had a substantial impact on the social order (see Box 8.2).

BOX 8.2
SCORECARD FOR THE LEFT

Are there meaningful differences within the "new Left" in Latin America? What do pink-tide movements have in common and where do they diverge? And do the variations matter?

An important new study seeks to explore these questions. The authors begin by tracing common threads within the new Left. With the partial (but conspicuous) exception of Hugo Chávez, all pink-tide leaders have upheld the basic institutions of political democracy, including reliance on free and fair elections. Unlike the revolutionaries of the 1960s and 1970s, none has advocated violent overthrow of the social or political social order. All have kept their countries open to foreign investment. All proclaim paramount desires to reduce poverty and inequality.

Yet important differences have emerged. A "moderate" streak, epitomized for these authors by Brazil and Chile, appeared in countries with relatively strong and institutionalized political parties. A more extremist trend, illustrated by Venezuela and Bolivia (and labeled "contestatory" rather than "radical"), emerged in societies with disintegrating, nonexistent, or personalistic party systems.

One clear divergence has involved political strategy. Moderate governments in Brazil and Chile have respected representative political institutions and sought common ground with the opposition. In contrast, the contestatory regimes of Chávez and Morales have sought to revamp the political framework (by rewriting national constitutions) and to eliminate strongholds of the opposition. Such tactics have intensified polarization.

At the same time, the Chávez–Morales approach has substantially enhanced the political role of previously marginal groups, such as indigenous populations and the urban poor. This has not occurred under the moderate Left. As shown by survey research, political inclusion in Venezuela and Bolivia has led to notable increases in popular support (and satisfaction with) democracy.

With regard to economic policy, the moderate Left has embraced the private sector and the importance of the market. For its part, the contestatory faction has instead sought to strengthen the role of the state. In Venezuela, for example, central government spending increased from 18 percent of GDP in 1998 to 34 percent in 2008.

Concertación governments in Chile and Lula in Brazil have presided over years of steady and strong macroeconomic performance, with average growth rates around 5 percent. Venezuela, and to a lesser extent Bolivia, have achieved spectacular results—with growth rates exceeding 10 percent in some years—but with erratic overall patterns. This might be due in part to the reliance on petroleum and hydrocarbon exports, which are subject to sharp fluctuations in prices.

As to social policy, the moderate Left has emphasized gradual poverty reduction through the deliberate use of CCTs. The contestatory Left has used similar instruments (as in Bolivia) and also grander, less institutionalized transfers to the poor (such as the "missions" in Venezuela). One major difference concerns land reform, which has been strongly advocated by Chávez and Morales but essentially ignored by their moderate counterparts.

"In sum," write the authors, the contestatory Left "has undertaken more ambitious initiatives on the political, economic, and social front and has managed to achieve considerable progress toward its goals in recent years. But it is unclear whether these accomplishments—especially the economic and social achievements—are sustainable. By contrast," the moderate Left "has taken smaller steps, yet on a more solid foundation....This patient approach may yield greater achievements in the long run."

Source: Kurt Weyland, Raúl L. Madrid, and Wendy Hunter, eds., *Leftist Governments in Latin America: Successes and Shortcomings* (New York: Cambridge University Press, 2010), Ch. 7.

The overall connection between social transfer programs and democracy is suggestive but unclear. The Oportunidades program in Mexico started under Ernesto Zedillo Ponce de León, the last of the *priista* presidents. To be sure, increasingly democratic regimes have greatly expanded the scope of CCTs. Yet authoritarian governments have also created top-down assistance programs, as in Venezuela, and not every country with CCTs could be classified as democratic. Ambiguity prevails.

INEQUALITY AND INCOME DISTRIBUTION

Socioeconomic inequality has presented an additional structural challenge. For a complex variety of (strongly debated) reasons, Latin America has exhibited the most unequal distribution of income (and wealth) in the entire world. Economic inequality in Latin America is worse than in sub-Saharan Africa, North Africa, the Middle East, and South Asia—and much worse than in the advanced industrial economies.[18] Like poverty, yawning differences between rich and poor have been denounced as a cause of economic underdevelopment, a moral disgrace, and a potential source of political instability. Even more than poverty, inequality is thought to engender social tension, as the well-being of "haves" can inspire acute resentment among the "have-nots."

According to a classic argument by Simon Kuznets, inequality constitutes a necessary phase in the process of economic development. As economic transformation takes place, some social groups are inexorably bound to move

---

[18] Luis F. López-Calva and Nora Lustig, eds., *Declining Inequality in Latin America: A Decade of Progress?* (New York and Washington, DC: United Nations Development Programme and Brookings Institution, 2010), 1–2.

ahead more rapidly than others.[19] Not everyone can benefit to the same degree at the same time. However, the political question is how long the rest of society must wait. When will less privileged sectors begin to catch up?

Changes in levels of inequality depend on both the haves and have-nots. Alleviation of inequality would require the have-nots to increase their incomes more rapidly than do the haves. Alternatively, exacerbation of inequality could occur under any one of several scenarios: (1) the haves get richer while the have-nots stay the same, (2) the haves stay the same but the have-nots suffer a decline, (3) the haves get richer and the have-nots suffer a decline, or (4) the haves get richer and the have-nots move ahead, but not as rapidly as the haves. These scenarios are likely to produce different levels of political tension. Condition (3) would probably be the most volatile and condition (4) the least volatile, with conditions (1) and (2) somewhere in between.

Because of such relationships, inequality has fomented complex political debates in Latin America. Sometimes evoking Marxist notions of class struggle, radicals have stridently denounced the concentration of wealth. They have advocated agrarian reform and land redistribution, they have supported working-class organizations, and, in frustration, they have issued calls for social revolution. Sometimes evoking Kuznets, conservatives have asserted that things will get better in the long run—whenever that might occur. And moderates, in the meantime, have acknowledged the moral and political need for greater social equity, hoping that, under conditions of economic growth, have-nots will manage to make up ground on the haves.

What has happened in Latin America? Has the onset of electoral democracy had a discernible impact on income distribution? Figure 8.6 approaches these questions by tracing patterns of income distribution for four major countries—Argentina, Brazil, Chile, and Mexico—from 1980 to 2010. The horizontal axis in the graph corresponds to change over time. The vertical axis presents values for a summary measure of maldistribution of income called the Gini index, which ranges from a theoretical point of zero (where income is equally distributed among all segments of the population) toward a maximum value of unity, or 1.0 (where a minimal portion of the population, presumably one individual, would garner all the income of the entire society). Think of it this way: The higher the Gini index, the worse the income distribution.

---

[19] Historical research has cast doubt on the empirical validity of the Kuznets hypothesis. For example, see Martin Shanahan and Margaret Correll, "In Search of Kuznets' Curve: A Reexamination of the Distribution of Wealth in the United States between 1650 and 1950," paper presented at the Third World Conference of Cliometrics (Munich, Germany, July 1997), and Nicola Rossi, Gianni Toniolo, and Giovanni Vecchi, "Is the Kuznets Curve Still Alive? Evidence from Italy's Household Budgets, 1881–1961," CERP Discussion Paper 2140, Centre for Economic Policy Research (London, 1999).

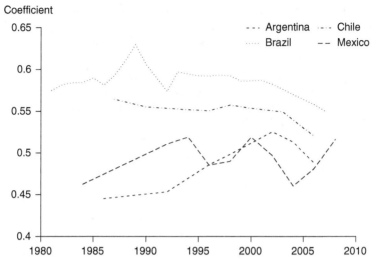

Figure 8.6 Patterns of income distribution: ABC countries and Mexico, 1980–2010

Source: World Bank, World Development Indicators.

Broadly speaking, trends over time take the shape of an inverted U-curve. For the most part, levels of inequality grew sharper during the 1980s and 1990s, as countries struggled to recover from the debt crisis of the 1980s—and met severe competition in the globalizing marketplace. The Gini index for Brazil spiked upward in the late 1980s and flattened out during the 1990s. After a steady rise in maldistribution from the late 1960s to the early 1980s under the Pinochet dictatorship, Chile showed a slight increase in the mid-1990s. Argentina showed a strong and steady rise in inequality from the mid-1980s to the turn of the century. The indicators for Mexico are somewhat erratic, but they also reveal an upward tendency from the mid-1980s to 2000 or so. (Year-to-year oscillations are probably due to variations in measurement techniques.) For Latin America as a whole, income inequality was became decidedly worse during the 1980s and 1990s.[20]

This unwelcome trend resulted from a variety of factors. First, poor people in Latin America were unable to protect themselves during the "lost decade" of the 1980s and against the neoliberal structural reforms of the 1990s. Second, increasing rewards for educational attainment increased earnings gaps between skilled and less skilled workers. And third, trade liberalization under the Washington Consensus had an indirect effect. As Luis López-Calva and Nora Lustig have noted, "The direct effect of trade

---

[20] See Programa de las Naciones Unidas para el Desarrollo (PNUD), *La democracia en América Latina: hacia una democracia de ciudadanas y ciudadanos* (New York and Buenos Aires: United Nations Development Programme, 2004), 40–41 and 124; and Karl, "Vicious Cycle," 137–138.

liberalization on wage inequality seems to have been small, [while] the indirect effect of trade and capital account liberalization through their impact on adoption of new skill-intensive technologies of production and organization might have been substantial."[21]

Patterns of change reversed course in the mid-1990s or early 2000s, depending on the country. As shown in Figure 8.6, levels of inequality started moving downward in Brazil and Chile after 2000 and in Argentina after 2003. Inequality in Mexico also moved downward around 2000, but then (as an exception to the rule) spiked upward again.

In point of fact, the regional decline in inequality turns out to have been a widespread phenomenon. According to an authoritative recent study, levels of inequality were reduced in no less than twelve out of seventeen countries of Latin America between 2000 and 2006. These shifts were systematic: Among those twelve countries, the average decline was around 1 percent per year. Ecuador, Paraguay, and Brazil made the greatest progress, while several countries—including Uruguay and Costa Rica—showed increases in inequality. By the year 2007, Venezuela had the least amount of inequality, with a Gini index of less than 0.45, followed by Uruguay and Argentina. Costa Rica, Peru, El Salvador, and Mexico were also under 0.50. At the other end of the spectrum were Brazil, Panama, Bolivia, and Honduras, which was close to 0.60.

Explanations for this trend must necessarily be tentative. One apparent factor was a reduction in the earnings gap between skilled and less skilled workers, itself the result of a long-term expansion of basic education that led to an upgrading of the work force. (Recall that democracies have strongly outperformed autocracies in the realm of public education.) Another factor was the effect and diffusion of CCTs, which helped bring people out of poverty and into national markets. Migrant remittances to Mexico and other countries provided another kind of income transfer to the poor.

Once again, the connection to democracy is unclear and indirect. Ultimately, the achievement of social equity, defined as a reasonable and fair distribution of income (or wealth), might depend on economic rather than political factors. But once again, this begs a fundamental question: Have democracies provided a more efficient and productive context for economic development than have autocracies? As revealed repeatedly throughout this chapter, the answer here is inconclusive.

Even in light of recent progress against poverty and inequality, fundamental questions remain: Are these improvements substantial enough? Will the positive trends persist? Will they enhance popular support for democratic forms of rule? For citizens who struggled so long against dictatorship, lifted their hopes so enthusiastically, and waited so patiently for social and economic justice, uncertainty continues to provoke frustration and anxiety.

---

[21] López-Calva and Lustig, *Declining Inequality*, 7–8.

CHAPTER 9

THE POLITICS OF
SOCIAL EQUITY

Does democracy promote equity? Does it empower the weak and disadvantaged? Such questions strike at the core of democratic governance. In principle, political freedoms and fair elections should enable the poor to advance their interests through parties, associations, and movements that can press for redistributive reform. By giving power to "the people," democracy should make it possible for common citizens to pursue their interests, increase their share of benefits, and thus reduce societal inequalities. Reflecting this conviction, democratic ideals embrace fundamental notions of justice, equity, and fairness.[1]

Has this happened in Latin America? This chapter approaches the question by focusing on three major groups: labor, women, and indigenous peoples. All these groups endured long histories of exclusion and discrimination: workers on the basis of class status, women on the basis of gender bias, and indigenous peoples on the basis of ethnic prejudice. In several key countries organized labor and indigenous communities suffered from horrendous campaigns of state-sponsored violence. Societies are therefore in debt to these groups. According to minimal standards of fairness, workers, women, and indigenous peoples should receive substantial benefits from the democracies they helped inaugurate and now support. How have they been faring?

Distinctions are important here. One is that, as shown later, organized labor in Latin America has a long and complex history of relations with the state. Worker unions were hierarchically organized, populist in orientation, and engaged in pragmatic bargaining with government authorities. In contrast, movements of women and indigenous peoples have been generally

---

[1] Within democratic theory there is, of course, considerable tension between the competing ideals of individual freedom and collective equity.

THE CONCEPT OF CIVIL SOCIETY

The notion of "civil society" has become a basic foundation for understanding contemporary democracy. In essence, it depicts an arena of citizen empowerment. According to one of its foremost analysts, Larry Diamond, it can be defined as follows:

> *Civil society is the realm of organized social life that is open, voluntary, self-generating, at least partially self-supporting, autonomous from the state, and bound by a legal order or set of shared rules.* It is distinct from "society" in general in that *it involves citizens acting collectively in a public sphere* to express their interests, passions, preferences, and ideas, to exchange information, to achieve collective goals, to make demands on the state, to improve the structure and functioning of the state, and to hold state officials accountable. Civil society is an intermediary phenomenon, standing between the private sphere and the state.

Unlike revolutionaries, actors in civil society recognize the principles of state authority and rule of law; unlike political parties, they do not seek high-level offices; unlike pressure groups, they are concerned with public goals rather than private ends. Rather than attempting to "conquer" the state, civil society seeks concessions, benefits, policy changes, relief, redress, justice, or accountability.

Source: Larry Diamond, *Developing Democracy: Toward Consolidation* (Baltimore: Johns Hopkins University Press, 1999), 221.

construed as "new" social movements. They have emerged from grassroots activism, they are independent and autonomous—and in many cases they regard the state as hostile, corrupt, or ineffective. They are expressions of what has come to be known as "civil society" (see Box 9.1).

As the evidence will show, these groups have chosen a broad array of means to pursue their ends. One prominent path has involved political parties, and another has been through social movements. They have made significant advances and suffered setbacks as well. None has achieved all the power or benefits that they rightfully deserve. Even under democracy, social justice remains elusive.

As a result, many leaders of disadvantaged groups in Latin America have been losing patience with democratic politics. Frustrated by the glacial pace of social progress and institutional reform, they have been rebuilding their popular bases and taking their demands back into the streets. Insofar as this trend provides citizens with freedoms of speech and association, it is a positive development; insofar as it threatens the legitimacy of democratic government, it might undermine prospects for regime consolidation.

LOSING GROUND: THE WORKING CLASS

The working classes of Latin America entered the political scene through a variety of mechanisms. One early route entailed mobilization by traditional political parties seeking electoral advantage—the Colorados in Uruguay, for instance, and the Liberals in Colombia. These awkward alliances yielded benefits for both politicians and laborers, but it was difficult to sustain such coalitions in light of social-class differences. They ultimately ended in stalemate or failure.

The 1930s proved to be a formative time. One emerging pattern involved "state incorporation" of organized labor. Under this scenario, the state was the principal actor: Its goal was to create a legalized and institutionalized labor movement that was depoliticized, controlled, and penetrated by the state. Union links to political parties were prohibited, and preexisting political currents within the labor movement were suppressed. The prototypical case occurred in Brazil, as Getúlio Vargas incorporated organized labor as part of the Estado Novo. A similar trend emerged under Lázaro Cárdenas in Mexico, where labor was brought under the fold of a ruling party that was itself an instrument of the state.

During the 1940s an alternative pattern took the form of "labor populism," which involved the electoral mobilization of labor with close links to a party or political movement, but without including the peasantry. In this context, a populist party or movement displaced traditional parties or the traditional political class; its ideology was strongly anti-oligarchical, but not to the point of altering property relations in the rural sector. The most conspicuous case was Peronism in Argentina. A more "radical" variant of the populist alternative involved the electoral mobilization of labor, a major effort to link unions to a party, and parallel incorporation of the peasantry, which led to a call for agrarian reform as well as labor rights. One clear-cut example appeared in Venezuela; by the 1940s, Chile offered another instance.[2]

During the 1940–1977 phase of democratization, there emerged a trade-off between labor and the state: (1) Labor cast its destiny with a political party and was thus dependent on the outcome of elections. (2) Labor would mobilize behind that party and provide a major boost at the polls; in cases of authoritarian or semidemocratic elections, as in Mexico from the 1940s through the 1980s, labor's participation helped to legitimize the outcome. (3) With victory secured, organized labor would receive a series of benefits—formal recognition of unions as bargaining units, the right to organize and strike, mandatory wage increases, the creation of union shops, intervention on behalf of labor in struggles with employers, and social security programs. This overall bargain tended to consolidate the role and strength of union

---

[2] See Ruth Berins Collier and David Collier, *Shaping the Political Arena: Critical Junctures, the Labor Movement, and Regime Dynamics in Latin America* (Princeton, NJ: Princeton University Press, 1991), esp. 161–168.

leadership, which was often highly centralized (and not very democratic). All in all, this was a fairly cozy relationship, one that kept employers on the defensive and, especially where labor was tied to the peasantry, a source of concern to landowners as well.

Organized labor became a major target of the bureaucratic-authoritarian regimes that overthrew electoral democracies in the 1960s and 1970s. It was seen as a threat to economic growth and sustainability and, perhaps even worse, as a hotbed of Marxist ideology. Military rulers thus unleashed furious attacks on existing labor unions in Argentina, Brazil, Chile, and Uruguay. They also sought to forge a new breed of leaders and unions that would facilitate fulfillment of the state-led projects of the 1920s and 1930s: a depoliticized labor movement that would be penetrated and controlled by the state.

Eventually, labor mounted heroic resistance. In Argentina, labor unions organized a series of general strikes that mobilized popular opinion against the military regime (and prompted the generals to undertake the ill-fated invasion of the Falkland/Malvinas Islands in 1982, a move that led to their defeat and disgrace). Reacting against the Pinochet regime, workers in Chile staged forty to ninety strikes per year during the 1980s. Unions in Uruguay mounted thirty strikes in 1983 and seventy-five in 1984. In Brazil, the workers of São Paulo, especially the metalworkers' union, led by an up-and-coming young leader with the nickname of Lula, organized mass rallies that sped the regime toward liberalization and eventual exit. During the 1970s and 1980s, labor had contentious relationships with every "exclusionary" authoritarian government in Latin America. Organized protests and strikes by trade unions were crucial in destabilizing authoritarianism and opening the way for democratization.[3]

One might have expected that as a result, labor would receive substantial benefits from the new post-1978 democracies throughout the region. That has not occurred. On the contrary, unions have faced a wave of neoliberal reforms that have endangered their economic welfare and compromised their political clout. More perplexing still is the fact that many of these reforms were implemented by parties that were once loyal allies, including the Peronists in Argentina and Acción Democrática in Venezuela. What had changed, and why?

Signs of Hard Times

A central determinant of labor's declining political influence stems from the changing shape of global, regional, and national economies. Since the

---

[3] Ruth Berins Collier, *Paths Toward Democracy: The Working Class and Elites in Western Europe and South America* (Cambridge: Cambridge University Press, 1999); and Paul W. Drake, *Labor Movements and Dictatorships: The Southern Cone in Comparative Perspective* (Baltimore: Johns Hopkins University Press, 1996).

early 1980s, Latin America has been undergoing a "dual transition," one political, the other economic. One refers to the onset and spread of electoral democracy. The other refers to the imposition of neoliberal economic reforms in accordance with the Washington Consensus: the reduction or near-elimination of protectionist barriers against foreign imports and investment (which threatened domestic industry), alteration in the economic role of the state (which could no longer protect organized labor), the removal of safety nets and security blankets (which made unemployment that much more severe), and the promotion of free-market economics (which led to a new private sector). All these changes hurt organized labor.

During the 1990s, employers in Latin America began to increase their focus on keeping labor costs low. As a result of increased competition from abroad and a decline in government subsidies, businesses were no longer in a position to keep "labor peace" as a high priority. Without state intervention and assistance, many firms reduced their payrolls by slashing wages or dismissing workers. In the face of such realities, organized labor has lost considerable leverage in the marketplace and power in politics. In sum, Latin America's dual transition to democracy and free-market economics simultaneously increased the voice of actors in civil society (such as labor) while giving them more reason to protest (declines in real wages, the disappearance of trade protection, and the privatization of many state-owned industries).

Numerous indicators point to a decline in the strength of organized labor. One underlying factor was the expansion of "informal" employment—day-to-day jobs that are ad hoc, insecure, and unprotected by labor regulations of any kind. In 1980, about 40 percent of Latin America's workers held informal employment; by 2000, the figure was approaching 50 percent.[4] This trend was highly problematic for unions insofar as workers in the informal sector were often self-employed and difficult, if not impossible, to organize.

Partly as a result, the percentage of workers belonging to unions—what is known as "union density"—has sharply declined in many countries. As shown in Figure 9.1, density dropped almost everywhere between the 1980s and the 1990s: from 48 percent to 25 percent in Argentina, from 38 percent to 16 percent in Uruguay, from 23 percent to 12 percent in Costa Rica, from 22 percent to 18 percent in Brazil, and from 25 percent to 14 percent in Venezuela. All these declines took place under electoral democracies. Only Chile showed an increase, from 11 percent under the heel of the Pinochet dictatorship to a still-modest level of 15 percent under democratic governments.[5] Generally speaking, workers did not have unions—and unions

---

[4] Emilio Klein and Víctor Tokman, "La estratificación social bajo tensión en la era de la globalización," *Revista de la CEPAL* (December 2000), 13.

[5] See also International Labour Organization, *World Labour Report, 1997–98: Industrial Relations, Democracy and Social Stability* (ILO: Geneva, 1997).

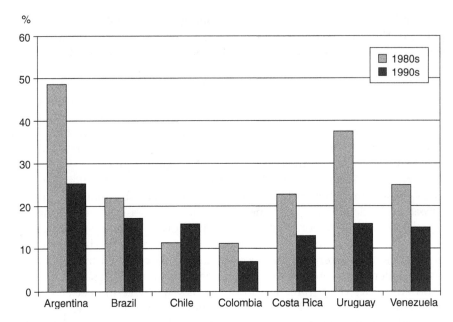

Figure 9.1 Union density in selected countries, 1980s–1990s

Sources: World Bank; International Labour Organization, *World Labour Report, 1997–98: Industrial Relations, Democracy and Social Stability* (Geneva: ILO, 1997), Statistical Annex, Tables 1.1 and 1.2, 235–238; and Paul G. Buchanan and Kate Nicholls, *Labour Politics in Small Open Democracies* (New York: Palgrave/Macmillan, 2003).

did not have workers. Both would suffer as a result. This downward trend continued into the twenty-first century.

Organized or not, workers were facing hard times. As revealed by Figure 9.2, the region as a whole endured a steady increase in unemployment from the 1980s through the turn of the century, with rates rising from 7 percent to approximately 9 percent and slipping back to 7 percent by 2007. Unemployment in Chile peaked in the early 1980s under the hard-fisted Pinochet regime, declined in the mid-1990s, then rose and fell once again. In contrast, Brazil showed a steady rise in unemployment from the 1980s to the early 2000s, hovering around 8 percent for several years before dropping to 7 percent. Democracy in Argentina suffered the most spectacular variations, with layoffs rising to nearly 20 percent in the mid-1990s and again in response to the crisis of 2002–2003, then dropping precipitously to the 7 percent range. Rates for Mexico exhibited a sharp rise during the peso crisis of 1994–1995, but then returned to levels of less than 5 percent (Mexico's operational definition of "unemployment" accounts in part for its lower overall level). Generally speaking, it would have to be said that political democracy was unable to assure job security for the working class.

Wages reveal a parallel trend. Setting real wages in the year 2000 as a base of 100, Figure 9.3 presents data on trends in ABC countries plus Mexico from

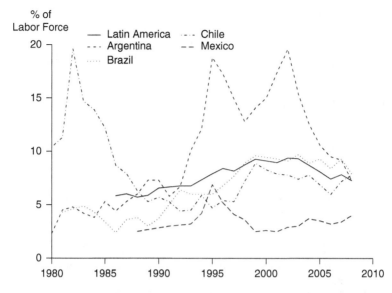

Figure 9.2 Unemployment in ABC countries and Mexico, 1980–2010

Source: International Labour Organization.

1980 to 2010. Chile displays a steady upward trend, climbing from the low 70s under Pinochet to approximately 105 by 2007. Brazil reveals a downward trend over time, with real rates peaking in the late 1990s and sliding downward thereafter. Argentina shows wild fluctuations, with real wages rising sharply in the early 1980s (after the restoration of democracy), holding steady during the 1990s, plunging downward during the crisis of 2002–2003, then rising sharply to 150 by 2007. As with unemployment, Mexico demonstrates the periodic impact of economic crisis—as real wages dropped markedly during the "lost decade" of the 1980s, recovered in the early 1990s, dropped again in response to the 1994–1995 pesos crisis, then climbed back over 100 after the turn of the century. Despite these variations, patterns nonetheless emerge. For Latin America as whole, average wage rates by the year 2000 had barely returned to the 1980 level. There was progress after that, especially in Argentina, but not so much in Brazil. With slight improvements after 2002, Chile and Mexico came closer to the norm.

High unemployment levels and the increasingly adversarial relationships between employers and unions were direct outcomes of neoliberal economic reforms in Latin America. Although this economic opening made Latin American businesses more competitive in general, it came at the cost of high jobless rates and a decline in both the real and perceived ability of unions to negotiate on the behalf of workers. The bottom line is plain to see: Despite the advent of electoral democracy, workers have not been faring well.

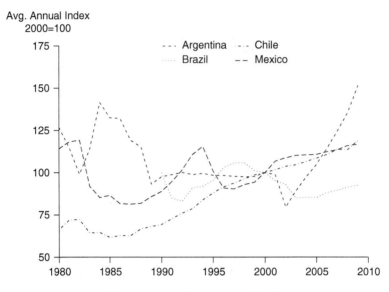

Figure 9.3 Wages in ABC countries and Mexico, 1980–2010

Source: International Labour Organization.

Zero-Sum Politics

Nor did labor have a wide range of choices. What could unions do? They could strengthen ties with partisan allies and press them to adopt strong prolabor platforms.[6] They could switch allegiance and court support from new or rival political parties. They could lobby congressional delegations and chief executives for alterations in policy. They could mount demonstrations and organize strikes—but in the prevailing economic environment, such moves incurred substantial risk of backlash. Labor was lacking leverage at this juncture.

At least in the medium term, labor's loss has been the private sector's gain. Generally speaking, the business community, especially large-scale business in Latin America, flourished during the 1990s. To be sure, some sectors struggled and failed: Small and medium-sized firms found it difficult to compete with foreign enterprise, and even larger companies could not survive without protection from the state. So there were shake-ups within the private sector as some firms went under and new ones came forward.

---

[6] In some instances, political parties defected from long-term alliances with labor. The most conspicuous case is the Peronist party in Argentina. On this see Stephen Levitsky, "From Labor Politics to Machine Politics: The Transformation of Party-Union Linkages in Argentine Peronism, 1983–1999," *Latin American Research Review* 38, 3 (2003): 3–36; and Gabriela Delamata, "Organizations of Unemployed Workers in Greater Buenos Aires," CLAS Working Paper #8 (Center for Latin American Studies, University of California, Berkeley, 2004).

And for the most part, members of Latin America's new business sector worked hand-in-hand with democratic governments. They did not take over or "conquer" the state, but they were able to advance their agendas and defend their interests through a variety of mechanisms: lobbying, personal contacts, campaign contributions, access to (or ownership of) mass media, and, more broadly, their endorsement of neoliberal economic reforms.[7] As critical allies for democratic leaders, entrepreneurs assumed a place of privilege in the pyramid of power. In the eyes of many political leaders, the business community has come to wield consummate influence in modern-day Latin America.[8]

WOMEN: MOVING UP

Contrary to prevailing stereotypes about Latin America, women have long played significant roles in the public arena. They have taken active part in party politics, they have joined up with revolutionary cadres, they have created social movements of their own, and they have achieved empowerment throughout the hemisphere. They have helped shape national agendas, stimulated public awareness, and influenced policy decisions. They have called autocratic rulers to account, undermined the legitimacy of authoritarian regimes, and thus helped to promote transitions toward electoral democracy.

To analyze this phenomenon, it is essential to distinguish between what have been called *feminine* (or women's) interests and *feminist* interests. As here defined, the purpose of feminine interests is to improve women's ability to fulfill traditional gendered roles—as mothers, nurturers, and helpmates—roles that are socially constructed. These have also been referred to as "practical" gender interests. According to Maxine Molyneux, such concerns generally "arise from the concrete condition of women's positioning within the gender division of labor," and they tend to be formulated "by the women who are themselves within these positions rather than through external interventions." Examples extend from neighborhood soup kitchens to public demonstrations demanding to learn the fate of family members who have been "disappeared" by military governments.

The idea behind feminist interests, in contrast, is to challenge and revise these social codes. They have also come to be known as "strategic" gender interests. They derive from broad analyses of women's subordination rather than concrete experience, and they entail "the formulation of an alternative,

[7]See Kurt Weyland, *Democracy without Equity: Failures of Reform in Brazil* (Pittsburgh, PA: University of Pittsburgh Press, 1996).

[8] Programa de Naciones Unidas para el Desarrollo, *La democracia en América Latina: hacia una democracia de ciudadanas y ciudadanos* (New York and Buenos Aires: United Nations Development Programme, 2004), 161, 164–165.

more satisfactory set of arrangements to those which exist." They focus not only on the immediate situation but also on its determinants, especially the social codes that define and enforce the gendered division of roles. They seek to alter the rules of the game.

As analysts have pointed out, the line between feminine and feminist interests tends to be blurred. In particular, the pursuit of "practical" gender interests can often lead to the articulation of "strategic" gender interests. Moreover, the content of Latin American feminism has differed from feminism in Europe and the United States. There is less emphasis on sexual liberation and economic equality and greater acceptance of the distinctiveness of womanhood. According to Francesca Miller,

> The belief in women's "different mission" lies at the heart of feminist movements in Latin America and differentiates it from the predominant form of feminism that developed in England and the United States, where equality with men was the goal, and gender differences were denied or at least played down. In the Latin American context, the feminine is cherished, the womanly—the ability to bear and raise children, to nurture a family—is celebrated.

Partly as a result, Latin American feminism has only rarely expressed systematic hostility toward men or become antimale.

Moreover, the struggle for women's interests—feminine, feminist, or both—has coexisted with struggles based on social class and ethnicity. This has given rise to considerable tension. A working-class woman of indigenous origin thus embodies different and sometimes competing interests to those of other women. And in many instances, class or ethnic interests have taken priority over women's goals.

There has been profound ambivalence about political participation. One opinion has held that politics (as practiced by men!) is inherently corrupt, a self-serving ritual of backroom deals, and that women's interests will be routinely ignored or underemphasized in the process of wheeling and dealing. Better to build social movements around women's interests than to enter party politics from a position of weakness. As women have moved ahead in politics, some of their sisters have shaken their heads in dismay.

An alternative view has insisted that, for better or worse, the path to power runs through politics. Sonia Alvarez, for example, has contended that participation in political institutions is essential to the advancement of women's interests under democratic rule. "The state," she writes,

> is *not* the executive committee of men, and therefore may act in the interest of particular groups of women (e.g., women of specific racial groups and classes) at a given historical conjuncture. Moreover, if state mediation of the conflicting interests of capitalism and patriarchy is sometimes contradictory, then gender-based social struggles can potentially exacerbate those contradictions. This feminist perspective on the relative autonomy of the state thus implies that class-based, racially based, and gender-based political struggles, led by social movements,

can and *must* take place both within and outside the political apparatus of the state.[9]

Like it or not, women have little choice but to plunge into the maelstroms of politics. And as Nikki Craske has said, women's participation in politics is not only about women's interests, it "is crucial to the quality of democracy itself."[10]

Patterns of Participation

Feminist currents first emerged in Latin America in the late nineteenth and early twentieth centuries, focusing on three sets of issues: women's civil status, labor laws, and education. Civil status was central because of patriarchal social codes: In some countries, women under thirty could not leave the parental home except to marry. Labor laws affected women because they worked long and hard in mills and factories, in the home, and as domestic servants. And because many women were teachers, they regarded educational opportunity as the key to social advancement. Reflecting the importance of these trends, an International Feminist Congress took place in Buenos Aires in 1910.

With the expansion of suffrage to adult males, women began to clamor for the right to vote. The suffragette movement was especially active in Chile. Women eventually acquired the vote, but not, for the most part, from democratic governments. On the contrary, it was a series of authoritarian regimes that granted suffrage to women from the 1930s through the 1950s. This pattern occurred in Ecuador (1929), Brazil (1932), Haiti (1950), Mexico (1953), Peru (1955), Colombia (1957), Paraguay (1961), and much of Central America. Perhaps the most well-known instance took place in Argentina (1947), where Evita Perón became one of the most powerful women in the history of the Western Hemisphere. Electoral democracies granted the vote to women in only three instances: Uruguay (1932), Venezuela (1947), and Chile (1949).[11]

This paradox has two explanations. First, it was generally assumed that women would vote for conservative parties and candidates and thus exert a moderating influence on electoral processes. Second, women were viewed as potential assets. As voters, they could be organized into electoral blocs, often through state-run political parties, and they could thus be counted on to legitimize one-sided elections. And in compliance with traditional gender roles, they could render social services through charitable works (in schools,

---

[9] Sonia Alvarez, *Engendering Democracy in Brazil: Women's Movements in Transition Politics* (Princeton, NJ: Princeton University Press, 1990), 31.

[10] Nikki Craske, *Women and Politics in Latin America* (New Brunswick, NJ: Rutgers University Press, 1999), 1.

[11] Costa Rica was in the process of becoming democratic when it extended suffrage to women in 1949.

1940s: Eva Perón dazzled throngs of admirers throughout Argentina with her glamorous appearance and populist ideology. (AP Photo/Archivo Clarín)

orphanages, neighborhoods, and elsewhere) and thus help strengthen autocratic regimes.

A "second generation" of women's activism emerged from the 1950s through the 1980s. Women took active part in revolutionary movements, constituting fully one third of the Sandinista fighting force in Nicaragua and a comparable share of armed rebels in El Salvador.

As brutal military regimes took hold, especially in South America, women found ways to resist. In Brazil, as Sonia Alvarez has said, women joined together in "militant motherhood" to denounce human-rights abuses. In Argentina, the "mothers of the Plaza de Mayo" held weekly vigils demanding information on relatives and loved ones who had "disappeared." In Chile, determined women found ways to express themselves through subversive forms of folk art (most notably *arpilleras*, tapestries made of burlap). All these protests began as classic expressions of "practical" and private interests—as efforts by mothers, wives, and grandmothers to nurture and protect their families. The mothers of the Plaza de Mayo, for instance, were not explicitly calling for the military to leave power, they were simply seeking information about family members. Yet their demands implicitly contained a subversive element, because they were attempting to hold the generals accountable for their actions. In this sense, their practical concerns acquired a strategic component. Ultimately, the courageous campaign of the *madres*—weekly vigils

1980s: Mothers of the Plaza de Mayo issued forceful demands for information about their missing children (*niños desaparecidos*)—and, in the process, helped undermine the military regime. (AP Photo/Eduardo Di Baia, File)

in downtown Buenos Aires, right in front of the presidential Casa Rosada and the majestic cathedral—helped undermine the regime.

Political Representation

Starting in the 1980s, the trend toward democratization produced ambivalent effects. Eager to recoup power, civilian men at first controlled the political arena, reserved high-ranking positions for themselves and their colleagues, and made only token concessions to women's demands. As one authority has noted, the process of regime transition resulted in the "demobilization" of social movements and their leaders in favor of political parties. Even so, women remained active in politics. They made up significant electoral constituencies, sometimes a majority of voters. They were increasingly educated and engaged in the work force. Feminist publications emerged in Mexico, Argentina, Chile, Brazil, and other countries.

As a result, women of Latin America gained increasing representation in formal positions of power, especially in congress. In 1990, according to

TABLE 9.1 Women in Latin American Legislatures, 1990–2010

Country	WOMEN (AS % TOTAL)*		
	1990	2000	2010
Argentina	5	27	38.5
Bolivia	9	12	25.4
Brazil	5	6	8.8
Chile	6	11	14.2
Colombia	9	12	—
Costa Rica	12	19	38.6
Dominican Republic	12	16	20.8
Ecuador	7	15	32.3
El Salvador	—	10	19.0
Guatemala	7	9	12.0
Honduras	—	9	18.0
Mexico	12	16	26.2
Nicaragua	19	10	20.7
Panama	8	10	8.5
Paraguay	4	3	12.5
Peru	6	20	27.5
Uruguay	6	12	15.2
Venezuela	10	10	—

*Lower house in case of bicameral legislature.
— = not available.

Sources: Women's Leadership Conference of the Americas, *Women and Power in the Americas: A Report Card* (Washington, DC: Inter-American Dialogue and International Center for Research on Women, 2001), 12–15; and Inter-Parliamentary Union.

Table 9.1, women occupied an average of less than 10 percent of seats in lower legislative houses; by 2000 the average had increased to 15 percent, approximately the same level as in the United States, and by 2010 it had climbed to 34 percent. Additionally, three Latin American democracies were among the top thirty countries in terms of female representatives: Costa Rica was tied for 11th, Argentina was 12th, and Ecuador was 20th.[12]

These gains resulted in part from the idea that women could provide a fresh alternative to stultified male leadership. According to one major survey, 66 percent agreed that women are more honest than men, and 85 percent agreed that women are good decision makers. Of respondents, 62 percent expressed the belief that women would do better than men at reducing poverty, 72 percent at improving education, 57 percent at combating corruption, 64 percent at protecting the environment, 59 percent at managing the economy, and 53 percent at conducting diplomatic relations. More than 90 percent claimed they would be willing to vote for a well-qualified candidate for

---

[12] Cuba ranked fourth—higher than any of the electoral democracies in this study. Inter-Parliamentary Union, at www.ipu.org/wmn-e/classif.htm.

president who happened to be a woman, and 69 percent believed that their country would elect a woman as president within the next twenty years.[13]

Also instrumental was the introduction of "quota laws," which require political parties to meet designated quotas for women within their slates of candidates (20 percent, 30 percent, etc.). Quotas were adopted for both domestic and international reasons. The domestic incentive reflected attempts by leaders, such as Carlos Saúl Menem in Argentina, to capture women as a voting bloc. The key international factor was the Fourth World Conference on Women, held in Beijing in 1995, which advocated quotas as a means of reducing the systematic underrepresentation of women in legislative bodies. In response to this challenge, chastened leaderships around the world introduced quotas for women's participation, either as a permanent or temporary measure, to increase the normative image of female representation in national parliaments.

By 2010 about two thirds of the nations of Latin America had quota laws (meaning, of course, that around one third did not). Argentina was the only nation to adopt a quota law prior to the Beijing meeting, and its results were impressive indeed: Women's representation in the lower house increased from 5 percent in 1990 to nearly 40 percent by 2010, with comparable results in the upper house as well. Costa Rica's 1997 law also proved to be effective, increasing women's representation in the country's unicameral legislature from 12 percent to 39 percent (slightly short of the designated 40 percent, but a substantial gain nonetheless). Similarly, Mexico's 1996 law (with subsequent revisions) led to notable advances. For the region as a whole, quota laws increased the share of women in parliament by an average of 8 percent or so.[14]

Backsliding and foot-dragging occurred. In most cases, advances for women have fallen well short of stipulated quotas. As political scientist Mala Htun has argued, these negative trends reflect deliberate efforts to weaken the effects of these laws. In Brazil, for example, the 30 percent figure was a *goal*, not a firm requirement. And in Mexico, loopholes in early versions of the law enabled parties to meet their quotas by nominating women for *suplente* (or "substitute") positions; in the 2000 elections for the chamber of deputies, women occupied 60 percent of the *suplente* slots and actually won only 16 percent of the regular seats.

Such experiences have shown that quota laws are most effective under three conditions. First, the quotas must be mandatory, not optional. Second, they must specify rules on the "placement" of women candidates—in every

---

[13] Women's Leadership Conference of the Americas, *Women and Power in the Americas: A Report Card* (Washington, DC: Inter-American Dialogue and International Center for Research on Women, 2001), 9.

[14] As of 2010, countries with quota laws were Argentina, Bolivia, Brazil, Costa Rica, the Dominican Republic, Ecuador, Honduras, Mexico, Panama, Paraguay, and Peru.

third slot on the party list, for example, rather than clustered either at the bottom or in *suplente* positions. Third, they must be enforceable: Parties must face the threat of losing seats in congress for failure to comply.

Although women have made substantial gains in congressional representation, this achievement faces a fundamental limitation: It is only as meaningful as the legislatures themselves. As revealed in Chapter 6 and elsewhere, congressional bodies in Latin America have been essentially "reactive" to executive initiatives—more negative than positive, more obstructionist than constructive. Moreover, women in these parliaments frequently find themselves relegated to family, health, or community (read: "feminine") committees. This gender segregation arguably perpetuates stereotypes, putting Latin America's female legislators in the perpetual role of *supermadre*, whose obligation is to "clean up" the dirty world of male-dominated politics. Increases in the legislative representation of females are positive developments, in other words, but they do not necessarily indicate that women succeeded in acquiring significant shares of real power.

The key lies in the executive branch. Gains have taken place. The first woman cabinet minister (without portfolio) was appointed in Cuba in 1948, followed by a female minister of justice in Chile in 1952. Argentina and Paraguay did not have female ministers until 1989. By 1990 women constituted 9 percent of Latin America's cabinet ministers, and by 2000 the figure had risen to 13 percent. In some countries—Chile, Colombia, Costa Rica, El Salvador, Honduras, Panama, and Venezuela—women held one fifth to one quarter of ministerial posts. Women took charge of major portfolios, such as foreign relations, in both Mexico and Chile. Perhaps most remarkably, Chile and Colombia have each had a female minister of defense!

There have been women presidents as well. To be sure, the first generation of women who became presidents—Isabel Martínez de Perón in Argentina, Violeta Barrios de Chamorro in Nicaragua, and Mireya Moscoso in Panama—acquired public profiles as widows of prominent men.[15] (And as Chamorro famously declared, "I am not a feminist nor do I wish to be one. I am a woman dedicated to my home, as [my husband] taught me.")

Shortly thereafter, a second generation of women stepped forward as serious presidential contenders. During the first decade of the twenty-first century, an impressive list of female politicians triumphed in national elections:

Michelle Bachelet, Chile (2006–2010)

Cristina Fernández de Kirchner, Argentina (2007–)

Laura Chinchilla, Costa Rica (2010–)

Dilma Rousseff, Brazil (2010–).

---

[15] Lidia Gueiler briefly served as president of Bolivia from November 1979 to July 1980; she was not directly elected, however, and she was overthrown by a military coup.

All these women had managed to build substantial political careers on their own (although Fernández of Argentina was preceded in the presidency by her husband, Néstor Kirchner). Women were poised to seek the presidency in other countries as well. Gender was no longer an insuperable handicap to political leadership.

As all the evidence indicates, legacies of *machismo* were not nearly as strong as stereotypes might suggest. At the very least, it must be said that women in Latin American politics were doing better than their sisters in the United States, which has not yet had a female president. And when did the Pentagon ever have a female commander?

Positions and Policies

Uneven advances in political representation for Latin American women were mirrored by uncertain accomplishments in the realm of policy. One indisputable and lasting achievement concerned agenda setting. Through social movements, public demonstrations, and legislative debates, women of Latin America made themselves heard. They stated their claims on society with eloquence and force. In so doing, they have raised the consciousness of women throughout the region, captured the attention of male decision makers, and inserted women's concerns onto national agendas. From this there is no turning back.

Second, they extracted policy concessions from traditionally patriarchal bastions of power. As in the case of São Paulo's Movimento de Luta por Creches (the Fight for Day Care Movement), they pressured governmental authorities into establishing day care centers, improving schools, and responding to a broad variety of "practical" (rather than strategic) demands. In Argentina and Chile, too, the continuing demands of mothers, wives, and grandmothers of disappeared persons obliged state authorities to continue delving into questions of accountability and guilt for human rights abuses under authoritarian regimes.

Third, women pressured national leaders into forming cabinet ministries devoted to the furtherance of women's interests. Originally imagined as "beach-heads" for broader assaults on male-dominated power establishments, these agencies also threatened to ghettoize female concerns. In Chile, the cabinet-level Servicio Nacional para la Mujer (SERNAM) had good access to other government agencies but only modest influence; the same held true for the Brazilian National Council for Women's Rights (CNDM). In Argentina, the Consejo Nacional de la Mujer had neither access nor influence. For the most part, according to Craske, women's ministries in Latin America were "structurally weak and not a major resource for furthering interests." The state could provide resources and legal frameworks, but the ministries themselves are not enough: "External pressure is needed to make the state work for women."[16]

---

[16] Craske, *Women and Politics*, 187–189.

Advances on specifically feminist agendas have come through varied channels. In a supreme irony, authoritarian military regimes—dictatorships that typically invoked patriarchal discourses as part of their claims on power—found themselves promoting women's interests. In their effort to "modernize" social and political structures, as Htun has shown, bureau-cratic-authoritarian leaders decided to update and reform long-standing legal codes. Their chosen instrument was a committee of prominent jurists, who could recommend sometimes sweeping changes that leaders could implement without the benefit (or inconvenience) of democratic debate. Within these obscure juridical realms, legal questions were considered to be "technical" and not political.[17] Under such contexts, authoritarian rulers in Argentina, Brazil, and Chile recognized civil capacity and property rights for women and imposed major reforms in the area of *patria potestad*, granting women and men equal responsibility for the care of children.[18]

Legalization of divorce presented greater challenges, especially in light of unyielding doctrinal opposition from the Roman Catholic Church. Where the prevailing regime (dictatorial or democratic) was in close alliance with the church, as in authoritarian Argentina and post-Pinochet Chile, there was no change in prohibitions on divorce. Where the regime was opposed to the church, as in authoritarian Brazil and democratic Argentina, progress became possible. As a result, divorce became legal in Brazil in 1977 and in Argentina in 1987. Otherwise progressive Chile would not legalize divorce until mid-2004.

Abortion was yet another matter. Given the strength of church opposition and the lack of support from male colleagues, few gains were made on this issue. As of 2010 only one Latin America nation—socialist Cuba—allowed abortions on demand.[19] A handful of countries, including such vibrant democracies as Uruguay and Chile, upheld complete and total prohibitions on the practice. Others permitted abortions only under special conditions, such as when the pregnancy resulted from rape or if the life or health of the mother was deemed to be "at risk" (judges and doctors were often reluctant to certify these conditions, however, so legal abortions were relatively rare). Throughout most of the region, legalization of abortion remained a central issue the feminist agenda.

---

[17] See Mala Htun, *Sex and the State: Abortion, Divorce, and the Family under Latin American Dictatorships and Democracies* (Cambridge: Cambridge University Press, 2003).

[18] *Patria potestad* refers to men's de facto control over a family's children. This was a legal norm in most of Latin America until the 1980s and 1990s.

[19] Mexico City (the Federal District) has also legalized abortion on demand, thanks to efforts by the left-leaning PRD. Rulings on abortion are made at the state or provincial level in Mexico.

GATHERING STRENGTH: INDIGENOUS PEOPLES

The latest phase of democratization in Latin America has witnessed the entrance of indigenous peoples into the political arena, especially in countries where they approach or exceed a majority of the population. Indigenous movements face a critical choice—whether to emphasize class and economic issues or to place the stress on ethnic and cultural identity. The former demands social justice as a matter of *equality* among citizens; the latter calls for recognition of *differences* among kinds of citizens.

This political emergence is of recent origin. During the colonial period, indigenous peoples responded to the Spanish conquest in a variety of ways: submission (with insubordinate subterfuges), flight, and armed rebellion. During the nineteenth century, economic liberalism resulted in the dispossession of indigenous peoples and their reduction to wage labor and debt peonage. Political participation, such as it was, usually took the form of *gamonalismo*, whereby a local *jefe* ("chief," perhaps indigenous, perhaps mestizo) would buy and sell votes in return for favors. A basic pattern was established by the 1930s: Indigenous populations were politically marginalized, socially and culturally besieged, and economically exploited. They were part of the economy, but not part of the nation.

Around the middle of the twentieth century, countries such as Mexico, Bolivia, and Ecuador undertook grandiose projects for economic and political development on a national scale. White and mestizo elites viewed indigenous peoples as an obstacle to be overcome, a problem to correct, because their "backward" beliefs and practices presented threats to modernization. Accordingly, states led active efforts to "encourage" indigenous peoples to reconceptualize themselves as "peasants," not as "Indians." In support of this strategy, states doled out patronage to indigenous communities: meager land reforms and agricultural subsidies. Thus reorganizing the economic incentives, elites hoped that indigenous peoples would accept their role in agricultural production as their primary identity. Ironically, the credit systems and land reforms allowed indigenous identities to survive in the midst of radical economic transformation at the national level.

What explains the recent rise in activism? As occurred with organized labor, indigenous populations were greatly affected by Latin America's "dual transition"—simultaneous economic and political change. The debt crisis of the 1980s and the ensuing implementation of neoliberal reforms imposed enormous hardships on indigenous communities. Perhaps more to the point, as Deborah Yashar has argued, the debt crisis and subsequent reforms dismantled many of the patronage systems and corporatist institutions that had (inadvertently) generated high levels of indigenous autonomy. Clientelistic links between states and indigenous communities came crashing down during the 1980s and 1990s. The results were devastating. Economically, families found it difficult to subsist; socially, downturns in the agricultural economy threatened the autonomy and stability of indigenous communities.

Communal land ownership was collapsing in the face of political reforms and market shocks. The picture was extremely bleak.

At the same time, democratization created new opportunities for indigenous organization. Without systematic threats of repression, political activism suddenly became feasible. Prolonged economic crisis led to the need for mobilization; democratization provided the space for political action. The specific form of political participation varied according to local circumstance, as shown by the cases of Bolivia, Ecuador, and Guatemala.

Bolivia: Party Politics

The trajectory of indigenous politics in Bolivia follows from three defining factors. First is relative size: Depending on definition, approximately 57 percent of the Bolivian population is "indigenous." Second was the forced conscription of indigenous males into the national military during the Chaco War (against Paraguay, 1932–1935), which brought men out of traditional villages and into the national community. Third was mobilization of the highland peasantry during the 1940s into agrarian *sindicatos* in support of a revolutionary movement that seized power in 1952. With this new government in place, indigenous leaders began pressing the MNR (Movimiento Nacional Revolucionario) to recognize their concerns and promote land reform. Acceding to these demands, the MNR promptly incorporated the peasantry as its principal mass political base; in tacit exchange, speakers of Aymara and Quechua insisted that they be called not *indios* but *campesinos*, or peasants. By the late 1950s, the indigenous peasant movement had become an integral part of the MNR's clientelistic political machine and actually served as a conservatizing force.

Thereafter, indigenous groups became objects of co-optation and repression. To maintain their electoral base, MNR presidents—and there were several—continued to nurture clientelistic relations with indigenous communities. A military government under General René Barrientos forged a "military-peasant" pact in the mid-1960s, only to unleash a campaign of repression after it broke apart in 1971. Within the political arena, Bolivia's indigenous population continued to define itself in social-class terms rather than in cultural terms.

That changed by the 1980s. During Bolivia's transition to democracy (1978–1982), the relationship between agrarian workers and the MNR deteriorated. In response, indigenous leaders began to explore new forms of representation. Levels of ethnic consciousness within indigenous communities were on the rise, providing a potential basis for ideological and cultural cohesion. As a result, indigenous peoples turned from class identification to ethnic tradition.

The symbolic figure of inspiration became Tupak Katiri, who took part in an indigenous rebellion against Spanish rule in 1781 (he was the nephew of one Tupac Amaru, after whom the uprising is generally named). During the 1960s, Katarismo developed initially as an alliance of peasants, students, and intellectuals seeking to break the traditional ties between the peasantry and the military, which suppressed authentic indigenous issues and voices. As it developed over time, according to John A. Peeler, Katarismo became "less a movement than a banner denoting the political and cultural assertion of Aymara identity."[20] Although it was subject to fragmentation, it was conspicuously successful in gaining adherents. By the 1990s at least six Katarista parties were active on the national scene. One notable beneficiary was the populist Conciencia de la Patria (CONDEPA) movement of radio commentator Carlos Palenque, who was three times elected mayor of La Paz and made serious runs for the presidency in 1989 and 1993. Katarismo was also becoming an important force within the nation's labor unions.

Factions developed within extant indigenous political parties and the new indigenous organizations. As early as the 1980s, there were two identifiable veins within Katarismo. One was an "Indianist" vein, which advocated strong indigenous cultural and social autonomy, denounced Westernization, and refused to integrate nonindigenous actors into their movement. Although this ideological conviction served to generate a consistent message of autonomy and self-determination, it also managed to alienate most Bolivians. A more moderate vein, represented by the Movimento Revolucionario Tupac Katari de Liberación (MRTKL) party, combined Western political liberalism with advocacy for indigenous issues. As a result, the MRTKL has been successful at creating alliances with mainstream political parties and winning national-level offices. In 1993 the MRTKL formed an alliance with the MNR, which won the presidential election of 1993, and "cogoverned" with the MNR until 1997.

Disenchanted with the MRTKL's moderate line and alienation of indigenous militants, some indigenous leaders in Bolivia circumvented the party and formed organizations of their own. In 1995, the Confederación Sindical Única de Trabajadores y Campesinos de Bolivia (CSUTCB) created its own political party, the Asamblea de la Soberanía de los Pueblos (ASP). Initially successful at the local level, the ASP won 3.7 percent of the national vote in 1997.

By 1999, the MRTKL had split into Quechua and Aymara factions, the latter reformed as the Movimiento al Socialismo (MAS) in 2001. Under the leadership of Evo Morales, charismatic spokesman for Bolivia's coca-leaf growers (*cocaleros*), MAS finished a close second in the 2002 presidential elections with 20.9 percent of the vote. Taking advantage of the polarization and paralysis that gripped the country in subsequent years, Morales and

---

[20] See John A. Peeler, "Social Justice and the New Indigenous Politics," in Susan Eva Eckstein and Timothy P. Wickham-Crowley, eds., *What Justice? Whose Justice? Fighting for Fairness in Latin America* (Berkeley and Los Angeles: University of California Press, 2003), 257–284.

President Evo Morales summons all of his persuasive powers to govern multiethnic Bolivia. (AP Photo/Juan Karita)

MAS continued to build political strength. In late 2005 the near-unthinkable occurred: Evo Morales, an indigenous spokesperson for indigenous interests, won the presidency with a first-round majority of 54 percent. This was an astonishing development.

In keeping with his campaign rhetoric, Morales became a hard-core member of Latin America's left-leaning "pink tide." Proclaiming solidarity with Hugo Chávez and Fidel Castro, he immediately signed up with ALBA (the "Bolivarian alternative"). Faced at home with strident autonomy movements, especially in the powerful region of Santa Cruz, Morales convened a constitutional assembly that eventually defined the Bolivian state as "unitarian social, plurinational and communitarian, free, independent, sovereign, democratic, intercultural, and decentralized with autonomies." It further stressed that "nations and indigenous peoples" have the right to self-determination and self-government. In addition, Morales significantly augmented state intervention in the economy, sharply increasing governmental shares in the hydrocarbons and mining sectors. In turn, expanding revenues provided funding for social transfer programs that reached nearly 2 million children and 730,000 senior citizens. He also proposed an ambitious project for agrarian reform. Buoyed by international demand, the economy grew at rates of 5 to 6 percent, even registering +3.5 percent in the otherwise disastrous year of 2009. Apparently as a reward for these achievements, Morales won the 2009 election with 62.5 percent of the vote.

Ecuador: Strength in Social Movements

Ecuador has been the site of sustained indigenous politics since the 1980s. As in Bolivia, indigenous peoples have two distinct histories, one in the highlands of the sierra and the other in the Amazon jungle regions. In contrast to Bolivia, however, indigenous groups have managed to overcome these differences and to forge a strong and durable national movement.

Activism began as early as the 1920s, when peasant *sindicatos*, in alliance with the communist party, voiced demands for economic justice within a Marxist framework emphasizing class struggle rather than cultural identity. During the 1940s, the Federación Ecuatoriana de Indígenas continued to express the class-based grievances of indigenous workers and peasants. Peasant groups engaged in land seizures and uprisings in the 1950s and 1960s. Governments responded with agrarian reform programs in the 1960s and early 1970s, creating divergent interests among those who did and did not benefit from the reform—and, in effect, breaking down the cohesion of the peasant unions. Yet the tradition of an assertive indigenous peasantry did not die. Rather, it transformed itself into a national indigenous movement.

In 1986, the Confederación de Nacionalidades Indígenas del Ecuador (CONAIE) succeeded in merging indigenous movements from both the sierra and Amazonia. Displaying impressive organizational capacity, CONAIE became the principal institutional force behind indigenous demonstrations and strikes that marked Ecuadorian politics during the 1990s.

In 1990, members of CONAIE occupied the central cathedral in Quito, and others closed down roads and shut down commerce and transportation for more than a week. The demands reflected their dual constituencies: They wanted the government to expedite indigenous land claims in the sierra and territorial claims in the Amazonian *oriente*. In 1994, CONAIE joined with other organizations to shut down the country for two whole weeks. In January 2000, CONAIE increased the intensity of its political demands, organizing nationwide protests that resulted in the overthrow of President Jamil Mahuad. In Ecuador, an indigenous social movement was not yet able to elect a president, but it was capable of bringing one down. CONAIE thus became a vital veto player on the national scene.

CONAIE's agenda was clear: Indigenous populations were no longer willing to tolerate the economic injustices levied on the agrarian sector as a result of neoliberal economic reforms. Additionally, indigenous groups continued to demand an end to systematic discrimination in education, government policy, and society at large. Theirs was a vibrant movement with an expanding mission and increasing membership. Where it might end was anyone's guess (see Box 9.2).

Guatemala: Civil War and Genocide

The indigenous peoples of Guatemala entered the national stage during the 1940s, when they joined with idealistic reformers to overthrow a despised dictator, Jorge Ubico. Free and fair elections, the first in the country's history, resulted in successive victories for Juan José Arévalo and Jacobo Arbenz. Intent on structural change, Arévalo and (especially) Arbenz launched extensive programs for land reform and encouraged the formation of peasant and

CONAIE: INDIGENOUS MOBILIZATION OUTSIDE AND INSIDE THE STATE

CONAIE (Confederación de Nacionalidades Indígenas del Ecuador) is a broad coalition of Ecuadorian indigenous groups formed in the 1980s by regional organizations of Amazonian and Andean indigenous peoples. CONAIE is most readily labeled a "social movement organization," although the organization has participated in elections as well.

CONAIE first gained national and international notoriety for its June 1990 uprising that shut down Ecuador's transportation infrastructure and brought economic activity to a halt for more than a week. In 1996, the Movimento de Unidad Plurinacional Pachakutik (MUPP), a political party created by CONAIE, ran candidates in national and local elections, winning eight of eighty-two congressional seats (making it the fourth-largest party) and sixty-eight seats in local elections. Although an increase in the size of the national assembly decreased the proportional representation of the MUPP's eight seats in 1998 (the assembly grew to 121 seats), the party continues to participate in national and local elections.

indigenous unions. All this came to a halt in 1954, when the U.S. government conspired with reactionaries to oust Arbenz from power and install a military government.

This was a turning point for Guatemala. The reformist forces of the political Center (as represented by Arévalo and Arbenz) were crushed. There remained only a Left and a Right, with the Right in the ascendancy. Landowners and foreign investors regained their power under the protection of military rule. In this highly polarized context, Guatemala's military rulers never embraced the kind of "reformist" agenda adopted by inclusionary regimes in Peru (1968–1975) and in Ecuador (1972–1978). There were some half-hearted attempts and co-optation and appeasement of the country's peasantry, but no meaningful change.

In defense of traditional indigenous communities, Guatemalan peasants had only one choice: armed rebellion. Governments responded with vicious repression. Paramilitary death squads carried out a murderous campaign against political dissenters. Sweep-and-destroy missions routinely destroyed entire villages at a time. The toll was absolutely horrendous: In a country with an average annual population of 10 million inhabitants, as many as 200,000 people were killed or disappeared between the 1960s and the 1990s, according to recent estimates, and an equivalent number of survivors fled to other countries. Subsequent investigations revealed that government forces were responsible for well over 90 percent of these murders. For reasons still not entirely clear, the Guatemalan state had launched a campaign of genocide against its Mayan people.

Formed in the 1980s, the Unión Revolucionaria Nacional de Guatemala (URNG) posed a serious political and military challenge. As the army attacked communities, residents could either flee (into exile or into the forests) or stay behind to resist. Entire villages could be "caught between two armies."

The repression of the 1970s and 1980s forced the creation of new and more assertive forms of indigenous mobilization. These came to include (1) community-level and grassroots movements, (2) popular organizations, and (3) Mayan cultural institutions. It was in this context that the stress on cultural identity gained strength. As in Bolivia and Ecuador, indigenous organizations moved from class-based identity to ethnic identity.

They also entered the electoral arena. Even as repression continued, the Frente Democrática Nueva Guatemala in 1995 elected six candidates to congress, including two Mayan women, and became the principal force of the national Left. Other Mayan groups supported Álvaro Arzú of the Partido de Avanzada Nacional. As president, Arzú eventually reached a peace accord with the UNRG, an agreement brokered by the United Nations—and one that committed Guatemala to the principles of a multicultural, multilingual society. To the extent that it was carried out, the peace accord came to represent a significant advance for Guatemala's indigenous peoples and, on paper at least, an assertion of social justice. As one analyst noted, "Because they achieved unprecedented weight, Mayan concerns became proportionately more prominent in the political discourse of Ladinos, among whom one may note a certain nervousness about the future."

Almost as soon as these accomplishments took place, they threatened to unravel. In a 1999 referendum on the indigenous accords and the constitution of Guatemala as a "multicultural, ethnically plural, and multilingual state," voters defeated the measures by a margin of 53 to 47 percent. Moreover, a substantial number of indigenous persons voted against the referendum, and many did not vote at all. This amounted to a stunning defeat for the indigenous cause. Adding insult to injury within the same year, voters elected as president a candidate of the Frente Republicano Guatemalteco, a party long controlled by former dictator Efraín Ríos Montt, who had unleashed genocidal campaigns against Mayan peoples in the early 1980s. As Kay Warren has noted, sympathetic observers and Mayan leaders alike were beginning to wonder if leftist popular movements and indigenous culturalist groups would "be able to maneuver successfully within the established system of political parties and electoral politics."[21] The answer seemed entirely unclear.

---

[21] Kay B. Warren, "Voting Against Indigenous Rights in Guatemala: Lessons from the 1999 Referendum," in Kay B. Warren and Jean E. Jackson, eds., *Indigenous Movements, Self-Representation, and the State in Latin America* (Austin: University of Texas Press, 2002), 149–180.

BOX 9.3
ZAPATISTAS: FIGHTING FOR INDIGENOUS AUTONOMY IN MEXICO

An armed uprising on January 1, 1994, in Mexico's southernmost state of Chiapas shocked that nation's leadership and much of the world. Naming their movement after Emiliano Zapata, legendary peasant leader in the Mexican Revolution of 1910, the insurgents presented a series of demands for indigenous rights. The government initially responded with an unsuccessful attempt at repression. Negotiations ensued, a stalemate developed, and it continues to this day. Here follows a ten-year review:

> With their rubber boots slapping at the slick cobblestones and faces hooded by mists and masks, they seemed like ghosts from a past that many do not recognize as being very present in contemporary Mexico. They advanced on the center of San Cristobal de las Casas, the capital of the Mayan highlands of Chiapas, in the early hours of New Year's Day, 1994, the start-up date for that beacon of globalization, the North American Free Trade Agreement—NAFTA.
>
> When dawn rose above the old colonial city, a black flag embroidered with a large five-pointed red star flew over the sacked municipal palace, as ski-masked rebels hunkered around small bonfires under its porticos....From the balcony of the wrecked palace, the Zapatista Army of National Liberation (EZLN)—for that is what they called themselves—declared war on the Mexican Army and promulgated a series of revolutionary "laws." At nightfall, as Mexican Air Force fighters circled San Cristobal, a curfew was declared. Then, before dawn, the rebels pulled back to lay siege to a military base on the outskirts of the city....
>
> Ten years later, the slogans spray painted upon San Cristobal's whitewashed walls are liable to be dedicated to Kurt Cobain rather than Zapatista leader Subcomandante Marcos. The international volunteers who saturated the jungle and the highlands, not to mention the cafes of San Cristobal, have mostly moved on to other battlefronts.
>
> ...Silences have marked the Zapatista decade. From January 1997 when Zedillo vetoed San Andrés [a set of negotiated accords] through July 1998, Marcos and the Comandantes did not utter a word outside their jungle mountain camps. During the 2000 presidential election, the Zapatistas were equally mum. From May 2001 through December 2002, the angry silence reigned. Silence is an Indian weapon, the Subcomandante is fond of reminding his public, but such lapses do not much sustain the EZLN's national and international notoriety. In a world that has been in permanent turmoil since 9/11/01, not a lot of people are listening to Indian silence....
>
> Mostly, the Zapatistas seem to want to grow their own corn and coffee and their communities in the way that they see fit. The rebels are, after all, Mayans, "the People of the Corn," and corn is rooted in this rebellion. It was only when the three NAFTA nations began discussing corn quotas, which the EZLN feared would displace Indian farmers from

the internal market, that they got around to declaring war. NAFTA and Salinas' revision of constitutional Article 27 to permit the privatization of the ejido "left us no alternative but to declare war," Marcos has often explained.

The brief show war the Indians fought, armed political theater really, was in fact a strategy for survival, as agribusiness giants like Cargill and Archer Daniels Midland closed in on the People of the Corn. Ten years later, the guns are out of sight (although last New Year's Eve, in the pine-scented Oventic auditorium, the militia men and women danced with them slung over their shoulders), but the Zapatista communities are themselves armed and loaded with resolve to resist and to survive the global monster. Perhaps the EZLN has not saved the world, but it has saved itself.

And was not their survival what the Zapatista rebellion was about in the first place?

Source: John Ross, "The Zapatistas at Ten," *NACLA Report on the Americas* 37, 3 (2003): 11.

The political mobilization of indigenous peoples has not occurred throughout all of Latin America. Their voices were muted in countries with relatively small indigenous populations. Even in Peru, where the indigenous account for nearly 40 percent of the population, indigenous organization has been modest (with the partial exception of Sendero Luminoso, an armed movement that sought to present indigenous demands through a Maoist class analysis).[22] In Mexico, a largely mestizo nation that is nonetheless home to the largest indigenous population in Latin America, organization has focused more on *campesino* concerns than on indigenous identities— although much debate surrounds the question of whether the Zapatista movement is essentially indigenous or *campesino* (see Box 9.3).

It is clear that democratization has made it possible for ethnic identities to form the basis for social cleavages and political activism. Moreover, indigenous parties have demonstrated an ability to develop viable electoral coalitions that blend indigenous issues with issues of broad appeal in their respective societies. What is not clear is where this will end. As John Peeler has surmised, thing could go either way: "Probably, the emergence of indigenous peoples onto the political stage will change little.... But possibly, the political emergence of the indigenous could change everything."[23]

During the most recent phase of democratization, social groups in Latin America thus experienced substantial shifts in their relative strengths and

---

[22] See Donna Lee Van Cott, "Turning Crisis into Opportunity: Achievements of Excluded Groups in the Andes," in Paul W. Drake and Eric Hershberg, eds., *State and Society in Conflict: Comparative Perspectives on Andean Crises* (Pittsburgh, PA: University of Pittsburgh Press, 2006), esp. 162.

[23] Peeler, "Social Justice," 279.

access to power. Labor has suffered the steepest declines. Unemployment has risen, union density has declined, and union–party linkages have weakened. Moreover, those unions that chose to support programs of neoliberal economic reform (as in Mexico and Argentina) have received precious little in exchange.

By comparison, the picture for women and indigenous peoples has improved. During the transition toward democracy, many leaders (of both groups) moved away from social movements and sought political office and power. The question, then, concerns the extent to which formal political representation—for instance, through legislative seats—has generated meaningful benefits for popular constituencies. Gains have been made and offices won, but there is still a long way to go. As a result, diehard grassroots activists have begun to wonder if democratic institutions can provide truly effective means of enhancing equity and achieving social justice.

CHAPTER 10

FREEDOMS, RIGHTS, AND ILLIBERAL DEMOCRACY

Freedoms and rights are cherished principles of liberal democracy. They enable citizens to articulate personal views about politics and to pronounce disagreement with established authorities. Public dissent is essential to the notion of accountability, which explains why authoritarian regimes make it their business to suppress discordant voices. In constitutional democracies, by contrast, the expression of dissent is considered not to be a privilege but a right—an "inalienable" right at that, one that cannot be removed or curtailed by the state. In practice, implementation of this idea entails the protection of fundamental freedoms, freedoms of speech, the press, assembly, partisan affiliation, religious belief, and so on.

What is the situation in contemporary Latin America? The analysis thus far has demonstrated that with some conspicuous exceptions, elections throughout the region became free and fair by the end of the twentieth century. In most countries people cast ballots without undue harassment, opposition parties challenged incumbent authorities, and sitting presidents (and their parties) were peacefully removed from power. The dominant form of political organization was "electoral democracy." The question is whether such regimes demonstrated sufficient respect and protection for citizens' rights as to meet the standards for "liberal" democracies. To what extent have citizens of Latin America enjoyed full democracy?

This chapter approaches these issues in several ways. It begins with a recapitulation of the concept of "illiberal democracy" as set forth in the introduction to this book. It moves on to evaluate freedom of the press in Latin America and examines the state of human rights, or "civil liberties," throughout the region. It then provides an empirical assessment of changing relationships between electoral democracy and civil liberties. The analysis clearly demonstrates that in recent decades the most prevalent form of governance in Latin America has been not liberal but illiberal democracy.[1]

GRADATIONS OF DEMOCRACY

As described in earlier chapters, the cycle of democratization that began in the 1970s extended to and beyond the end of the twentieth century. Competitive elections clearly became the instrument of choice for allocating political power. To illustrate the point, Figure 10.1 traces the rise of electoral democracy from 1972 through 2008. The curves depict a steady increase in the number of democracies from the late 1970s through the 1980s and 1990s, and then a plateau from 2002 to 2008—by which time seventeen of nineteen countries were holding free and fair elections, the sole exceptions being Haiti and Venezuela.

In and of themselves, however, democratic elections do not necessarily guarantee full protection of citizens' freedoms and rights. For whatever reason, people might voluntarily elect tyrants. They might be duped into electing tyrants. They might accept or tolerate tyrannical behavior on the part of elected rulers. Has this occurred in Latin America?

For purposes of this analysis, electoral systems can be classified as *democratic,* with free and fair elections; *semidemocratic,* where elections were free but not fair; or nondemocratic, if elections were nonexistent, openly fraudulent, or staged by authoritarian regimes.[2] Citizens' rights can also be construed as *extensive, limited,* and *minimal.* Extensive guarantees of citizen rights correspond to "liberal" polities; partial but systematic limitations on rights characterize "illiberal" regimes; and minimal rights reflect hard-line levels of repression.

As shown in Table 10.1, a cross-tabulation of elections and citizen rights generates a composite picture of the two variables. The purpose here is to explore the relationship between these vital dimensions of democracy. On theoretical and empirical grounds, two of the nine cells became null categories—repressive democracy and liberal dictatorship. The result is a sevenfold classification.

Political regimes that combine free and fair elections with extensive protection of civil liberties qualify as full, or "liberal," democracies. At the other extreme, authoritarian regimes have no meaningful elections. Hard-line autocracies, or *dictaduras* (such as the bureaucratic-authoritarian regimes of South America), impose relentless repression to the point such that civil liberties are minimal; traditional dictatorships, sometimes

---

[1] Fareed Zakaria, "The Rise of Illiberal Democracy," *Foreign Affairs* 76, 6 (November/December 1997): 22–43.

[2] Andreas Schedler, ed., *Electoral Authoritarianism: The Dynamics of Unfree Competition* (Boulder, CO: Lynne Rienner, 2000).

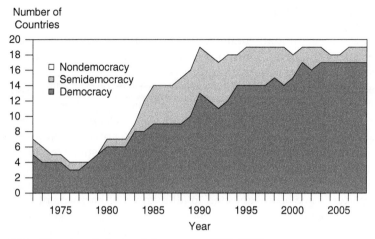

Figure 10.1 The rise of electoral democracy, 1972–2008

TABLE 10.1 Elections, Rights, and Political Regimes

	CHARACTER OF ELECTIONS		
Citizen Rights	*None*	*Free Not Fair*	*Free and Fair*
Minimal	Hard-Line *dictadura*	Repressive semidemocracy	<Null>
Limited	Moderate *dictablanda*	Restrictive semidemocracy	Illiberal democracy
Extensive	<Null>	Permissive semidemocracy	Liberal democracy

known as *dictablandas,* allow the partial enjoyment of civil liberties, but only within prescribed limits.[3] As a matter of conceptual definition and empirical observation, autocracies do not promote extensive civil liberties; if they did, they would not be truly autocratic. Semidemocracies can coexist with a fairly broad range of civil liberties, and partly for this reason they tend to be short-lived. Special importance relates to the category of "illiberal democracy," which combines free and fair elections with partial but systematic restrictions of civil liberties. This situation represents a fundamental paradox. And as shown later, it also constitutes a persisting and pervasive reality.

---

[3] This terminology was first coined by Guillermo O'Donnell and Philippe C. Schmitter in *Transitions from Authoritarian Rule: Tentative Conclusions about Uncertain Democracies* (Baltimore: Johns Hopkins University Press, 1986), 13–14.

FREEDOM OF THE PRESS

One of the most fundamental requirements for constitutional democracy is freedom of the press. Only unfettered media can provide citizens with alternative sources of information. This permits people to circumvent official propaganda and Orwellian doublespeak, to form independent judgments, and to hold incumbents accountable for actions and policies.

Press freedom is not to be taken for granted. Even in societies with independent media, journalism can be a hazardous occupation. News reporting might be more or less objective, but editorials can be subjected to rigid censorship. In Latin America as well as other areas of the developing world, investigative journalism is in its infancy. As grim headlines reveal, writers and reporters have been subjected to all manner of harassment and intimidation: They have been fired, kidnapped, tortured, and assassinated.

According to the Committee to Protect Journalists (CPJ), a highly respected watchdog group, no fewer than 458 journalists around the world lost their lives in the line of duty during the 1990s. The single most dangerous area for correspondents was Eastern Europe and the former Soviet Union (including Russia). With eighty-two total deaths, Latin America also proved to be a perilous place, nearly on par with the Middle East and North Africa and substantially more hazardous than Asia and continental Africa. As shown in Table 10.2, Colombia was the most dangerous country in the region. Observing the heavy toll on fellow workers, one correspondent in Bogotá sadly noted that "The question my colleagues and I ask is, who will be left to report?"

Mexico emerged as the most dangerous country for journalists after the turn of the century, just as it began holding free and fair elections. Colombia held second place, and Brazil—also democratic—tied with Honduras for third. Even more startling, perhaps, is the fact that the total number of assassinations jumped from 83 in the 1990s to 157 from 2000 through 2010. Electoral democracy might have prevailed in the early twenty-first century, but freedom of the press did not.

Central governments bore varying degrees of responsibility for this grisly record. National authorities were no doubt involved in many instances, but some of the killings were carried out by groups beyond the control of the state—guerrillas, for instance, or unauthorized paramilitary units. Some assassinations were ordered by landowners or businesspeople threatened by journalistic exposés. Still other murders occurred at the behest of local and provincial officials, party leaders, or, in a number of cases, military officers. (For example, a radio journalist in rural Brazil was shot to death in March 2000 after he accused the local mayor of corruption.) Death threats constituted an especially common means of official and semiofficial intimidation.

Governments held indirect responsibility as well. To uphold standards of justice, state authorities were supposed to identify, detain, and punish the

TABLE 10.2 Numbers of Journalists Killed, 1990–2010

	KILLINGS	
Country	*1990–1999*	*2000–2010*
Colombia	36	41
Peru	12	3
Mexico	10	46
Brazil	8	12
Haiti	4	8
Argentina	3	1
Guatemala	3	9
Venezuela	2	6
Chile	1	0
Dominican Republic	1	4
Honduras	1	12
Paraguay	1	2
Costa Rica	0	1
Uruguay	0	1
Nicaragua	0	1
Ecuador	0	2
Totals	83	157

Sources: Committee to Protect Journalists, *Attacks on the Press in 1999* (New York: CPJ, 2000), 23; and cpj.org/killed/americas.

murderers. If successful, these measures would be the most effective way to deter future attacks on members of the media. In all too many instances, this did not occur, because the government was either unable or unwilling to mount an effective investigation and prosecution. In either case, the overall message would be the same: Disgruntled parties could assault the press with virtual impunity.

Among the worst offenders in the late 1990s was the administration of Alberto K. Fujimori in Peru. While he was still in power, according to the CPJ, Fujimori ran an iron-fisted "infotatorship." One of its pillars was a docile press that would report only favorable information about the regime, a regime that in electoral terms would qualify as a semidemocracy. Analyzing events of 1999, the CPJ reported that "Fujimori's intelligence arm has engaged in assassination plans, death threats, wiretapping, surveillance, and smear tactics to harass and imperil journalists, often forcing them into exile. Investigative reporters looking into government corruption and collusion between drug traffickers and the military have been hit with charges of espionage, treason, and terrorism invoked to discredit and deter their work."[4]

---

[4] Committee to Protect Journalists, *Attacks on the Press in 1999* (New York: CPJ, 2000), 62–63.

Other governments, even freely and fairly elected ones, resorted to more subtle means of curbing the press. Several countries, including Bolivia, Honduras, El Salvador, Nicaragua, and Panama, all electoral democracies, required official licensing of journalists. The putative goal was to ensure professional standards and responsible behavior on the part of the press. The underlying purpose was to silence the voices of a potentially obstreperous opposition. The implication was clear: Cross an invisible line and you lose your accreditation. It was a means of muzzling the press.

Another way to curtail the media was through outright censorship. Panama had draconian "gag laws" dating back to 1969. In El Salvador, Juan José Dalton, son of the revered poet Roque Dalton, was removed from the editorial board of *El Diario de Hoy* after he published an article criticizing the government party. In Honduras, Rossana Guevara found that her dog had been poisoned after she investigated cases of official corruption, and soon afterward she was fired from her job. The Venezuelan constitution of 1999 required that the media publish only "truthful information" (*información veraz*), whatever that might mean. In October 2000, a local judge in the Brazilian state of Acre banned local press coverage of municipal elections on the grounds that such reporting would constitute political propaganda. Attempts at censorship often led to surveillance of journalists.

The most surprising and spectacular case of censorship took place in Chile, an electoral democracy that was by the late 1990s widely praised for its respect for citizen rights and freedom of expression. Even under the *Concertación*, however, ownership of the media was still concentrated in the hands of a few corporations with close ties to the Pinochet regime. In 1999 Alejandra Matus published *The Black Book of Chilean Justice*, the result of six years of research into the failings and complicity of the judiciary system. An outraged member of the Supreme Court, Servando Jordán, took it upon himself to charge Matus with violation of a state security law and banned the book from circulation. Police confiscated the entire press run on April 14, less than two days after publication. That same day, Matus boarded a plane to Argentina to avoid arrest. The CEO and editor of the publishing company, Planeta, were briefly detained in June in connection with the case. Amid a public outcry, the U.S. government (under Bill Clinton) granted political asylum to Matus. In December 2000, undeterred by international opinion, a Santiago judge upheld the arrest warrant against Matus and the banning of the book.

Chilean President Eduardo Frei Ruiz-Tagle soon submitted a bill to the congress to revise the state security law, but many said it did not go far enough: It would still leave "disrespect" as an offense under the penal code, impose stiff penalties for defamation of high officials, and leave open the possibility of banning publications. Reform would not come rapidly.

Antidefamation Laws and Policies

The issue of press freedom came to a head over questions of defamation of governmental authorities. As noted by the CPJ, a vibrant press requires a strong judiciary:

While Latin American reporters have become extremely good at exposing wrongdoing, they cannot count on the courts to investigate, prosecute, and ultimately punish the people whom they expose. In most countries, the judiciary remains notoriously weak, and is often unable or unwilling to investigate cases brought to its attention. As a result, journalists who expose corruption become sitting ducks. Since negative press coverage is one of the few effective sanctions against criminal behavior in Latin America, discrediting the press is an excellent way for criminals to avoid accountability.[5]

As a result, exposure of official wrongdoing was often more dangerous to the journalists than to the perpetrators (see Box 10.1).

The central issue revolved around the question of libel. According to traditional legal canons in Latin America, disrespect toward governmental authorities (*desacato*) was regarded as a criminal offense. Vague in scope and content, this provided an excellent and effective cover for incumbents. Within international circles, however, meaningful protection of journalists involved two standards. One concerned "actual malice," under which plaintiffs must prove not only that the published information is false, but also that the journalists knew or should have known that it was false at the time of publication. The other was "neutral reporting," which held that plaintiffs cannot sue journalists for accurately reproducing information from an explicitly mentioned source, whether the information turns out to be accurate or not.

Cases regarding libel and alleged defamation of officials occurred with frequency. In Argentina, President Carlos Saúl Menem filed criminal charges in 1992 against investigative reporter Horacio Verbitsky for *desacato*. Verbitsky appealed to the Inter-American Commission on Human Rights (IAHR), which ruled in his favor. After subsequent negotiations, the Argentine government agreed to repeal its *desacato* law, which it did the following year. Several years later, Verbitsky, as secretary general of a press freedom organization, proposed a separate settlement regarding three different defamation cases and called for the introduction of "actual malice" and "neutral reporting" standards. Soon after taking office in 1999, President Fernando de la Rúa asked the legislature to take immediate action, but the bill stalled in committee after local journalists implicated eleven senators in a bribery scandal, thus prompting a backlash against the press. In the meantime, television talk show host Bernardo Neustadt was found guilty of defamation

---

[5] Marylene Smeets, "Overview of the Americas," *Attacks on the Press in 1999* (New York: Committee to Protect Journalists, 2000), first page.

BOX 10.1

GUATEMALA: PRESIDENTIAL REVENGE ON WOMEN JOURNALISTS

In April 1999, a mysterious program called "Hoy por Hoy" ("Right Now") appeared on Guatemalan radio. The format consisted of gossip and political chitchat, and the hosts seemed to have it in for journalists. One of them described Dina Fernández, a columnist and editor at Guatemala's biggest daily, *Prensa Libre*, and her mother, Dina García, as loose women and bad journalists.

The personal attacks seemed to come from nowhere. Nobody, not even the director of the radio station that broadcast "Hoy por Hoy," knew who was responsible for its contents. But suspicion immediately fell on Guatemalan president Álvaro Arzú Irigoyen, who already had a very hostile relationship with the press. Arzú had succeeded in damaging critical publications by depriving them of government advertising. And he had allowed the government-funded television and radio program "Avances" ("Progress") to be used for partisan political purposes, trumpeting the government's achievements and attacking the press for unfavorable coverage of his regime.

Certainly, the staff of the Guatemala City daily *El Periódico* suspected government involvement. On June 17, the paper's front page carried the headline "Who's behind 'Hoy por Hoy'?" as well as a photo of a perplexed-looking Mariano Rayo, special adviser to the president. Using a neat deduction, the accompanying article established that Rayo had established the company responsible for the controversial program.

On June 18, Fernández addressed Rayo directly in her column: "You have dishonored the government and the governing party," she wrote. "It has been demonstrated, once again, that there are people [in your government] who attempt to destroy the press, maybe not murdering us as before, but disqualifying and asphyxiating us."

On June 23, the opposition Guatemalan Republican Front (FRG) summoned Rayo to a hearing in Congress. Having endured a lengthy grilling about the program, he was asked to leave the government. Rayo then submitted his resignation to President Arzú, who refused to accept it. And even while the government party's ethics committee was looking into the case, the party's executive committee confirmed Rayo, who was not a party member before the "Hoy por Hoy" scandal broke, as one of its preferred candidates in the November elections to the legislative assembly. Predictably, the ethics committee absolved him, and Rayo was elected deputy. "In any other country this would have destroyed his aspirations," said Fernández. "Here they reward him....There's no American happy ending: Mariano Rayo will live happily ever after."

Source: Marylene Smeets, "Speaking Out: Postwar Journalism in Guatemala and El Salvador," *Attacks on the Press in 1999* (New York: Committee to Protect Journalists, 2000), 221–222.

for a disparaging remark that a *guest* on his program had made about a local judge. Months later a court upheld a judgment against Neustadt in the amount of U.S. $80,000.

In February 2000, the Supreme Court of Chile convicted journalist José Ale of insulting Supreme Court judge Servando Jordán under the state security law. In 1998, Ale had written that during Jordán's two-year term as chief justice "the prestige of the Chilean judiciary fell to one of its lowest levels ever." Two weeks before the conviction (which carried an eighteen-month suspended prison sentence), the judge who drafted the decision called Ale a "professional slanderer." Ale was later pardoned by incoming President Lagos, but the court had made its point.

Almost everywhere, penalties for defamation were extremely severe. The Brazilian legislature not only slapped enormous fines on convicted journalists but planned to punish officials who leaked information with dismissals, hefty fines, and three-year bans on holding public office. In the Dominican Republic, defamation was punishable by jail terms of up to six months; in Ecuador, prison terms could be for as long as three years; in Honduras, the normal punishment was one year in jail, but up to twelve years for those who "offend the President of the Republic." Even in Uruguay, where press freedom was widely respected, the penal code called for sentences of up to three years for defamation, contempt, or seditious libel offenses—or longer if the crime was committed in publicly disseminated writings. And in Venezuela, the Chávez regime has attempted to browbeat the press through intimidation, harassment, detention, and cooptation (see Box 10.2).

Analytical Overview

In light of pervasive constraints on media, a watchdog organization known as Freedom House began to measure degrees of press freedom in all societies around the world. The annual reports define three categories: not free, partly free, and free.[6] As its name suggests, Freedom House employs the tools of investigative journalism to uphold the rights of journalists everywhere.

For Latin America, Table 10.3 presents country-by-country ratings of press freedom for 2002 and 2009. The display is compelling. Only three countries out of nineteen—Chile, Costa Rica, and Uruguay—achieved "free" scores in both 2002 and 2009. Four other countries—Bolivia, the Dominican Republic, Panama, and Peru—slipped from "free" to "partly free" status. No less than ten nations, from Argentina through Paraguay, were rated as "partly free" in both years. Venezuela dropped from "partly free" to "not free," and Haiti

---

[6] Freedom House measures harassment or intimidation on a scale of 0 to 100, and collapses the results into three basic categories: not free (scores of 61–100), partly free (31–60) and free (0–30).

BOX 10.2

VENEZUELA: HEY MR. PRESIDENT!

Hugo Chávez has waged a running battle with Venezuela's vibrant media. There are two major national dailies, *El Universal* and *El Nacional*, a handful of Caracas papers, several regional publications, and a few online news sites. Three private TV stations broadcast nationwide, and others deliver regional coverage. The press has vigorously criticized Chávez, and he has responded by lashing out at what he calls the "media of the oligarchy." Most vulnerable are radio and TV, because the government controls frequency allocation.

Chávez has tried to take over the press. He has a weekly radio call-in show, "Aló, Presidente," averaging four hours in length. Whenever Chávez wants to talk, television and radio stations nationwide must preempt regular programming. Sometimes he shows up unannounced at radio and TV stations. His denunciations of the press give supporters license to attack journalists, denouncing them as "journalists of the rich." Phone lines are tapped, and security agents have been seen trailing some reporters.

Chávez kept silent when a military judge ordered the arrest of the lawyer and columnist Pablo Aure Sánchez for allegedly insulting the military in a letter to *El Nacional* published in January 2001. Aure Sánchez described the armed forces as weak and unworthy, more "castrated" (*castrados*) than "military" (*castrenses*). Shortly thereafter military intelligence agents detained the columnist at his home. The defense minister was particularly outraged by Aure's claim that public esteem for the military had sunk so low that "we imagine them parading...in multi-colored panties," apparently in reference to an ongoing campaign in which women's underwear (in a variety of festive hues) was being delivered to military officers to insult their manhood. The minister stoutly insisted that Aure Sánchez was not the object of political persecution. "I'm not a politician, nor do I aspire to be one, nor do I want to be one," he said. "I'm a soldier." Amid a public outcry, Chávez later replaced the minister.

"Press freedom is more or less respected," according to Manuel Alfredo Rodríguez, a well-regarded columnist, "because [to restrict it] would create universal alarm. He [Chávez] is walking on a razor's edge." Chávez would become less tolerant as time went by.

Source: Marylene Smeets, "Venezuela: Radio Chávez," *Attacks on the Press in 2000* (New York: Committee to Protect Journalists, 2001), 17–24.

moved in the reverse direction. For the region as a whole, freedom of the press was in decline.

The data thus convey a basic point. Electoral democracy was a necessary but not sufficient condition for full freedom of the press. Free media might exist only under electoral democracies, but not all electoral democracies uphold free media. On the contrary, the press enjoyed full freedom less than half the time in countries with free and fair elections. This combination—free elections without free media—conforms precisely to the profile of "illiberal democracy."

TABLE 10.3 Ratings for Freedom of the Press, 2002–2009

Country	2002	2009
Chile	Free	Free
Costa Rica	Free	Free
Uruguay	Free	Free
Bolivia	Free	Partly free
Dominican Republic	Free	Partly free
Panama	Free	Partly free
Peru	Free	Partly free
Argentina	Partly free	Partly free
Brazil	Partly free	Partly free
Colombia	Partly free	Partly free
Ecuador	Partly free	Partly free
El Salvador	Partly free	Partly free
Guatemala	Partly free	Partly free
Honduras	Partly free	Partly free
Mexico	Partly free	Partly free
Nicaragua	Partly free	Partly free
Paraguay	Partly free	Partly free
Venezuela	Partly free	Not free
Haiti	Not free	Partly free

Source: Freedom House at www.freedomhouse.org

THE UNEVEN RULE OF LAW

Aside from such restrictions on the free flow of information, citizens of Latin America have endured pervasive constraints on human rights. Particularly evident has been arbitrary action on the part of security forces, most notably the police. Arrests have been made for little or no reason, violence has been employed with little or no provocation, and the judicial system—weak, inefficient, and often corrupt—has failed to uphold the basic rights of citizens. One consequence of such practices has been to exclude citizens from meaningful participation in the political arena, what has come to be known more broadly as the "public sphere" (see Box 10.3).

There were exceptions to this rule. In three countries—Chile, Costa Rica, and Uruguay—governments respected and protected the human rights of citizens. Chile, of course, was embroiled in public controversy about the detention of former dictator Augusto Pinochet and human rights abuses under his authoritarian regime; at the very least, this heightened public and official sensitivity to the need for upholding fundamental rights. Costa Rica, not a highly polarized society, boasted an unusually effective judiciary system and standard of law. Similarly, Uruguay managed to uphold the rights of citizens to a respectable degree.

More typically, however, democratic governments failed to provide even-handed and effective rule of law. Take the case of Argentina, a country with a vibrant and voluble citizenry. After a frightful period of military

BOX 10.3

CONTRACTION OF THE PUBLIC SPHERE

An important and significant way of thinking about the quality of democracy in present-day Latin America is to focus on what has come to be known as "the public sphere"—the arena in which citizens organize themselves, take part in politics, advocate their causes, and pursue their goals and interests. It is, in other words, "a contested participatory site" in which ordinary people "form a public body and engage in negotiations and contestations over political and social life."

As Philip Oxhorn has observed, public spheres can be characterized according to their inclusiveness (who takes part) and their utility (whether participants can achieve their goals). And the problem, he finds, is that the public sphere in Latin American democracies is "limited in ways that contribute to a growing distance between a political elite and the people they are supposed to represent."

Two factors account for this state of affairs. One is the progressive weakening of the state, of mass organizations (such as labor unions), and of incentives for collective mobilization over the past quarter-century. Given the absence of social safety nets, economic insecurity discourages lower-class workers from taking part in the public sphere: "the necessity of day-to-day survival may make public participation and collective action seem at best a luxury one can no longer afford and at worst a wasted effort." In the meantime, uneven application of the rule of law has exacerbated social-class differences: According to one analyst, "Police and other institutions of the criminal justice system tend to act as 'border guards,' protecting the elites from the poor."

A second key factor is popular alienation from formal politics, as shown by voter apathy and abstention. As political contests unfold, people have no active part: They are reduced to being "consumers" of public discourses rather than active protagonists in national dramas. They become not citizens but spectators. As a result, the quality of democracy is gravely weakened.

Source: Philip Oxhorn, "When Democracy Isn't All That Democratic: Social Exclusion and the Limits of the Public Sphere in Latin America," *North-South Agenda Papers* 44 (Miami, FL: North-South Center, University of Miami, April 2001).

---

rule, electoral democracy returned in 1983. But by the late 1990s, its people faced systematic constraints on fundamental freedoms. According to the U.S. Department of State, the Argentine government, ardently pro-American in its foreign policy, "generally respected the human rights of its citizens; however, there were problems in some areas."

There continued to be instances of extrajudicial killings, torture, and brutality by the police, although the authorities prosecuted a number of persons for such actions. Police also arbitrarily arrested and detained citizens, prison conditions are poor, and lengthy pretrial detention is a problem. The judicial system is inefficient and is subject at times to political influence and to inordinate delays in trials. There were numerous threats—and several acts of violence—against journalists. Police used violence against demonstrators. Violence and discrimination against women also are problems. Child abuse and child prostitution continued to increase. Discrimination against indigenous people persists, and there were instances of anti-Semitism. Child labor is a problem. In addition, the legacy of the human rights abuses of the 1976–83 military regime continued to be a subject of intense national debate, particularly the arrest of former junta leaders on charges of taking or seizing babies born to dissidents in detention and giving them to supporters for adoption.[7]

Despite a strong recommendation from the IAHR, the Argentine government failed to compensate the families of two individuals who vanished after being taken into custody by the police in 1990 (well after the return of democratic rule). The local court had also urged the government to investigate the disappearances and bring the responsible parties to justice. Nothing of the sort occurred.

A similar situation prevailed in Brazil, where the government "generally respected the human rights of its citizens" but "there continued to be numerous serious abuses." Police agents routinely committed extrajudicial killings, tortured suspects, and arrested people arbitrarily. Not only that: "Police were also implicated in criminal activity of all kinds, including killings for hire, death squad executions, and kidnappings for ransom." And punishment was rare. Indeed, a special court system for uniformed police contributed to a widespread climate of impunity, as it was clear that convictions would be few and far between. A study of São Paulo's special courts for uniformed police uncovered more than 1,000 "missing" and "delayed" cases involving crimes against civilians, including murder and torture. A newspaper investigation of 300 cases found 100 murder charges among them, some delayed for up to twelve years. Justice was proving to be elusive.

In Guatemala the picture was even more dismal. Extrajudicial killings and judiciary incompetence were commonplace. In February 1999, a "Historical Clarification Commission" published a report that found that government forces were responsible for 93 percent of the human rights abuses committed during the country's decades-long civil conflict. Participants in the study were promptly harassed, intimidated, and driven to exile. The government of Álvaro Arzú took an ambivalent and legalistic stance and refused to adopt recommendations for means of improving the human rights situation and carrying out reforms within the military. Around this same time, a sociologist named María Ramírez Sánchez became the victim of a professional killing—apparently because of her research into military atrocities in the Guatemalan countryside.

---

[7] U.S. Department of State, *Country Reports on Human Rights Practices for 1999* (Washington, DC: U.S. Government Printing Office, 2000), 573–574.

Police in Guatemala arrest demonstrators during the course of an election campaign. (AP Photo/Rodrigo Abd)

Several electoral democracies had even worse records. One example was Colombia, where the situation was bluntly described by U.S. officials as "poor."

> Government forces continued to commit numerous, serious abuses, including extrajudicial killings, at a level that was roughly similar to that of 1998. Despite some prosecutions and convictions, the authorities rarely brought officers of the security forces and the policy charged with human rights offenses to justice, and impunity remains a problem. At times the security forces collaborated with paramilitary groups that committed abuses; in some instances, individual members of the security forces actively collaborated with members of paramilitary forces by passing them through roadblocks, sharing intelligence, and providing them with ammunition. Paramilitary forces find a ready support base within the military and police, as well as local civilian elites in many areas.[8]

Moreover, the use of "faceless" prosecutors and witnesses in cases involving kidnapping, extortion, drug trafficking, and high-profile human rights abuse, adopted in an effort to protect officials and witnesses from violent retribution, constituted a clear violation of basic rights to fair trials. In mid-1999 the practice was restricted to a "specialized jurisdiction," but it would

---

[8] Ibid., 658.

continue to violate the rights of the accused. In addition, there were unconfirmed reports of security forces harassing and threatening human rights groups.

The Dominican Republic also had serious problems. Police committed extrajudicial killings with near impunity and routinely used excessive force to break up demonstrations (leading to at least nine citizen deaths). Security forces arbitrarily arrested and abused not only suspects but also their relatives, broke into private quarters without cause to search for suspects, and regularly refused to obey judicial orders. Examples of the abuses are chilling. One reported instance was an extrajudicial killing:

> The police shot and killed Fausto Torres Estévez, whom they sought in connection with the murder of a fellow officer earlier the same day. According to the Policía Nacional, Torres Estévez was a known delinquent in Santiago, and in possession of a 12-gauge shotgun with which he tried to fight off the police patrol. However, according to neighbors and other witnesses, Torres Estévez was walking when a vehicle suddenly swerved to stop in front of him and several men carrying firearms leaped out and began shooting. When he was dead, they put his body in the trunk of their vehicle and drove him to the morgue. No investigation has been reported.

Another was an eyewitness report of torture in the prisons:

> Shortly after her release from 2 years' confinement on drug-related charges, "Miss Najayo 98" Angela de la Cruz spoke of practices she witnessed at the Mexico section of the San Pedro de Macorís prison, including torture. The most graphic was the use of a punishment called "the toaster," where guards laid prisoners, shackled hand and foot, on a bed of hot asphalt for the entire day and, if they screamed, beat them with a club. The army administers San Pedro de Macorís prison.[9]

Most tellingly, perhaps, there was little evidence of governmental efforts to stop these practices. Quite the opposite: Attempting to suppress information, Dominican police detained a journalist who had published a list of extrajudicial killings.

As might have been expected, electoral semidemocracies provided even fewer protections for civil and political rights than did the beleaguered democracies. During 1999 the government of Ecuador declared or extended states of emergency and ordered participants in a nationwide strike back to work; in July of that year security forces opened fire on an indigenous protest against austerity measures, killing at least one person and injuring scores of others. Haiti presented an utterly dismal scene of rampant abuse and shortcomings in oversight. And Peru, still in the grip of Fujimori's "infotatorship," withdrew from the jurisdiction of the IAHR.

---

[9] Ibid., 723–724.

Perhaps the most telling case was Mexico. Although the long-dominant PRI claimed to rule in the name of the people, the human rights situation in 1999 presented a disquieting panorama:

> Continued serious abuses include extrajudicial killings; disappearances; torture and other abuse; police corruption and alleged involvement in narcotics-related abuses; poor prison conditions; arbitrary arrest and detention; lengthy pretrial detention; lack of due process; judicial inefficiency and corruption; illegal searches; attacks and threats against journalists; some self-censorship; assaults, harassment, and threats against human rights monitors; violence and discrimination against women; child prostitution and abuse; discrimination against indigenous people; violence and discrimination against religious minorities; violence against homosexuals; limits on worker rights; extensive child labor in agriculture and in the informal economy; and trafficking in persons.[10]

This was a pretty bleak picture.

Dissidence was dangerous. In January 1999, unknown assassins murdered a human rights activist in the state of Sinaloa. In March, federal judicial police killed a former local official and adviser to the PRD, the left-wing opposition party. In April, uniformed soldiers killed two farmers. In May, a PRD senator and the leader of an indigenous rights movement were shot, both in the state of Oaxaca. In June, a police officer killed an activist affiliated with the PAN, the right-wing opposition party. In October, a prominent member of the Zapatista National Liberation Front (FZLN, the political branch of the EZLN), was found dead in a cell in a Tijuana detention facility. Also in October, a group of men armed with AK-47 assault weapons opened fire on an Acapulco city counselor-elect and his family en route to a PRD election victory celebration. And in November of that year, President Ernesto Zedillo, soon to oversee the country's transition to electoral democracy, admitted to the UN High Commissioner for Human Rights that Mexico endured "serious human rights violations."

The Roles of Courts

Courts have often been complicit in this uneven rule of law. This has been a fundamental deficiency in Latin American politics. In a democratic system based on checks and balances, the judiciary must perform essential roles: protecting the rights of citizens, upholding constraints on abuses of power, and, in particular, providing an institutional counterweight to the executive branch. Judges have not always complied with these responsibilities.

Legal communities have frequently supported and justified nondemocratic rule. In fact one recurring feature of authoritarian regimes has been the insistence on legality (or, at least, the appearance of legality). Dictators routinely seize or exercise power in the name of the national constitution,

---

[10] Ibid., 835.

or, if necessary, they have a new one written. They control the composition of higher courts, especially the supreme court, purging or intimidating noncompliant judges. They hire teams of highly skilled lawyers to explicate the legalistic foundations of undemocratic rule. As Beatriz Magaloni has observed, these practices are part and parcel of authoritarian domination:

> Autocrats employ courts to enforce their commands directed to bureaucratic subordinates and the citizenry, but they normally do not resort to these institutions to arbitrate conflicts among members of the ruling elite...autocrats face a dilemma–creating a system of courts strong enough to allow top-level state officials to monitor lower-level officials and judges, but weak enough to prevent citizens from enforcing their rights vis-à-vis the regime.[11]

The judiciary thus becomes an instrument of political discipline and social control. And to a considerable extent, authoritarian government relies not on the rule *of* law, but on rule *by* law.

Particularly egregious instances have involved the legalistic approval of "dirty wars" waged by military rulers. After the 1976 coup in Argentina, the general immediately purged the Supreme Court and appointed docile justices who went on to approve the use of military tribunals for cases of suspected subversion, on the ground that the country was in a state of war. Even more unsettling was the case of Chile, where the Supreme Court was not purged—but still approved the murderous practices of the Pinochet regime, which proclaimed its adherence to the 1925 constitution and imposed a state of siege. In September 1973 the president of the Supreme Court proclaimed his "most intimate satisfaction" with the military's pledge to respect and enforce the rulings of the court. Accepting the claim that the country was at war, the Court abdicated its right to review the decisions of the military tribunals. Judicial compliance with authoritarian rule continued through the 1980s. Despite the flagrant and widespread disregard of human rights, the Court accepted citizen claims to habeas corpus in two or three tenths of one percent of all cases. As Lisa Hilbink has concluded, "the overwhelming pattern was passivity, deference to the executive, and an apparent commitment to order over liberty."[12]

The advent of electoral democracy has led to only partial improvements. Depending on political circumstances, justices in higher courts have continued to support the president in power—or his or her likely successor.[13]

---

[11] Beatriz Magaloni, "Enforcing the Autocratic Political Order and the Role of Courts: The Case of Mexico," in Tom Ginsburg and Tamir Moustafa, eds., *Rule by Law: The Politics of Courts in Authoritarian Regimes* (New York: Cambridge University Press, 2008), 180–181.

[12] Lisa Hilbink, *Judges Beyond Politics in Democracy and Dictatorship: Lessons from Chile* (New York: Cambridge University Press, 2007), 156.

[13] Gretchen Helmke, "The Logic of Strategic Defection: Court-Executive Relations in Argentina under Dictatorship and Democracy," *American Political Science Review*

Checks and balances have remained very weak. Characteristically employing a technical and legalistic discourse, judges have engaged in overtly partisan calculations. Politics has been justified in the name of anti-politics.

Especially chilling, in many countries, has been the legal response to extrajudicial killings by security forces, most frequently by the police. In the Brazilian state of São Paulo, for example, the police killed more than 7,500 people in the alleged line of duty. As cases went to trial, sitting justices tended to accept police accounts at face value. Poor families were unable to afford the costs of legal representation, and judges often treated them with disrespect. Conviction rates were unconscionably low—under 5 percent in some cities of Brazil and around 20 percent in Buenos Aires. The courts were not defending citizens.

Opportunistic politicians promoted hard-line tactics by the police. As popular concerns mounted over crime waves and public insecurity, leaders defended ruthless tactics against supposed delinquents and undesirables. As the governor of Buenos Aires province crowed in the late 1990s, the only way to deal with criminal elements was to *meta bala*—give them bullets, or mow them down. "It is necessary," he said on one occasion, "to enter into all the villas with the [police] agents to put an end to crime. The police are capable, it's simply necessary to give them instructions and combat decisions. But let us give them the norms they need: we can't have a situation where a policeman enters one of those places and kills someone and then some lawyer of the criminal appears and says it's the policeman who is the murderer."[14] Social order was clearly more important than personal liberty.

Progress has taken place in recent years. Mexico began a significant process of judicial reform in 1994, and courts have achieved a "slight increase in autonomy" from the executive as a result. The 1998 detention of Augusto Pinochet and ensuing human rights litigation exerted a galvanizing effect on lawyers and judges in Chile and throughout the hemisphere. In Mexico and well as in Colombia, however, judges and legal authorities have faced constant threats of violence or assassination from drug traffickers. Although countries such as Uruguay and Costa Rica have strong traditions of judicial independence, such instances are relatively rare. Equally illustrative is the packing of Venezuelan higher courts by Hugo Chávez. A truly impartial application of the law remains a basic challenge for modern-day Latin America.[15]

96, 2 (June 2002): 291–303; and Helmke, *Courts under Constraints: Judges, Generals, and Presidents in Argentina* (New York: Cambridge University Press, 2005).

[14] Daniel M. Brinks, *The Judicial Response to Police Killings in Latin America: Inequality and the Rule of Law* (New York: Cambridge University Press, 2008), 119.

[15] As Brinks has noted, "São Paulo presents a clear challenge to the notion that democracy comes all of a piece. Political rights are alive and vibrant in São Paulo, and yet the police routinely violate fundamental civil rights and, in practical terms, remain above the law." *Judicial Response*, 142.

THE CHANGING CONTENT OF ELECTORAL DEMOCRACY

The analysis now turns to the overall relationship between electoral democracy and civil liberties. Once again, studies by Freedom House shed critical light on this issue. Since the early 1970s, this organization has published annual reports that assess the actual level of "freedom" around the world along two dimensions: political rights (the right to form and join political parties and cast votes without harassment) and civil liberties (freedom of religion, expression, the press, assembly and organization, etc.). Both are scored on a 7-point scale, with 1 being most free and 7 being least free.

The assessment of civil liberties is especially important.[16] According to the working definition, the concept refers to "freedoms to develop views, institutions, and personal autonomy apart from the state." The Freedom House checklist for civil liberties includes such items as these:

- freedom of expression and belief, including an independent media (in effect, freedom of the press)
- rights of assembly, association, and organization
- an impartial rule of law and the protection of human rights (including "freedom from extreme government indifference and corruption")
- personal autonomy and economic rights (e.g., choice of residence and employment, property rights, equality of opportunity, especially educational opportunity, and freedom from exploitation).[17]

The assessment of civil liberties thus moves from the electoral arena to basic elements of citizenship. To be sure, the criteria include some issues that might lie beyond the capacity of governments, such as freedom from exploitation, which might depend on forces of the market, and the equitable rule of law, which might be threatened by drug traffickers or other illicit groups. In general, the Freedom House survey provides useful and usable measurements of democratic practice. For this analysis, the seven-point scores on civil liberties have been collapsed into three categories: ratings of 1 or 2 indicate the availability of "extensive" civil liberties, 3 to 4 reflect "partial" civil liberties, and 5 to 7 correspond to "minimal" civil liberties.

Accordingly, Table 10.4 displays cross-tabulations of ratings on "civil liberties" for Latin American countries with type of electoral regime from 1972,

---

[16] The Freedom House treatment of "political rights" is more or less identical to this study's criteria for classifying electoral regimes (that is, they represent "the right of all adults to vote and compete for public office, and for elected representatives to have a decisive vote on public policies").

[17] *Freedom in the World, 1999–2000.*

TABLE 10.4 Electoral Regimes and Civil Liberties, 1970s–2000s

Civil Liberties	REGIME		
	Autocracy	Semidemocracy	Democracy
1972–1979			
Minimal	22	0	0
Partial	90	1	10
Extensive	0	1	28
Totals	112	2	38
1980–1989			
Minimal	15	1	0
Partial	59	30	41
Extensive	1	4	39
Totals	75	35	80
1990–1999			
Minimal	3	11	0
Partial	3	39	100
Extensive	0	2	32
Totals	6	52	132
2000–2008			
Minimal	2	9	0
Partial	1	9	90
Extensive	0	0	60
Totals	3	18	150

Source: Author's calculations.

when Freedom House first launched its survey, through 2000. The results are presented by decade: 1972–1979, 1980–1989, 1990–1999, and 2000–2008. Observations consist of country-years.

The overall patterns conform to commonsense expectations. Electoral democracies tended to have relatively expansive civil liberties, dictatorships tended to restrict civil liberties (with varying degrees of harshness), and semidemocracies tended to impose systematic but partial restrictions on civil liberties.

But there is more to the findings than that. Particularly striking is the steady emergence of electoral regimes that can be classified as democratic but that provide only partial protection for civil liberties. During the 1970s, ten out of thirty-eight "democratic" country-years (26 percent) showed only partial respect for civil liberties. In the 1980s, the proportion rose to forty-one out of eighty country-years (or 51 percent). By the 1990s, 100 out of 132 democratic country-years (more than 75 percent!) displayed partial protection of civil liberties. And during the 2000s, 90 out of 150 democratic country-years (60 percent of the total) corresponded with partial protection of citizen rights. The relationship between electoral democracy and civil

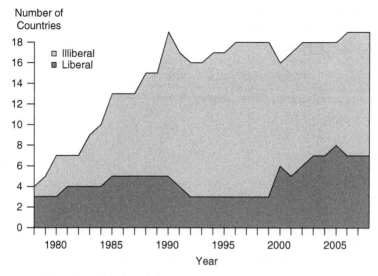

Figure 10.2 Liberal and illiberal democracy, 1978–2008

liberties declined steadily from the 1970s through the 1990s and remained at low levels after the turn of the century.[18]

From a different perspective, Figure 10.2 tracks the relative position of liberal and illiberal democracies in Latin America from 1978 through 2008. Notably conspicuous is the expansion over time of illiberal democracy. In 1980, there were three liberal democracies and three illiberal democracies; by 1990 there were four liberal democracies and nine illiberal democracies; and by the year 2000, there were six liberal democracies and nine illiberal democracies. Illiberal democracy thus became the most common, pervasive, and visible form of political organization throughout the region.

It affected not only the least important (and least developed) countries of Latin America, but also its most substantial nations. From the 1980s to the 2000s, electoral democracies with restricted civil liberties included eight South American countries:

Argentina, 1990–1999, 2001

Bolivia, 1983–2008

Brazil, 1990–2004

Colombia, 1978–2008

Ecuador, 1985–1987, 1991–1995, 2001–2008

---

[18] As shown by the decline in gamma coefficients, from +.994 for the 1970s to +.898 for the 1980s and +.854 for the 1990s; the computation for 2000–2008 is skewed by lopsided marginal values.

Paraguay, 1993–2008

Peru, 1980–1991, 2001–2008

Venezuela, 1989–1998

Elsewhere, the listing included eight other countries:

Dominican Republic, 1984–1999

El Salvador, 1994–2008

Guatemala, 1996–2008

Haiti, 1990

Honduras, 1998–2008

Mexico, 2000–2001, 2006–2008

Nicaragua, 1990–2008

Panama, 1994–1998.

To state the case another way, over the course of the past two decades, as the still-current cycle of democratization reached its highest point, only three countries—Chile, Costa Rica, and Uruguay—qualified consistently as "liberal democracies," that is, electoral democracies with expansive civil liberties. They represented less than 16 percent of nations in the region and an even smaller share of the population.

PATHWAYS TO FULL DEMOCRACY

Over time, illiberal democracy revealed two dominant tendencies. One was to stay in place, with democratic elections accompanied by systematic restrictions on citizen rights. This proved to be a durable phenomenon. The other was to give way to move toward liberal democracy. In Latin America, the path to authentic democracy usually passed through illiberal democracy. How and why did this occur?

One recent study has explored the conditions under which these illiberal-to-liberal transitions have taken place.[19] Research uncovered two key determinants: widespread economic distress and the presence of election years. This combination of factors often enabled electoral victory by opposition candidates, who then proceeded to dismantle existing constraints on citizen rights—sometimes fulfilling campaign promises, sometimes seeking to bolster their own popularity (or both). Elections came to play crucial roles in the improvement of the quality of democratic life in Latin America.

---

[19] Peter H. Smith and Melissa L. Ziegler, "Liberal and Illiberal Democracy in Latin America," *Latin American Politics and Society* 50, 1 (Spring 2008): 31–57, also published in William C. Smith, ed., *Latin American Democratic Transformations: Institutions, Actors, and Processes* (Malden, MA: Wiley-Blackwell, 2009), 13–33.

Even then, liberal democracy occasionally reverted to illiberal democracy, as leaders or security forces clamped down on popular movements, press freedoms, and political dissidence. Cases in point include the Dominican Republic in the early 1980s, Argentina and Ecuador around 1990–1991, and Mexico in 2006—when escalation of the drug wars led to widespread violence and abuse of human rights.

Venezuela proved to be a special case. The 1989 *caracazo* and its aftermath provoked a shift from liberal to illiberal democracy that endured for most of the 1990s. By rewriting the nation's constitution, the triumphalist regime of Hugo Chávez altered the rules of the political game and installed what is here referred to as a restrictive semidemocracy in 1999. Polarization and intransigence led to a brief phase of intensified repression (2000–2001) followed by a return to less harsh, restrictive semidemocracy (2002–2008). Under *chavismo*, national elections have had predetermined outcomes and citizen rights have been subjected to increasing degrees of repression and constraint.

Taken together, these findings suggest a two-step process in overall transitions from authoritarianism to authentic democracy. The first step takes place when outgoing autocrats attempt to control the terms of their exit by establishing "protected" democracies of one sort or another—either illiberal or semidemocratic. This is the typical result of dictator-with-dissident negotiations that have often produced "pacted" democracies in Latin America. It is most decidedly a top-down process. More specifically, it entails a series of movements along the electoral axis: from no elections to rigged (or semidemocratic) elections to free-and-fair elections with continuing constraints on citizen rights (illiberal democracy). The second step occurs when popular protest accelerates, often in response to economic distress, polarization intensifies, and citizens cast votes (or other signs of approval) for opposition candidates. This phase is reminiscent of what O'Donnell and Schmitter referred to as "the resurrection of civil society" in their still-classic treatise on transitions.[20] The expansion of civil liberties is most commonly a bottom-up process. It marks the culmination of political change—and the onset of liberal democracy.

Case studies reveal three basic patterns of change. One group of countries—Argentina, Chile, Ecuador, and Uruguay—took direct routes from authoritarian dictatorship to liberal democracy. These countries had an extended democratic past in common. At the moment of transition, the prospect of democracy offered little uncertainty; it was a known quantity. Albeit with interruptions, electoral democracy first took root in Argentina and Uruguay in the 1910s; Chile followed in the 1930s, as did Ecuador in the 1940s. During all the transitions under review, outgoing military rulers were engaged in negotiations with incoming democrats; understandings

---

[20] O'Donnell and Schmitter, *Transitions*, Ch. 5.

were formed and "pacts" were established, most explicitly in the case of Uruguay but in the other countries as well.[21]

And as the generals prepared to leave office, the political Left appeared to pose little danger. Ecuador's military regime (1972–1979) had espoused a reformist/populist ideology that was willing to accept left-of-center civilian leadership. Throughout the Southern Cone, in contrast, years of repression had greatly weakened the Left—and persuaded survivors to adopt a pragmatic political course. (According to a much-quoted maxim, there was not much left of the Left.) In Uruguay the Tupamaro urban guerrilla movement had been crushed; labor unions and leftist parties retained their organizational capacity, but they willingly accepted the moderating terms of the "Naval Club Pact." In Chile the Socialists entered into the *Concertación*, a centrist coalition that included Christian Democrats. Argentina, perennially a special case, showed little left-wing inclination. The Peronist party had always been more populist than Marxist. And in its brutal wars against "subversion," the military regime had successfully exterminated large cadres of potential leftist leadership. On the assumption that Peronists would win the upcoming elections, in fact, the Argentine generals engaged in intensive discussions with party leaders—only to watch the Radicals triumph at the polls! And when the Alfonsín administration mounted a threat against the armed forces, the defining issue concerned human rights abuses, rather than socioeconomic restructuring. Herewith a sobering truth: Pact-making requires accurate political intelligence. This the generals lacked, and they would pay a price for that.

A second pattern entailed incremental stages of transition to democracy. Some nations had endured lengthy periods of authoritarian domination, and political alignments were unclear. These conditions cast a pall of uncertainty over the future. Brazil had enjoyed brief periods of electoral democracy in the 1940s and 1950s, punctuated regularly by military interventions, but the coup of 1964 led to more than twenty years of continuous autocracy. As elections took place under military tutelage in 1985, Brazil moved into a semidemocratic phase (1985–1989). During this time the party system was fluid, unstructured, and fragile. There followed a prolonged period of illiberal democracy (1990–2003). As civil liberties improved under Lula's government, Brazil finally became a liberal democracy in 2004.

Similarly, Mexico emerged from its long-standing dominant-party autocracy under the PRI with a decade of semidemocratic rule (1988–1999), when Carlos Salinas de Gortari and Ernesto Zedillo triumphed in one-sided presidential elections. The stunning victory of Vicente Fox then inaugurated a two-year period of illiberal democracy (2000–2001) that eventuated in a liberal democracy (2002–2005). Mexico reverted to illiberal democracy in 2006,

---

[21] See Peter H. Smith and Matthew C. Kearney, "Transitions, Interrupted: Routes toward Democracy in Latin America," *Taiwan Journal of Democracy* 6, no. 1 (July 2010): 137–163.

however, as drug wars and police impunity led to widespread violations of human rights and the rule of law and as increasing violence against journalists weakened freedom of the press.

Such political trajectories involved negotiation and renegotiation at almost every step. Because the future was unclear—much less clear, anyway, than it appeared to be in the cases of direct transition to democracy—stock-taking, renegotiation, and adjustment took place along the way. To the extent that democratization requires an element of mutual trust, experiments with semi-democratic and illiberal governance can be regarded as confidence-building measures among contending parties. Once it became clear that the other side was not going to set the house on fire, it became possible to accept the prospect of alternation in power. It was equally possible to relax constraints on citizen rights. Democracy thus came on the installment plan.

The third basic pattern entailed transitions culminating in illiberal democracy. Some cases revealed the outlines of a clear-cut bargain: Elections could be free and fair, but constraints on citizen rights would stay in place. Dictators were willing to concede presidential office to untested civilians, so long as the social order remained intact. Moreover, the sponsorship of democratic elections at the time of their exit would confer retroactive legitimacy on their period of authoritarian rule, especially in the eyes of the international community. This was a tempting reward. Illiberal democracy also flourished among the least developed countries of the region, as in Central America and Paraguay.

In these contexts, confidence-building proved to be a slow and uncertain process; political parties and interest groups did not establish sufficient mutual trust to permit a transition to liberal democracy. Moreover, illiberal democracy represented a convenient and durable solution from the standpoint of societal elites. On the one hand, it benefited from the legitimacy of free and fair elections, and on the other hand, it possessed the added virtue of constraining civil liberties. In Simón Bolívar's famous phrase, it offered an intermediate compromise "between tyranny and chaos." Its signature measures included restrictions on the media and on grass-roots organizations, an uncertain (often arbitrary) rule of law, and low-level but systematic abuse of human rights.

Illiberal democracy took deep root in places lacking democratic histories. These societies had no collective recollections of "golden eras" in the past. In sharp contrast to Chile and Uruguay, such nations as Haiti and Honduras lacked blueprints, scripts, playbooks, and texts. They were starting from scratch. Particularly in Central America, where civil wars had polarized societies in the 1980s, contending parties had little if any trust in one another. By the early twenty-first century, illiberal democracy was as far as they would go.

Beyond mistrust among elites, these societies revealed another common feature—the presence of large marginal populations. In some cases (Ecuador, Guatemala, Peru) these historically excluded sectors were largely indigenous; in other countries they consisted primarily of *campesinos* and, to a lesser extent, of migrant workers in the cities. As a result of their size and potential importance, these marginal sectors represented real or imagined threats to the prevailing social order. The uncertainties inherent in full-fledged democracy created widespread fear and apprehension, especially among upper-class and ruling groups. Herewith a dilemma of power: Illiberal democracy would not have the strength (or the will) to challenge established elites, but it would have the strength (and the will) to keep the unruly masses in place.

And for the most part, these marginal sectors were not highly mobilized. They were unorganized and dispersed. Worker unions and peasant organizations were weak. Political party systems were inchoate and unrepresentative. Expressions of people power were intermittent and sporadic. In such contexts it would be inappropriate to speak of a potential "resurrection" of civil society; the more suitable question would concern its provocation and formation. Broadly speaking, there was insufficient demand for broad extensions of citizen rights.

Illiberal democracy thus became a dominant form. And as Fareed Zakaria once predicted, this was not a passing phenomenon.

> Illiberal democracy is a growth industry....Far from being a temporary or transitional stage, it appears that many countries are settling into a form of government that mixes a substantial degree of democracy with a substantial degree of illiberalism. Just as nations across the world have become comfortable with many variations of capitalism, they could well adopt and sustain varied forms of democracy. Western liberal democracy might prove to be not the final destination on the democratic road, but just one of many possible exits.[22]

Would this be the future of Latin America?

---

[22] Zakaria, "Rise of Illiberal Democracy," 24. See also Marina Ottaway, *Democracy Challenged: The Rise of Semi-Authoritarianism* (Washington, DC: Carnegie Endowment for International Peace, 2003).

CHAPTER 11

THE PEOPLE'S VERDICT

What do the people of Latin America think of their democracy? Do they sub-scribe to the principles of free and open competition? What is the nature and basis of popular support for political democracy? Is it widespread through-out society or restricted to specific groups and classes? Is it stable and strong or contingent on instrumental considerations? Especially in times of dif-ficulty, might the citizens of Latin America be willing to accept authoritar-ian regimes? And what do their assessments suggest about prospects for consolidation of democracy?

These are issues of major concern. One might wonder why. Democracy grants power to the people; people use power to promote their interests; hence, people should support democracy. This logic is especially compelling in the United States and Western Europe, where it is broadly assumed that democracy constitutes the only legitimate form of government. There are critiques, of course, but no plausible alternative. In such societies, democracy is simply the only game in town.

Such a consensus does not exist in Latin America. Most democracies throughout the region are of recent origin, dating from the 1980s or 1990s. Many are novel experiments rather than time-tested traditions. Moreover, there have been difficult times: Democracy is not always associated with progress and prosperity. And as a result of historical experience, there exists a conceivable option: authoritarian rule under a party, a junta, or a charis-matic strongman. There is no reason to take democracy for granted.

This greatly complicates the challenge of consolidation. It is the consolida-tion of democracy that, above all, demands the support of citizens. It involves the institutionalization and perpetuation of democracy into an indefinite future. Legitimization requires deep-rooted loyalty and a generalized con-viction that, for all its faults, democracy should and must survive.

This chapter explores the content and structure of political attitudes in contemporary Latin America. Systematic analysis of public opinion surveys yields unsettling results. Citizens throughout the region express considerable disenchantment with present-day democracy. Moreover, they do not proclaim unconditional and principled support for democratic institutions. Their backing is conditional: They want practical results. And to the extent that results fall short of expectations, they place the blame on governing elites and representative institutions. Although this is understandable, it is also problematic.

The delivery of tangible benefits might not depend on, or be within the grasp of, Latin America's political leadership. This is especially true in regard to economics: In a globalizing world, the region's destiny largely depends on developments elsewhere around the globe (including the United States). To a lesser extent, it is also true concerning the imposition of law and order: Drug-trafficking rings and criminal gangs have virtually unfettered access to financial and paramilitary resources. Improving state performance is more easily said than done.

The present configuration of popular attitudes in Latin America is more conducive to illiberal than to liberal democracy. Citizens want what they need. They are less concerned about restrictions on civil or political rights, unless, of course, it is their own rights that are at stake. Many people appear willing to accept the curtailment of democratic freedoms in exchange for effective and constructive leadership. Illiberal democracy has a popular following.

THE CONCEPT OF POLITICAL CULTURE

Exploration of these issues moves into the realm of what has come to be known as "political culture." Such a phrase might seem strange or contradictory. There is nothing very cultured about politics. Yet in this context the term *culture* does not refer to high-minded artistic expression—it refers to fundamental beliefs and attitudes within a society. More to the point, the idea of political culture can be defined as "a people's predominant beliefs, attitudes, values, ideals, sentiments and evaluations about the political system of their country and the role of the self in the system."[1] What do people think about politics? What do they want from government? What are the foundations of their views?

There are many ways of studying beliefs. Historians, anthropologists, and sociologists, among others, employ textual analysis and participant observation to provide in-depth examination of the contents and nuances of shared values and attitudes.[2] In contrast, political scientists often rely

---

[1] Larry Diamond, *Developing Democracy: Toward Consolidation* (Baltimore: Johns Hopkins University Press, 1999), 163. See also Larry Diamond, ed., *Political Culture and Democracy in Developing Countries* (Boulder, CO: Lynne Rienner, 1993).

[2] See Daniel H. Levine, ed., *Constructing Culture and Power in Latin America* (Ann Arbor: University of Michigan Press, 1993); and Amparo Menéndez Carrión, "The Transformation of Political Culture," in Manuel Antonio Garretón and Edward Newman, eds., *Democracy in Latin America: (Re)Constructing Political Society* (Tokyo: United Nations University Press, 2001), 249–277.

on the quantitative exploration of public opinion surveys. Although these two approaches differ in method and style, they are highly complementary. Qualitative studies offer guidelines about what to look for in large-scale surveys, while quantitative analysis helps to reveal the extent to which members of a population share the outlooks or values in question.

Empirical political science scholarship dates from the early 1960s, when Gabriel Almond and Sidney Verba published a book entitled *The Civic Culture*. This was a broad comparative study of public opinion in five nations—the United States, Britain, Germany, Italy, and Mexico. Applying then-new methods of survey research and computerized analysis, Almond and Verba set out to identify clusters of attitudes and beliefs that would provide firm foundations for democracy. (These were urgent questions at the time: the "second wave" of democratization was still sweeping the world, decolonization was bringing independence to scores of new states, and the United States and the Soviet Union were strenuously competing for political influence throughout the third world.) And indeed, the authors found that key attitudes, such as trust in other people and a sense of personal efficacy, formed the core of a "civic culture" that was essential for modern democracy. Central to their interpretation was a distinction between "participant," "subject," and "parochial" political cultures—the greater the level of participation, the stronger the basis of democracy. Not surprisingly, perhaps, they found that participant values were most apparent in the United States and least evident in Italy, which exhibited an "alienated" political culture, and in Mexico, characterized by a mixture of "alienation and aspiration."[3]

This was a landmark study. Through the systematic use of public opinion surveys, *The Civic Culture* provided a solid basis for the study of political culture. Precisely because of its importance, the book also attracted a good deal of criticism. Theorists argued that the key to democratic stability in large and complex societies was not the extension of political participation, but constraints on popular activism according to class, race, and gender. Comparative specialists suggested that celebration of U.S.-style political virtue was an ethnocentric exercise and a foregone conclusion from the outset. Historians observed that a cross-national focus on culture did little to explain patterns of change over time. Experts on Mexico noted that by focusing only on urban communities, the sample excluded a large share of the national population.[4] Others raised questions about the direction of causality: Does

---

[3] *The Civic Culture: Political Attitudes and Democracy in Five Nations* (Boston: Little, Brown, 1965, first published by Princeton University Press in 1963), especially Chapters 1 and 11. On Mexico see also Robert Scott, "Mexico: The Established Revolution," in Lucian W. Pye and Sidney Verba, eds., *Political Culture and Political Development* (Princeton, NJ: Princeton University Press, 1965).

[4] See Ann L. Craig and Wayne A. Cornelius, "Political Culture in Mexico: Continuities and Revisionist Interpretations," in Gabriel A. Almond and Sidney Verba, eds., *The Civic Culture Revisited* (Boston: Little, Brown, 1980).

democracy result from a culture of trust, efficacy, and participation? Or do these virtues result from positive experiences with democracy?[5]

Area specialists tended to ignore or dismiss the total enterprise. First, they were reluctant to embrace anything that might resemble the facile and demeaning notions of "national character" that had once been so prevalent in the field of Latin American studies. Second, they tended to interpret political change as the result of class struggle or shifting social coalitions: What mattered in this view were material interests, not popular beliefs or attitudes (which, in Marxist terms, might merely have been "opiates" to mollify the masses). Third was the painful fact that from the mid-1960s to the 1980s, Latin America fell under the sway of brutal authoritarian regimes. The preferences or values of the citizenry seemed of little relevance. Besides, it was difficult (if not impossible) for independent scholars to conduct surveys under such conditions. Finally, considerations about political culture were discredited by a series of impressionistic studies that proposed that Latin American society had inherited an "Iberic-Mediterranean" tradition—a cultural outlook that prized order over liberty, harmony over competition, and societal interests over individual rights. According to this school, authoritarianism came to Latin America because its people embraced it.

Then began the recent cycle of electoral democracy. As citizens throughout South America mounted vigorous and courageous protests against authoritarian domination, interest began to grow in the subject of popular opinion. As elections approached, including those initially intended to prolong the rule of dictators, polls gave citizens the strength and conviction to vote their tormentors out of power (see Box 11.1). As campaigns took place in transitional democracies, pollsters became crucial to the fate of individual candidacies and electoral coalitions. Partly as a novelty and fad, political surveys began to take deep root in the newly democratic ambience of Latin America.

Caution is required here: Electoral polling is not the same as research on public opinion. Polling tends to meet short-term, practical goals, such as assessing the feasibility of an electoral campaign, identifying interests of constituencies, and determining who is ahead and who is behind (the so-called "horse-race" approach). In contrast, the study of public opinion explores long-term, conceptual concerns about political orientations in general rather than perceptions of specific candidates or issues. It was polling that made such rapid headway in Latin America. The analysis of public opinion remained in its infancy.

By the late 1980s, U.S. and European scholars had proclaimed a "renaissance" for the study of political culture. The self-evident role of religious and societal values in Poland, East Asia, and the Islamic world was offering

---

[5] Edward N. Muller and Mitchell A. Seligson, "Civic Culture and Democracy: The Question of Causal Relationships," *American Political Science Review*, 88, no. 3 (September 1994): 635–652.

BOX 11.1

POLLING AND POLITICS

Public opinion research is an essential tool of contemporary social science. It can also be, in its own right, a democratizing force.

Polling gives voice to ordinary citizens. In contrast to elections, which allow people to make a choice among preselected candidates for political leadership only at specified intervals, surveys allow citizens to express their views in a continuous way on substantive issues and public policies. Especially in societies undergoing political transition, the publication of polling results can stimulate and empower civil society by fostering awareness of key issues, by sharpening perceptions of leaders, and by promoting social solidarity. Once citizens recognize that their views are shared by a substantial number of compatriots, perhaps even a majority, they feel less isolated, less vulnerable, less helpless, and more determined to resist governmental abuse, intimidation, and repression.

At the same time, public opinion research can provide an instrument for social and political control. For nondemocratic regimes, it has been a means of social surveillance, as in the Soviet Union under the communists and in Brazil and Chile under the generals. And even in modern democracies, it tends to lull citizens into complacency rather than provoking them to action. Survey instruments call for passive responses to a range of issues and choices determined by elites; as such, they tend to foreclose and delimit public debate, and in the end, they tend to legitimate prevailing policy rather than challenge it. Through a process known as the "spiral of silence," it has been shown, survey participants tend to offer opinions that are socially acceptable and conventional. They do not want interviewers or anyone else to regard them as extremist or unusual; they want to go along with the majority.

Polling has played a special role in contemporary Latin America. From the 1960s through the 1980s, it was used by authoritarian rulers—partly to detect pockets of opposition, and also to assess degrees of popular acceptance and support. And as the current wave of democratization gathered strength in the 1980s, the study of public opinion rose to highly privileged status. Within the public arena, it became something of a novelty; it had the allure of "scientific" accuracy, with its deployment of dizzying arrays of numbers; and it enjoyed international acceptance. Of course, these very qualities made polling subject to abuse, manipulation, and sloppy methodology. But they also meant that polls would become key factors within the political arena.

eloquent testimony to the significance of cultural factors. In terms reminiscent of Almond and Verba, Ronald Inglehart advanced the propositions that "different societies are characterized to very different degrees by a specific syndrome of political cultural attitudes; that these cultural differences are relatively enduring, but not immutable; and that they have major political consequences, being closely linked to the viability of democratic institutions." Moreover, he asserted, "the evolution and persistence of mass-based democracy requires the emergence of certain supportive habits and attitudes among the general public." Such attitudes included interpersonal trust and overall satisfaction with life. Using systematic surveys from Europe—the "Eurobarometer" series dating from the 1970s—Inglehart found strong empirical associations between popular culture and democratic stability. In his words, "those societies characterized by high levels of life satisfaction (as well as interpersonal trust, tolerance, etc.) would be likelier to adopt and maintain democratic institutions than those whose publics lacked such attitudes. Conversely, democratic institutions would be more likely to flounder in societies with low levels of satisfaction, trust, and so on."[6] On the basis of such evidence, an understanding of political culture was therefore essential to a comprehension of democracy.

This chapter bears a complex relationship to mainstream scholarship on political culture. It relies on the quantitative analysis of a large-scale survey, like most studies, but it departs from orthodox approaches in two important ways. One concerns the question of causality. Essentially, the study sets out to examine how the peoples of Latin America evaluate and react to the performance of electoral democracies. It thus treats popular opinion not as an independent *cause* of democratic politics, but as an *effect*. (Formally expressed, public opinion here becomes the "dependent" variable, and democratic performance, as outlined in earlier chapters, constitutes the "independent" variable.) At the same time—once again, more in keeping with scholarly convention—the chapter speculates about the potential impact of these attitudes on the prospects for consolidation of democracy. Second, this essay adopts an agnostic stance with regard to the existence of value clusters that might (or might not) fit together into a political culture. The idea of a "culture" assumes a consistency, coherence, and congruence among beliefs that might or might not exist. In consequence, this investigation makes no attempt to categorize Latin American societies as "parochial" or "subject" or "participant." It is based, instead, on the assumption that citizens know what they want and understand what they see.

In this spirit, the chapter explores fundamental themes in popular attitudes toward politics:

- Support for democracy in principle
- Satisfaction with democracy in practice
- Ideological leanings
- Evaluations of key political institutions
- Perceptions of major societal problems
- Levels of protest and activism.

---

[6] Ronald Inglehart, "The Renaissance of Political Culture," *American Political Science Review* 82, no. 4 (December 1988): 1203–1230. See also Inglehart, *Modernization and Postmodernization: Cultural, Economic, and Political Change in 43 Societies* (Princeton, NJ: Princeton University Press, 1997).

MEANING VS. SIGNIFICANCE

The concept of statistical "significance" often sows more confusion than enlightenment. Based on probability theory, it offers a shorthand way of estimating the likelihood that results obtained from a public opinion survey (or any other quantitative sample) represent a statistical fluke.

Take Figure 11.1, which presents distributions of data for 1997 and 2007 according to two variables: preference for democracy and nationality. It is drawn from samples of more than 20,000 respondents in eighteen countries of Latin America for each of the two years. Analysis requires a leap of faith: that it is possible to extend results in the graph to the overall populations of the region as a whole (more than 550 million). This assumes that the samples are drawn at random from those populations or are demonstrably equivalent to random samples.

The question then becomes: What are the chances that the real association between these two variables for the total populations is actually zero? This is known as the "null hypothesis." Using laws of probability, it is possible to calculate the likelihood that the null hypothesis applies to the populations at large. Simple rules of thumb apply: The stronger the observed relationship and the larger the sample size, the less the chance that the null hypothesis holds true.

On the basis of these computations, researchers determine the "significance" of their findings by the extent to which they can plausibly reject the null hypothesis. The most common criterion for rejection is a probability of less than 5 out of 100 (or .05). A more demanding criterion is less than 1 out of 100 (.01). In such cases it is reported that the findings from the sample are "significant at the .05 level" or "significant at the .01 level."

So far so good. The problem is the language. *Statistical significance is not the same as substantive meaning.* The calculations merely determine probabilities about the null hypothesis. They do *not* show that the observed results are interesting, important, or valuable.

Undue emphasis on "statistical significance" can distort interpretation in at least three ways:

- by ignoring the potential importance of zero or near-zero relationships
- by placing too much stress on sample size (and not enough on sample quality)
- by distracting attention from the interpretative meaning of correlations within the sample.

Unless stated otherwise, findings reported in this chapter are significant at the .01 level.

For most of these variables, background research has explored correlations with demographic and social characteristics of respondents, such as social class, educational level, gender, urban versus rural location, economic outlook, and self-defined political ideology. Most of the resulting correlations yield no meaningful results. As explained here, the most suggestive findings relate to social class. In contemporary Latin America, socioeconomic status emerges as a key determinant of popular perceptions of political democracy.

The empirical data for this undertaking come from the Latinobarómetro, or Latin Barometer, an annual survey of public opinion modeled on the Eurobarometer and initiated in the mid-1990s. Currently extending to eighteen countries, the Latinobarómetro (or Barómetro) is widely regarded as the most extensive gauge of popular attitudes throughout the region.[7] Findings for the 2007 survey (used in this chapter) cover more than 20,000 respondents; for selected variables, results for that year will be compared with data from 1996–1997. Given this analytical strategy, Barómetro data can yield suggestive insights into trends and developments across countries, across demographic and social groups, and, within limits, over a decade of far-reaching change.

DEMOCRACY IN PRINCIPLE

There is popular support for political democracy in Latin America, but it is neither strong nor extensive. A key question in the Barómetro (and in other surveys) asks respondents whether they think democracy "is preferable to any other form of government" or whether, "under some circumstances, an authoritarian regime can be preferable to a democratic one." With its abstract and hypothetical phrasing, the item seeks to assess dimensions of support for democracy as a general principle. The results for 2007 proved to be somewhat unsettling: Across the region as a whole, 55 percent expressed unconditional preference for democracy, 18 percent could imagine authoritarian rule under some conditions, and—even more revealing—20 percent replied that "for people like me, it doesn't matter." (Another 7 percent didn't have an answer to the question.) Over one fifth of Latin Americans expressed marginalization or alienation from the political process.

Breakdowns by year and country appear in Figure 11.1. As of 2007, support for democracy ranged from a high of 83 percent in Costa Rica to a low of 32 percent in Guatemala. Figures for major countries came to 60-plus percent in Argentina, Bolivia, and Venezuela; close to 50 percent in Chile, Mexico, Peru, and Colombia; and 44 percent in Brazil. El Salvador and Paraguay came in at less than 40 percent. At the same time, acknowledgment that an authoritarian regime might be preferable "under some circumstances" ranged from 6 percent in Costa Rica to more than 20 percent in Chile and

---

[7] Also of major importance is the Latin American Popular Opinion Project (LAPOP), directed by Mitchell A. Seligson at Vanderbilt University. In addition see Roderic Ai Camp, ed., *Citizen Views of Democracy in Latin America* (Pittsburgh, PA: University of Pittsburgh Press, 2001).

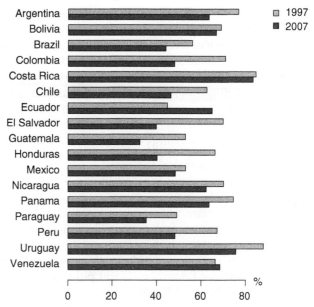

Figure 11.1 Preference for democracy, 1997–2007

Argentina, Bolivia, Brazil, Colombia, Costa Rica, Chile, Ecuador, El Salvador, Guatemala, Honduras, Mexico, Nicaragua, Panama, Paraguay, Peru, Uruguay, Venezuela

1997 2007

0 20 40 60 80 %

Argentina and well over 30 percent in Paraguay and Guatemala! More than a quarter-century after the initiation of the current cycle of democratization in Latin America, tolerance for autocracy still had a fairly strong foothold.

Such findings contrast sharply with results in advanced industrial democracies, as in Europe and the United States, where support for democratic legitimacy tends to be upward of 80 to 90 percent. Latin America reveals a complex pattern: Support for democracy is moderate, and it varies from country to country. Some of this might be due to ambiguities with the term *democracy*, which is bound to mean different things in different countries, but the overall implication is nonetheless telling: Democratic loyalty was limited.

Equally indicative is a marked decline in support for democracy. As the data show, the proportional preference for democracy slipped downward in all but two countries between 1997 and 2007. The greatest slippages occurred in Colombia, Guatemala, El Salvador, Honduras, Peru—and even Chile, widely hailed as an exemplary case of democracy incarnate. (Apparently some Chileans still admired the Pinochet dictatorship and others were becoming disappointed with the post-Pinochet *Concertación*.) Smaller drops were seen in Argentina, Brazil, Mexico, Panama, Paraguay, and Uruguay. Bolivia, Costa Rica, and Mexico more or less held their own. Yet the basic point is clear: Popular support for democracy in Latin America was a good deal less "enduring" than in Western Europe and North America.

Rising support appeared in two countries, Ecuador and Venezuela, both of which elected pink-tide presidents in between the survey years. These outcomes could well reflect the results of popular mobilization and mass participation during and after those turning points. Yet the picture seems ironic in the case of Venezuela, where Hugo Chávez has resorted to quasi-authoritarian measures to sustain his hold on power. In such a context, one might imagine that a declaration of support for democracy in principle could constitute a critique of nondemocratic political practice. Responses to an otherwise innocuous opinion survey could encapsulate statements of protest.

The Relevance of Social Class

Barómetro surveys reveal the pervasive and enduring impact of social-class differences. Throughout the developing world, particularly Latin America, extensive poverty and persisting inequality have led to the formation of hierarchical societies. Socioeconomic status remains a source and symbol of prominence, prestige, and power. The emergence of "middle sectors" over the past half-century has not altered this fundamental fact. It therefore stands to reason that social-class status would have a far-reaching impact on attitudes toward democracy and politics.

Data from the 2007 Barómetro have been manipulated (or "massaged" or "transformed") in such a way as to create an ordered-nominal variable with four socioeconomic groupings: an upper class (about 5 percent of the total), an upper-middle class (39 percent), a lower-middle class (44 percent), and a lower class (11 percent). (See Box 11.3.) The classification is based on a combination of subjective and objective criteria. It substantially underestimates the relative size of population that is poor and overestimates the middle classes, a common deficiency in survey research on the region. To avoid consequent problems we restrict the present analysis to comparisons of proportional distributions across the social-class groupings.[8]

Table 11.1 thus presents a cross-tabulation between social-class background and preference for political democracy. Several observations emerge. First, all class groupings expressed decisive preferences for democracy over all other forms of government. Second, there was a clear-cut ordering of support by social status: 66 percent in the upper class, about 60 percent among the middle groups, and 54 percent within the lower class. Third, tolerance for authoritarianism was fairly consistent across the groups: 18 to 19 percent for the upper and middle categories, declining to about 15 percent amount the poor. And finally, there was a stepwise increase in levels of resignation ("it doesn't matter"): 16 percent among the upper class, 18 percent in the upper-middle, 21 percent among the lower-middle, and—most stunning—over 31 percent within the lower class. Political marginalization was a social-class phenomenon.

These are remarkable results. The social stratum that might have felt threatened by democracy, the upper class, was in fact the most supportive;

---

[8] Estimates for the total population could be achieved by judicious "weighting" of the data.

ON THE MEASUREMENT OF SOCIAL CLASS

Social class is one of the most crucial concepts in modern social science (see Box 2.2 in Chapter 2). It is also one of the most difficult to put to empirical use—to "operationalize," in the language of the trade.

The Latin Barometer contains two items that bear directly on this question. One is an assessment by the interviewer of the respondent's "socio-economic level"—based on the appearance of the home, the quality of furniture, and the interviewee's "general appearance." The other is a self-assessment by the respondent of economic status—a ten-point scale ranging from 1 (*poorest*) to 10 (*richest*), which we have collapsed into three categories (1–3 = lower, 4–7 = middle, and 8–10 = upper). The first indicator is presumed to be objective, the second is subjective.

As might be expected, the results are not entirely consistent. We have therefore combined the two variables to create a composite variable for "social class" as follows:

- Upper: "rich" in self-identification and "good" or "very good" in interviewer assessment ($n = 572$)
- Upper-middle: "middle" in self-identification and "good" in interviewer assessment ($n = 5,110$)
- Lower-middle: "middle" in self-identification and "not bad" in interviewer assessment ($n = 5,842$)
- Lower: "poor" in self-identification and "bad" or "very bad" in interviewer assessment ($n = 1,601$).

This process of winnowing brings the total number of usable observations down from 20,212 to 13,125 (a reduction of approximately 35 percent). It does not yield a true "random sample" of the population at large, given the over-representation of the middle classes (a chronic problem in the Latin Barometer and in survey research in general). It is nonetheless possible to make valid comparisons *across* the four socioeconomic groupings.

and the sector that might presumably have felt empowered by democracy, the lower class, was least supportive—and by far the most resigned. By the early twenty-first century, the ideals of democracy appeared to have more appeal among the wealthy than among the poor. This was a topsy-turvy world.

DEMOCRACY IN PRACTICE

What about real-life democracy? Can democracy survive hard times? Will people sustain democratic legitimacy under trying circumstances?

One approach to this question comes through an assessment of generic "satisfaction" with the performance of democracy. Over the years, the

TABLE 11.1 Social Class and Preference for Democracy, 2007

	SOCIAL CLASS			
Preference for Democracy	*Upper*	*Upper-Middle*	*Lower-Middle*	*Lower*
Always preferable	66.0	62.7	60.0	54.4
Authoritarianism maybe	18.4	19.0	19.3	14.5
Doesn't matter	15.6	18.3	20.6	31.2
Total	100.0	100.0	100.0	100.0

TABLE 11.2 Social Class and Satisfaction with Democracy, 2007

	SOCIAL CLASS			
Satisfaction with Democracy	*Upper*	*Upper-Middle*	*Lower-Middle*	*Lower*
Very satisfied	16.8	8.6	8.5	6.4
Fairly satisfied	34.9	31.6	31.2	25.4
Not very satisfied	34.2	43.8	45.1	43.7
Not at satisfied	14.2	16.0	15.2	24.6
Total	100.0	100.0	100.0	100.0

Note: Columns might not add up to 100.0 because of rounding

Barómetro has asked respondents to indicate whether they were "very satisfied, fairly satisfied, not very satisfied or not satisfied at all with the way democracy works in [your country]?" This item is very different from the abstract question of whether democracy, as a system, is preferable to any other form of government; it probes the question of democracy in practice.

In the late 1990s only 37 percent of respondents were "very" or "fairly" satisfied with the operation of democracy; about 60 percent were "not very satisfied" or "not at all satisfied," with 3 percent undecided. By 2007 the results showed only the slightest improvement: 40 percent were satisfied to one degree or another and 60 percent were not. Disenchantment was still running strong.

As shown in Table 11.2, socioeconomic position has exerted a strong influence on these collective opinions. By 2007 more than half of the upper class, 52 percent, was (very or fairly) satisfied with the workings of political democracy, compared with 40 percent of the middle-class groups and only 32 percent of the lower class. Conversely, less than 15 percent of the high-status groups were thoroughly dissatisfied, compared with nearly one quarter of the poor.

Once again, a central paradox appears: Although democracy is often thought to strengthen the hand of common people and the poor, it was the rich—the upper crust of Latin American society—that was most content with its actual performance.

TABLE 11.3 Social Class and Satisfaction with Democracy: Selected Countries, 2007

Country	SOCIAL CLASS				
	Upper	Upper–Middle	Lower-Middle	Lower	Upper-Lower
Argentina	37.5	33.9	32.7	28.1	+ 9.4
Brazil	41.9	30.0	32.9	37.7	+ 4.2
Colombia	40.9	34.6	37.2	32.9	+ 8.0
Costa Rica	58.2	47.3	48.0	48.5	+ 9.7
Dominican Republic	55.4	52.5	49.5	53.0	+ 2.4
Ecuador	68.2	35.3	47.9	15.5	+ 52.7
Honduras	45.0	29.6	31.8	32.8	+ 12.2
Paraguay	23.5	9.8	6.4	8.3	+ 15.2

Note: Figures represent proportions expressing themselves to be "very" or "fairly" satisfied with the performance of democracy in their country.

This counterintuitive relationship appears on a country-by-country basis as well as for the region as a whole. For selected countries in the 2007 Barómetro, Table 11.3 demonstrates the point by displaying the percentage of respondents within each social class who expressed themselves as "very" or "fairly" satisfied with the workings of democracy.[9] In addition, the right column shows differences between the upper and lower segments of society: Positive signs show that the upper class was more satisfied than the lower.

Results confirm the region-wide findings. Almost everywhere, the upper class expressed substantial degrees of satisfaction—40 percent or more in six of the eight cases (and in many of the other instances with insufficient data). And in every single country under consideration, the upper class was more satisfied than the lower class. Margins of difference ranged from 2.4 percent in the Dominican Republic to 52.7 percent in Ecuador, with most others between 5 and 15 percent. Once again, Latin America's upper classes approved more fully of the workings of democracy than did the lower classes. Clearly, they did not perceive the onset of democracy as a fundamental threat; just as clearly, the poorest elements did not regard democracy as an unwavering path toward social justice and popular *reivindicación* of downtrodden masses.

Part of this puzzle might stem from vagueness in the phrasing of the question. Responses about satisfaction might reflect not so much deliberate judgments on the mechanisms of democracy, but general feelings about the current situation in society—a vaguely defined status quo. To the extent that this holds true, it would help explain why the most privileged sectors of society, those in the upper and upper-middle classes, should express the

---

[9] The criterion for inclusion of countries was a minimum of twenty-five observations in each of the social-class groupings.

greatest degree of contentment with the prevalent state of affairs. After all, they were reaping disproportionate benefits.

Case Study: Insights from Argentina

The original inspiration for this social-class analysis came from Argentina. As of 1988, when the late Edgardo Catterberg undertook a major survey, things seemed to be looking good for that nation: Political discourse was civil, the still-restive military was coming under control, and the economic crisis that would bring down Raúl Alfonsín's government was still in the future. On the whole, one might have expected Argentine citizens to be feeling optimistic.

Yet their notions of democracy were sharply qualified. A large majority of Argentine citizens endorsed the idea of widespread "participation" in democratic life, and many expressed doubt about the need for "tolerance" of dissenting views and opposition rights. According to Catterberg's classification, only 52 percent of Argentines would qualify as true "democrats," supportive of both participation and tolerance. About 5 percent were "elitists," supportive of tolerance but not participation; 8 percent were out-and-out "authoritarians," with little use for either participation or tolerance; and 35 percent were "populists," who endorsed participation but not tolerance.[10]

These divergent conceptions of democracy bore a clear relationship to socioeconomic position. Argentina's upper class had the largest percentage of elitists (8 percent), as one might have expected, but also the largest percentage of democrats (78 percent), which one would not have expected. Within the middle class, 66 percent were democrats, and 27 percent were populists. The lower classes, both the organized working class and the "unstructured" strata, were less committed to democracy, with proponents at around 50 and 35 percent. They also had higher shares of populists, whereas the lowest layer of society also displayed a notable tendency toward authoritarianism. Such patterns dispel ideas about the middle class as the principal bastion of democracy, and they provide substantial evidence for the existence of "working-class authoritarianism."[11]

Almost by definition, populists would uphold tyrannies of the majority. They would support free and fair elections—and allow the winners to trample on the rights of the losers. Quite explicitly, they would lend their support the "illiberal" democracy discussed throughout this book.

POLITICAL IDEOLOGY

---

[10] Edgardo Catterberg, *Argentina Confronts Politics: Political Culture and Popular Opinion in the Argentine Transition to Democracy* (Boulder, CO: Lynne Rienner, 1991).
[11] This concept originated with S. M. Lipset's *Political Man: The Social Bases of Politics* (Garden City, NY: Anchor Books, 1963), Ch. 4.

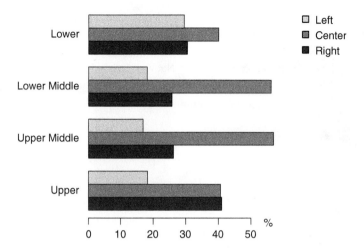

Figure 11.2 Ideology and social class, 2007

A widely accepted proposition in contemporary political science argues that ideological outlook depends on social class. In efforts to defend their privileges, the rich adopt conservative stances in favor of the status quo; in attempts to improve their position, the poor support reformist or radical platforms that seek to modify or overthrow the status quo. At bottom, philosophical discourses on the relative merits of capitalism and socialism reflect contradictions and conflicts of material interest. Where you stand depends on where you sit.

Is this what happens in Latin America? Figure 11.2 explores this question by showing the relationship between ideological self-placement and social class in the 2007 Barometer survey.[12] The graphics show a modest but consistent pattern. Over 40 percent of upper-class respondents placed themselves on the "Right," compared with 26 percent of the middle sectors and, surprisingly, 30 percent of the poor. In contrast, about 30 percent of the lower-class group put themselves on the "Left," as did only 17 to 18 percent of the upper- and middle-class respondents. For these same strata, the most commonly claimed position was the political Center (which came in a very close second within the upper class, too).

Generally speaking, Latin America was exuding a moderate mood. In support of this view, Figure 11.3 displays the relationship between political ideology and satisfaction with the workings of democracy. About 40 percent of the Left was "very" or "fairly" satisfied with the system's performance—slightly more than the Center (37 percent) and not too much less than the

---

[12] Respondents were asked to place their political beliefs on a left–right scale from 0 to 10. We collapsed the results into three categories: 0–3 = Left, 4–6 = Center, 7–10 = Right.

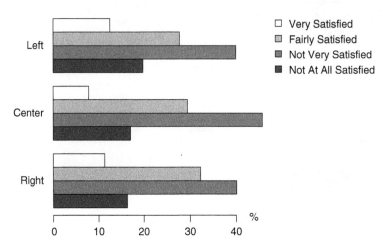

Figure 11.3 Ideology and satisfaction with democracy, 2007

Right (44 percent). And although 20 percent of respondents on the Left were "not at all satisfied," the same held true for 17 percent of the Center and 16 percent of the Right.

These were modest differences. Both the rich and the poor staked out positions on behalf of their interests, but not in extremist degrees. For the most part, the right was not calling for reinstatement of repressive military regimes; the left was not seeking to topple governments through violent revolution and guerrilla movements. Polarization was relatively mild. The dominant position was, in fact, the political center.

TRUST IN INSTITUTIONS

Popular assessments of political institutions provide a means of breaking down broad-based evaluations of democratic performance. As shown earlier, Latin American citizens displayed considerable discomfiture with current situations in their countries—almost 60 percent expressing some level of systemic dissatisfaction. This result then begs a question: Do judgments vary across specific institutions?

Figure 11.4 approaches this question by presenting proportions of respondents expressing "some" or "a lot" of confidence in national institutions as of 1996 and 2007. The political system was not faring very well. By 2007 only 39 percent of respondents expressed confidence in "the government," a slight improvement over a decade before, while just 43 percent proclaimed support for "the president." Support for security forces also climbed a bit—reaching 51 percent for the military and 39 percent for the police. In contrast, confidence in the judiciary and in the legislature dipped to less than 30 percent, and approval for political parties slipped to less

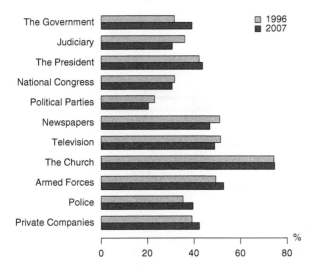

Figure 11.4 Levels of trust in institutions, 1996–2007

than 20 percent. From the standpoint of democratic legitimacy, these were disturbing results: Citizens were losing faith in checks and balances and in channels of representation.

Confidence in the media was stronger but nonetheless mixed. By 2007, around 45 percent of respondents expressed faith in newspapers and television, a slight drop from the mid-1990s (56 percent proclaimed support for radio, a more widespread and popular source of public information throughout the region). Support for the private sector edged up a bit to 41 percent. By far the highest score went to the church, with an approval rating of 74 percent, essentially unchanged from a decade before.

Disenchantment with political institutions was widespread throughout the region. At the same time, this phenomenon varied by social class. As shown in Table 11.3, nearly 20 percent of the upper class expressed "a lot" of confidence in the government and over 30 percent conveyed "some" degree of trust—well over 50 percent. Middle sectors displayed substantially lower levels of confidence, and only one third of the lower class expressed any degree of support. (A similar relationship applied to confidence in political parties.) Here as in other realms, political perceptions varied according to privilege and social rank. Once again, a counterintuitive interpretation emerges: Elites showed little if any fear of democracy.

ROOTS OF DISENCHANTMENT

Why so much dissatisfaction? One clue comes from a Barómetro item asking people to identify "the most important problem" confronting their countries. Respondents were allowed to mention only one issue, the single most urgent issue as of 2007. Table 11.4 arrays the results.

TABLE 11.4 Perceptions of Most Important Problems, 2007

Problem	%
Economic	
Inflation	3.1
Unemployment, underemployment	18.9
Poverty/inequality	9.0
Income distribution	1.9
Economic and financial problems	10.8
Other	2.3
Subtotal	**45.9**
Political	
Terrorism/violence	2.2
Corruption	10.7
Drug trafficking	0.4
Crime/public security	17.1
Political crisis	5.0
Other	0.4
Subtotal	**35.7**
Other	
Education	3.7
Health	2.4
Environment	0.5
Drug consumption	1.9
Other	5.6
Don't know/No answer	4.3
Subtotal	**18.4**
Total	**100.0**

Source: Latinobarómetro, 2007 (total N = 20,212).

Concerns fell into three categories: economic (46 percent of the total), political (36 percent), and other miscellaneous or other (18 percent). With the economic realm, citizens gave top priority to three major problems: employment (19 percent), poverty and inequality (9 percent), and macroeconomic and financial problems (11 percent). Political concerns focused sharply on two issues, public safety (17 percent) and corruption (11 percent), whereas terrorism and drug trafficking captured much less attention than threats of political stalemate (5 percent). Other problems, ranging from health and education to drug consumption, failed to generate much public interest.

Economic distress provided a crucial source of disenchantment. Among respondents who predicted that their economic situation would substantially improve, 51 percent pronounced satisfaction with the workings of democracy, and 49 percent expressed dissatisfaction, suggesting that economic gratification alone was not enough to guarantee approval for system performance. Among those who said their situation was likely to get "much worse," only 17 percent expressed approval of the workings of democracy, and 83 percent proclaimed dissatisfaction.

Emphasis on economic performance derives from the existence of an implicit compact between state and society: The government is expected to promote the economic welfare of its citizens. As Argentina's Alfonsín declared in a well-remembered campaign speech, "With democracy you eat, you educate, and you cure." As goes the economy, so goes support for the regime. (Note, once again, that this refers not to support for the person or party in power; it refers to the entire system of democracy.) Yet there remains the fact that the region's political leaders, especially democratically elected leaders, often exert little control over the economic destinies of their nations. As Latin America was increasingly buffeted by the winds of global economic forces, as in the global meltdown of 2008–2009, popular support for democratic governance was hanging in the balance.

As revealed in other studies, political corruption loomed as a major issue. This was more than a matter of pilfering the public treasury. Corruption means that political leaders are pursuing personal gain at the expense of collective benefits, that they are placing individual interests above the needs of their constituencies, and that, in societies plagued by inequity and poverty, they are making private deals instead of fulfilling public pledges. It is not just that money is changing hands. Corruption represents a fundamental violation of the public trust. It also underscores the helplessness of citizens: No matter how they vote, they have little control over public officials. And as Barometer data reveal, over 60 percent of respondents believed that their government had made "little" or "no" progress in reducing corruption in the prior two years, and less than 10 percent thought that government had made "a lot" of progress.

Extending the point, Table 11.5 demonstrates the connection between political corruption and satisfaction (or dissatisfaction) with democracy. Among those who believed that government had made "much" recent progress in reducing public corruption, 53 percent described themselves as "very" or "fairly" satisfied with the workings of democracy, as did 50 percent of those who perceived "some" progress in the fight against corruption. Among those who saw "little" progress, only 35 percent expressed satisfaction with the political system; among those who detected no progress just 21 percent were satisfied. (They might have lowered expectations in the belief that corruption was so deeply ingrained in the political community as to defy any efforts to root it out.) The overall pattern was clear: The greater the perception of official corruption, the greater the dissatisfaction with the political regime. This was a fundamental issue for the legitimization of democratic politics.

The implication is self-evident: Preference for democracy in Latin America is contingent, not absolute. It depends not only on philosophical principles but also on system performance. And after the turn of the century, more than a quarter-century after the onset of the current cycle of democracy, the situation was becoming tenuous. Dissatisfaction was undermining popular belief in the innate legitimacy of democratic rule.

TABLE 11.5 Corruption and Satisfaction with Democracy, 2007

| | PROGRESS IN REDUCING CORRUPTION | | | |
Satisfaction with Democracy	Much	Some	Little	None
Very satisfied	21.2	11.4	6.5	4.8
Fairly satisfied	31.9	38.6	28.8	17.8
Not very satisfied	34.2	39.0	49.2	46.0
Not at satisfied	12.7	11.0	15.5	31.3
Total	100.0	100.0	100.0	100.0

Note: Question concerns perceived reduction of corruption among state officials over the previous two years. Columns might not add up to 100.0 because of rounding.

ACTIVISM AND PROTEST

Does disenchantment lead to popular protest? Do people stand up for their rights? Everything else being equal, it seems reasonable to assume that democratization would encourage citizens to take an active part in the public arena.

Has this been the case in Latin America? Figure 11.5 presents graphic results on people's willingness to engage in specific forms of political protest—signing a petition, joining an authorized demonstration, or taking part in an unauthorized demonstration. Taken together, the queries thus create a scale of escalating proactivism.

As the data show, only 17 percent reported that they had ever signed a petition—and 47 percent said that they would "never" do such a thing. Just over 13 percent had taken part in authorized rallies, and over half said they would never do so. Merely 7 percent had taken part in an unauthorized demonstration, and nearly two thirds—64 percent, to be precise—said they would never do so. This last item is especially telling, because it indicates the extent to which people of Latin America would be overtly willing to challenge established authority. The basic answer is, not very.

Such findings are far from conclusive. They reflect responses to a questionnaire about hypothetical conditions, not actual behavior, and the wording of some items is ambiguous (Sign a protest letter *to whom*? Attend *what kind* of demonstration? Would they *dare* or *care* to take these actions?). Despite such limitations, the data do not portray an eager populace joyously embracing democratic opportunities to speak up or out to figures of political authority.

Nuances are significant. Levels of protest have been much higher in Argentina and Bolivia than in Mexico, Brazil, or El Salvador. And there are different kinds of protest. Expressions of "disaffected radicalism" denounce not only specific policies or leaders, but the fundamental legitimacy of the democratic system; in contrast, protest as a "strategic resource" represents just another form of conventional participation in contemporary democratic settings. And according to one study, recent surges of activism—including

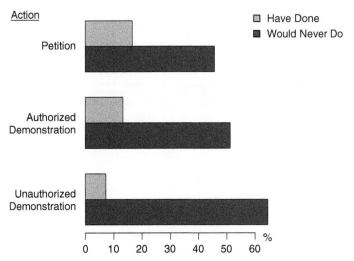

Figure 11.5 Propensity for protest, 2007

street blockages by *piqueteros* in Argentina and mass demonstrations by *campesinos* in Bolivia—have come to form part of the national repertoires of conventional political participation.[13] At the same time, protests in other countries of the region have taken more radical turns and threatened the validity of democratic politics.

Generally speaking, this was not an activist society. In contrast with conventional stereotypes, which evoke images of temperamental, passionate, hot-blooded Latin Americans, the survey depicts a citizenry that was careful, cautious, and somewhat withdrawn from the public arena. Possible explanations for this outcome are diverse. Average citizens might have little interest in politics. Especially in "illiberal" democracies, they might be fearful of governmental retribution. Perhaps even more to the point, they might assume that their entreaties would be in vain. Distrust in governmental institutions led to a sense of personal inefficacy. Electoral democracy was not empowering its citizens.

Taken together, the findings in this chapter have unsettling implications for the future consolidation of democracy throughout the region. As stated earlier, popular attitudes in Latin America are more conducive to illiberal than to liberal democracy. Transformation of the present-day illiberal democracy into a truly liberal democracy would require at least two separate things: insistence on the protection of rights, rather than the acquisition of benefits, and a societal commitment to extend such rights to others, so that they reach all sectors of the national community. The prognosis has to be cautious at best.

---

[13] Mason Mosely and Daniel Moreno, "The Normalization of Protest in Latin America," *AmericasBarometer Insights: 2010* (no. 42).

PART IV

DEMOCRACY CONSIDERED

Democratic nations care but little for what has been, but they are haunted by visions of what will be; in this direction their unbounded imagination grows and dilates beyond all measure. ... Democracy, which shuts the past against the poet, opens the future before him.

—ALEXIS DE TOQUEVILLE

Well begun is half done.

—ARISTOTLE

CHAPTER 12

THE DIALECTIC OF DEMOCRACY

This has been a complex tale. Democracy has come to Latin America through persistent struggle against formidable odds—economic underdevelopment, inhospitable international environments, and state-sponsored violence. It is a story of heroic resistance, determination, and commitment—of unyielding beliefs in the virtues of justice and freedom. It is also a story of opportunism, venality, intransigence, and intolerance. In part, as well, it is a story of failed expectations—of promises betrayed, aspirations dashed, and hopes disappointed.

Have things improved over time? As formulated at the outset of this study, the specific question is this: How does the most recent cycle of democracy compare with earlier episodes? Has it been more (or less) responsive to the will of the people? Has it imposed more (or less) effective policies? Is it more (or less) likely to endure? Why?

Addressing such issues, this chapter offers a synthesis of key trends over the course of the twentieth century. It begins with a summation of principal findings, presents a conceptual argument, and moves on to an analysis of continuity and change. Most of the comparison focuses on differences between the second (1940–1977) and third (1978–present) phases of democratization. And as will become apparent, the discussion is a highly interpretive exercise. It represents my personal attempt to uncover patterns of change, identify underlying factors, and comprehend the structure and significance of Latin American democracy.

The basic conclusion—indeed, a central thesis of this book—has two components. First is the idea that democracy became more widespread (and to some extent more durable) throughout Latin America because it had been tamed. From the 1940s to the 1970s, democracy was seen by elites as "dangerous." It amounted to a social provocation. From the 1980s through the 1990s, that was no longer the case. Elites could embrace democracy because it did not effectively challenge their interests. In particular, widespread endorsement of the Washington Consensus assured the perpetuation of pro-capitalist, free-market pathways of development. Reversing Woodrow Wilson's famous statement that it was at one time imperative "to make the world safe for democracy," democracy had now been made safe for the world.

But then a backlash occurred—and herewith the second component of the argument. Starting with the 1998 election of Hugo Chávez in Venezuela, voters in many countries rejected the neoliberal orientations of prevailing "market democracies" in quest of social justice. They wanted states that would be strong enough to serve the people. Unconvinced by trickle-down theories of economic development, they wanted meaningful alternatives. Suspicious of overeducated elites and sometimes duplicitous leaders, they demanded more effective representation and participation in decision-making processes. Apprehensive about proclamations of U.S. hegemony in the post–Cold War international order, they wanted leaders who would be willing to assert their nation's sovereign interests in the pursuit of a kinder, gentler, and more egalitarian world. Taking advantage of their rights within electoral democracy, they were demanding political change.

Thus emerged the "new Left" in Latin America. It was a direct and deliberate reaction to the regional prevalence of conservative, rightist, and center-right politics in the 1980s and 1990s. It surged rapidly throughout the 2000s. It did not have a coherent dogma or espouse uniform policies; on the contrary, it was subject to divergence and division. Broadly speaking, though, it reflected a dialectical pattern in Latin American democracy, a process of push-and-pull that shaped and reshaped prevailing terms of political contestation.

This interpretation views the surge of the "pink tide" not as the product of populist mystification or psychological derangement (as some have suggested), but as a rational and understandable response to prevailing conditions. This does not mean that new-left policies have always been effective and that new-left leaders have been paragons of virtue. What it means, instead, is that we can seek clues to patterns of Latin America's political change by focusing on context, conditions, and alternatives. With its bold reform agenda, the new Left of the 2000s appeared as a response to the cautious, overly timid democracies of the 1990s; and in turn, the hypercautious democracies of the 1990s took their shape as a response to the allegedly "dangerous" democracies of the 1960s and 1970s and the military interventions they provoked. History has its pendulums.

FINDINGS IN REVIEW

The initial task of this study was to trace the timing and levels of democratization over the course of the century. Focusing at first on the electoral component of democracy, the operational strategy has been to plot the incidence of democratic, semidemocratic, oligarchic, and nondemocratic regimes for nineteen countries of Latin America from 1900 through 2000. Illustrative graphs offered year-by-year displays of numbers of countries with each regime type (Chapter 1). In a comparable vein, Figure 12.1 reveals the same

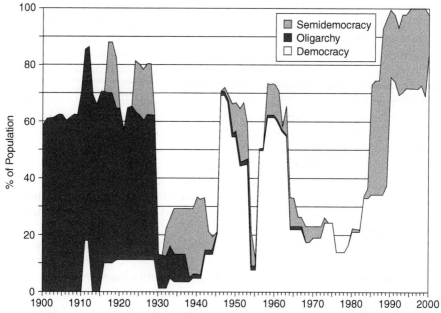

Figure 12.1 Cycles of political change in Latin America, by population, 1900–2000

basic trends but now with controls for population size: The vertical axis measures approximate percentages *of people* of the region living under each type of regime, and the horizontal axis once again represents change over time.

The overall patterns are much the same. Democracy rises over time, starting fairly early in the century and reaching a peak at the end. Nearly 90 percent of the region's population was living under electoral democracy by 2000. To be sure, the curves in Figure 12.1 are sharper and steeper than are those in Figure 1.1: The resulting configuration places more emphasis on the "cycles" of change and somewhat less on the linear trend. This difference stems largely from the effects of two major countries, Argentina and Brazil, both of which underwent fairly frequent changes of regime (Brazil, in fact, contained nearly 40 percent of the region's population).[1]

Each of the three cycles involved distinctive social-class coalitions. During the initial phase (1900–1939), socioeconomic elites were seeking to mobilize middle-class and (to a lesser extent) lower-class groups either

---

[1] The weighting scheme was based on population figures as of 1950, the midpoint of the century. With Cuba included in the denominator, Brazil's share of the regional population drops to 34 percent, and the combined population for Brazil plus Argentina amounts to 45 percent of the regional total. Although Mexico had the second-largest population in Latin America, it had little impact on Figure 12.1 because it underwent infrequent alterations of regime.

to gain partisan advantage or to co-opt potential sources of opposition. During the second phase (1940–1977), middle-class groups sought access to power through tactical alliances with working-class elements, including organized labor. The most recent phase (1978–2000) has been more heterogeneous in this regard, and class coalitions have been less visibly drawn. It was in this phase, as well, that negotiations or "pacts" between outgoing authoritarians and incoming civilians facilitated the process of transition but also tied the hands of succeeding democratic governments (Chapter 2). In part for this reason, military rulers agreed to return to their barracks, although the armed forces continued to represent a significant political factor (Chapter 3). Throughout most of the twentieth century, international factors—and the policy of the United States—exerted negative impacts on the prospects for democracy in Latin America, although the post–Cold War decade of the 1990s offered a partial exception to this rule (Chapter 4).

Generally speaking, elections have gone smoothly during the post-1978 cycle. After consideration of a parliamentary alternative, leaders throughout the region decided to maintain (or restore) presidentialist systems of politics (Chapters 5 and 6). Almost everywhere, suffrage extended to all adult citizens. Institutional reforms frequently included presidential reelection and majority runoff (MRO) systems. Voter turnout was strong in "founding" elections after the restoration of democracy, but it subsequently displayed considerable variation, even in countries where voting was mandatory. Competition was nonetheless keen, and voters showed little hesitation in ousting incumbents (or their parties) from office. One result was interruption of continuity in policy. Even so, people were using ballots to express their preferences (Chapter 7).

Latin America was not an easy place to govern. Late in the twentieth century, neither democracies nor dictatorships had much success in stimulating economic growth. States were less powerful than they had been before. Democratic leaders proved more effective than did autocrats in improving social conditions, especially regarding health and welfare, but their accomplishments fell short of overall needs. Poverty and inequality stubbornly persisted, but a burst of growth in the 2000s led to hopeful improvements in both areas (Chapter 8). As citizens confronted a nearly continuous state of economic uncertainty, presidential approval ratings fluctuated with often bewildering speed.

Effective representation came to show a distinctive social bias. As organized labor lost strength, the working class found itself on the sidelines of politics. Without access to conventional political parties, indigenous groups formed social movements to promote their interests and press their demands (with conspicuous success in Bolivia). Having played major roles in toppling authoritarian regimes, women finally gained representation in political institutions, especially legislatures, and several became presidents (most prominently in Brazil), but there was still a long way to go. In the meantime,

August 2003: President Álvaro Uribe of Colombia decorates troops during the ceremonial inauguration of a monument to soldiers killed in the country's war against guerrilla groups and paramilitary forces. (AP Photo/Ministry of Defense, Javier Casella)

the private sector—the business community—wielded enormous influence over and within the new democracies (Chapter 9).

Freedoms and rights were constricted. In many electoral democracies, freedom of the press was under near continual siege. There were constraints on civil rights as well. Indeed, the most common form of political regime in the 1990s and early 2000s was "illiberal democracy," an arrangement that combined the free and fair election of national leaders with systematic restrictions on the exercise of basic rights. As the public sphere contracted, citizenship was proving to be incomplete (Chapter 10).

For all these reasons, Latin Americans avowed only conditional support for political democracy—in principle and, especially, in practice. Generally approving of democracy in the abstract, they expressed considerable dissatisfaction with the actual performance of democratic leaders and regimes. They were particularly contemptuous of corruption and mismanagement. Members of the working class, those who had suffered so seriously under authoritarian rule, pronounced deep disappointment over the policy failures of democratic governments. Almost everywhere, comfort with democracy followed social-class lines: The higher one's social standing, the greater the satisfaction with the performance of democracy. After the turn of the century, many Latin Americans were so despairing that they would not even bother to protest (Chapter 11).

CHANGING SHAPES OF DEMOCRACY

In summary, the analysis has shown far-reaching changes in the configuration of political democracy in Latin America since the beginning of the twentieth century. It has uncovered limited and tentative movements toward electoral democracy between the turn of the century and the late 1930s, substantial democratic gains (with authoritarian reversals) between the 1940s and the mid-1970s, and a region-wide surge in democratization from the late 1970s to the present. It has demonstrated changes in the durability of political forms, with electoral democracy becoming stronger over time, autocratic rule becoming weaker, and oligarchic republicanism all but disappearing by the middle of the century.

The study also has revealed significant variations in effective levels of popular "representation"—very modest in the initial stage, expansive in the second stage, and systematically restricted in the third and most recent stage. This observation leads to a core interpretation, which rests on several propositions, or hypotheses:

H_1: These distinct dimensions of democracy—scope, durability, and representation—are related to one another.

H_2: The greater the level of effective representation, the greater the likelihood that political democracy will threaten established interests (at both national and international levels).

H_3: The less the level of effective representation, the less the likelihood that political democracy will threaten established interests (at national and international levels).

H_4: The less threatening the democracy, the greater its spread.

H_5: The less threatening the democracy, the longer its survival.

To illustrate this line of argumentation, Figure 12.2 presents a schematic depiction of what might be considered the changing "shape" of political democracy in twentieth-century Latin America. As constructed here, the concept of shape has three dimensions:

- extensiveness or "spread"—the pervasiveness of democratic politics, as measured by the number of countries with democratic experience (also by the proportion of country-years corresponding to electoral democracy)
- durability—the duration of electoral regimes, as measured by length of periods and by year-to-year survival rates
- representation—the degree to which social sectors and classes, especially the popular classes near the bottom of the social scale, are represented in the political regime.

Variation along these dimensions produces different patterns for different time periods.[2]

---

[2] The figure employs a six-point scale for each variable; entries represent my qualitative judgments, which are based (in large part) on quantitative data.

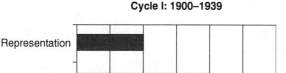

Cycle I: 1900–1939

Figure 12.2 Profiles of political democracy in Latin America

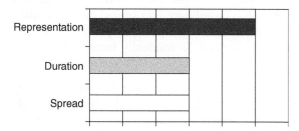

Cycle II: 1940–1977

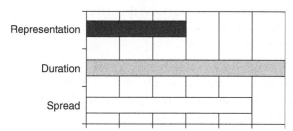

Cycle III: 1978–2000

As applied to Latin America, this scheme produces three sharply distinct "shapes" of political democracy in the twentieth century. During the early years (1900–1939), the picture shows (1) very limited spread, (2) substantial levels of durability, and (3) limited degrees of representation. Only three countries adopted electoral democracy. Most of these experiments ended in military coups, and effective participation extended from the upper classes only part way through the middle classes. For the second period (1940–1977), the scheme reveals (1) a somewhat more expansive spread, (2) reduced durability, and (3) a relatively high degree of representation. During this period, we should recall, the number of electoral democracies never exceeded 50 percent. Survival rates for democratic regimes were modest and somewhat skewed by the long duration of democratic regimes in Colombia, Venezuela, and Costa Rica. (Aside from these three exceptional instances, democratic life spans were rather short.) And given the strength of labor unions, the presence of opposition parties, the existence of ideological debate, and relative freedom of the press, the scope of political representation during this cycle was rather high.

The overall shape of the third and final period (1978–2000) was altogether different. Electoral democracy became very extensive, spreading to three quarters of the countries under consideration and to nearly 90 percent of the people. Durability increased, particularly as the threat of military intervention appeared to decline. But even so, these were relatively "narrow" democracies—as the span of ideological contention became more restricted, as mass-based parties and movements were excluded from power, and as popular voices were left in the wings of the political stage.

To be sure, this interpretation employs a particular notion of cause and effect—the idea that participation has an influence on spread and durability. One could entertain an alternative notion, the idea that spread, durability, or both have an influence on participation. In modestly formal terms, this gives rise to competing propositions:

- Proposition 1: The narrowness of contemporary democracy accounts for both its spread and durability; that is, with effective constraints on popular demands, democracy has posed little threat to established interests. (In this formulation, representation is the independent variable.)

- Proposition 2: The spread and durability of electoral democracy provide an atmosphere that will facilitate, even nurture, the effective participation of mass-based parties and movements over time. (Here, of course, representation becomes a dependent variable.)

Implicitly, Proposition 1 envisions limited democracy as an enduring and persisting component of the political landscape. By contrast, Proposition 2 helps explain the rise of the new Left and also advances the idea that illiberal electoral democracy will, with time, give way to liberal democracy.

DEMOCRACY IN THE ERA OF MASS POLITICS

The emergence of "mass politics" in the 1930s and 1940s—earlier (and later) in some locales and countries—had far-reaching effects on Latin America. It intensified demands on the state, altered the terms of public discourse, and challenged the legitimacy of existing regimes. As early as the 1910s, the eruption of the "social question" threatened ruling elites and plunged competitive oligarchies into crisis. And in the 1930s, the decade of the Great Depression, mass movements and popular protests helped bring about the downfall of fledgling electoral democracies throughout the Southern Cone. First-cycle democracies were not overthrown because they threatened established interests; on the contrary, they were deemed incapable of containing social pressures from below.

1940–1977: Dangers of Democracy

Mass politics came to culmination during the 1940–1977 cycle of democracy. One defining factor was large-scale mobilization. As agricultural exports declined in the 1930s, displaced rural workers migrated to cities in search of work. As urban populations swelled and industrial production advanced in the 1940s and 1950s, factory workers joined together in labor unions. Some organizations had ties to leftist political parties, socialist or even communist, as in the case of Chile; others had links to centrist parties or with the state itself, as in Brazil; and in Argentina, organized labor became a founding member of the Peronist movement and party. Workers could exercise influence through votes at the ballot box or through the use or threat of large-scale strikes. In differing ways, organized labor became a significant political actor in major countries of the region.

Unrest surged in the countryside, too. In Brazil, "peasant leagues" came forth to demand agrarian reform. Calls for redistribution of land—*tierra para quien la trabaje*—emerged in Chile and Colombia. In the highlands of the Andes, peasants began seizing estates of absentee landowners. The clamor for agrarian reform not only reshaped agendas of national politics. Possessed of the right to vote, peasants—and workers—could affect the outcome of national elections. Often espousing explicitly socialist views, parties of the Left had substantial electoral followings.

Lurking in the background was revolutionary fervor. Largely inspired by the Cuban Revolution, more than thirty armed guerrilla movements emerged in Latin America from the 1950s to the 1970s. Their goal was to accomplish by force what could not be achieved by the vote. Anti-imperialism and anti-Americanism were staples of everyday discourse, and Marxist thought, in a variety of guises, dominated intellectual circles. In the United States, alarmist commentators breathlessly proclaimed that the whole of Latin America was on the "brink" of revolution, with barely "ten minutes to midnight."[3]

Democratic leaders engaged in sweeping rhetoric, and sometimes populistic demagoguery. Fiery speakers such as Víctor Raúl Haya de la Torre in Peru and Jorge Eliecer Gaitán in Colombia ignited huge crowds with compelling appeals for social justice, economic development, and national dignity. And in country after country, politicians with mass followings assumed presidential power: Jacobo Arbenz in Guatemala, Juan Perón in Argentina, João Goulart in Brazil, and Rómulo Betancourt in Venezuela.

---

[3] For a diverse sampling see Daniel James, *Red Design for the Americas: Guatemalan Prelude* (New York: Day, 1954); Gary MacEóin, *Latin America, The Eleventh Hour* (New York: P. J. Kennedy, 1962); Milton S. Eisenhower, *The Wine Is Bitter: The United States and Latin America* (Garden City, NY: Doubleday, 1963); and John Gerassi, *The Great Fear: The Reconquest of Latin America by Latin Americans* (New York: Macmillan, 1963).

Grandiose policies followed. Agrarian reform became a key goal of democratic governments in Guatemala, Venezuela, Chile, and Colombia. Programs for worker entitlement came forth in Argentina, Brazil, Chile, and Uruguay. Progressive taxation was proposed in the belief that it would both bolster state revenues and enable redistribution of income. Nationalization of foreign-owned assets took place in the name of national sovereignty. During this period, the state was relatively strong, and there was a reasonable chance that policies could be implemented.[4]

On occasion, authoritarian governments adopted similar programs. In name, if not in fact, Mexico's dominant-party regime based its claim to power and legitimacy on the legacies of the 1910–1920 revolution. And in Peru, the military regime of General Juan Velasco Alvarado sought to impose sweeping changes on economy and society. But in general, it was the democrats, not the autocrats, who espoused or mounted substantial programs of social reform.

Who felt threatened by such developments? Most directly challenged were the socioeconomic elite, the owners of land and captains of industry. This was the group that would have the most to lose from redistributive policies, programs designed to take from the rich and give to the poor. Moreover, democratic politicians often reviled the upper classes as parasitical and selfish "oligarchies," undeserving wielders of power and privilege. (Actually, they made a tempting target, not only because of their behavior but also because they were very few in number; in electoral democracies, this was a decided disadvantage.) Not surprisingly, upper-class representatives denounced radical programs as naive, counterproductive, or—typically— "socialistic" in orientation.

Middle classes were often divided. Some elements supported democratic calls for social change. Others were fearful and resistant. It should be remembered that Latin America's "middle classes" did not occupy the "middle" of the social pyramid. On the contrary, they held positions of relative privilege (see Box 2.2 in Chapter 2). Serious alteration of the social structure could lead to considerable losses in prestige, influence, and, perhaps, prosperity. This anxiety was probably more acute among upwardly mobile members of the middle class, those who had just moved up from popular strata or those who were aspiring to climb upward to the vicinity of the upper-class elite.

Additional opposition came from the military (except in such inclusionary cases as 1968–1975 Peru and 1972–1978 Ecuador). Military officers instinctively distrusted democratic politicians, who (1) seemed more interested in winning elections than in protecting *la patria*, (2) denounced the armed forces for their longtime collusion with the traditional oligarchy, and (3) once in office, sometimes attempted to assert executive authority over the military. All such actions threatened to subvert the honor and the autonomy of the

---

[4] For an elegant description of such policies see Albert O. Hirschman, *Journeys Toward Progress: Studies of Economic Policy-Making in Latin America* (New York: Twentieth Century Fund, 1963).

armed forces. So when prominent civilians issued public pleas for military interventions against demagogic and "irresponsible" politicians, the generals did not hesitate for long.

Last but not least was the United States. This cycle of democratization took place under the shadow of the Cold War, which stretched from the mid-1940s to the late 1980s. During this entire period the U.S. government stood resolutely against any government that could vaguely be described as left-leaning, socialist, or communist. This determination was only strengthened by the surprising and stunning triumph of the Cuban Revolution in 1959. Accordingly, Washington took action to promote, support, or bring about the overthrow of reformist and left-of-center democratic regimes in Guatemala (1954), Brazil (1964), the Dominican Republic (1965), and Chile (1973). Where it occurred, expropriation of U.S.-owned assets (with or without compensation) added yet another incentive for American intervention. Further, U.S. authorities openly embraced authoritarian rulers or military regimes in Argentina, Brazil, Chile, Uruguay, Venezuela, and elsewhere.

For different but convergent reasons, these four elements thus regarded democracy as dangerous. It posed a variety of threats. Most fundamental was the possibility that it would lead to radical policy measures. Another was that it would serve as a kind of "Trojan horse" for revolutionary groups. Still another was that democracy would lack the will or capacity to crush insurgent guerrilla movements. Whether it was too strong or too weak, democracy was a source of danger. It would have to go.

It was because of such threats that U.S.-approved military coups took place. Repressive and long-term bureaucratic-authoritarian regimes seized power in Brazil (1964), Argentina (1966 and 1976), Chile (1973), and Uruguay (1973). These coups occurred primarily for domestic reasons: With or without applause from Washington, they would probably have taken place. Had democracy not appeared to pose a danger, there would have been no need to intervene. To be precise, what led to drastic action was a *perception* of threat, which must be distinguished from the actual *existence* of threat—and there is little doubt that Latin American militaries and the U.S. government both held exaggerated fears of leftist takeovers and communist subversion. Yet the point still stands: Democratic governments in Latin America from the 1940s to the 1970s pursued agendas and imposed policies far different from those of the first wave of successor democracies from the 1980s onward.

1978–Present: Democracy Made Safe

The most recent phase of democratization has enshrined the principles of free and fair elections and the putative virtues of cautious, centrist policy programs. Competition for office has been strenuous, and fraud has been greatly reduced. In this procedural sense, democracy gained strength throughout the region. According to substantive criteria, however, democracy made only modest headway. It was no longer a social provocation or a threat.

Explanation begins with the dynamics of transition. In countries under military regimes, especially in South America, transitional "compacts" imposed strict limits on subsequent policies. In particular, as Schmitter and O'Donnell counseled, it was imperative for incoming democrats to pledge that "the property rights of the bourgeoisie [would be] inviolable." Such an understanding has clearly prevailed in Argentina, Brazil, Chile, and Uruguay. And in cases where democracy arrived through an electoral route, as in Mexico, the bargain would go without saying (after all, Vicente Fox had occupied executive positions in the Coca-Cola company).[5] As a result, elected leaders often took office not only with positive policy programs, but also with a clear-cut sense of *what they could not do.*

Popular forces lost coherence and strength. Partly as a result of neoliberal economic policies, organized labor no longer wielded political power. Classical peasant movements virtually disappeared. The voices of the poor and other less advantaged sectors fell into an almost eerie silence. Elected governments imposed systematic constraints on freedom of the press. And as free and fair elections swept the region in the 1990s, they led to the widespread installation of "illiberal democracy."

The political Left plunged into steep decline. The end of the Cold War discredited left-wing ideology: Socialist ideals and Marxist analyses became tainted by association with the corruption and collapse of the Soviet regime. In Argentina and elsewhere, leftist movements had been literally decimated by the barbarities of military rule. With few exceptions, left-wing parties watched their share of the vote plummet in country after country throughout the 1990s.

As Fidel Castro's aging regime in Cuba became increasingly isolated (and irrelevant) and as once-idealistic Sandinista leaders suffered electoral defeats in Nicaragua, the cult of social revolution vanished from the scene. Armed resistance to oppression lost romantic appeal.[6] By the end of the century, classical guerrilla movements survived only in Colombia (partly because they obtained financial resources through drug trafficking). Besides, it was one thing to take to the mountains against such ruthless tyrants as Fulgencio Batista and Anastasio Somoza; it made less sense to mount violent attacks against such elected leaders as Raúl Alfonsín, Ricardo Lagos, and Vicente Fox.

For the time being, at least, progressive intellectuals were unable to forge programmatic alternatives to neoliberal orthodoxy. Leader after leader

---

[5] Similar bargains were struck in "pacted" transitions in Colombia and Venezuela during the 1950s, which helps explain the longevity of the subsequent regimes.

[6] The only new movement to emerge during the 1990s was the Zapatista uprising in Mexico, but that was essentially a defensive rebellion rather than an offensive campaign to take over the state. As such, it is the exception that proves the rule.

renounced their political pasts. In Argentina, Carlos Saúl Menem imposed a sweeping reversal of Peronist policies; in Brazil, Fernando Henrique Cardoso, once a leading exponent of the neo-Marxist conception of *dependencia*, dismissed his academic writings as irrelevant to the tasks at hand; and in Chile, Ricardo Lagos emphasized that he would enter the presidential office not as the second socialist (after Salvador Allende) but as the third consecutive candidate of the centrist *Concertación*. Confronted by the incentives of electoral competition, once-prominent leftists migrated toward the center of the political spectrum.

Not that it would have made much difference. In view of the neoliberal reforms of the 1980s and 1990s, the Latin American state was no longer as strong as it had been. There is little doubt that some free-market reforms had positive effects: Many governments of the region had bloated payrolls, intervened excessively in economic affairs, and managed state-owned companies with grotesque inefficiency. Yet the neoliberal programs of the Washington Consensus often went further than that, stripping states of the capacity to make coherent policy, sustain much-needed social programs, and manage the direction of national affairs. Thus the bottom line: Even if democratic leaders of the 1980s and 1990s had wanted to pursue radical programs—of, for instance, land reform or income redistribution—they would have not commanded the resources to put them into place. "Economic policy is not determined democratically," as one leader recently said (under condition of anonymity). "There is a set of rules everyone must follow....If you don't, you do so at your own peril."

In sum, the illiberal democracies of post-1977 Latin America were shaped by two distinctive factors. One was the determination of political elites to avoid what they regarded as the pitfalls of the past. This led incoming civilians to accept bargains with outgoing dictators, to construct forms of institutional design that would restrict the prospects of "extremist" tendencies, and to impose (or consent to) systematic constraints on dissident voices and groups. A second factor was economic liberalization and globalization. Confronted by little practical choice, Latin American leaders, authoritarians on the way out and democrats on the way in, succumbed to pressures from international financial organizations to abide by the Washington Consensus. This led to substantial reduction in the power of the state. In other words, the combined effect of the region's "dual transition" was to impose clear limits on the reach and impact of democratic politics.

To grasp the historical contrast consider the Alliance for Progress, a reformist program for the region that was launched by John F. Kennedy in 1961. It called for land reform, labor rights, frontal attacks on poverty, government-to-government cooperation, and state activism in economic affairs. These were mainstream ideas during the 1960s and 1970s. But by the 1990s, with a new cycle of democratization in full swing, proposals of this sort were routinely dismissed as utopian exaggerations of a bygone populist era. They were seen as naive, impractical, and far-fetched—by international economists, by sentinels of the Washington Consensus, and, partly in reaction to these developments, by democratic politicians in Latin America. The activist agenda of the 1960s had no place in the 1990s.

As a result, democracy no longer posed a threat. Socioeconomic elites could rest in the assurance that they were safe (recall the survey analysis showing that among all social sectors, the upper class was most supportive of electoral democracy). Members of the middle class could remain confident that the rules of social ascent would stay intact. Military establishments expressed occasional resistance to calls for human rights prosecutions but drew comfort from that fact that much of this clamor came from abroad—whereas democratic governments hastened to claim that transitional compacts foreswearing such trials were matters of national sovereignty. And finally, the United States had little to fear during the decade of the 1990s. Democracy was tame.

And it was this timid quality, in turn, that helped explain the spread and the longevity of democracy throughout the region. It had become acceptable to powerful elites. There was no deep-rooted reason either for military *golpes* or for U.S. military intervention. Episodes of the 1990s serve to prove the point. Only the Haitian coup of 1991 sought to alter the direction of national policy. The Peruvian coup of 1992 was an *autogolpe* by the sitting president, Alberto Fujimori, who remained in office for the following eight years. And the Ecuadoran intervention of 2000 was intentionally brief, a short-term action to stabilize political turmoil before turning over power to a civilian. For Latin America as a whole, these were placid times.

Latin America thus ended the twentieth century with electoral democracies that were more efficient at selecting political leaders than at representing popular wishes. As the Argentine sociologist Torcuato di Tella quipped in 1999, "What seem to be required in Latin America these days are democracies that cannot govern." It was a playful remark, and an insightful one as well.

1998–Present: Democracy Turns Left

Moods were dark as the twenty-first century arrived. Implementation of the Washington Consensus had reduced inflation, but sustained development remained illusory. Economic growth for the region as a whole was close to zero in 2001, –0.4 percent in 2002, and a paltry +2.2 percent in 2003. Argentina, Uruguay, and Venezuela endured sharp and sudden downturns. With the exceptions of Costa Rica and Argentina in 2003 (with Argentina still recuperating from the calamities of 2001–2002), no country surpassed the 5 percent benchmark at this time. The two most populous nations, Brazil and Mexico, languished at less than 2 percent growth, and Chile, the poster child for neoliberal reform, barely managed 3.9 percent.

These trends yield a startling observation: Over the span of an entire generation, Latin Americans under electoral democracy experienced virtually no improvement in per capita income. Allowing for population growth (and controlling for inflation), GDP per capita in 2003 was just about the same as it had been in 1980. Meanwhile, the rate of poverty actually increased, from 40 percent in 1980 to 48 percent in 1990 and then to 44 percent in 2002, which signified an enormous expansion in the absolute number of people below the poverty line, from 136 million in 1980 to more than 220 million in 2002 (see Figures 8.4 and 8.5). Levels of inequality meantime continued climbing to world-record levels. In these most elementary senses, democracy was not meeting the needs of its citizens. "Democracy works well in that there are elections, free speech and a free press," said Carmen Velásquez, a former schoolteacher selling fruits and vegetables on the streets of Lima. "But there is a lot of discontent among the poor."

Partly as a consequence of economic distress, criminality and violence were spreading throughout the region. Public safety became a central concern among all social classes. From Mexico City to Buenos Aires, crime waves in metropolitan areas surged throughout the 1990s. In particular, poverty and unemployment were resulting in property crimes—and in kidnappings, usually to extort large ransoms from well-to-do families. Homicide was also on the rise. Around the end of the twentieth century, well over 100,000 murders were taking place each year in Latin America. This amounted to 25.1 homicides per 100,000 inhabitants, the highest rate of any region in the world. (Only Africa came close; other world areas showed rates of less than 10 per 100,000.) The problem was not just that democratic governments could not provide citizens with economic prosperity; they could not protect the people from criminal violence and quotidian dangers.

Endemic frustration became evident through a much-publicized study of public opinion conducted by the United Nations Development Programme.[7] Based on more than 18,000 interviews conducted in 2002, the analysis found that only 57 percent of respondents throughout Latin America believed that "democracy is preferable to any other form of government." More to the point, 55 percent of the people, well over half, would support an authoritarian government "if it could resolve economic problems." A nearly identical number, 56 percent, agreed that "economic development is more important than democracy." As already shown in Chapter 11, popular support for democratic rule in Latin America depends in large part on practical results: If performance falters, support declines.

The survey offered additional insight into relationships between leaders and citizens. A total of 43 percent of respondents indicated they would be willing to have their president "go beyond the law" in the pursuit of national interests: 37 percent agreed that the president could "impose order through force," 37 percent were willing to have the president "control the

---

[7] Programa de las Naciones Unidas para el Desarrollo [United Nations Development Programme], *La democracia en América Latina: hacia una democracia de ciudadanas y ciudadanos* (New York and Buenos Aires: PNUD/UNDP, 2004), also published in English.

mass media" (*medios de comunicación*), and 36 percent would allow the president to bypass legislatures and political parties (*que deje de lado al Congreso y los partidos*). Taken together, such attitudes reveal widespread acceptance of top-down restrictions on democracy, resulting in what Guillermo O'Donnell has called "delegative democracy" and what Fareed Zakaria has labeled "illiberal democracy."

Disenchantment formed the bottom line. Citizens of Latin America were demanding change. They wanted strong, proactive governments that would be able and willing to challenge socioeconomic elites and to represent popular interests. Unconvinced by conventional wisdom about the virtues of free-market economics, they were seeking plausible alternatives to the Washington Consensus. They were calling for frontal attacks against poverty, inequality, and embedded forms of social injustice. They were discontent with what they regarded as subservience to the United States. In place of prudence, they were advocating boldness, daring, and a bit of political audacity.

Yet they were willing to rely on democratic institutions. In place after place and time after time, they expressed their preferences in voting booths. They did not call for violent revolution. They did not engage in large-scale riots. They did not advocate class warfare (although some said that they did). They did not attempt to overthrow the political system or the social order. They were seeking activist reform, not unattainable utopias.

Given the opportunity, citizens therefore cast their ballots in favor of the "new Left." Democracy thus revealed a dialectical process. The trend began in 1998 in Venezuela, as recounted earlier, with the presidential victory of Hugo Chávez. It gained momentum with the subsequent triumphs of Lula in Brazil and Néstor Kirchner in Argentina. It picked up additional strength in 2005–2006, with a string of victories in Bolivia, Uruguay, and Ecuador—plus hair's-breadth defeats in Mexico and Peru. Later triumphs followed in El Salvador, Paraguay, and eventually Peru. Neither an organized nor a doctrinaire movement, the "pink tide" became a defining feature of the hemispheric political scene.

As the evidence shows, this overall trend gave rise to significant differences, particularly between "moderates" (led by Lula) and "radicals" (led by Chávez). But a basic point remains: Leaders and supporters wanted to reinvigorate democracy, to amplify the range of practical policy options, and, on occasion, to challenge the interests of entrenched upper classes and international forces. After all, what good was a democracy if it could not be dangerous?

As 2010 drew to a close, Latin American democracies displayed kaleidoscopic variation. Avowed conservatives held power in Colombia, Mexico, and much of Central America; new-left advocates prevailed in Bolivia, Ecuador, Venezuela, and elsewhere. Other governments resisted facile classification. On a practical level, these differences tended to complicate and even prevent regional efforts at diplomatic collaboration. And on an intellectual level, they provided lasting testimony to the creativity, imagination, and determination of political activity in Latin America. It is a complex and difficult place to understand, and that is why it remains the object of so much fascination.

THE FUTURE OF DEMOCRACY

The time has come to look ahead. What is the future of Latin American politics? As presented here, a principal goal of long-term analysis is to detect underlying trajectories of change. The point is not only to describe how things have been, it is also to understand the logic of transformation and thus generate informed speculation about where things might be going. Will democracy survive? In what form? With what results?

This epilogue approaches these questions in several ways. It begins with an analysis of recent trends in the international environment and then traces political developments within the region. It offers an assessment of prospects for the "consolidation" of democracy in Latin America and briefly sketches alternative scenarios for the future of the region. The prognosis is mixed, but possibilities for progress nonetheless remain.

THE INTERNATIONAL ENVIRONMENT

Terrorist attacks on the World Trade Center in New York and the Pentagon in Washington, DC, on September 11, 2001, would have immediate and funda-mental effects on the United States and the world. Within a matter of days, President George W. Bush launched an all-out war on terrorism. Vowing to use military force as necessary, he set ambitious and far-reaching goals. "Our war on terror begins with Al Qaeda," the president said, "but it does not stop there. It will not end until every terrorist group of global reach has been found, stopped, and defeated." Promising to challenge and dismantle "the global terror network," Bush went on to declare that "Our response involves far more than instant retaliation and isolated strikes. Americans should not expect one battle, but a lengthy campaign, unlike any other we have seen. It may include dramatic strikes, visible on television, and covert operations, secret even in success." Moreover, Bush proclaimed, "Every nation in every region now has a decision to make. Either you are with us, or you are with the terrorists. From this day forward, any nation that continues to harbor or support terrorism will be regarded by the United States as a hostile regime." There was only one choice—black or white. The president made no mention of international law, world tribunals, or the United Nations.

Within a month, the United States launched military strikes against Afghanistan. In short order, a U.S.-led coalition was able to patch together a government of sorts. That turned out to be the easy part. Al Qaeda was another matter. The elusive Osama bin Laden remained at large, less prominent leaders were holding his organization together, and hundreds if not thousands of shock troops were poised to launch further attacks. Escalating its antiterrorist campaign, the Bush administration in March 2003 undertook a massive invasion of Iraq. What the Pentagon called the "long shadow war" was taking ominous shape.

The "global war on terror" led to sweeping changes in regional priorities for U.S. foreign policy. Central and South Asia and the Middle East—broadly speaking, the Muslim world—vaulted to the top of the ladder. Latin America lost huge amounts of ground. The region fell off the proverbial radar screen and suffered from inattention as Argentina and the rest of South America plunged into economic and institutional crises. Initially embraced as a special partner, Mexico saw its hopes completely dashed for significant reform of U.S. immigration policy. "In these difficult times," said a disappointed Vicente Fox in May 2002, "Latin America seems to have been abandoned to its fate."

In this context U.S. policy was formed around a single issue—the attacks and aftermath of September 11 (or 9/11, as the date came to be known). That was the sole criterion for alignment with (and gratitude from) the Bush administration. Gone were concerns about human rights, democratic practice, or related issues. The only relevant question was whether governments would enlist in the American-led antiterrorist campaign. To peoples still living under autocratic rule, this might seem like a betrayal. In time, this could come back to haunt the United States.

More specifically, the war on terror raised profound doubts about commitments to democracy. After 9/11, the key issue for the advanced industrial world became security. All kinds of states—traditionally democratic and blatantly authoritarian, from the United Kingdom to Pakistan to Saudi Arabia—were bound together in this common cause. Military forces engaged in programs of "homeland security." Legal rights of suspects were abrogated. And there was an understandable temptation for leaders around the world, from Russia to Colombia, to label their opponents as "terrorists."

As a result, the international environment was no longer supportive of democratization in Latin America (or other parts of the world). Seen in historical perspective, in fact, the decade of the 1990s, extending from the end of the Cold War to mid-2001, was proving to be an exceptional period, a time when global factors and international forces assisted and promoted democratic change with unusual commitment and effectiveness. That was

BOX E.1

OPPORTUNITIES FOR THE UNITED STATES?

It could be argued that ongoing processes of democratization in Latin America present the United States with a historic opportunity—a chance to demonstrate its commitment to democracy and human rights and, in the process, to help lay the foundations for long-term stability throughout the region. Aside from altruistic motivations, the perpetuation and consolidation of democracy throughout the Western Hemisphere would appear to promote U.S. interests in "homeland security" and protection from international terrorist threats.

What should the United States do?

First, the United States would have to discard what might be called the "cherished assumption"—the idea that democracies everywhere will necessarily support the policies of the United States (which claims to be the world's leading democracy). That is not the way democracies work. If voters do not wish to support U.S. policies, their leaders will not do so, either. Washington must accept that basic truth.

Second, Washington should attempt to bolster the institutions of democracy rather than base its policy on the actions or personalities of individual leaders. It is no secret that the U.S. government has had scant regard for Hugo Chávez in Venezuela or Jean-Bertrand Aristide in Haiti. But that does not justify behind-the-scenes efforts to throw these once-elected leaders out of office.

Third, the U.S. government should accelerate bilateral and multilateral efforts to strengthen democratic institutions throughout the region. This would entail campaigns to build independent judiciaries, for instance, and congressional oversight committees. The idea should be to help construct appropriate checks and balances and more efficient systems of citizen representation.

Fourth, the United States should anticipate the implications of deepening democracy in Latin America. For the most part, Washington has been able to work and deal with executive leaders in highly centralized systems. As opposition parties, legislative bodies, nongovernmental organizations, and grassroots movements become more and more involved in policy debates throughout Latin America, the more difficult it will be for Latin American governments to speak with a single voice. And the more that impoverished and disadvantaged segments of Latin American society gain effective political voice, the more they will challenge neoliberal economic policies and prevailing conventional wisdoms. This points to a profound irony: The more the Latin American policy process comes to resemble that of the United States, the more contentious will be the region's dealings with the United States.

---

no longer the case. And although the Bush administration ardently claimed that its goal was to bring democracy to Iraq and thus transform the Arab world, its actions showed little true regard for pluralistic politics within the Middle East or anywhere else (see Box E.1). The promotion of "homeland security" was posing fundamental threats to the freedoms and rights of peoples throughout the world. The subsequent administration of President

Barack Obama substantially improved the diplomatic atmosphere, but the essential policies remained intact. Democratic forces in Latin America were facing an international environment that was hostile at times and neutral at best.

Economic Dimensions

One of the most startling developments of the early twenty-first century was the economic rise of the People's Republic of China (PRC). This would have major implications for Latin America. China's rapidly expanding consumer market displayed a boundless appetite for agricultural goods, and the country's industrial sector needed voluminous supplies of raw materials, especially minerals and petroleum.

Latin America was ready to provide these things. Starting in 2000, Chinese imports from the region grew by 60 percent a year, reaching $50 billion by 2005. The PRC developed especially close commercial ties with Argentina, Brazil, Chile, and Peru. By 2006 China was taking in 12 percent of all Chilean exports. In that same year Embraer, the Brazilian jet manufacturer, concluded a huge contract with Beijing, as China was becoming Brazil's second largest and fastest growing export market. In early 2007 Venezuela formed a joint investment fund for the construction of infrastructure projects and oil refineries. And in March 2007 Beijing launched its ultimately successful candidacy to join the board of the Inter-American Development Bank.

These new opportunities helped fuel substantial economic expansion. In 2004, the Latin American growth rate climbed to 6.1 percent, the highest level in decades. For 2005 it was 5.0 percent, in 2006 and 2007 it was 5.8 percent, and in 2008 it was 4.1 percent—still a respectable rate. It was entirely understandable that presidents, ministers, entrepreneurs, and journalists came to regard the PRC as a "trade angel" and showed unmistakable signs of "China fever." Here was the answer to the region's problems.

The Crash of 2007–2009

Then came the financial crash of 2007–2009. Beginning in the United States, the recession affected the global economy and wrought havoc throughout the world. It provoked rising unemployment, a sharp drop in international trade, and slumping commodity prices. Hardship struck everywhere.

The proximate cause was linked to reckless lending practices by financial institutions and the widespread "securitization" of real estate mortgages in the United States. Despite the risks inherent in "subprime" loans, mortgage-backed securities were marketed around the world. A broad-based credit boom fed a global speculative bubble in real estate and equities, which served to reinforce these risky lending practices. In the meantime, financial uncertainty was exacerbated by sharply increasing oil and food prices.

The exposure of subprime loan losses in 2007 precipitated the crisis, as risky loans and overinflated asset prices became fully apparent. In late 2008 panic broke out in financial markets with the fall of Lehman Brothers, one of Wall Street's most venerable institutions. As stock market shares and housing prices plummeted, prominent investment houses and commercial banks in the United States and Europe suffered huge losses and faced prospects of bankruptcy. With little choice, the incoming administration of U.S. President Barack Obama developed a multibillion-dollar "stimulus package" to forestall further deterioration of financial markets, restore liquidity, encourage confidence, and establish a foundation for eventual recovery.

Even so, the crash had a resounding and immediate impact on Latin America. Economic "growth" in 2009 for the region as a whole was negative, at –1.8 percent. Hardest hit was Mexico, partly because of its continuing trade dependence on the United States, with a decline of more than 6 percent (part of this drop was also due to drug-related violence, which led to a decisive slowdown in tourism). Oil-rich Venezuela also endured a decline of 2.3 percent, and Chile, even with its burgeoning Asian ties, had a loss of 1.8 percent. Other beneficiaries of the commodity boom, Brazil and Argentina, showed barely positive growth rates of 0.3 percent and 0.7 percent. To be sure, this was not nearly as bad as the "lost decade" of the 1980s, but it was a serious setback for leading countries of the region.

Transnational Crime

Amidst these changing contexts, a powerful force has come to pose a direct danger to democratic governance—transnational criminal activity. Underground international elements not only operate outside the boundaries of the law, they also challenge the reach of the law. Building upon sophisticated networks, they tend to be mobile, elusive, and strong. They sometimes establish de facto rule over geographic territories, carving out semi-sovereign "republics" under their primitive control. They frequently overwhelm public security forces, outgunning local police and even military units. They weaken state authority through corruption, intimidation, and assassination of public officials. Often operating with impunity, transnational criminal organizations have undermined the capacity, will, and legitimacy of constitutional states.

One of the most profitable activities has been smuggling—of people, weapons, money, drugs, anything that moved. Often charging outlandish fees, *coyotes* have sneaked undocumented migrants across the border from Mexico into the United States. Taking advantage of poverty-stricken young women, transnational rings have recruited prostitutes in Colombia, Panama, and the Dominican Republic and shipped them throughout the Americas and other world regions. In search of exorbitant profits, arms smugglers have furnished high-grade weapons to violent criminal organizations. Cashing in on all such operations, unscrupulous bankers and financiers have laundered the illicit profits of underground groups. Globalization has its darker side.

Street gangs have come to threaten public safety. After starting out with petty crime, ambitious gangs have moved on to kidnapping, extortion, and contract killing. Eventually they have come to exert brutal power over low-income neighborhoods in major cities—the *favelas* of Rio de Janeiro, the *villas miserias* of Buenos Aires, and the *barrios* of Lima and Mexico City. Particularly notorious is the MS-13 (*Mara Salvatrucha*) in El Salvador, which had its point of origin in the deportation of young criminals from the United States. As Ana Arana has explained, "Ultraviolent youth gangs, spawned in the ghettos of Los Angeles and other U.S. cities, have slowly migrated south to Central America, where they have transformed themselves into powerful, cross-border crime networks."[1] Armed with AK-47s and machetes, gangs have spread their tentacles to Honduras and Guatemala back through Mexico and back into the United States. No wonder that citizens of Latin America express persistent concerns about day-to-day security.

The most conspicuous (and lucrative) form of international crime is, of course, drug trafficking. This is a preeminently transnational activity. Except for pharmaceuticals, drugs are typically produced in one part of the world, transported through another, and consumed in still another. The result has been the formation of complex and formidably efficient "commodity chains." As just one example, coca leaf has historically been harvested in the high Andes (Bolivia, Peru, Colombia), processed in lowland Colombia, and transmitted to northern Mexico or to Caribbean islands for eventual distribution in the United States. Despite vigorous antidrug policies, trafficking has remained a source of enormous power and profit. U.S. consumption remains at high levels. Reliable reports estimate that Mexican DTOs (drug trafficking organizations) have more than one hundred wholesale outlets throughout the United States. Where there is demand, there will be supply.

Latin American governments have sought to contain the drug trade and re-establish political authority by unleashing "wars" against the DTOs, usually by enlisting the armed forces as well as the police. Colombia endured a decade of all-out violence from the 1990s into the early years of this century. Now that Central America has become a transit route for shipments of cocaine, the isthmus has also witnessed a growth of criminality and violence.

But the hardest hit country, as of this writing, has been Mexico. Upon taking office in December 2006, President Felipe Calderón declared an open war on the top half-dozen DTOs. First under George W. Bush and then under Barack Obama, the U.S. government has given unstinting moral support and material assistance to this campaign. Unable to rely on the police, Calderón assigned forty-five thousand soldiers to the task. Traffickers responded with lethal force. The result has been a complex and multifaceted war: soldiers

---

[1] Ana Arana, "How the Street Gangs Took Central America," *Foreign Affairs* 84, 3 (May/June 2005): 98. *Mara* is slang for "gang," and *trucha*—literally, "trout" in Spanish—refers to a shrewd or clever person.

against DTOs, police against DTOs, DTOs against DTOs, with innocent bystanders caught in the murderous crossfire. While engaged in hot pursuit of enemies, security forces have frequently abused the human rights of citizens. By the end of 2010 more than thirty thousand Mexicans had lost their lives, many of them murdered and mutilated in gruesome fashion. The carnage took a terrible toll on the nation as a whole—its economy, its democracy, and the fabric of its society.

Mexico's distressing plight offers but an extreme example of challenges faced throughout the hemisphere. From the Tierra del Fuego to the Rio Grande, from Argentina to the Dominican Republic, transnational criminal activity continues to threaten the effective rule of law. This would be a struggle without end.

POLITICAL DEVELOPMENTS

Events move rapidly in politics, and much can happen in short periods of time. The purpose here is to update the narrative about democratization and, more specifically, to identify patterns and trends. Have events of the past several years altered the direction of Latin American politics?

Democratic Tendencies

Electoral democracy continued to expand. After a brief military interlude in early 2000, Ecuador managed to reinstate free and fair elections, as did Peru after the peremptory departure of Alberto Fujimori in that same year. By late 2003, Latin America had seventeen electoral democracies, two semi-democracies, and no autocracies. (Cuba, as always, remained in a class by itself.) After a temporary pause in the late 1990s, the path of democratic change picked up once again.

Survival rates were high as well. Of the fifteen countries that qualified as electoral democracies in 2000, only one—a marginal case at that—underwent authoritarian reversals over the ensuing decade. There were crises, to be sure, and rumors of attempted coups, but no systemic alterations of regime. (Argentina suffered a brief relapse into semidemocracy during 2002, but regained its democratic standing by 2003.) Of the democracies founded during or just after the second cycle of the twentieth century (1940–1977), three continued to thrive: Costa Rica, Colombia, and the Dominican Republic. (Under the populist sway of the *chavista* movement, by contrast, Venezuela became a semidemocracy in 1999.) Of the eight democracies installed early in the post-1978 cycle, five—Argentina, Bolivia, Brazil, Chile, and Uruguay—were essentially intact, now boasting an average life span of well over twenty years. And with the conspicuous exception of Haiti, free elections were still taking place in countries where democracy arrived during the 1990s, although it remained too early to assess the longevity of these experiments. Generally speaking, electoral democracy was holding up.

In some countries democratic leaders made conspicuous progress in curtailing the political role of the armed forces. This process was especially apparent in Chile and Argentina, where public repudiation of Cold War atrocities continued to stain the image of the professional military. Meanwhile a new generation of officers—too young to have taken part in the "dirty wars," their promotions long delayed by senior cadres—tolerated and sometimes tacitly supported the prosecution of retired generals for human rights abuses. In Central America and the Andes, however, the armed forces continued to wield impressive amounts of influence. Throughout much of Latin America, the military remained a major player in the power game of politics.

An illustrative example came from Honduras, where members of the armed forces removed Manuel Zelaya from the presidency (and the country) in July 2009. The putative explanation was that Zelaya was intending to hold a popular referendum on institutional reform in alleged violation of the nation's constitution; the more compelling factor was conservative opposition to Zelaya's political alignment with Hugo Chávez and the Bolivarian Alliance for the Americas. Particularly striking about this episode is the fact that military officers did not seize control of the presidential palace. On the contrary, they turned effective power over to the official who was next in line, the leader of the congress. Clearly, soldiers were operating not with the intention of establishing a military regime, but in the service of a disgruntled faction of civilian leadership. This was a coup by the armed forces, but not a takeover.

Democracy was in the meantime making modest gains. As of 1999 only four nations—Chile, Costa Rica, Panama, and Uruguay—qualified as liberal democracies. Argentina and the Dominican Republic joined these ranks in the following year. Mexico entered this group in 2002, at which time Argentina temporarily dropped out, only to return in 2003. Several of these cases entail borderline judgments, so the results are somewhat biased. Even so, the findings suggest that liberal democracy was making modest progress. (See also Figure 10.2 in Chapter 10.) Once installed, in any case, it was not subject to authoritarian backsliding; it could give way to illiberalism or even semidemocracy, but not outright autocracy. Liberal democracy was proving to be its own best source of protection.

In this light, Figure E.1 displays the collective array of political regimes as of 2008. There were by this time seven liberal democracies, ten illiberal democracies, two semidemocracies, and no autocracies. Once again, the display confirms a basic point: Illiberal democracy remained the dominant form of political regime in Latin America.

Free and fair elections provided partial outlets for swelling discontent. In several key countries, citizens threw their support to antiestablishment candidates of dissidence—leftist, populist, or otherwise, what came to be known as the "new Left." Thus emerged the "pink tide" in regional politics. Ideologies in such instances were neither crucial nor precise; what

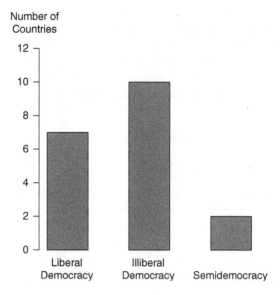

Figure E.1 Political regimes in Latin America, 2008

mattered was the prospect of change through popular empowerment. Much as Venezuelans voted for Chávez and Brazilians supported Lula, Argentines endorsed Néstor Kirchner in 2003, Uruguayans voted for Tabaré Vázquez in 2004, and Bolivians gave their backing to Evo Morales in 2005. Citizens did not always get what they wanted, as radical *politicians* could not (or would not) always impose effective radical *policies*. But the people's preferences were clear. They wanted a new start.

At the same time, popular frustration took a troublesome turn. After the turn of the century, two freely elected presidents—Fernando de la Rúa in Argentina (2001) and Gonzalo Sánchez de Losada in Bolivia (2003)—resigned in the face of violent protest against their economic policies. Early in 2004, a hapless Jean-Bertrand Aristide of Haiti fled his country as armed rebels closed in on the nation's capital. Such episodes revealed the rising importance of mass demonstrations and spontaneous (often violent) protest. Political crises were not being resolved through institutional means. Dissidents were going outside the system to achieve their goals; power was moving to the streets. As the *New York Times* editorialized, "Sacking a president usually makes things worse. Politicians will not make unpopular decisions—or decisions that offend powerful groups—if they must face the political guillotine every day. While many protesters want to destroy everything and start from zero, Latin America needs more continuity, not less. Also, with the presidency in constant play, opposition leaders will not make constructive compromises, instead manipulating every issue to try to win power."

These popular upheavals were not directed only against incumbent chief executives. At bottom, the reliance on crowds, demonstrations, and occasional violence reflected dissatisfaction with institutional channels of representation. Parties, legislatures, and constitutional mechanisms were not providing citizens with adequate means of expression. People were demanding to be heard—and raising their voices in the process.

THE QUESTION OF CONSOLIDATION

This panorama brings up fundamental questions. Will Latin American democracies endure? Might they become more genuinely democratic? Will "illiberal" democracies throughout the region become more "liberal"? What are the prospects for authoritarian reversals?

Such queries revolve around the issue of "democratic consolidation," an intuitively appealing concept that is fraught with ambiguity. What is meant by the consolidation of democracy? Does the notion imply that "consolidated" democracies are free from risk of overthrow, that they are no longer subject to modification, or that they have reached a utopian stage of ideal fulfillment? Is the concept a useful analytical tool, a teleological construct, or simply an illusion?[2]

It depends on what is meant. The simplest criterion for evaluating democratic consolidation is longevity. The longer democracy survives, the longer it is likely to survive. As leaders and publics become increasingly accustomed to the give-and-take of pluralistic politics, they should become increasingly tolerant of its imperfections and uncertainties. Once democracy acquires the status of a national "tradition," its durability increases. Continuity breeds continuity.

An alternative formulation measures longevity not in terms of calendar years but by the number of successive (and successful) elections. Instead of focusing on survival over time, this criterion deals with the management of competition. Free and fair elections beget free and fair elections. It becomes tempting, of course, to stipulate a minimum number of genuine elections required for "consolidation" of a democratic system: two, three, four? Not surprisingly, such hypothetical exercises in political arithmetic tend to shed more heat than light on the underlying question.[3]

---

[2] See Guillermo O'Donnell, "Illusions about Consolidation," *Journal of Democracy* 7, no. 2 (1996): 34–51.

[3] Samuel P. Huntington went so far as to propose a "two-turnover test," according to which "a democracy may be viewed as consolidated if the party or group that takes power at the time of transition loses a subsequent election and turns over power to those election winners, and if those election winners can then peacefully turn over power to the winners of a later election." *The Third Wave: Democratization in the Late Twentieth Century* (Norman: University of Oklahoma Press, 1991), 266–267.

The principal problem with emphases on longevity and number of elections is that they focus so narrowly on the *electoral* component of politics. They pay no explicit attention to the *quality* of democratic life. It would be entirely possible for an "illiberal" democracy, such as Colombia or Brazil, to meet the terms of this test. It would also be entirely possible for a fully "liberal" democracy, such as Chile after Pinochet, to obtain a failing score.

The obvious remedy is to concentrate not only on elections but also on improvement of the quality of democratic politics, what has come to be known as the "deepening" of democracy. As will soon be seen, however, this cure can raise as many problems as the original illness.

Deepening Democracy?

The idea of deepening has multiple meanings. As used here, it refers to four sets of issues: the dispersion of governmental powers, the effectiveness of representation, respect for citizen freedoms and rights, and the strengthening of states. All these dimensions represent critical challenges for the construction and consolidation of robust democracy "beyond the ballot box."

Take the problem of government powers. A fundamental question concerns the existence and the effectiveness of institutional checks and balances on executive authority. Can other branches of government establish meaningful limits on presidential power? Can the legislatures monitor executive implementation of laws and take action against transgressions of congressional will? Can the judiciary determine and preserve constitutional restraints on presidential power? To accomplish such missions, congress and the courts would need to become fully autonomous, rather than dependent on executive largess, and capable, provided with adequate staff and resources. Improvements have been made in recent years, but the overall picture is bleak: Nowhere in Latin America is there anything that remotely resembles the U.S. General Accounting Office, a fiercely independent organization that serves as a watchdog over budgetary expenditures. Without such checks and balances, of course, the path toward "delegative democracy" remains completely open.

This leads to the question of representation. Key institutional channels for the expression of popular will are legislatures and political parties, and neither one is very effective. Congresses in Latin America tend to be reactive rather than proactive, more obstructionist than constructive, and more focused on narrow interests than on broad issues of national policy. Parties tend to be either highly centralized, under the tight control of an internal hierarchy, or fragmented, with individual candidates seeking advancement of personal careers. As a result, legislatures and parties are held in low and declining esteem by citizens throughout the region. As frustration mounts, citizens find they have very few opportunities for expressing their will through plebiscites or referenda "from below." Not surprisingly, they often end up turning to the streets.

A third dimension refers to the protection of citizen freedoms and rights. This is an absolutely essential condition for the eventual achievement of liberal rather than illiberal democracy in Latin America. Here, again, the record tends to be spotty. Although some countries have made positive strides in recent years, illiberal democracy remains the most common form of political practice in the region. The rights of public dissent, including demands for accountability, freedom of the press, and participation in opposition activities, tend to be honored in the breach. Criticisms of government authorities are routinely dismissed as unpatriotic slander, and police and law enforcement agencies continue to repress oppositionist tendencies. Latin America still has a long way to go.

Fourth is the issue of "stateness." Democratic states cannot effectively implement the popular will unless they are reasonably strong. Under classical political theory, it was necessary to forge strong states to countermand nondemocratic bastions of power (such as exclusive oligarchies, military establishments, and business monopolies). Democratic states must also have the capacity to maintain law and order, protecting citizens and punishing criminals. Having been progressively weakened over the past quarter-century, Latin American states are unable to accomplish these fundamental missions. They are not strong enough, not autonomous enough, and not resourceful enough. It is not sufficient to invoke the mantra that states should now be "lean and mean"—they are lean, all right, to the point that they are incapable of being mean. According to one pithy summation, "A powerless state is a powerless democracy."[4]

A caveat is necessary at this point. Democratic states require strength to mitigate two of Latin America's most long-standing and excruciating social problems: poverty and inequality. Capacity is necessary for the development of effective social programs, such as conditional cash transfers (CCTs), for long-term investments in education, and for progressive fiscal policies. Desirable as they are, however, poverty alleviation and inequality reduction are not intrinsic to the process of deepening. Democracy is and must remain a political construct, a means of allocating political power. It is often said that democracy is incompatible with poverty and inequality, and, indeed, the viability of democratic politics might be threatened by the persistence of these conditions. Yet this formulation makes an implicit distinction between democracy (as a form of government) and its socioeconomic setting (which might affect the form of government). Poverty reduction will probably improve the prospects for the survival of democracy; as a matter of definition, however, it is not required for democracy to achieve this result.

In sum, present-day democracy in Latin America tends to be shallow. Electoral democracy has taken root throughout most of the region, but it

---

[4] Programa de Naciones Unidas para el Desarrollo (PNUD), *La democracia en América Latina: hacia una democracia de ciudadanas y ciudadanos* (New York and Buenos Aires: United Nations Development Programme, 2004), 189.

is not a very deep democracy. Checks and balances are few, representative institutions are weak, states are not very strong, and freedoms and rights are restricted. Improvements have occurred, but much still remains to be done.

Survival, Institutionalization, and Legitimation

A final theme concerns acceptance of democratic rules of the game. This concerns not only elections, but also dimensions of deepening, and it applies not only to elites, but also to the public at large. With regard to democratic practices, it is essential to distinguish among three patterns: survival, institutionalization, and legitimation.

Survival means just what it says. Democratic elections might survive from one year to the next, for example, but they might always be at risk. There could be recurrent possibilities of fraud, voter harassment, military veto, or, most important, refusal by losers to accept defeat. Violent demonstrations might make it necessary for nonpartisan authorities (or international organizations) to verify and certify results. In short, there could still be widespread and constant doubt about the authority of the electoral process. Competitive elections might take place over time, but always under the shadow of uncertainty. In and of itself, repetition does not guarantee continuity.

A more lasting impact comes from *institutionalization*. This takes place when rules of the game are made explicit, when they are enforced, and when they eventually become self-enforcing. Under these circumstances, the fate of an election does not depend on the generosity of the winner and the graciousness of the loser. It depends, instead, on such impersonal factors as (1) acknowledgment of clear-cut stipulations about voter eligibility and ballot counts, (2) rulings of a nonpartisan election board, and (3) if necessary, appropriate law enforcement to assure that street demonstrations remain more or less peaceful. Electoral processes thus comply with unambiguous rules that draw authority from the prospect of evenhanded enforcement. Institutions, not personalities, determine eventual outcomes.

The next (and highest) stage comes from *legitimation*, which occurs when people accept democratic procedures as appropriate and fair. They come to believe in the rules. (It is this process of internalization that lies at the core of much writing about "civic values" and "political culture.") Moreover, citizens no longer entertain alternative forms of government; nothing else is possible. In the oft-quoted phrase of Juan Linz and Alfred Stepan, democracy becomes legitimate when it is "the only game in town."[5] Political actors do not merely tolerate democracy, they actively embrace it and reject alternatives. This is the ultimate test of consolidation.

---

[5] Juan J. Linz and Alfred Stepan, *Problems of Democratic Transition and Consolidation: Southern Europe, South America, and Post-Communist Europe* (Baltimore: Johns Hopkins University Press, 1996), 5.

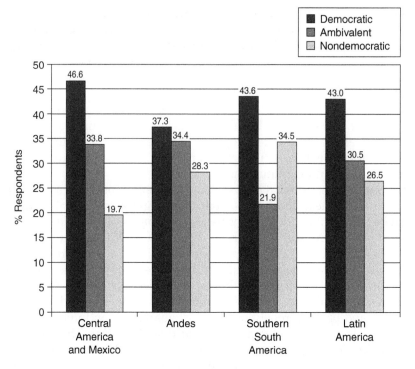

Figure E.2   Political orientations in Latin America

Source: Programa de las Naciones Unidas para el Desarrollo (PNUD), *La democracia en América Latina: hacia una democracia de ciudadanas y ciudadanos* (New York and Buenos Aires: United Nations Development Programme, 2004), 141.

In exploration of this point, analysts of the 2004 UNDP public opinion survey have identified three categories of political orientation in Latin America: "democrats," whose responses to a whole battery of questions indicated consistent support for democracy; "nondemocrats," whose cumulative responses revealed preferences for authoritarianism over democracy; and the "ambivalent" ones, whose replies were either ambiguous or contradictory. For Latin America as a whole, about 43 percent of respondents qualified as democrats—a plurality, but by no means a majority. Approximately 27 percent held nondemocratic attitudes, and 30 percent were ambivalent. As shown in Figure E.2, there was notable variation by subregion, with the Andean region being less democratic in orientation than southern South America (the area from Chile to Brazil) or Central America plus Mexico.[6]

Such findings have sobering implications. Popular support for democratic politics in Latin America is shown to be partial, fragile, and uncertain. "Democracies are not facing a coup d'etat but a slow death," said Dante

---

[6] PNUD, *La democracia en América Latina*, 138–145.

Caputo, a former foreign minister of Argentina and director of the study project. "It's dangerous when democracy becomes irrelevant because it does not solve day-to-day problems." Even without military intervention, democracy could become increasingly "illiberal" or semidemocratic and slide in the direction of autocracy. Democracy is nowhere near the only game in town. Legitimation remains a challenge for the distant future.

ALTERNATIVE SCENARIOS

What now? Where is Latin America heading? There are no facile answers to such questions. Judging from long-term trends and recent trajectories, however, it should be possible to offer some educated guesses about future directions of Latin America's politics.

Three alternative scenarios come to mind: standing fast, backsliding, and moving ahead. This is, of course, a massive simplification. There is no reason to assume that the region as a whole will pursue any particular path. Different countries are likely to follow different routes—at different times and at different speeds. Even so, the categorization can help facilitate informed anticipation of potential futures.

Standing Fast

This scenario anticipates that Latin America will remain more or less where it stands, with a predominant pattern of electoral democracy that is (1) widespread but (2) shallow, and, most important, (3) illiberal. Individual countries might switch positions from time to time, as semidemocracies become electoral democracies (or the opposite) or as electoral democracies become more liberal (or illiberal). Yet the basic picture would remain the same. Illiberal democracy would still be the most common form of politics.

Backsliding

Alternatively, Latin America might move in undemocratic directions— as electoral democracies become semidemocratic, as liberal democracies become illiberal, and as already-existing illiberal democracies become less and less protective of citizens' rights. This path was initially blazed by Alberto Fujimori in Peru, and, according to many observers, it is now being followed by Hugo Chávez in Venezuela.

This kind of trajectory does not require a classic military coup, nor does it culminate in straightforward authoritarianism. On the contrary, it is likely to begin with top-down assertions of authority by elected leaders, through either an outright *autogolpe* (as in Peru) or a constitutional *golpe* (as in Venezuela). To be sure, executives need the support of the armed forces for such aggressive maneuvers, and the military would probably end up with an essential role, tutelary if not domineering, in the resulting regimes.

It is equally important to understand, however, that the practice of illiberal democracy acquires its ultimate legitimacy from popular acceptance of the "delegative democracy" that effectively concentrates power in the chief executive. Such regimes become de facto dictatorships with popular consent.

Moving Ahead

The most optimistic scenario predicts that Latin America will continue to develop and consolidate democracy. Free and fair elections will take place everywhere throughout the region. Democracy will deepen, citizens will enjoy civil rights, states will become stronger, and the rule of law will be more impartial. Liberal democracy will replace illiberal democracy as the political norm.

This could happen. The question is whether it will and what conditions might encourage such a happy outcome. What the region needs is a "virtuous circle" of developments: global economic recovery, international support for human rights, continued reduction in poverty and inequality, more expansive popular participation in the political arena, and social support for tolerance and democratic values. Such a combination of factors would not only strengthen electoral democracy, but also enhance the likelihood of transitions from illiberal to liberal democracy as well.

How can democracy thrive? The answer, if there is one, lies within Latin America. This is a region where democracy has arisen and survived against formidable odds. It is a region where citizens have struggled persistently for fundamental rights. It is a region where a vast range of political experiments—leftist, centrist, rightist—have converged together in the direction of democracy. It is a region of the unexpected, and it might well surprise the world once again.

APPENDIX 1: CLASSIFICATION OF ELECTORAL REGIMES, 1900–2000

As indicated in the text, years for nineteen countries of Latin America from 1900 through 2000 have been classified according to the following scheme:

- electoral democracy = free and fair elections at the national level
- electoral semidemocracy = elections free but not fair, or elections not the real basis of political power
- oligarchic republicanism (or competitive oligarchy) = elections fair but not free, limited to dominant elites and restricted to less than half the adult male population
- otherwise = nondemocracy.

Classifications cover consecutive years under each type of regime. The initiation of "democratic," "semidemocratic," or "oligarchic" periods is coded according to year of first national election. Nondemocracy is a residual category except for years of military coups, which are positively coded as nondemocratic. Years of military occupation by a foreign power (e.g., the United States) are also coded as nondemocratic.

This categorization is based on qualitative judgments. It is based on firsthand familiarity with some cases, extensive reading in secondary sources, and in-depth consultations with professional colleagues. There is room for disagreement on specific instances and borderline cases. At the same time, I am confident that the cumulative patterns are accurate.

Reassurance comes from a comparison of this categorization with that of Adam Przeworski and his associates, who employed similar criteria to classify country-years for 141 countries over the forty-one-year-period from 1950 through 1990.[1] When both sets of variables are dichotomized (by collapsing their "democratic" categories and by omitting the semidemocratic and oligarchic categories), cross-tabulation yields an enormously positive and strong association, with a gamma coefficient of +.994. And when the categorization is treated as an ordered nominal variable, thus including data

---

[1]Adam Przeworski, Michael E. Alvarez, José Antonio Cheibub, and Fernando Limongi, *Democracy and Development: Political Institutions and Well-Being in the World, 1950–1990* (Cambridge: Cambridge University Press, 2000), esp. 55–69.

for all 779 country-years, the gamma coefficient comes out to +.963.[2] In other words, my categorization closely matches that of the Przeworski team.

Ultimately, of course, the validity of the classification used for this project depends on the plausibility, rigor, and consistency of the standards.[3] Herewith the results:

Argentina

1900–1915	Oligarchic
1916–1929	Democratic
1930–1931	Nondemocratic
1932–1942	Semidemocratic
1943–1945	Nondemocratic
1946–1950	Democratic
1951–1954	Semidemocratic
1955–1957	Nondemocratic
1958–1961	Semidemocratic
1962	Nondemocratic
1963–1965	Semidemocratic
1966–1972	Nondemocratic
1973–1975	Democratic
1976–1982	Nondemocratic
1983–2000	Democratic

Bolivia

1900–1919	Oligarchic
1920–1930	Nondemocratic
1931–1933	Oligarchic
1934–1939	Nondemocratic
1940–1942	Semidemocratic
1943–1946	Nondemocratic
1947–1950	Semidemocratic
1951	Nondemocratic
1952–1955	Semidemocratic

---

[2]Categories were ordered as follows: nondemocratic, oligarchic, semidemocratic, democratic.

[3]For thoughtful exploration of these points, see Gerardo L. Munck and Jay Verkuilen, "Conceptualizing and Measuring Democracy: Evaluating Alternative Indices," *Comparative Political Studies* 35, no. 1 (February 2002): 5–34, with discussion on 35–57; also Gerardo L. Munck, *Measuring Democracy: A Bridge between Scholarship and Politics* (Baltimore: Johns Hopkins University Press, 2009).

1956–1963	Democratic
1964–1982	Nondemocratic
1983–2000	Democratic

Brazil

1900–1929	Oligarchic
1930–1945	Nondemocratic
1946–1953	Democratic
1954–1955	Nondemocratic
1956–1963	Democratic
1964–1984	Nondemocratic
1985–1989	Semidemocratic
1990–2000	Democratic

Chile

1900–1923	Oligarchic
1924–1932	Nondemocratic
1933–1972	Democratic
1973–1988	Nondemocratic
1989–2000	Democratic

Colombia

1900–1909	Nondemocratic
1910–1920	Oligarchic
1921	Nondemocratic
1922–1937	Oligarchic
1938–1941	Semidemocratic
1942–1948	Democratic
1949–1952	Semidemocratic
1953–1957	Nondemocratic
1958–2000	Democratic

Costa Rica

1900–1916	Oligarchic
1917–1919	Nondemocratic
1920–1947	Oligarchic
1948–1952	Semidemocratic
1953–2000	Democratic

Dominican Republic

| 1900–1923 | Nondemocratic |
| 1924–1929 | Oligarchic |

1930–1961	Nondemocratic
1962	Democratic
1963–1965	Nondemocratic
1966–1977	Semidemocratic
1978–2000	Democratic

Ecuador

1900	Nondemocratic
1901–1905	Oligarchic
1906	Nondemocratic
1907–1910	Oligarchic
1911–1912	Nondemocratic
1913–1924	Oligarchic
1925–1939	Nondemocratic
1940–1943	Semidemocratic
1944–1947	Nondemocratic
1948–1960	Democratic
1961–1967	Nondemocratic
1968–1971	Semidemocratic
1972–1978	Nondemocratic
1979–1995	Democratic
1996–1999	Semidemocratic
2000	Nondemocratic

El Salvador

1900–1912	Oligarchic
1913	Nondemocratic
1914–1930	Oligarchic
1931–1979	Nondemocratic
1980	Semidemocratic
1981–1983	Nondemocratic
1984–1993	Semidemocratic
1994–2000	Democratic

Guatemala

1900–1922	Nondemocratic
1923–1925	Oligarchic
1926	Nondemocratic
1927–1929	Oligarchic
1930–1944	Nondemocratic
1945–1953	Democratic
1954–1965	Nondemocratic

1966–1973	Semidemocratic
1974–1985	Nondemocratic
1986–1995	Semidemocratic
1996–2000	Democratic

Haiti

1900–1989	Nondemocratic
1990	Democratic
1991–1994	Nondemocratic
1995–2000	Semidemocratic

Honduras

1900–1902	Oligarchic
1903	Nondemocratic
1904–1906	Oligarchic
1907	Nondemocratic
1908–1910	Oligarchic
1911	Nondemocratic
1912–1918	Oligarchic
1919	Nondemocratic
1920–1922	Oligarchic
1923–1924	Nondemocratic
1925–1931	Oligarchic
1932–1948	Nondemocratic
1949–1955	Oligarchic
1956–1957	Nondemocratic
1958–1962	Semidemocratic
1963–1980	Nondemocratic
1981–1997	Semidemocratic
1998–2000	Democratic

Mexico

1900–1910	Nondemocratic
1911–1912	Democratic
1913–1916	Nondemocratic
1917–1919	Semidemocratic
1920–1923	Nondemocratic
1924–1928	Semidemocratic
1929–1987	Nondemocratic
1988–1999	Semidemocratic
2000	Democratic

Nicaragua

1900–1983	Nondemocratic
1984–1989	Semidemocratic
1990–2000	Democratic

Panama

1900–1918	Nondemocratic
1919–1930	Oligarchic
1931	Nondemocratic
1932–1940	Oligarchic
1941	Nondemocratic
1942–1948	Oligarchic
1949	Nondemocratic
1950	Oligarchic
1951	Nondemocratic
1952–1967	Oligarchic
1968–1983	Nondemocratic
1984–1985	Semidemocratic
1986–1989	Nondemocratic
1990–1993	Semidemocratic
1994–2000	Democratic

Paraguay

1900–1989	Nondemocratic
1990–1992	Semidemocratic
1993–2000	Democratic

Peru

1900–1913	Oligarchic
1914	Nondemocratic
1915–1918	Oligarchic
1919–1933	Nondemocratic
1934–1944	Semidemocratic
1945–1947	Democratic
1948–1955	Nondemocratic
1956–1961	Democratic
1962–1963	Nondemocratic
1964–1967	Democratic
1968–1979	Nondemocratic
1980–1991	Democratic
1992	Nondemocratic
1993–2000	Semidemocratic

Uruguay

1900–1902	Nondemocratic
1903–1918	Oligarchic
1919–1933	Democratic
1934–1938	Semidemocratic
1939–1972	Democratic
1973–1984	Nondemocratic
1985–2000	Democratic

Venezuela

1900–1945	Nondemocratic
1946–1948	Democratic
1949–1957	Nondemocratic
1958–1998	Democratic
1999–2000	Semidemocratic

APPENDIX 2: MILITARY COUPS IN LATIN AMERICA, 1900–2000

This inventory lists military coups for nineteen countries of Latin America from 1900 through 2000. For the purposes of this study, military *golpes de estado* are considered successful overthrows of established governments by members of the national armed forces through the use or threat of force. This definition stresses two components: (1) the illegal overthrow of a pre-existing government and (2) the role of military leadership. It focuses on *military coups*, not all extraconstitutional changes in government. It does not include the following:

- unsuccessful coup attempts (of which there were many)
- governmental overthrows by foreign powers (that is, through U.S. military invasion)
- civilian-led coups that did not rely primarily on military force (e.g., the 1992 *autogolpe* in Peru)
- governmental overthrows by revolutionary movements (e.g., Mexico in 1911, Bolivia in 1952, Nicaragua in 1979) or by popular insurrections or civil wars (e.g., Costa Rica in 1948)
- changes of leadership within military juntas (e.g., Argentina in 1944 and 1982)—unless they reflect substantial disagreement, use of violence, or both (e.g., Venezuela in 1952).

Coups are classified by year. Multiple transfers of power within a single year are counted as one; otherwise the results would give excessive weight to intramilitary skirmishes (which tended to occur with frequency in small countries). Technically speaking, then, the inventory lists "coup-years" rather than the total tally of coups per se.

It should come as no surprise that sources are not entirely consistent. I have relied heavily on Dieter Nohlen, ed., *Enciclopedia electoral latinoamericana y del caribe* (San José, Costa Rica: Instituto Interamericano de Derechos Humanos, 1993), and a variety of supplementary works:

Mauricio Solaún, *Sociología de los golpes de estado latinomericanos* (Bogotá, Colombia: Universidad de los Andes, 1969)

Mauricio Solaún and Michael A. Quinn, *Sinners and Heretics: The Politics of Military Intervention in Latin America* (Urbana: University of Illinois Press, 1973)

Warren Dean, "Latin American *Golpes* and Economic Fluctuations, 1823–1966," *Social Science Quarterly* 51 (June 1970): 70–80.

Martin C. Needler, "Political Development and Military Intervention in Latin America," *American Political Science Review* 40 (September 1966): 616–626.

All of which yielded the following results:

Argentina: 1930, 1943, 1955, 1962, 1966, 1976

Bolivia: 1930, 1934, 1936, 1943, 1946, 1951, 1964, 1969, 1970, 1971, 1978, 1979, 1980, 1981, 1982

Brazil: 1930, 1937, 1945, 1954, 1955, 1964

Chile: 1924, 1925, 1927, 1931, 1932, 1973

Colombia: 1900, 1909, 1921, 1953, 1957

Costa Rica: 1917, 1919

Dominican Republic: 1902, 1903, 1906, 1911, 1914, 1916, 1930, 1963

Ecuador: 1906, 1911, 1912, 1925, 1931, 1935, 1937, 1944, 1947, 1961, 1963, 1972, 2000

El Salvador: 1913, 1931, 1944, 1948, 1960, 1961, 1979

Guatemala: 1921, 1922, 1926, 1930, 1931, 1954, 1957, 1963, 1982, 1983

Haiti: 1902, 1908, 1911, 1912, 1913, 1914, 1915, 1946, 1950, 1956, 1986, 1988, 1990, 1991

Honduras: 1903, 1907, 1911, 1919, 1924, 1956, 1957, 1963, 1972, 1975, 1978

Mexico: 1913, 1914, 1920

Nicaragua: 1909, 1910, 1911, 1912, 1926, 1936, 1947

Panama: 1931, 1941, 1949, 1951, 1968, 1983

Paraguay: 1902, 1904, 1905, 1908, 1911, 1912, 1921, 1936, 1948, 1949, 1954, 1989

Peru: 1914, 1919, 1930, 1931, 1933, 1948, 1962, 1963, 1968, 1975

Uruguay: 1973

Venezuela: 1908, 1936, 1945, 1948, 1952.

SUGGESTED READINGS

This bibliography offers a selected guide to basic readings on democracy and democratization in Latin America. The first section presents theoretical and comparative studies. Subsequent sections correspond to the organization of this book: historical perspectives, 1900–2000, the electoral arena, and qualities of democracy. Although these categories overlap in some cases, it is hoped that this layout will facilitate the search for relevant material.

In addition to sources cited here, readers are strongly encouraged to explore professional journals, among them the *American Journal of Political Science*, the *American Political Science Review, Comparative Politics, Desarrollo Económico* (Buenos Aires), *Foreign Affairs, Foreign Policy*, the *Hispanic American Historical Review*, the *Journal of Democracy*, the *Journal of Latin American Studies*, the *Latin American Research Review, Latin American Society and Politics, Política y Gobierno* (Mexico City), and *World Politics*.

THEORETICAL AND COMPARATIVE STUDIES

Acemoglu, Daron, and James A. Robinson. *Economic Origins of Dictatorship and Democracy*. New York: Cambridge University Press, 2006.

Anderson, Lisa, ed. *Transitions to Democracy*. New York: Columbia University Press, 1999.

Collier, Ruth Berins. *Paths Toward Democracy: The Working Class and Elites in Western Europe and South America*. Cambridge: Cambridge University Press, 1999.

Dahl, Robert A. *Polyarchy: Participation and Opposition*. New Haven, CT: Yale University Press, 1971.

Diamond, Larry. *Developing Democracy: Toward Consolidation*. Baltimore: Johns Hopkins University Press, 1999.

———. *Political Culture and Democracy in Developing Countries*. Boulder, CO: Lynne Rienner, 1993.

_____. The Spirit of Democracy: The Struggle to Build Free Societies Throughout the World. New York: Times Books/Henry Holt, 2008.

Diamond, Larry, and Marc F. Plattner, eds. *Civil-Military Relations and Democracy*. Baltimore: Johns Hopkins University Press, 1996.

———, eds. *The Global Resurgence of Democracy*, 2nd edition. Baltimore: Johns Hopkins University Press, 1996.

Diamond, Larry, Marc E. Plattner, Yun-han Chu, and Hung-mao Tien, eds. *Consolidating the Third Wave Democracies*. Baltimore: Johns Hopkins University Press, 1997.

Gill, Graeme. *The Dynamics of Democratization: Elites, Civil Society, and the Transition Process*. New York: St. Martin's Press, 2000.

Haggard, Stephan, and Robert R. Kaufman. *The Political Economy of Democratic Transitions*. Princeton, NJ: Princeton University Press, 1995.

Haggard, Stephan, and Mathew D. McCubbins, eds. *Presidents, Parliaments, and Policy.* Cambridge: Cambridge University Press, 2001.

Huntington, Samuel P. *The Third Wave: Democratization in the Late Twentieth Century.* Norman: University of Oklahoma Press, 1991.

Inglehart, Ronald. *Modernization and Postmodernization: Cultural, Economic, and Political Change in 43 Societies.* Princeton, NJ: Princeton University Press, 1997.

Lijphart, Arend. *Democracies: Patterns of Majoritarian and Consensus Government in Twenty-One Democracies.* New Haven, CT: Yale University Press, 1984.

———. *Patterns of Democracy: Government Forms and Performance in Thirty-Six Countries.* New Haven, CT: Yale University Press, 1999.

Linz, Juan J., and Alfred Stepan, eds. *The Breakdown of Democratic Regimes.* Baltimore: Johns Hopkins University Press, 1978.

———. *Problems of Democratic Transition and Consolidation: Southern Europe, South America, and Post-Communist Europe.* Baltimore: Johns Hopkins University Press, 1996.

Munck, Gerardo L. *Measuring Democracy: A Bridge between Scholarship and Politics.* Baltimore: Johns Hopkins University Press, 2009.

O'Donnell, Guillermo A., Philippe C. Schmitter, and Laurence Whitehead, eds. *Transitions from Authoritarian Rule: Prospects for Democracy.* Baltimore: Johns Hopkins University Press, 1986.

Pridham, Geoffrey. *Transitions to Democracy: Comparative Perspectives from Southern Europe, Latin America and Eastern Europe.* Aldershot, UK: Dartmouth, 1995.

Przeworski, Adam. *Democracy and the Market: Political and Economic Reforms in Eastern Europe and Latin America.* New York: Cambridge University Press, 1991.

———. *Sustainable Democracy.* Cambridge: Cambridge University Press, 1995.

Przeworski, Adam, Michael E. Alvarez, José Antonio Cheibub, and Fernando Limongi. *Democracy and Development: Political Institutions and Well-Being in the World, 1950–1990.* Cambridge: Cambridge University Press, 2000.

Przeworski, Adam, Susan C. Stokes, and Bernard Manin, eds. *Democracy, Accountability, and Representation.* Cambridge: Cambridge University Press, 1999.

Rueschemeyer, Dietrich, Evelyne Huber Stevens, and John D. Stephens. *Capitalist Development and Democracy.* Chicago: University of Chicago Press, 1992.

Schedler, Andreas, Larry Diamond, and Marc Plattner, eds. *The Self-Restraining State: Power and Accountability in New Democracies.* Boulder, CO: Lynne Rienner, 1999.

Whitehead, Laurence, ed. *The International Dimensions of Democratization: Europe and the Americas.* New York: Oxford University Press, 2001.

HISTORICAL PERSPECTIVES, 1900–2000

Bowman, Kirk S. *Militarization, Democracy, and Development: The Perils of Praetorianism in Latin America.* University Park: Pennsylvania State University Press, 2002.

Camp, Roderic Ai, ed. *Democracy in Latin America: Patterns and Cycles.* Wilmington, DE: Scholarly Resources, 1996.

Collier, David, ed. *The New Authoritarianism in Latin America.* Princeton, NJ: Princeton University Press, 1979.

Diamond, Larry, Jonathan Hartlyn, Juan J. Linz, and Seymour Martin Lipset, eds. *Democracy in Developing Countries: Latin America,* 2nd edition. Boulder, CO: Lynne Rienner, 1999.

Fitch, J. Samuel. *The Armed Forces and Democracy in Latin America*. Baltimore: Johns Hopkins University Press, 1998.

Hunter, Wendy. *Eroding Military Influence in Brazil: Politicians Against Soldiers*. Chapel Hill: University of North Carolina Press, 1997.

López-Alves, Fernando. *State Formation and Democracy in Latin America, 1810–1900*. Durham, NC: Duke University Press, 2000.

Loveman, Brian. *For La Patria: Politics and the Armed Forces in Latin America*. Wilmington, DE: Scholarly Resources, 1999.

———. *The Constitution of Tyranny: Regimes of Exception in Spanish America*. Pittsburgh: University of Pittsburgh Press, 1993.

Loveman, Brian, and Thomas M. Davies, Jr., eds. *The Politics of Antipolitics: The Military in Latin America*. Wilmington, DE: Scholarly Resources, 1997.

Lowenthal, Abraham F., ed. *Exporting Democracy: The United States and Latin America, Themes and Issues*. Baltimore: Johns Hopkins University Press, 1991.

Lowenthal, Abraham, and J. Samuel Fitch, eds. *Armies and Politics in Latin America*. New York: Holmes & Meier, 1986.

Mares, David R. *Violent Peace: Militarized Interstate Bargaining in Latin America*. New York: Columbia University Press, 2001.

———, ed. *Civil-Military Relations: Building Democracy and Regional Security in Latin America, Southern Asia, and Central Europe*. Boulder, CO: Westview Press, 1998.

O'Donnell, Guillermo A. *Modernization and Bureaucratic-Authoritarianism: Studies in South American Politics*. Berkeley, CA: Institute of International Studies, 1973.

Peeler, John. *Building Democracy in Latin America*, 3rd rev. edition. Boulder, CO: Lynne Rienner, 2009.

Pion-Berlin, David, ed. *Civil-Military Relations in Latin America: New Analytical Perspectives*. Chapel Hill: University of North Carolina Press, 2001.

Remmer, Karen. *Military Rule in Latin America*. Boulder, CO: Westview Press, 1991.

Sikkink, Kathryn. *Mixed Signals: U.S. Human Rights Policy and Latin America*. Ithaca, NY: Cornell University Press, 2004.

Skidmore, Thomas E., Peter H. Smith, and James N. Green. *Modern Latin America*, 7th rev. edition. New York: Oxford University Press, 2010.

Smith, Peter H. *Talons of the Eagle: Dynamics of U.S.-Latin American Relations*, 3rd rev. edition. New York: Oxford University Press, 2008.

Smith, Tony. *America's Mission: The United States and the Worldwide Struggle for Democracy in the Twentieth Century*. Princeton, NJ: Princeton University Press, 1994.

Stepan, Alfred. *The Military in Politics: Changing Patterns in Brazil*. Princeton, NJ: Princeton University Press, 1971.

———. *Rethinking Military Politics: Brazil and the Southern Cone*. Princeton, NJ: Princeton University Press, 1988.

THE ELECTORAL ARENA

Alcántara Sáez, Manuel, and Flavia Friedenberg, eds. *Partidos políticos en América Latina*, 3 vols. Salamanca, Spain: Ediciones Universidad de Salamanca, 2001.

Carey, John M. *Legislative Voting and Accountability*. New York: Cambridge University Press, 2009.

Carey, John M., and Matthew Soberg Shugart, eds. *Executive Decree Authority*. Cambridge: Cambridge University Press, 1998.

Colomer, Josep M. *Political Institutions: Democracy and Social Choice*. Oxford: Oxford University Press, 2001.

Dietz, Henry A., and Gil Shidlo, eds. *Urban Elections in Democratic Latin America*. Wilmington, DE: Scholarly Resources, 1998.

Di Tella, Torcuato S. *Los partidos politicos: Teoría y análisis comparativo*. Buenos Aires, Argentina: A–Z Editora, 1998.

Drake, Paul W., and Eduardo Silva, eds. *Elections and Democratization in Latin America, 1980–85*. La Jolla: Center for Iberian and Latin American Studies and Center for U.S.-Mexican Studies, University of California, San Diego, 1986.

Kitschelt, Herbert, Kirk A. Hawkins, Juan Pablo Luna, Guillermo Rosas, and Elizabeth J. Zechmeister. *Latin American Party Systems*. New York: Cambridge University Press, 2010.

Lijphart, Arend, ed. *Parliamentary Versus Presidential Government*. Oxford: Oxford University Press, 1992.

Lijphart, Arend, and Carlos H. Waisman, eds. *Institutional Design in New Democracies: Eastern Europe and Latin America*. Boulder, CO: Westview Press, 1996.

Linz, Juan J., and Arturo Valenzuela, eds. *The Failure of Presidential Democracy*, 2 vols. Baltimore: Johns Hopkins University Press, 1994.

Mainwaring, Scott, and Timothy R. Scully, eds. *Building Democratic Institutions: Party Systems in Latin America*. Stanford, CA: Stanford University Press, 1995.

Mainwaring, Scott, and Matthew Soberg Shugart, eds. *Presidentialism and Democracy in Latin America*. Cambridge: Cambridge University Press, 1997.

Middlebrook, Kevin J., ed. *Conservative Parties, the Right, and Democracy in Latin America*. Baltimore: Johns Hopkins University Press, 2000.

———, ed. *Electoral Observation and Democratic Transitions in Latin America*. La Jolla: Center for U.S.-Mexican Studies, University of California, San Diego, 1998.

Morgenstern, Scott. *Patterns of Legislative Politics: Roll-Call Voting in Latin America and the United States*. Cambridge: Cambridge University Press, 2003.

Morgenstern, Scott, and Benito Nacif, eds. *Legislative Politics in Latin America*. Cambridge: Cambridge University Press, 2002.

Pérez-Liñán, Aníbal. *Presidential Impeachment and the New Political Instability in Latin America*. New York: Cambridge University Press, 2007.

Samuels, David. *Ambition, Federalism, and Legislative Politics in Brazil*. Cambridge: Cambridge University Press, 2003.

Schedler, Andreas, ed. *Electoral Authoritarianism: The Dynamics of Unfree Competition*. Boulder, CO: Lynne Rienner, 2006.

Shugart, Matthew Soberg, and John M. Carey. *Presidents and Assemblies: Constitutional Design and Electoral Dynamics*. Cambridge: Cambridge University Press, 1992.

Shugart, Matthew Soberg, and Martin Wattenberg, eds. *Mixed-Member Electoral Systems: The Best of Both Worlds?* Oxford: Oxford University Press, 2001.

Ugalde, Luis Carlos. *The Mexican Congress: Old Player, New Power*. Washington, DC: Center for Strategic and International Studies, 2000.

QUALITIES OF DEMOCRACY

Agüero, Felipe, and Jeffrey Stark, eds. *Fault Lines of Democracy in Post-Transition Latin America*. Miami, FL: North-South Center, 1998.

Alvarez, Sonia. *Engendering Democracy in Brazil: Women's Movements in Transition Politics*. Princeton, NJ: Princeton University Press, 1990.

Baldez, Lisa. *Why Women Protest: Women's Movements in Chile.* Cambridge: Cambridge University Press, 2002.

Brinks, Daniel M. *The Judicial Response to Police Killings in Latin America: Inequality and the Rule of Law.* New York: Cambridge University Press, 2008.

Camp, Roderic Ai, ed. *Citizen Views of Democracy in Latin America.* Pittsburgh: University of Pittsburgh Press, 2001.

Catterberg, Edgardo R. *Argentina Confronts Politics: Political Culture and Public Opinion in the Argentine Transition to Democracy.* Boulder, CO: Lynne Rienner, 1991.

Chalmers, Douglas A., Carlos M. Vilas, Katherine Hite, Scott B. Martin, Kerianne Piester, and Monique Segarra, eds. *The New Politics of Inequality in Latin America: Rethinking Participation and Representation.* New York: Oxford University Press, 1997.

Collier, Ruth Berins, and David Collier. *Shaping the Political Arena: Critical Junctures, the Labor Movement, and Regime Dynamics in Latin America.* Princeton, NJ: Princeton University Press, 1991.

Craske, Nikki. *Women and Politics in Latin America.* New Brunswick, NJ: Rutgers University Press, 1999.

Domínguez, Jorge I. *Democratic Politics in Latin America and the Caribbean.* Baltimore: Johns Hopkins University Press, 1998.

Domínguez, Jorge I., and Abraham F. Lowenthal, eds. *Constructing Democratic Governance: Latin America and the Caribbean in the 1990s.* Baltimore: Johns Hopkins University Press, 1996.

Domínguez, Jorge I., and Michael Shifter, eds. *Constructing Democratic Governance in Latin America.* Baltimore: Johns Hopkins University Press, 2003.

Drake, Paul W. *Labor Movements and Dictatorships: The Southern Cone in Comparative Perspective.* Baltimore: Johns Hopkins University Press, 1996.

Drake, Paul W., and Eric Hershberg, eds. *State and Society in Conflict: Comparative Perspectives on Andean Crises.* Pittsburgh: University of Pittsburgh Press, 2006.

Durand, Francisco, and Eduardo Silva, eds. *Organized Business, Economic Change, and Democracy in Latin America.* Coral Gables, FL: North-South Center Press, 1998.

Eckstein, Susan Eva, and Timothy P. Wickham-Crowley, eds. *What Justice? Whose Justice? Fighting for Fairness in Latin America.* Berkeley and Los Angeles: University of California Press, 2003.

Escobar, Arturo, and Sonia E. Alvarez, eds. *The Making of Social Movements in Latin America: Identity, Strategy, and Democracy.* Boulder, CO: Westview Press, 1992.

Foweraker, Joe, Todd Landman, and Neil Harvey. *Governing Latin America.* Cambridge: Polity Press, 2003.

Helmke, Gretchen. *Courts under Constraints: Judges, Generals, and Presidents in Argentina.* New York: Cambridge University Press, 2005.

Hilbink, Lisa. *Judges Beyond Politics in Democracy and Dictatorship: Lessons from Chile.* New York: Cambridge University Press, 2007.

Htun, Mala. *Sex and the State: Abortion, Divorce, and the Family under Latin American Dictatorships and Democracies.* Cambridge: Cambridge University Press, 2003.

Inter-American Development Bank. *Development Beyond Economics: Economic and Social Progress in Latin America.* Baltimore: Johns Hopkins University Press for the Inter-American Development Bank, 2000.

Jaquette, Jane S., ed. *The Women's Movement in Latin America: Participation and Democracy,* 2nd edition. Boulder, CO: Westview Press, 1994.

Jaquette, Jane S., and Sharon L. Wolchik, eds. *Women and Democracy: Latin America and Central and Eastern Europe.* Baltimore: Johns Hopkins University Press, 1998.

Lawson, Chappell H. *Building the Fourth Estate: Democratization and the Rise of a Free Press in Mexico*. Berkeley and Los Angeles: University of California Press, 2002.

López-Calva, Luis F., and Nora Lustig, eds. *Declining Inequality in Latin America: A Decade of Progress?* New York and Washington, DC: United Nations Development Programme and Brookings Institution, 2010.

Mainwaring, Scott, and Christopher Welna, eds. *Democratic Accountability in Latin America*. New York: Oxford University Press, 2003.

Méndez, Juan E., Guillermo O'Donnell, and Paulo Sérgio Pinheiro, eds. *The (Un) Rule of Law and the Underprivileged in Latin America*. Notre Dame, IN: University of Notre Dame Press, 1999.

O'Donnell, Guillermo, Jorge Vargas Cullell, and Osvaldo M. Iazzetta, eds. *The Quality of Democracy: Theory and Applications*. Notre Dame, IN: University of Notre Dame Press, 2004.

Oxhorn, Philip, and Graciela Ducatenzeiler, eds. *What Kind of Democracy? What Kind of Market? Latin America in the Age of Neoliberalism*. University Park: Pennsylvania State University Press, 1998.

Programa de las Naciones Unidas para el Desarrollo (PNUD). *La democracia en América Latina: hacia una democracia de ciudadanas y ciudadanos*. New York and Buenos Aires: United Nations Development Programme, 2004.

Schneider, Ben Ross. *Business Politics and the State in Twentieth-Century Latin America*. Cambridge: Cambridge University Press, 2004.

Smith, Peter H., ed. *Drug Policy in the Americas*. Boulder, CO: Westview Press, 1992.

Smith, Peter H., Jennifer L. Troutner, and Christine Hünefeldt, eds. *Promises of Empowerment: Women in Asia and Latin America*. Lanham, MD: Rowman & Littlefield, 2004.

Stokes, Susan C. *Mandates and Democracy: Neoliberalism by Surprise in Latin America*. Cambridge: Cambridge University Press, 2001.

———, ed. *Public Support for Market Reforms in New Democracies*. Cambridge: Cambridge University Press, 2001.

Van Cott, Donna Lee, ed. *Indigenous Peoples and Democracy in Latin America*. New York: St. Martin's Press, 1994.

Vellinga, Menno, ed. *The Changing Role of the State in Latin America*. Boulder, CO: Westview Press, 1998.

Warren, Kay B., and Jean Jackson, eds. *Indigenous Movements, Self-Representation, and the State in Latin America*. Austin: University of Texas Press, 2002.

Weyland, Kurt. *The Politics of Market Reform in Fragile Democracies: Argentina, Brazil, Peru, and Venezuela*. Princeton, NJ: Princeton University Press, 2002.

———. *Democracy Without Equity: Failures of Reform in Brazil*. Pittsburgh: University of Pittsburgh Press, 1996.

Weyland, Kurt, Raúl L. Madrid, and Wendy Hunter, eds. *Leftist Governments in Latin America: Successes and Shortcomings*. New York: Cambridge University Press, 2010.

Zakaria, Fareed. *The Future of Freedom: Illiberal Democracy at Home and Abroad*. New York: Norton, 2003.

INDEX

Key: Location of item in text = plain numbers (e.g., 123 or 123–24); Location of item in footnotes = page plus note number (e.g., 123n2); Location of item in illustrations = italicized page numbers (e.g., *123*); Location of item in tables = page number plus italicized *t* (e.g., 123*t*); Location of item in figures = page number plus italicized *f* (e.g., 123*f*).